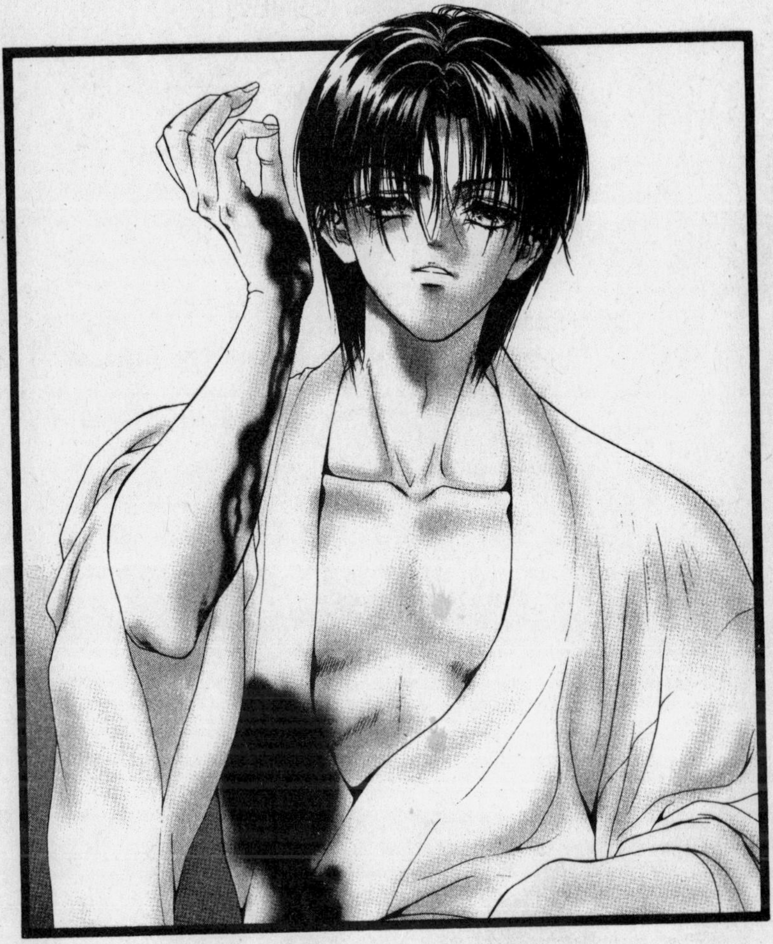

Cross Vol. 5
Created by Sumiko Amakawa

Translation - Yuko Fukami
English Adaptation - Len Wein
Copy Editors - Eric Althoff and Hope Donovan
Retouch and Lettering - Rafael Najarian
Production Artist - Fawn Lau
Cover Design - Kyle Plummer

Editor - Bryce P. Coleman
Digital Imaging Manager - Chris Buford
Production Managers - Jennifer Miller and Mutsumi Miyazaki
Managing Editor - Lindsey Johnston
VP of Production - Ron Klamert
Publisher and Editor-in-Chief - Mike Kiley
President and C.O.O. - John Parker
C.E.O. - Stuart Levy

A ⦿ TOKYOPOP® Manga

TOKYOPOP Inc.
5900 Wilshire Blvd. Suite 2000
Los Angeles, CA 90036

E-mail: info@TOKYOPOP.com
Come visit us online at www.TOKYOPOP.com

ISBN: 1-59532-231-0

First TOKYOPOP printing: January 2006
10 9 8 7 6 5 4 3 2 1
Printed in the USA

Cross

Volume 5

created by
Sumiko Amakawa

HAMBURG // LONDON // LOS ANGELES // TOKYO

Summary and Character Introduction

Summary

Takara Amakusa, son of an expert exorcist father and a mother whose family have been exorcists through the ages, is already a first-rate exorcist attending high school. He has tried to send Shizuha Matsuri, on whose body the "Scriptura" appears, to a safe place to protect her from a heretic organization, but instead, she has become a teacher at Holy Cross Academy High School, where Takara is a student.

One day, Shizuha finds Sister Caterina's pendant, which starts a chain of strange events that seem to be connected to both Caterina's past and the mysterious pendant, but...

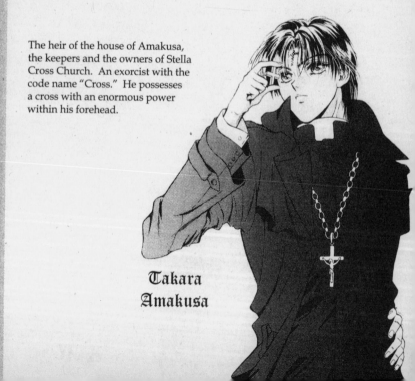

The heir of the house of Amakusa, the keepers and the owners of Stella Cross Church. An exorcist with the code name "Cross." He possesses a cross with an enormous power within his forehead.

Takara Amakusa

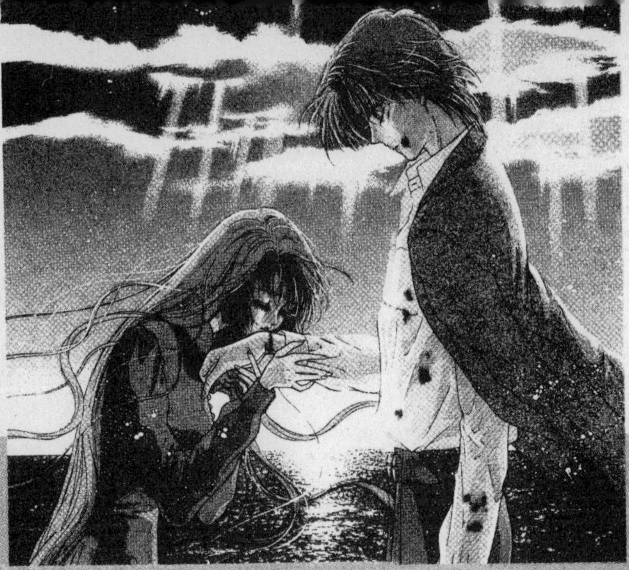

Gerardo Bernardo Serlio

Takara's father and also a first-class exorcist.
He is a priest of Stella Cross Church.

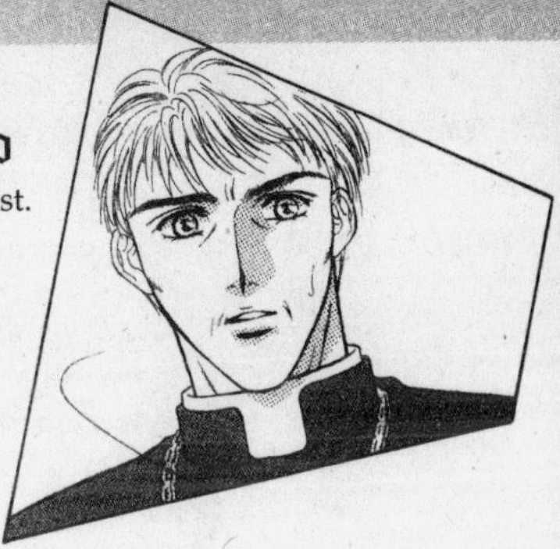

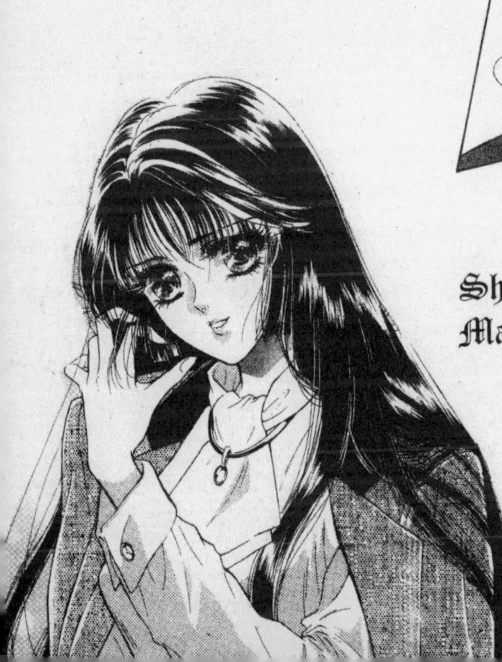

Shizuha Matsuri

Manipulated by a heretical organization, her own parents tried to sacrifice her. She escaped and was saved by Takara. Later, she became a teacher at Takara's high school.

Cross

Table of Contents

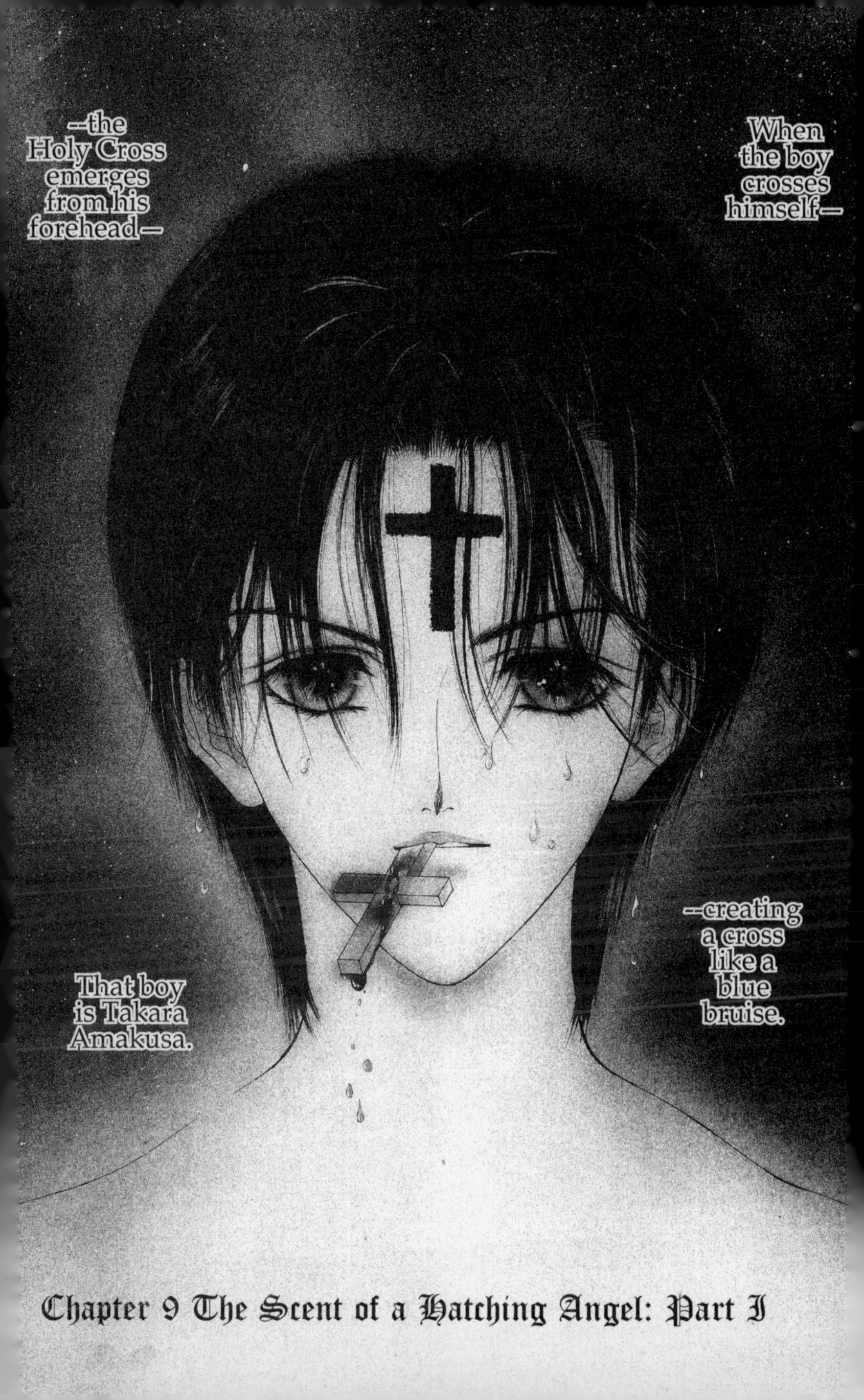
When the boy crosses himself—
--the Holy Cross emerges from his forehead—
--creating a cross like a blue bruise.
That boy is Takara Amakusa.
Chapter 9 The Scent of a Hatching Angel: Part I

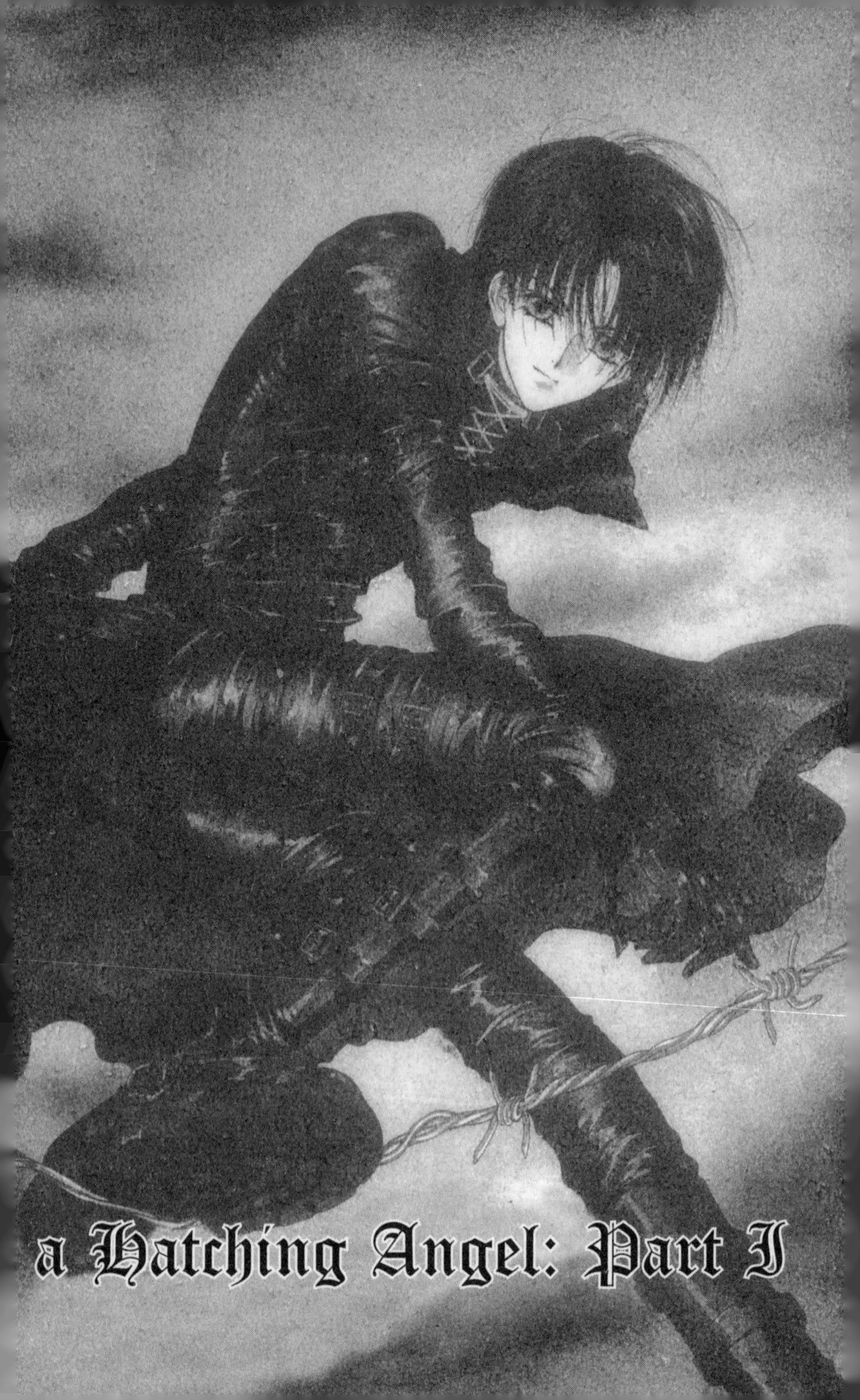

a Hatching Angel: Part I

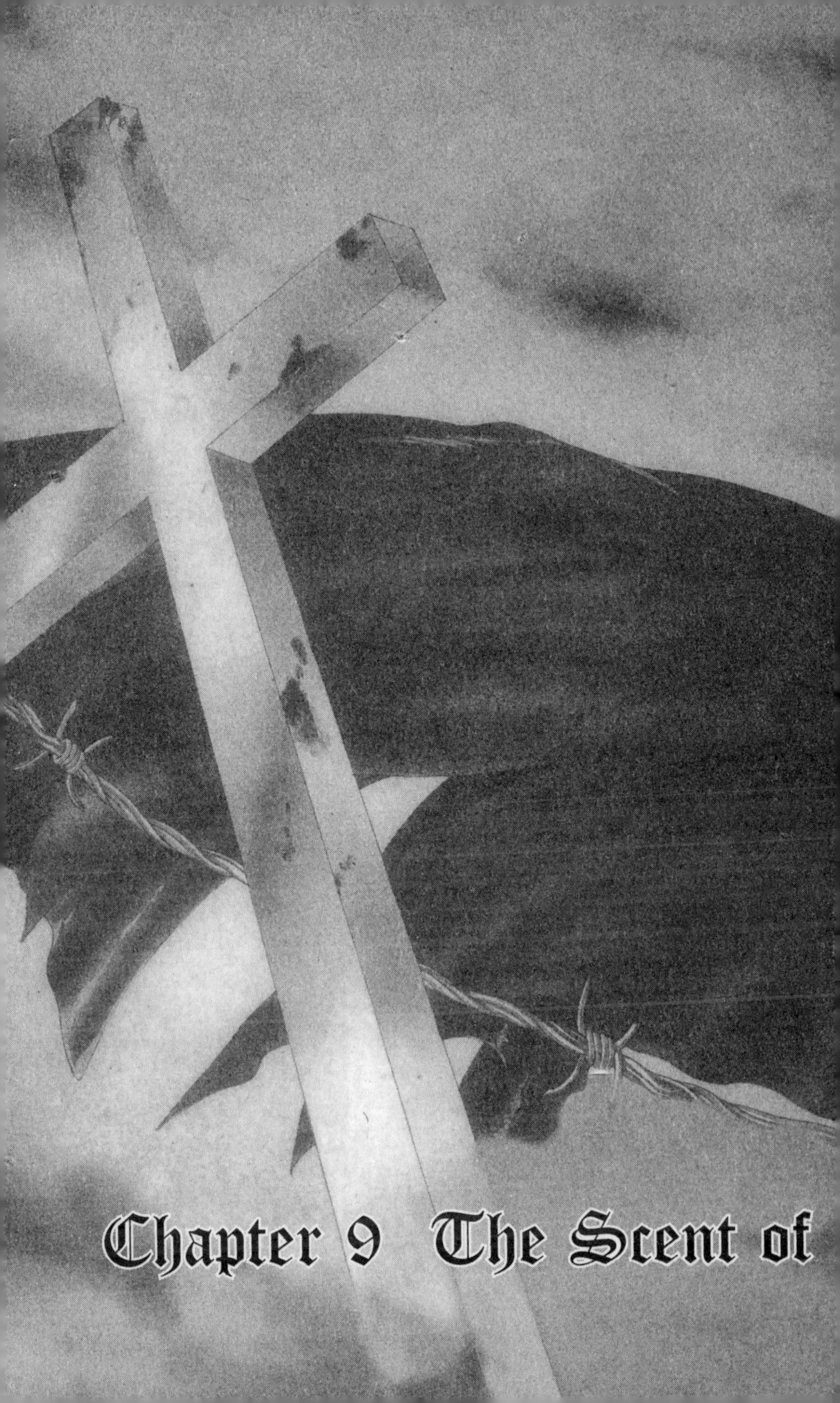

Chapter 9 The Scent of

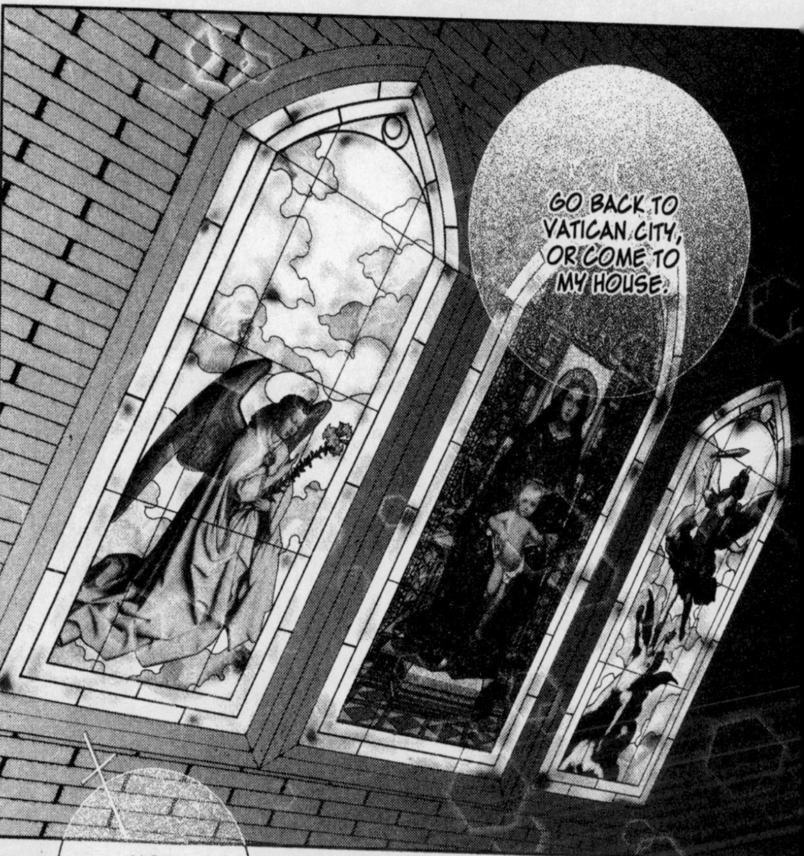
GO BACK TO VATICAN CITY, OR COME TO MY HOUSE.

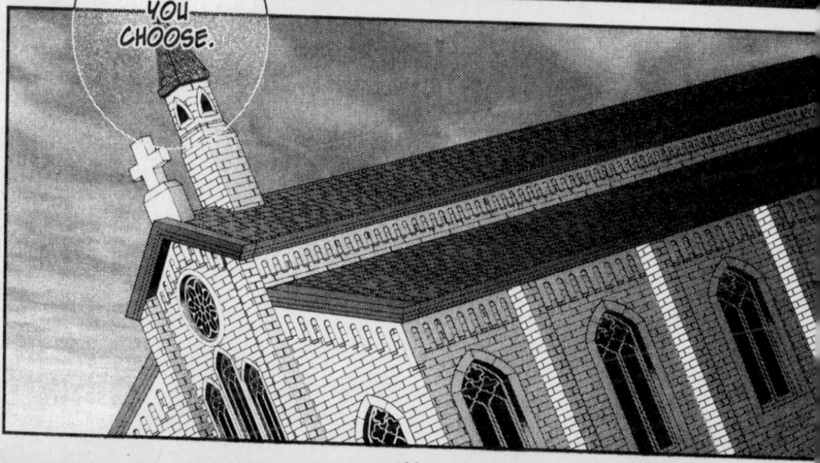
YOU CHOOSE.

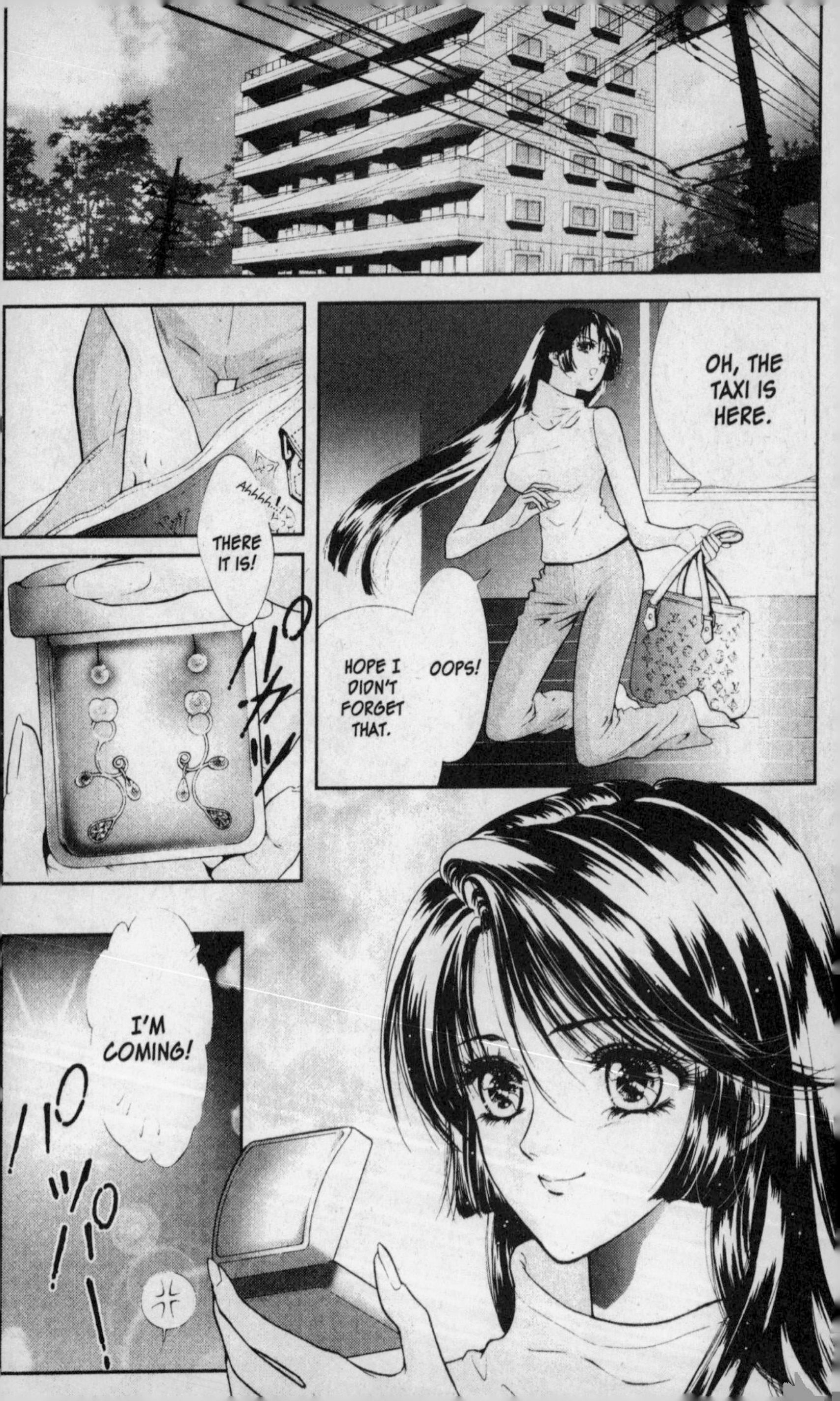

OH, THE TAXI IS HERE.
OOPS!
HOPE I DIDN'T FORGET THAT.
THERE IT IS!
I'M COMING!

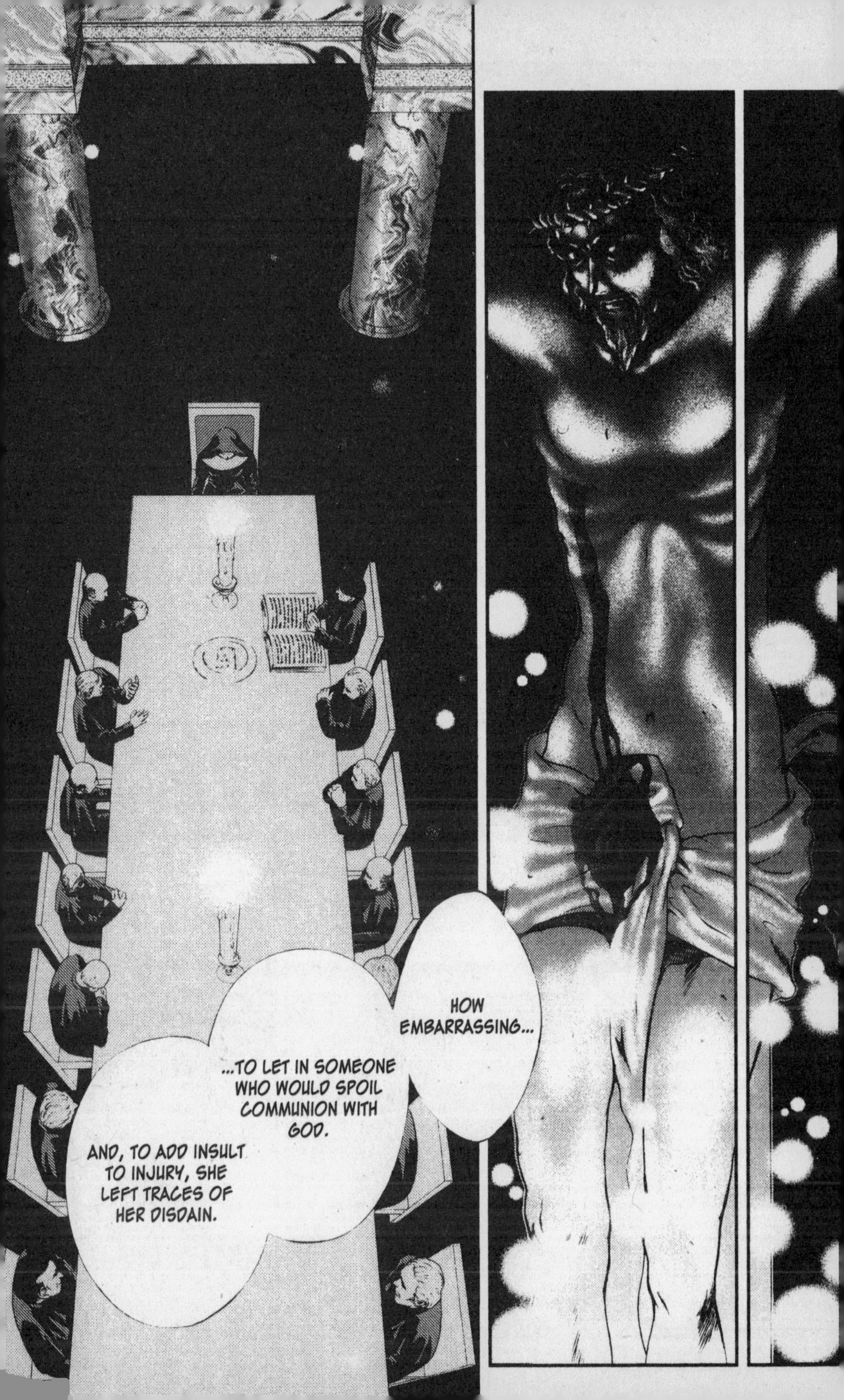
HOW EMBARRASSING...
...TO LET IN SOMEONE WHO WOULD SPOIL COMMUNION WITH GOD.
AND, TO ADD INSULT TO INJURY, SHE LEFT TRACES OF HER DISDAIN.

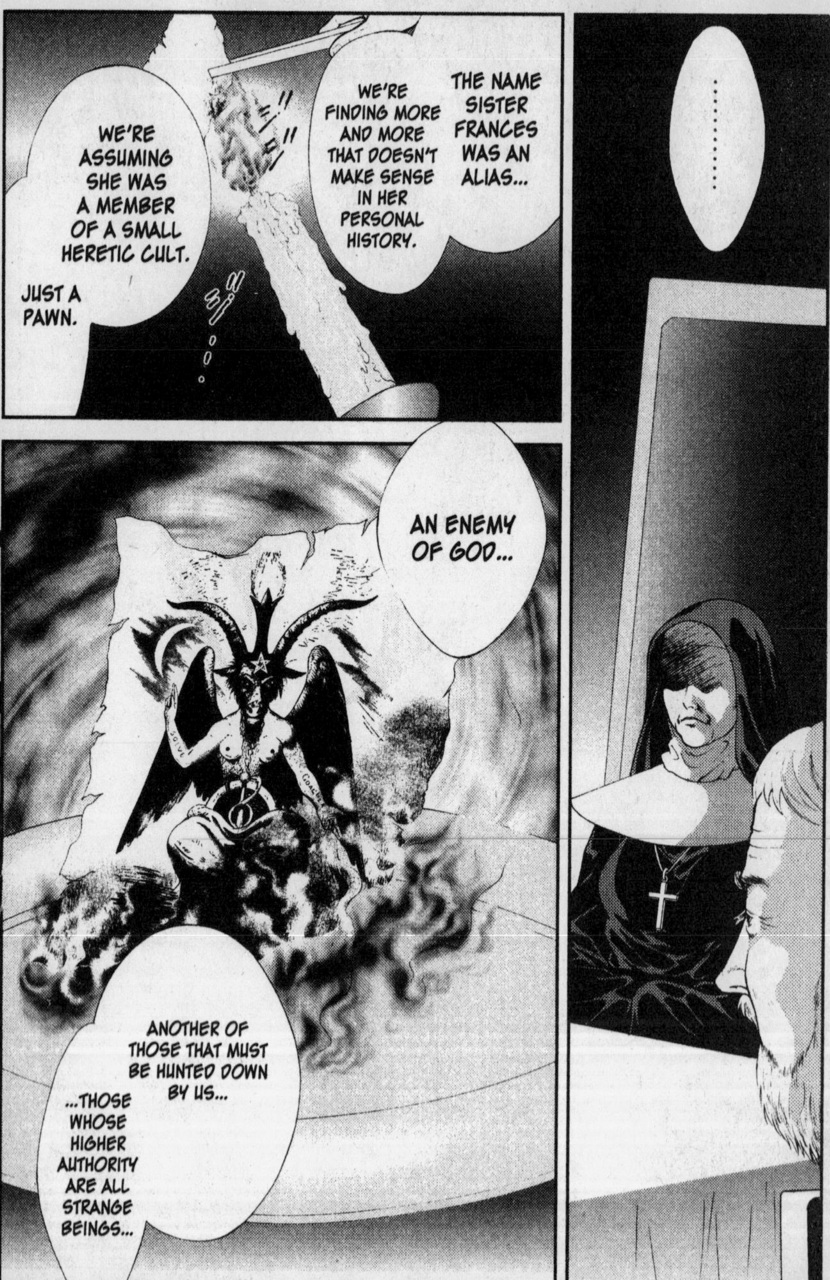

......
THE NAME SISTER FRANCES WAS AN ALIAS...
WE'RE FINDING MORE AND MORE THAT DOESN'T MAKE SENSE IN HER PERSONAL HISTORY.
WE'RE ASSUMING SHE WAS A MEMBER OF A SMALL HERETIC CULT.
JUST A PAWN.
AN ENEMY OF GOD...
ANOTHER OF THOSE THAT MUST BE HUNTED DOWN BY US...
...THOSE WHOSE HIGHER AUTHORITY ARE ALL STRANGE BEINGS...

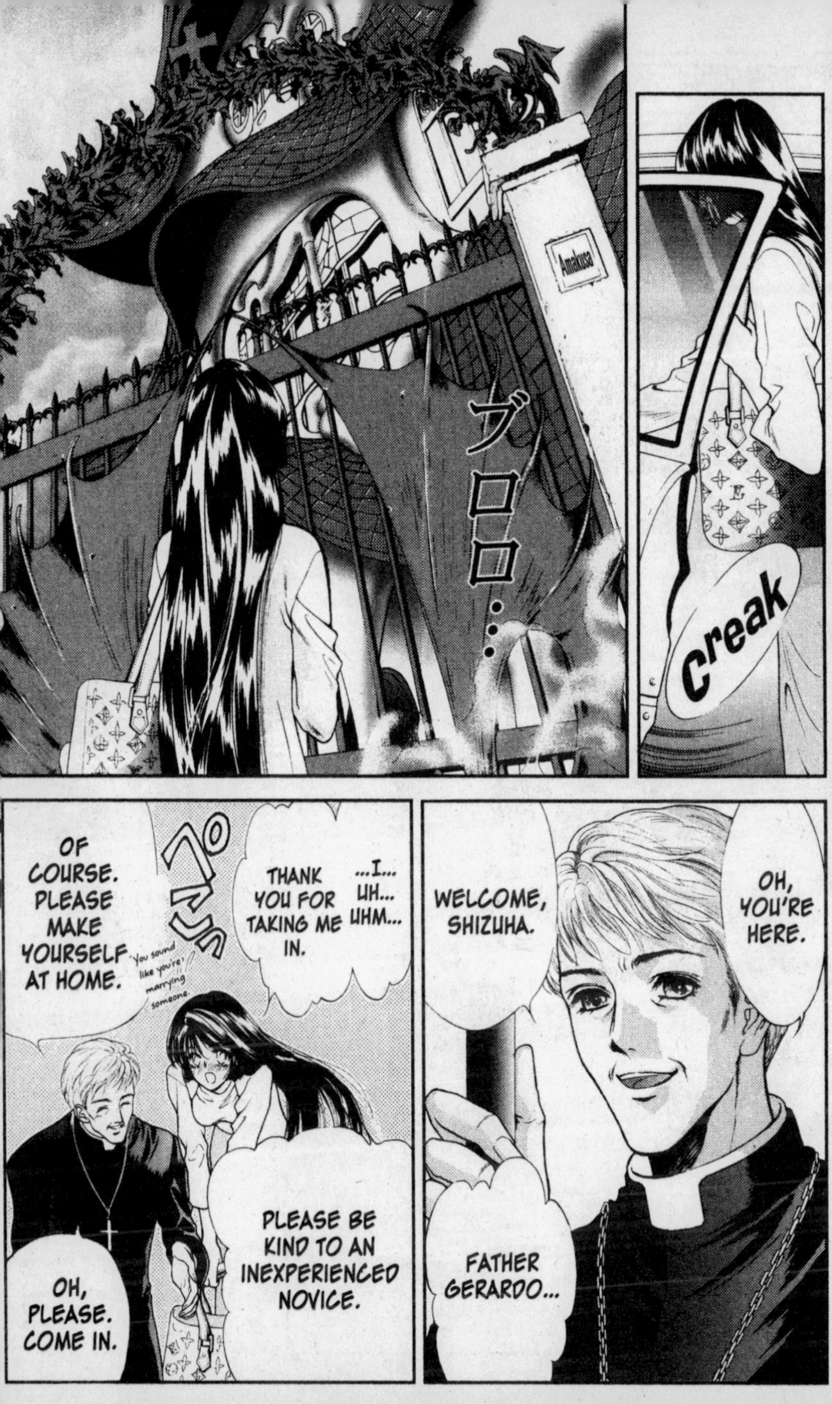
creak
Amakusa
ブロロ…
OH, YOU'RE HERE.
WELCOME, SHIZUHA.
FATHER GERARDO...
...I... UH... UHM...
THANK YOU FOR TAKING ME IN.
ペこり
OF COURSE. PLEASE MAKE YOURSELF AT HOME.
You sound like you're marrying someone.
PLEASE BE KIND TO AN INEXPERIENCED NOVICE.
OH, PLEASE. COME IN.

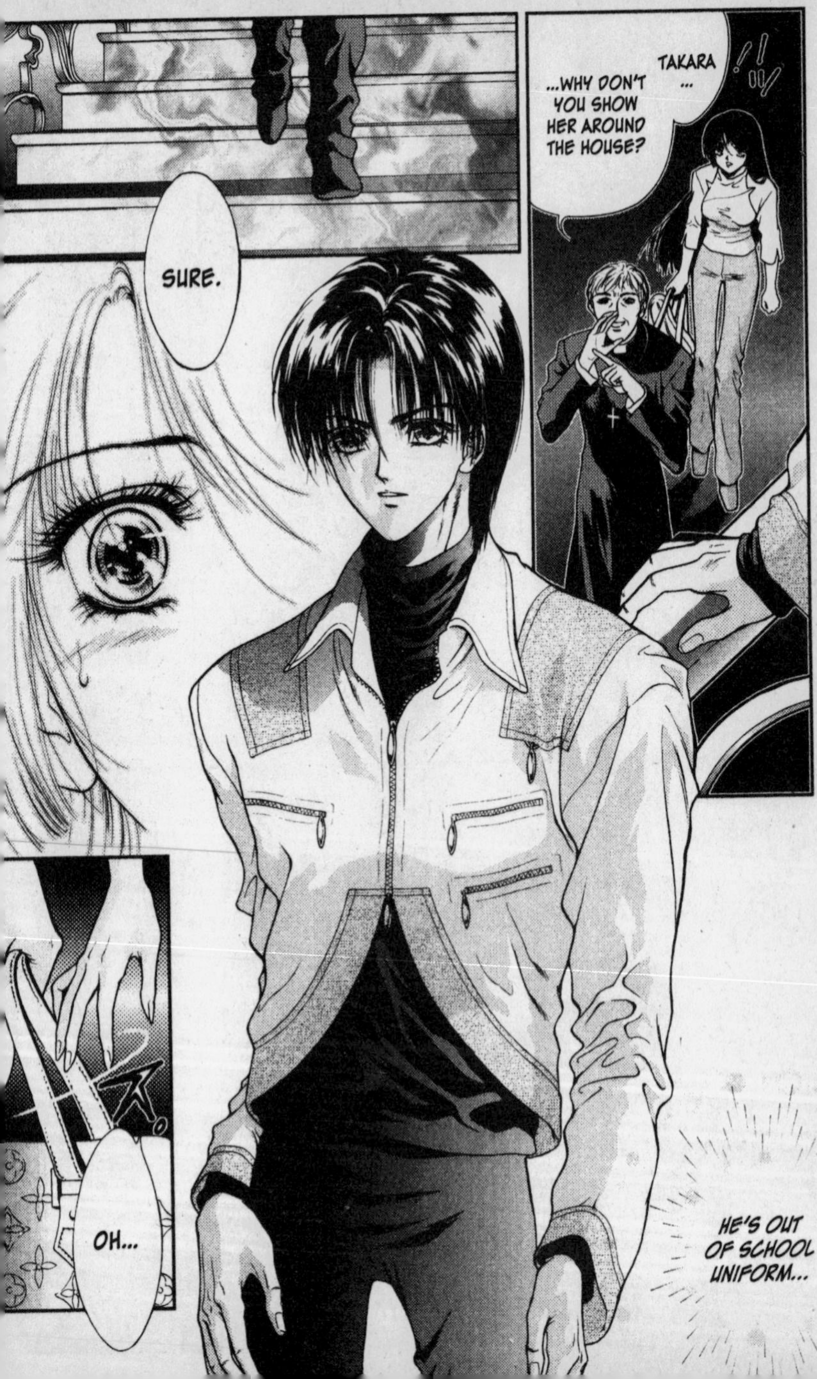
TAKARA ...
...WHY DON'T YOU SHOW HER AROUND THE HOUSE?
SURE.
HE'S OUT OF SCHOOL UNIFORM...
OH...

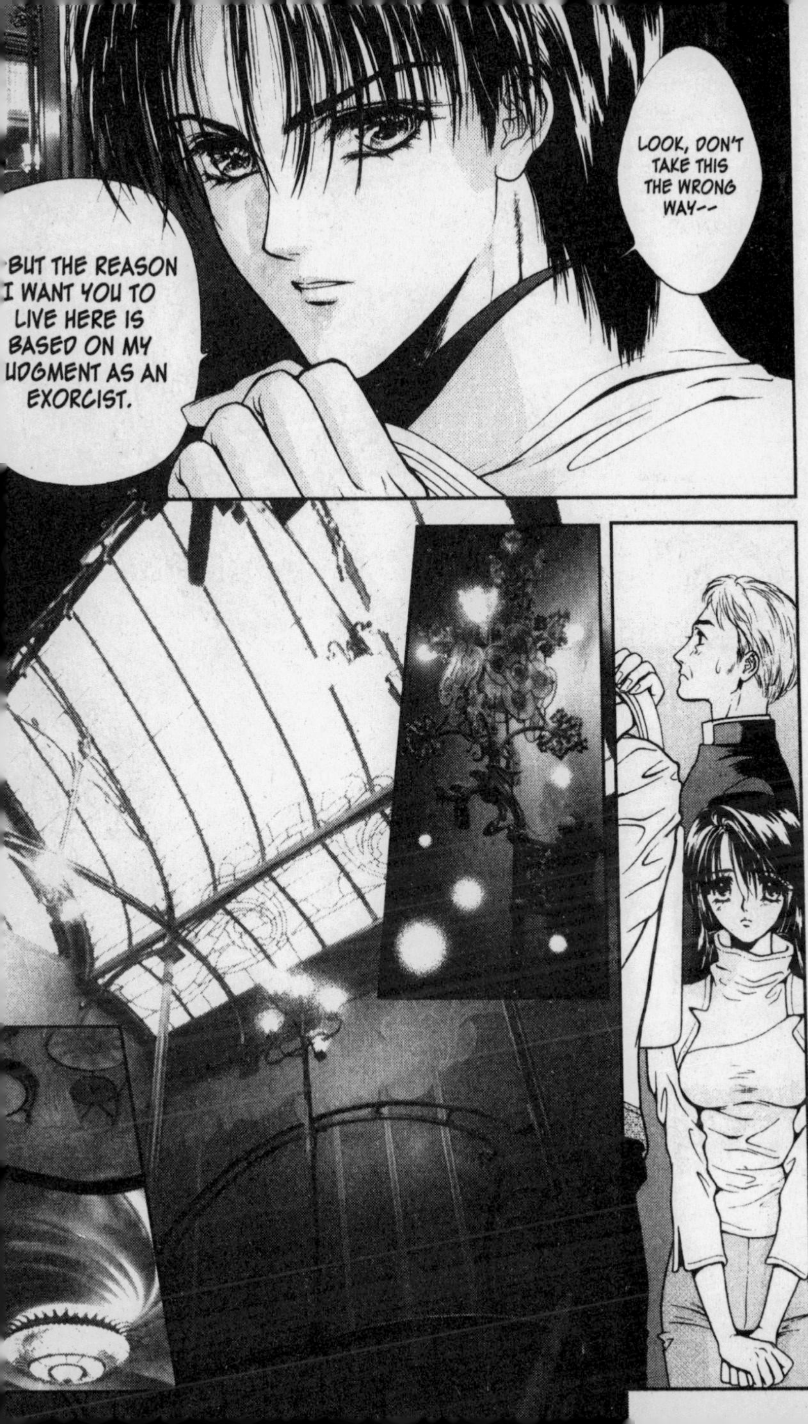
LOOK, DON'T TAKE THIS THE WRONG WAY--
BUT THE REASON I WANT YOU TO LIVE HERE IS BASED ON MY UDGMENT AS AN EXORCIST.

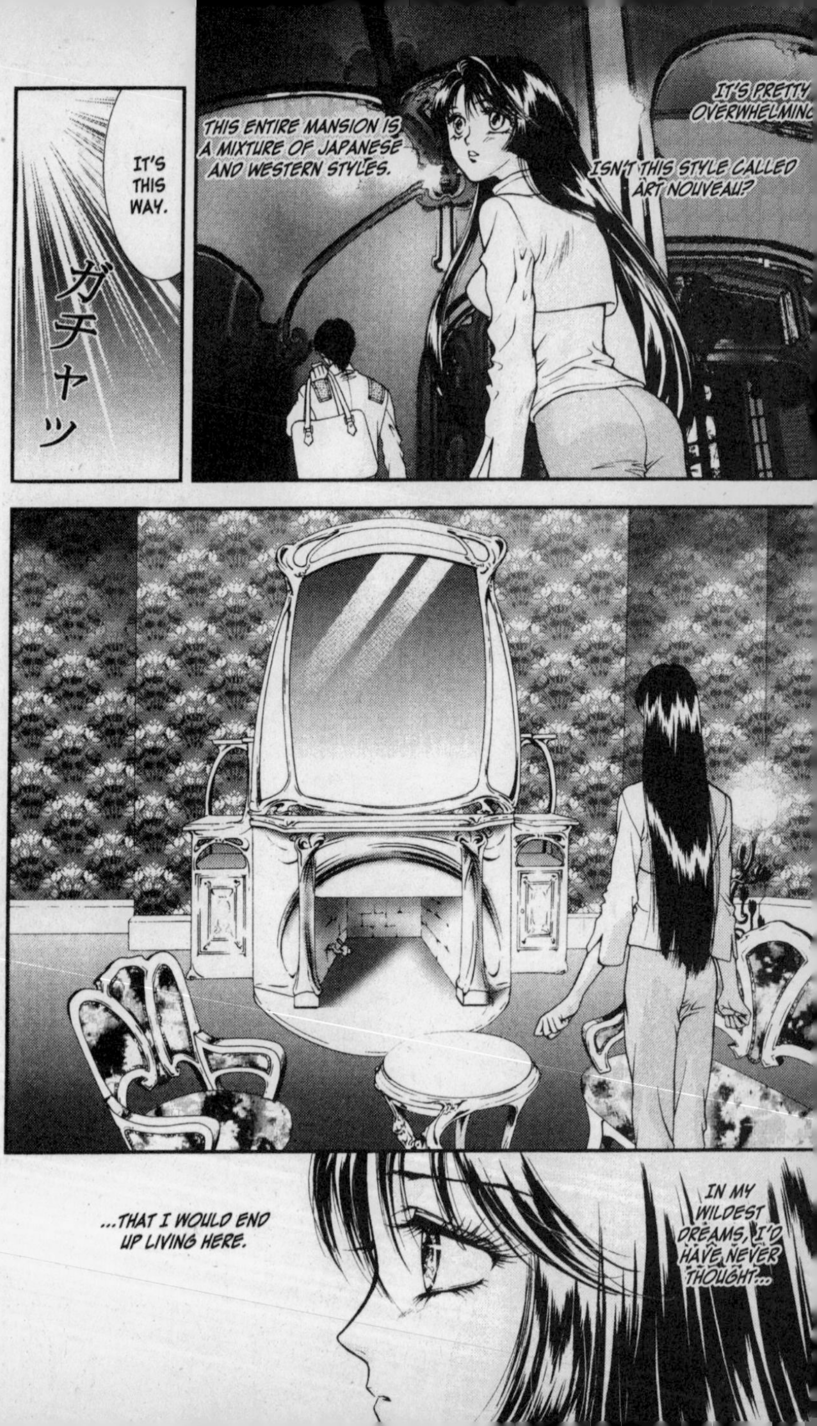
IT'S PRETTY OVERWHELMING
ISN'T THIS STYLE CALLED ART NOUVEAU?
THIS ENTIRE MANSION IS A MIXTURE OF JAPANESE AND WESTERN STYLES.
IT'S THIS WAY.
ガチャッ
IN MY WILDEST DREAMS, I'D HAVE NEVER THOUGHT...
...THAT I WOULD END UP LIVING HERE.

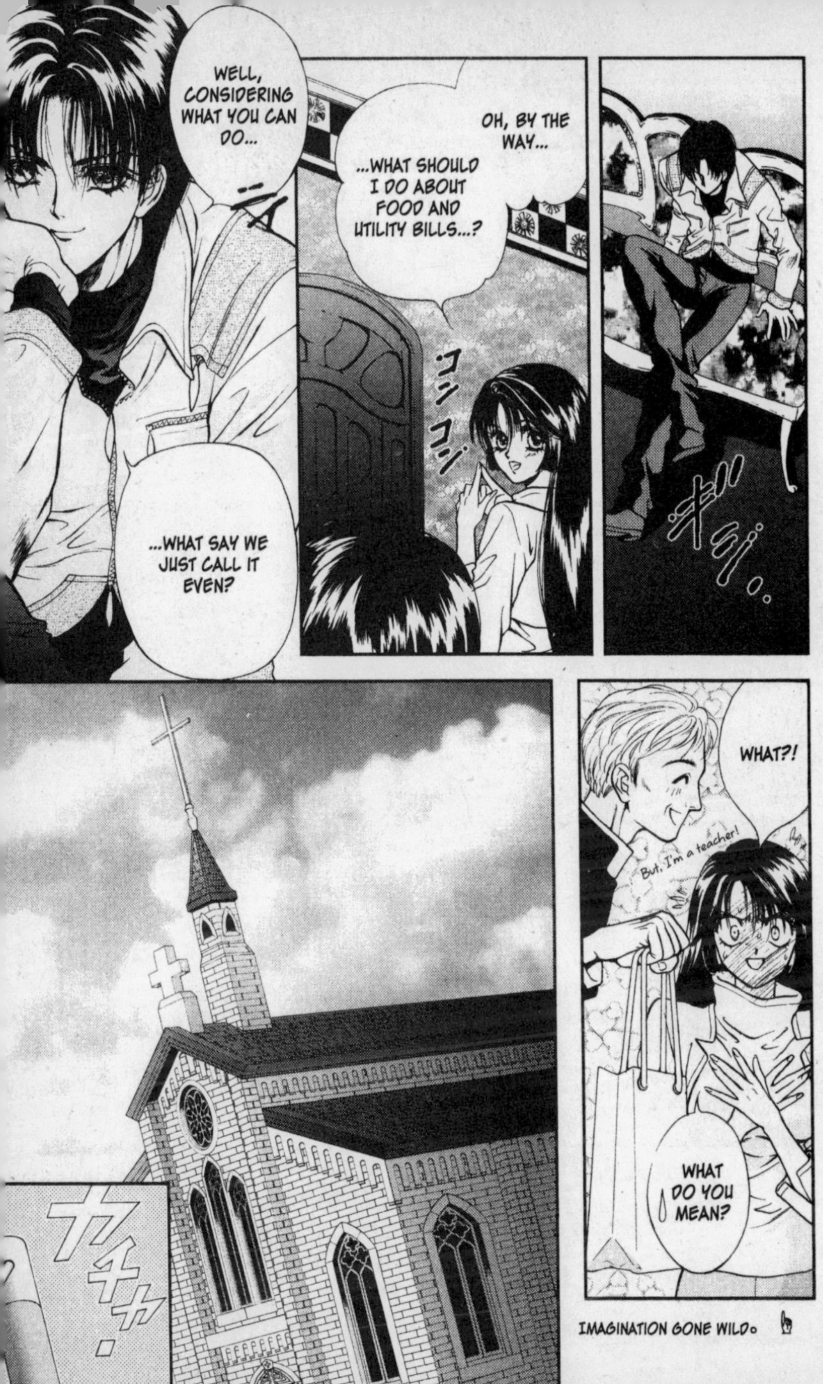
OH, BY THE WAY...
...WHAT SHOULD I DO ABOUT FOOD AND UTILITY BILLS...?
WELL, CONSIDERING WHAT YOU CAN DO...
...WHAT SAY WE JUST CALL IT EVEN?
WHAT?!
But, I'm a teacher!
WHAT DO YOU MEAN?
IMAGINATION GONE WILD。

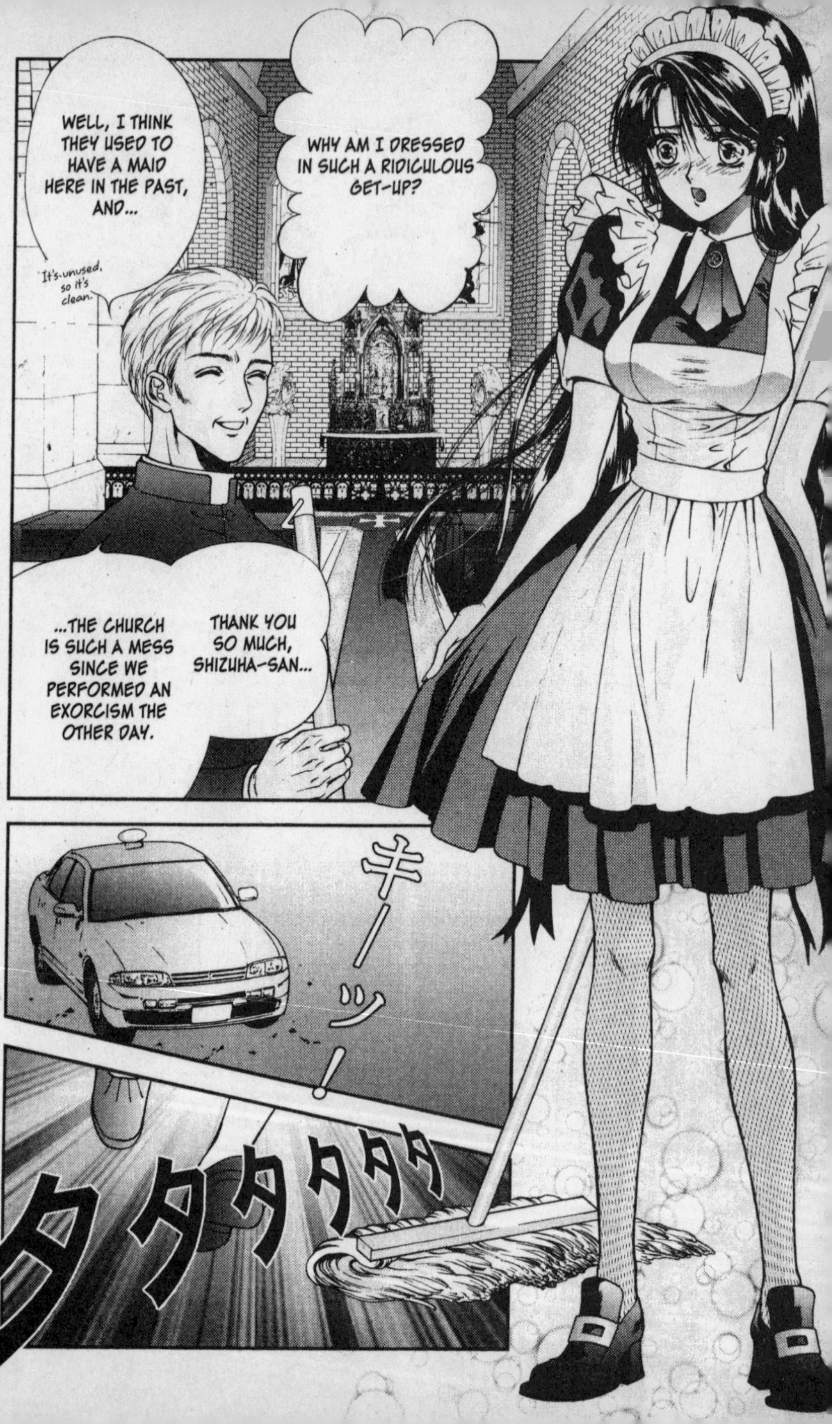
WHY AM I DRESSED IN SUCH A RIDICULOUS GET-UP?
WELL, I THINK THEY USED TO HAVE A MAID HERE IN THE PAST, AND...
It's unused, so it's clean.
THANK YOU SO MUCH, SHIZUHA-SAN...
...THE CHURCH IS SUCH A MESS SINCE WE PERFORMED AN EXORCISM THE OTHER DAY.
キーッ!
タタタタタタ

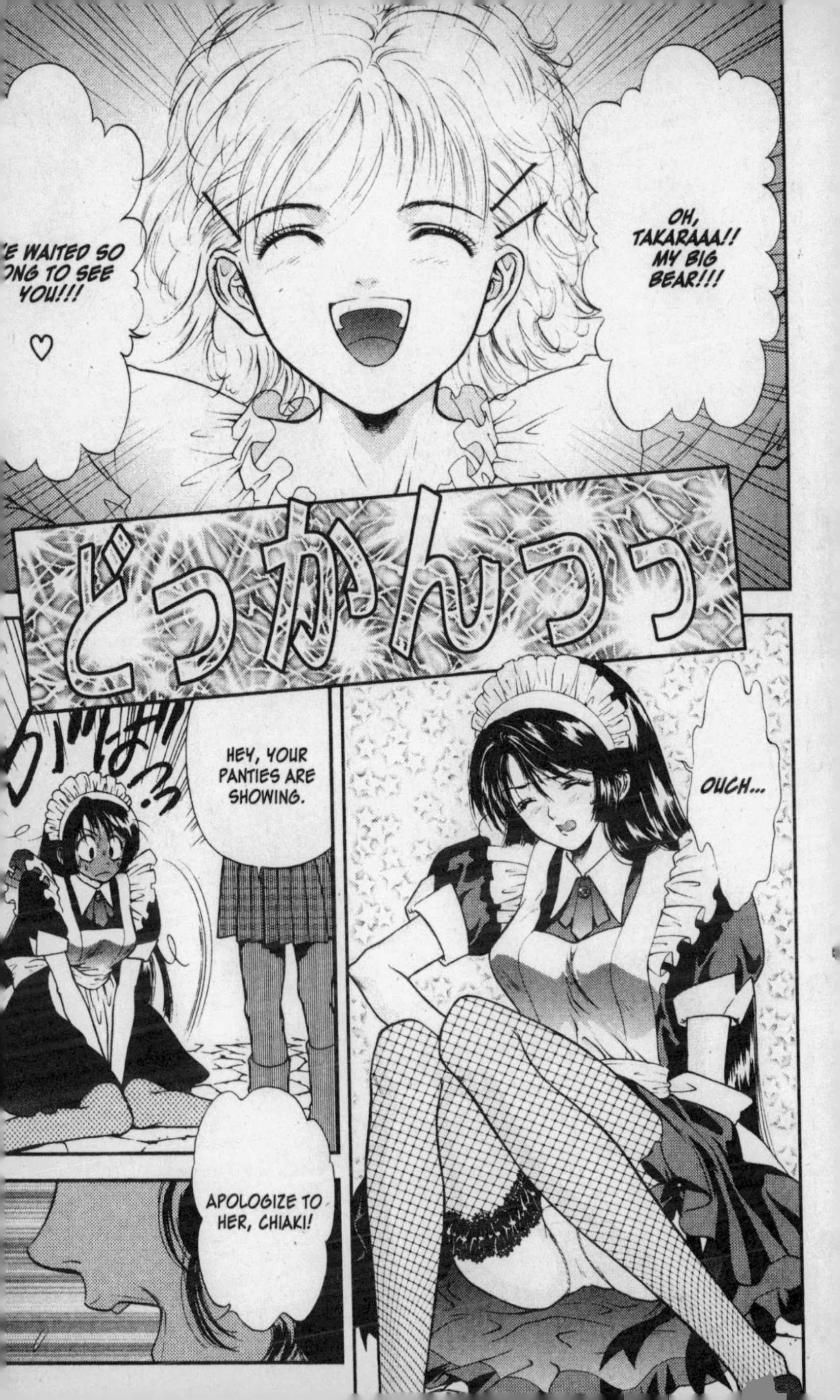
OH, TAKARAAA!! MY BIG BEAR!!!
E WAITED SO ONG TO SEE YOU!!! ♡
どっかんっっ
OUCH...
HEY, YOUR PANTIES ARE SHOWING.
APOLOGIZE TO HER, CHIAKI!

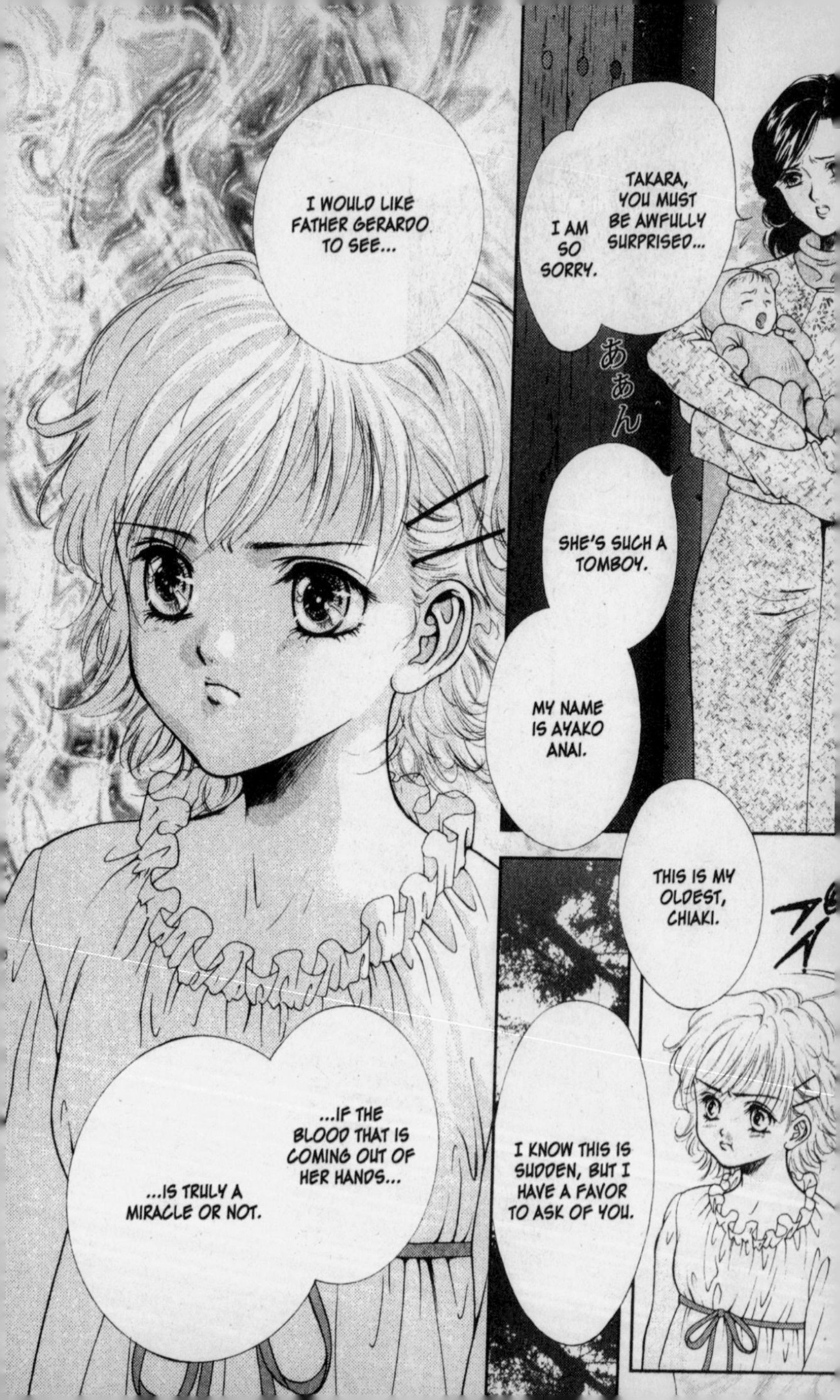
TAKARA, YOU MUST BE AWFULLY SURPRISED...
I AM SO SORRY.
ああん
SHE'S SUCH A TOMBOY.
MY NAME IS AYAKO ANAI.
THIS IS MY OLDEST, CHIAKI.
プイ
I KNOW THIS IS SUDDEN, BUT I HAVE A FAVOR TO ASK OF YOU.
I WOULD LIKE FATHER GERARDO TO SEE...
...IF THE BLOOD THAT IS COMING OUT OF HER HANDS...
...IS TRULY A MIRACLE OR NOT.

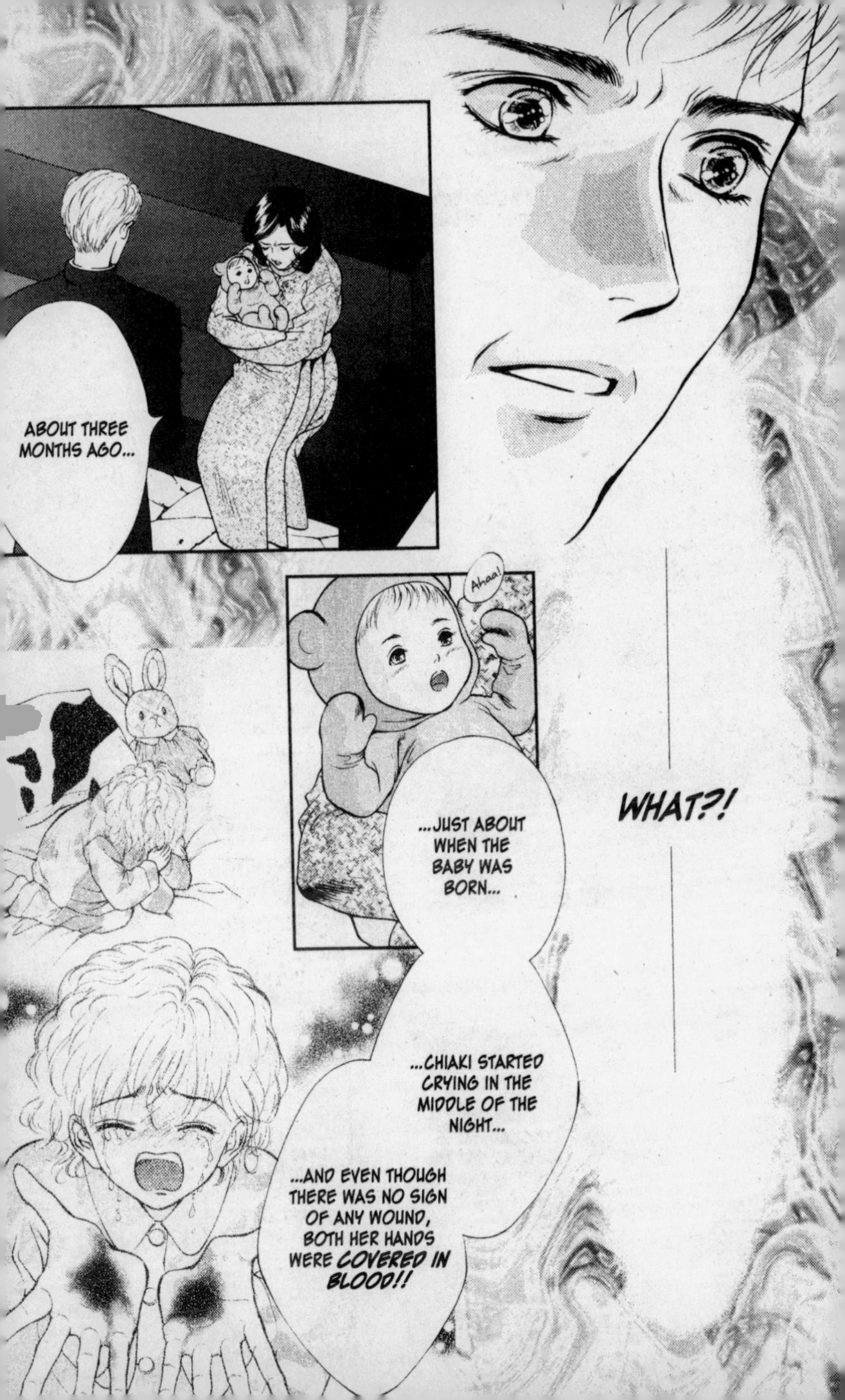
WHAT?!
ABOUT THREE MONTHS AGO...
Ahaa!
...JUST ABOUT WHEN THE BABY WAS BORN...
...CHIAKI STARTED CRYING IN THE MIDDLE OF THE NIGHT...
...AND EVEN THOUGH THERE WAS NO SIGN OF ANY WOUND, BOTH HER HANDS WERE COVERED IN BLOOD!!

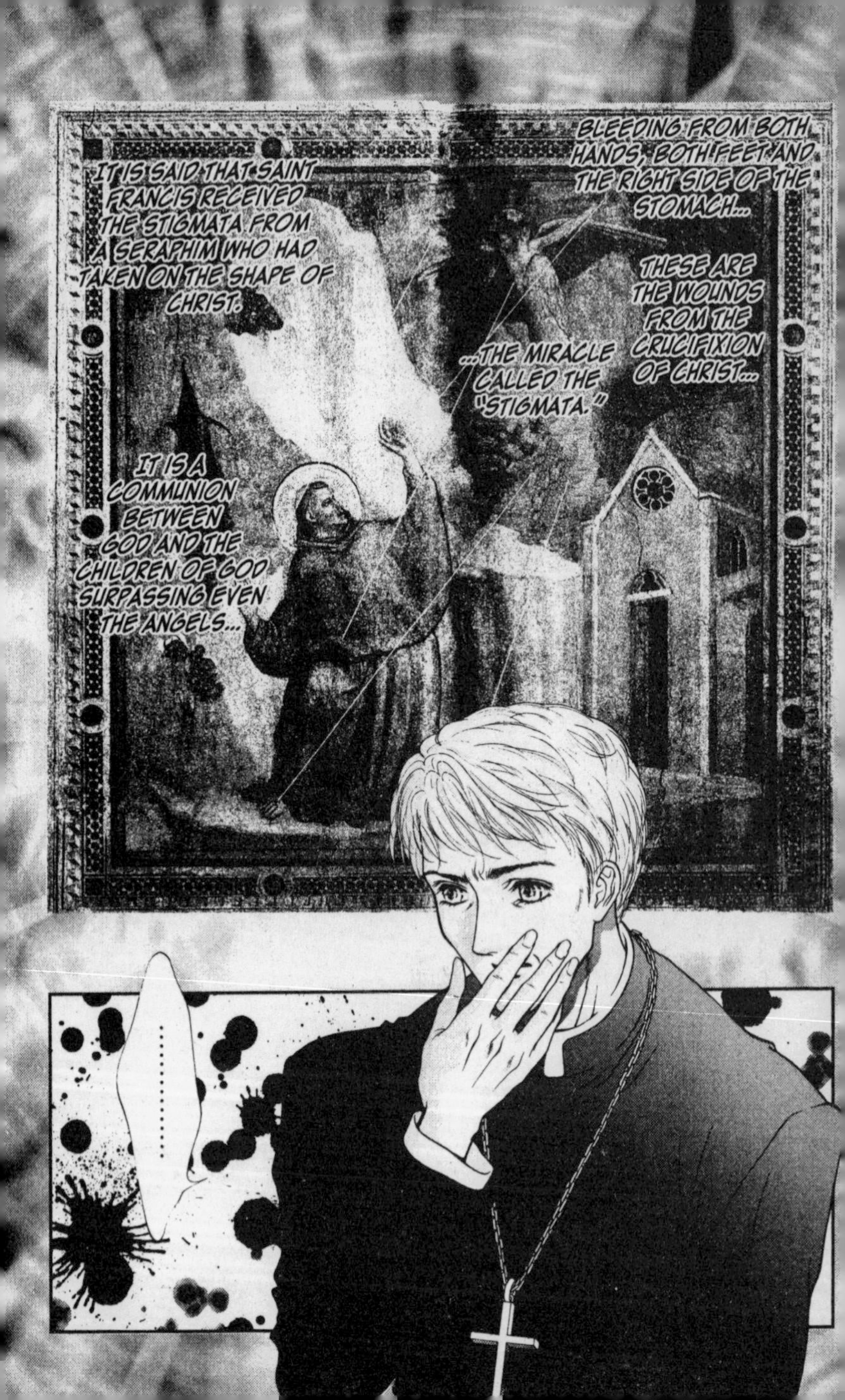
BLEEDING FROM BOTH HANDS, BOTH FEET AND THE RIGHT SIDE OF THE STOMACH...
IT IS SAID THAT SAINT FRANCIS RECEIVED THE STIGMATA FROM A SERAPHIM WHO HAD TAKEN ON THE SHAPE OF CHRIST.
THESE ARE THE WOUNDS FROM THE CRUCIFIXION OF CHRIST...
...THE MIRACLE CALLED THE "STIGMATA."
IT IS A COMMUNION BETWEEN GOD AND THE CHILDREN OF GOD SURPASSING EVEN THE ANGELS...
......

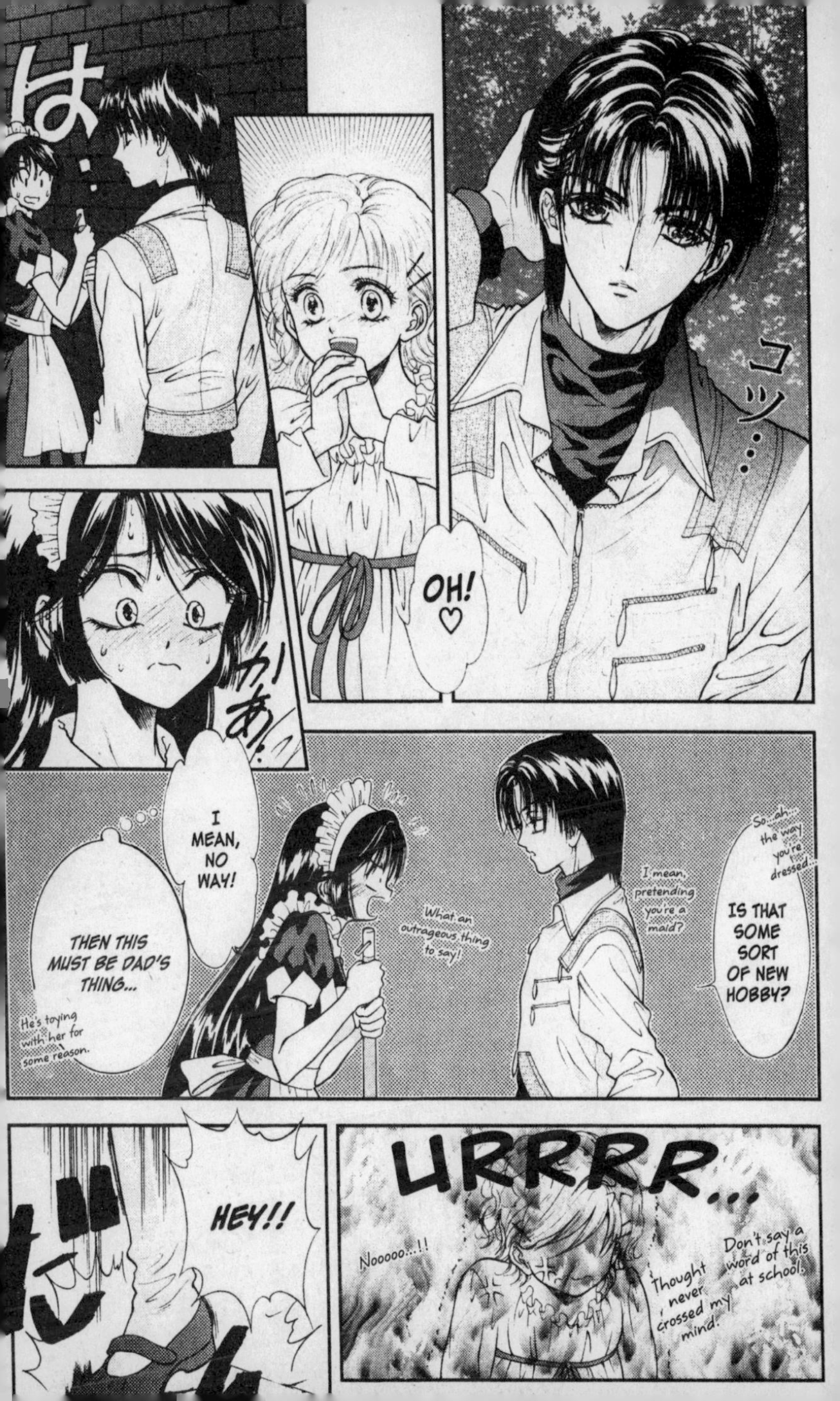

コツ…
OH! ♡
は
かあっ
So...ah... the way you're dressed...
IS THAT SOME SORT OF NEW HOBBY?
I mean, pretending you're a maid?
What an outrageous thing to say!
I MEAN, NO WAY!
THEN THIS MUST BE DAD'S THING...
He's toying with her for some reason.
URRRR...
Don't say a word of this at school.
Thought never crossed my mind.
Nooooo...!!
HEY!!

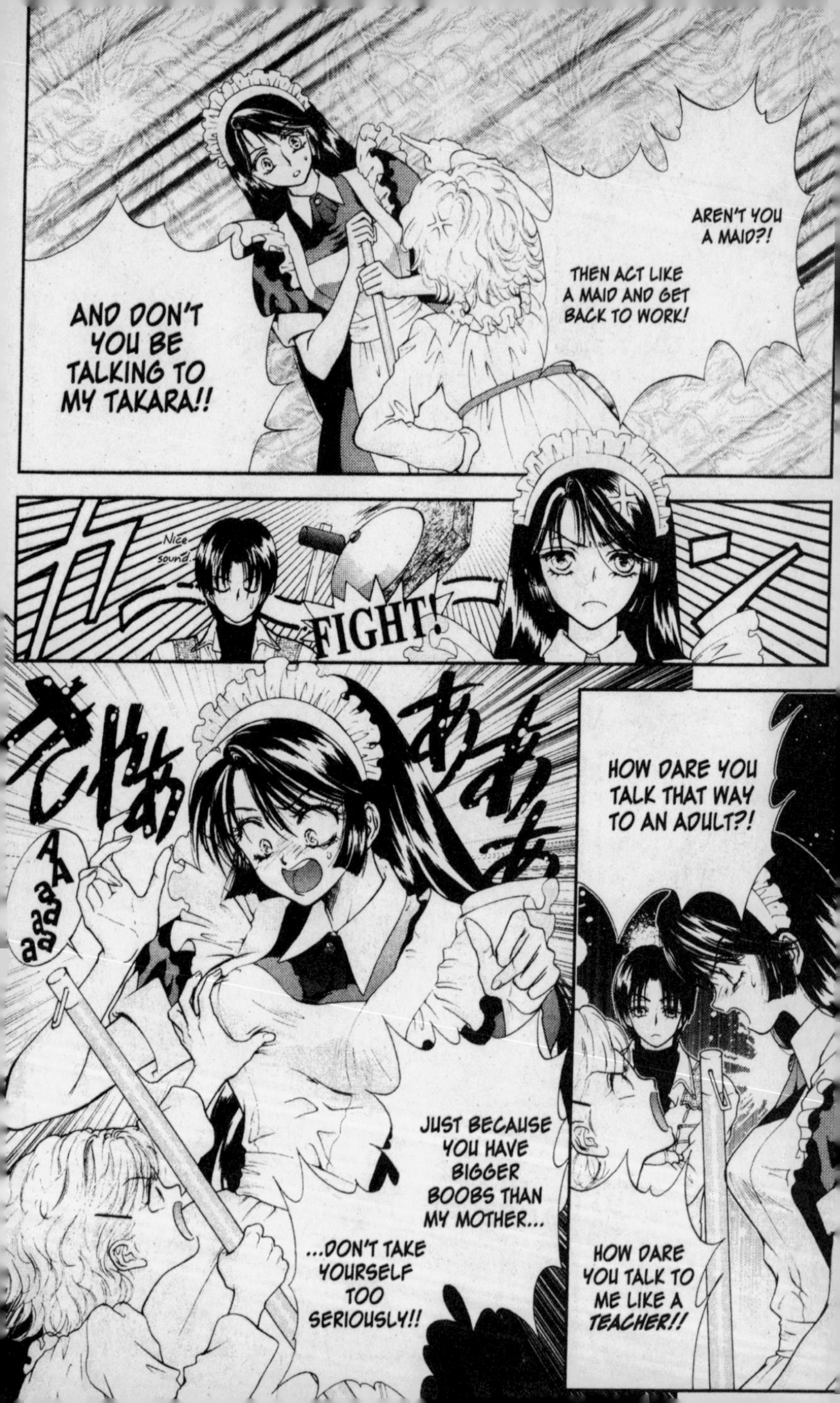
AREN'T YOU A MAID?!
THEN ACT LIKE A MAID AND GET BACK TO WORK!
AND DON'T YOU BE TALKING TO MY TAKARA!!
FIGHT!
Nice sound.
HOW DARE YOU TALK THAT WAY TO AN ADULT?!
HOW DARE YOU TALK TO ME LIKE A TEACHER!!
AAaaaa
JUST BECAUSE YOU HAVE BIGGER BOOBS THAN MY MOTHER...
...DON'T TAKE YOURSELF TOO SERIOUSLY!!

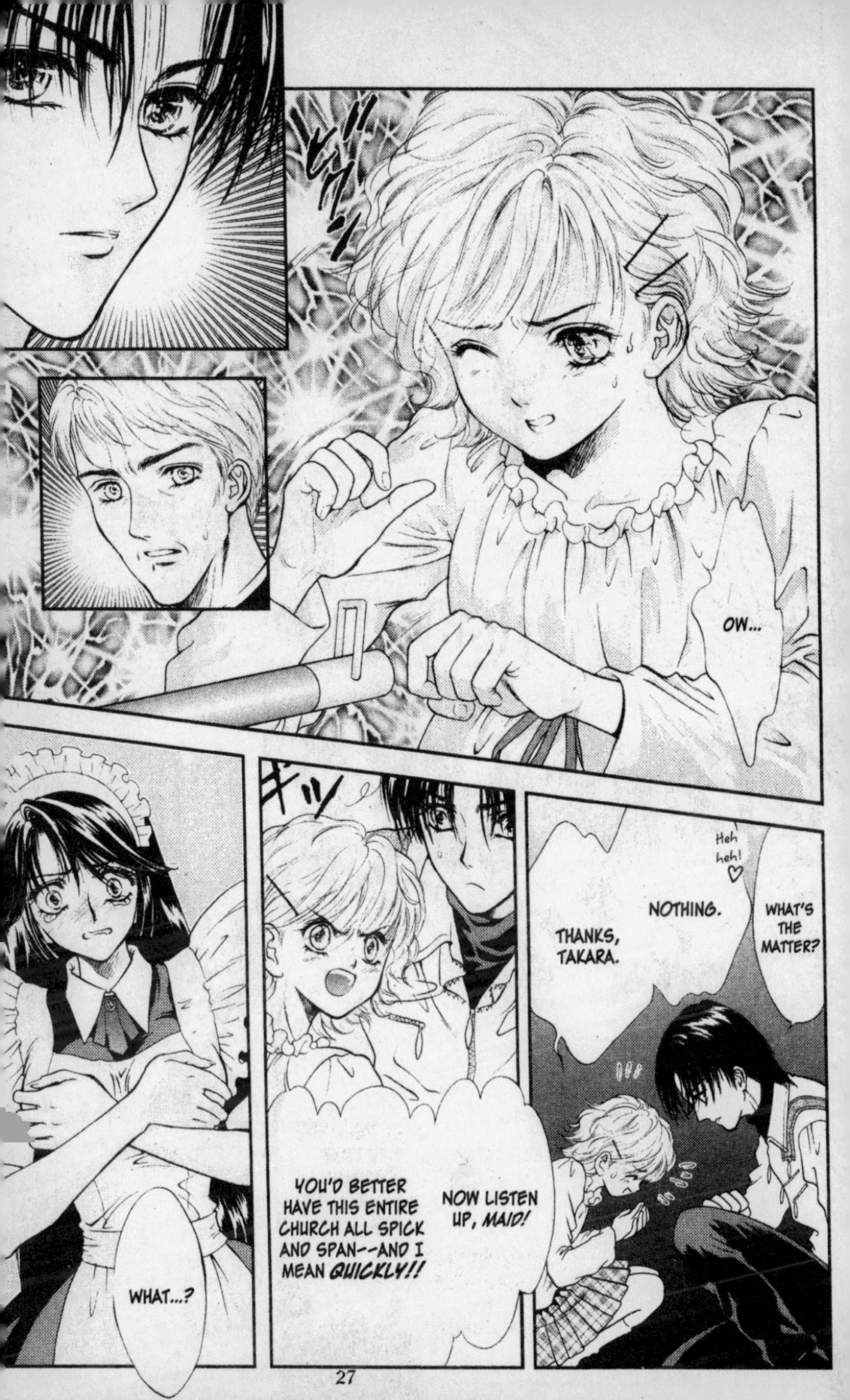
OW...
WHAT'S THE MATTER?
Heh heh! ♡
NOTHING.
THANKS, TAKARA.
NOW LISTEN UP, *MAID!*
YOU'D BETTER HAVE THIS ENTIRE CHURCH ALL SPICK AND SPAN--AND I MEAN ***QUICKLY!!***
WHAT...?

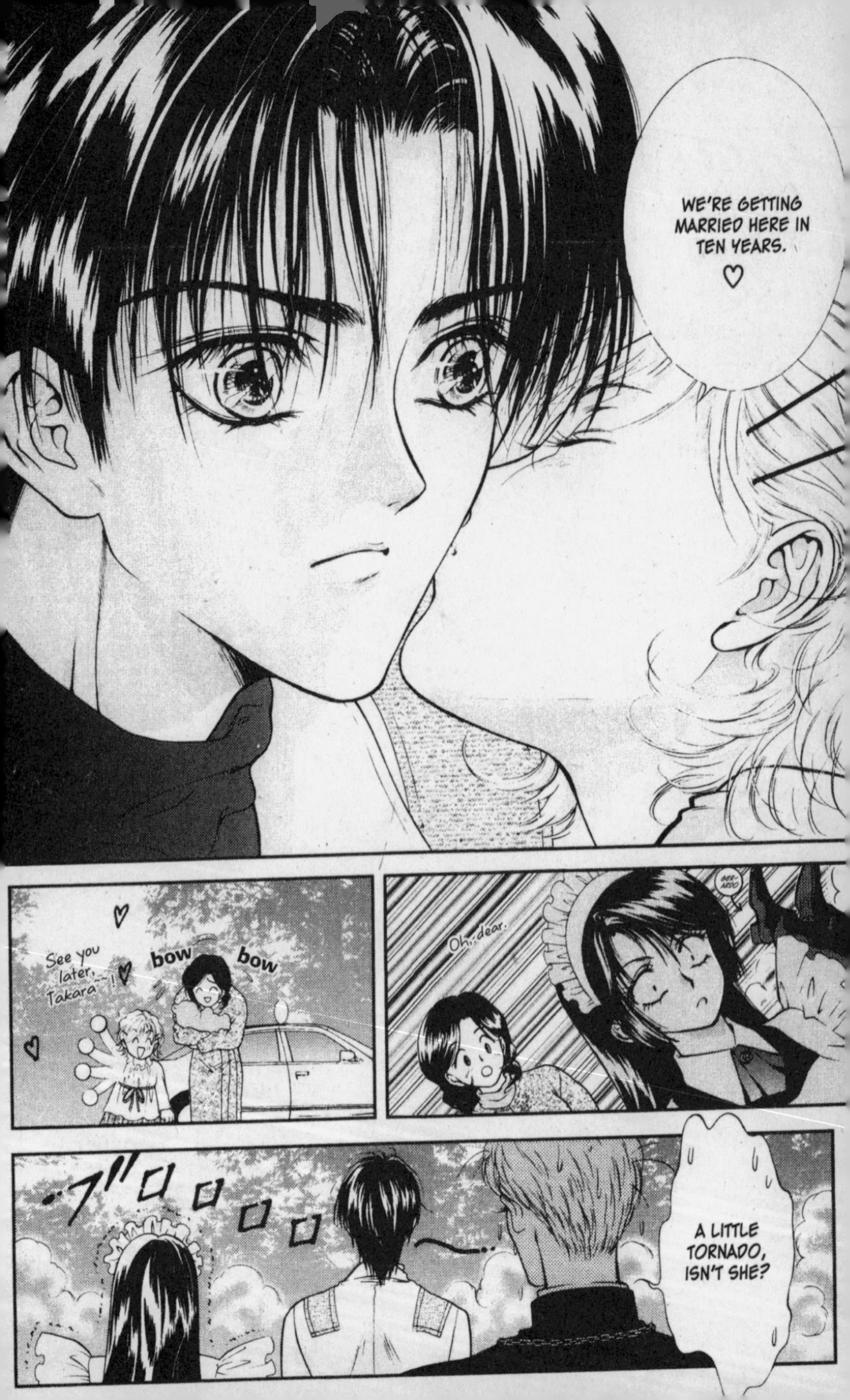
WE'RE GETTING MARRIED HERE IN TEN YEARS. ♡
GER-ARDO
Oh, dear.
See you later, Takara~~! ♡
bow
bow
ブロロロロ
A LITTLE TORNADO, ISN'T SHE?

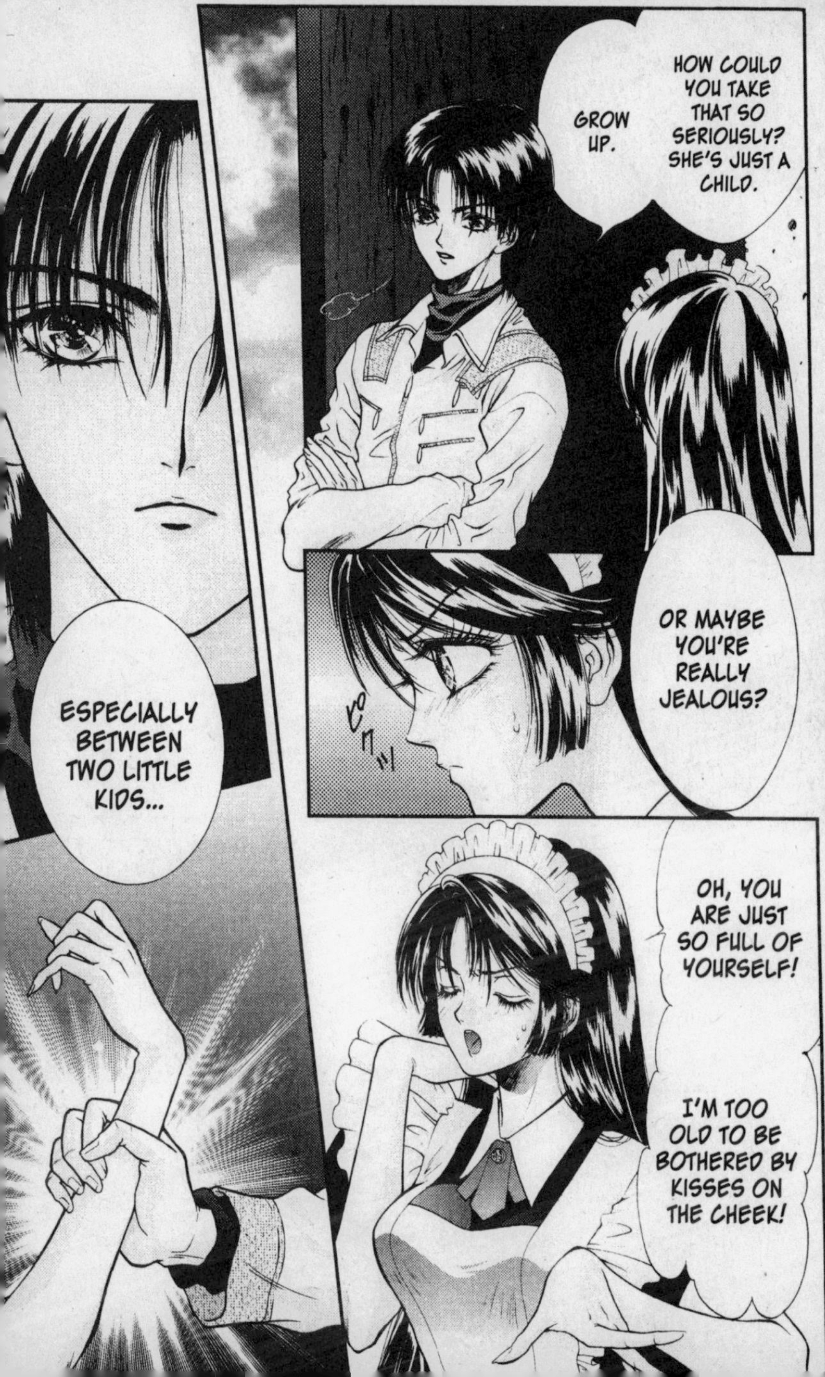
HOW COULD YOU TAKE THAT SO SERIOUSLY? SHE'S JUST A CHILD.
GROW UP.
OR MAYBE YOU'RE REALLY JEALOUS?
OH, YOU ARE JUST SO FULL OF YOURSELF!
I'M TOO OLD TO BE BOTHERED BY KISSES ON THE CHEEK!
ESPECIALLY BETWEEN TWO LITTLE KIDS...

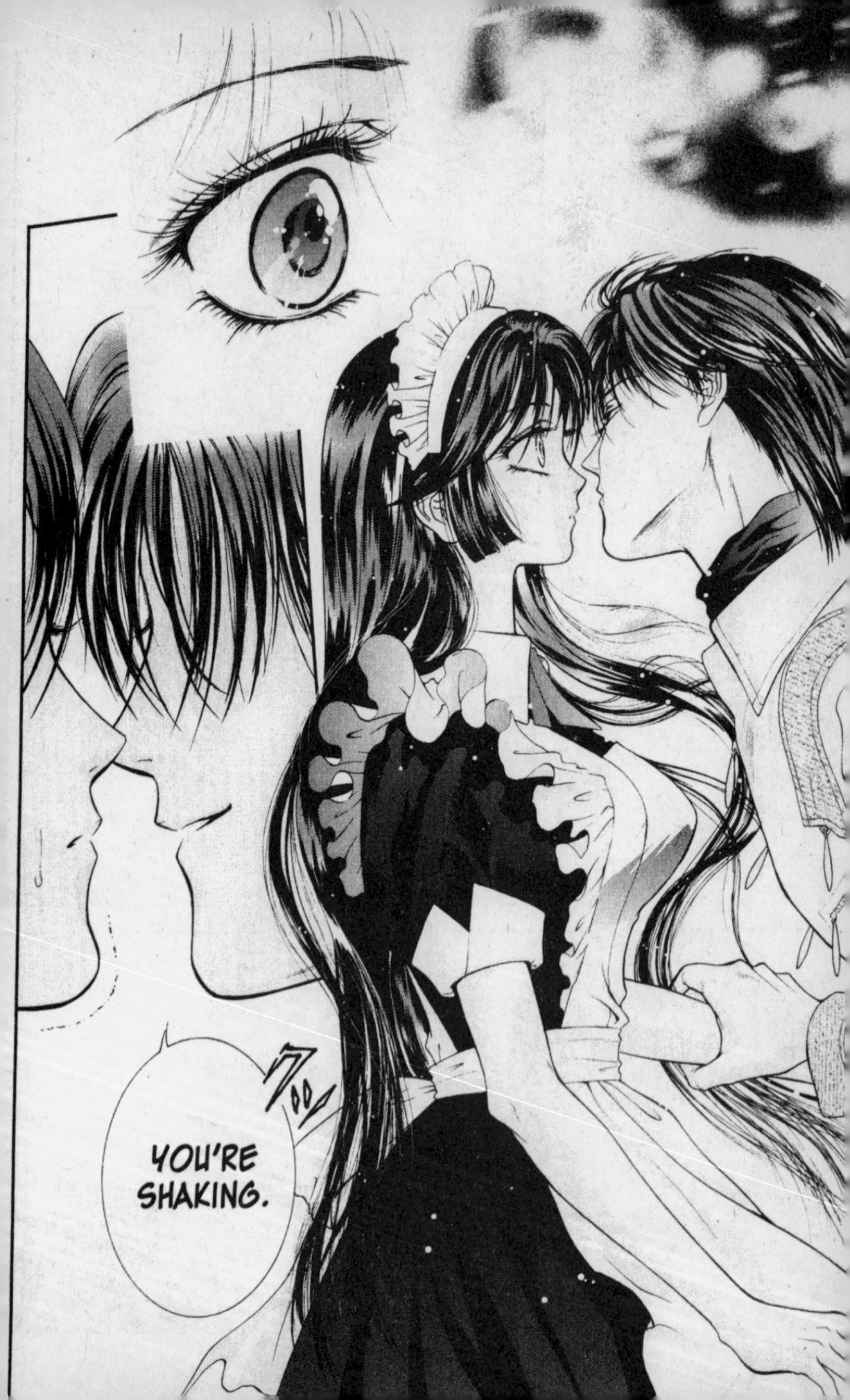
YOU'RE
SHAKING.

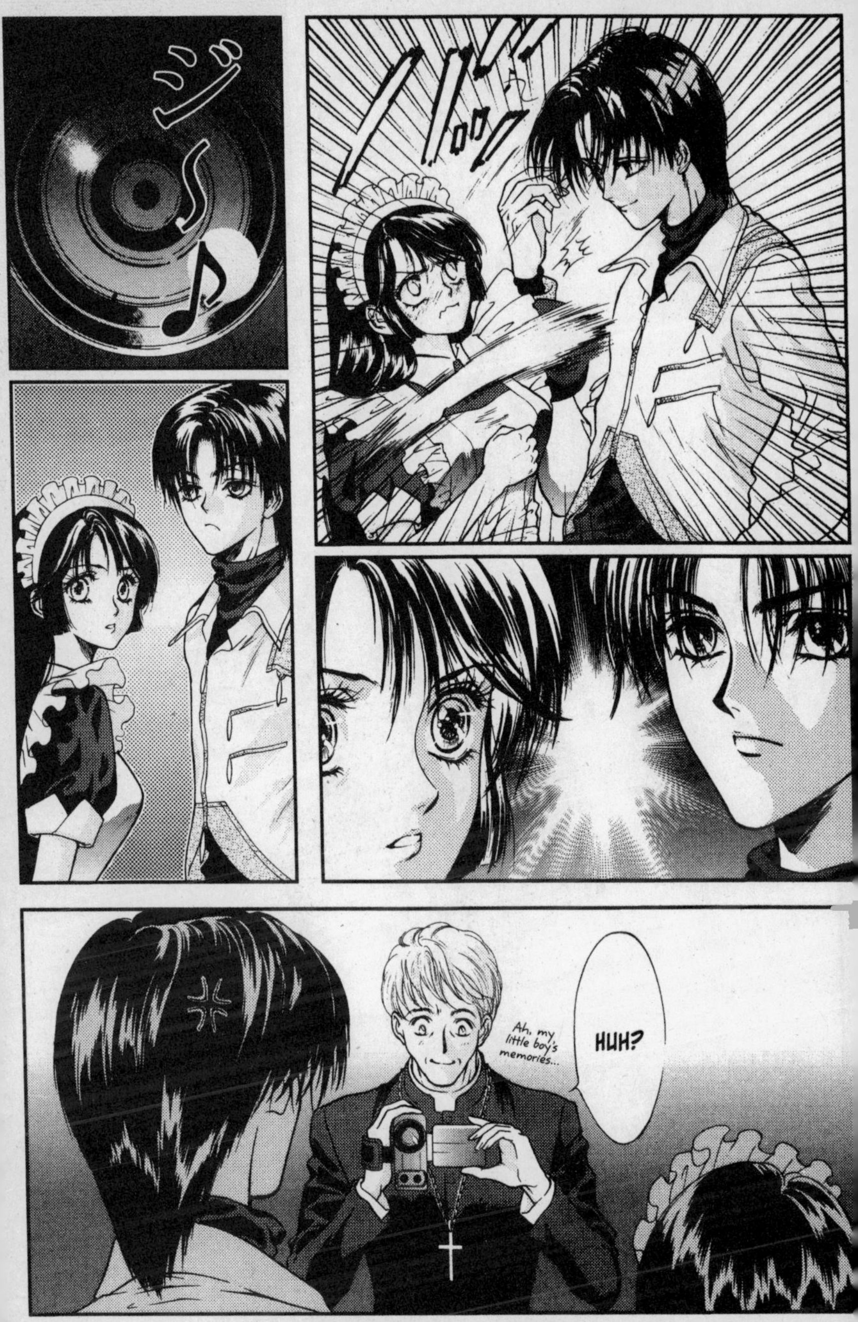
ジ
HUH?
Ah, my little boy's memories...

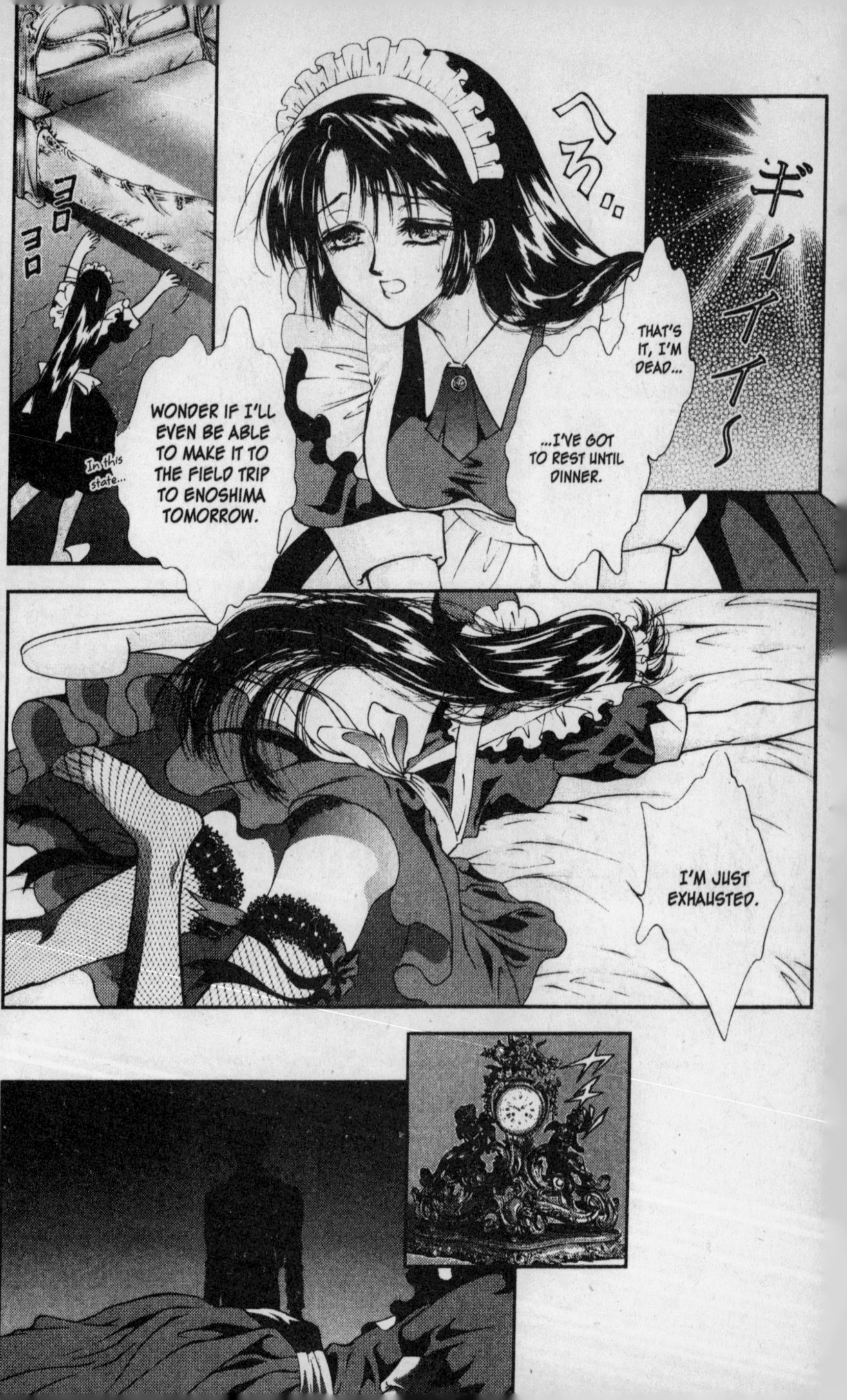
ギイイイー～
へろ。。
THAT'S IT, I'M DEAD...
...I'VE GOT TO REST UNTIL DINNER.
ヨロヨロ
In this state...
WONDER IF I'LL EVEN BE ABLE TO MAKE IT TO THE FIELD TRIP TO ENOSHIMA TOMORROW.
I'M JUST EXHAUSTED.

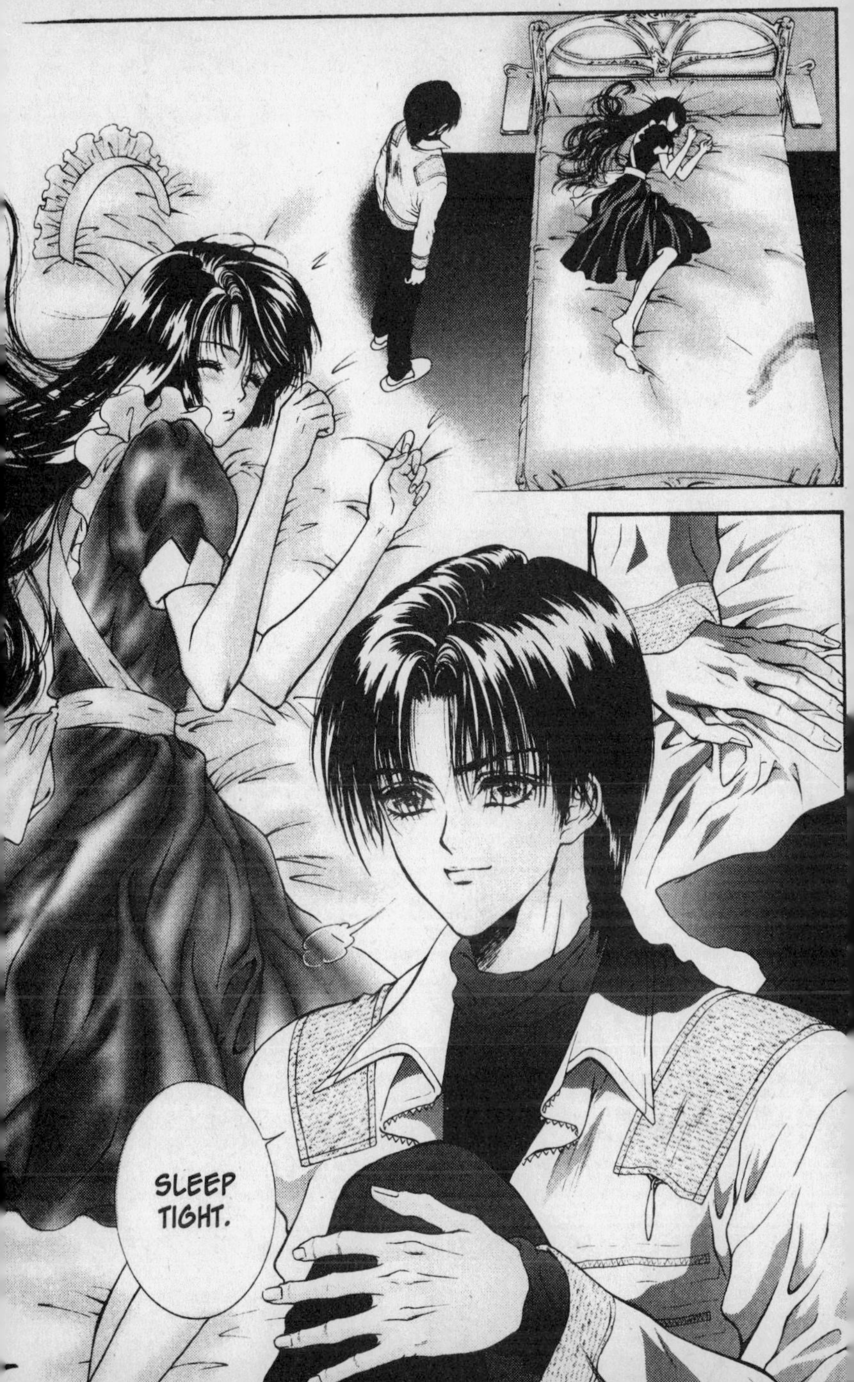
SLEEP TIGHT.

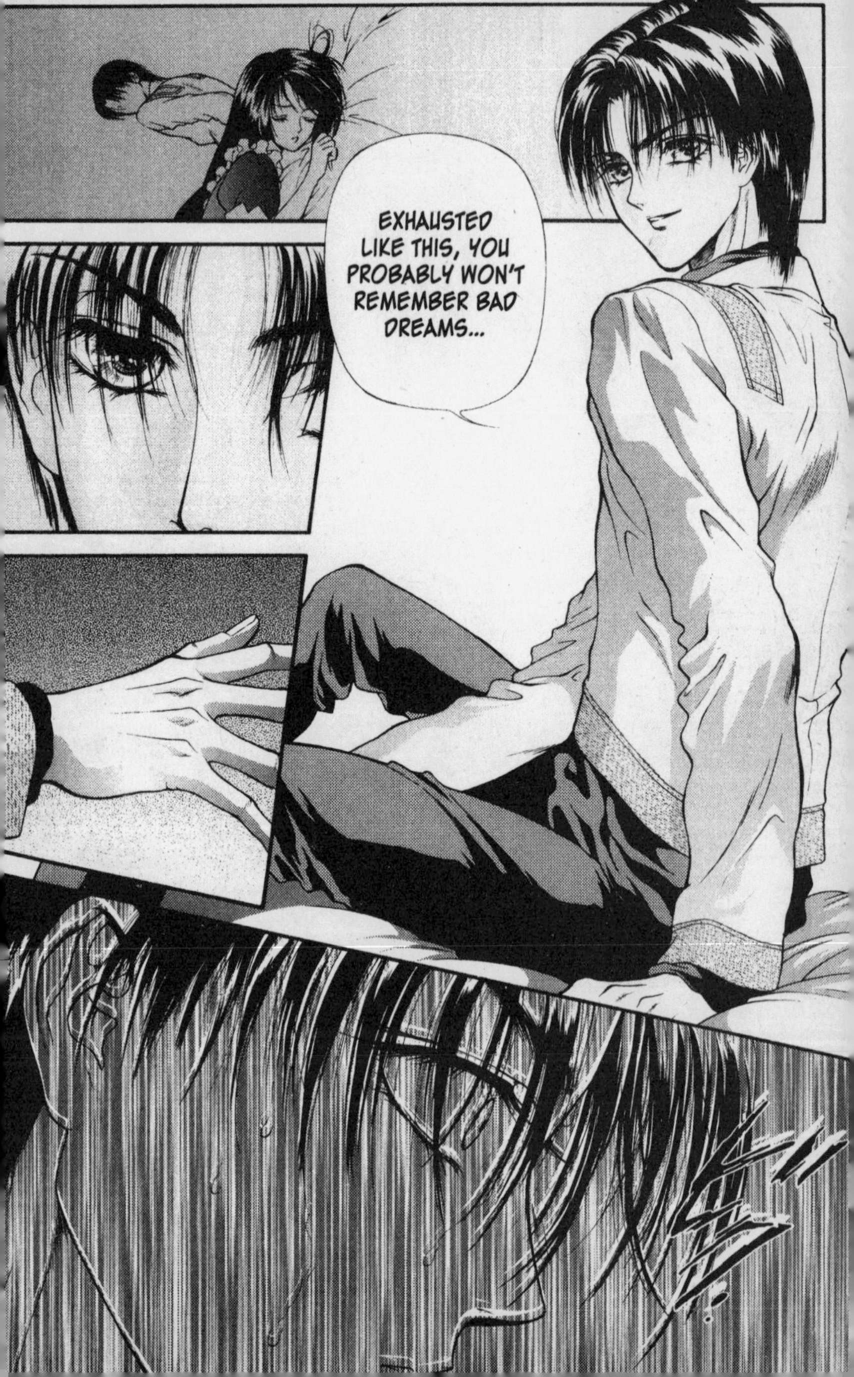
EXHAUSTED LIKE THIS, YOU PROBABLY WON'T REMEMBER BAD DREAMS...

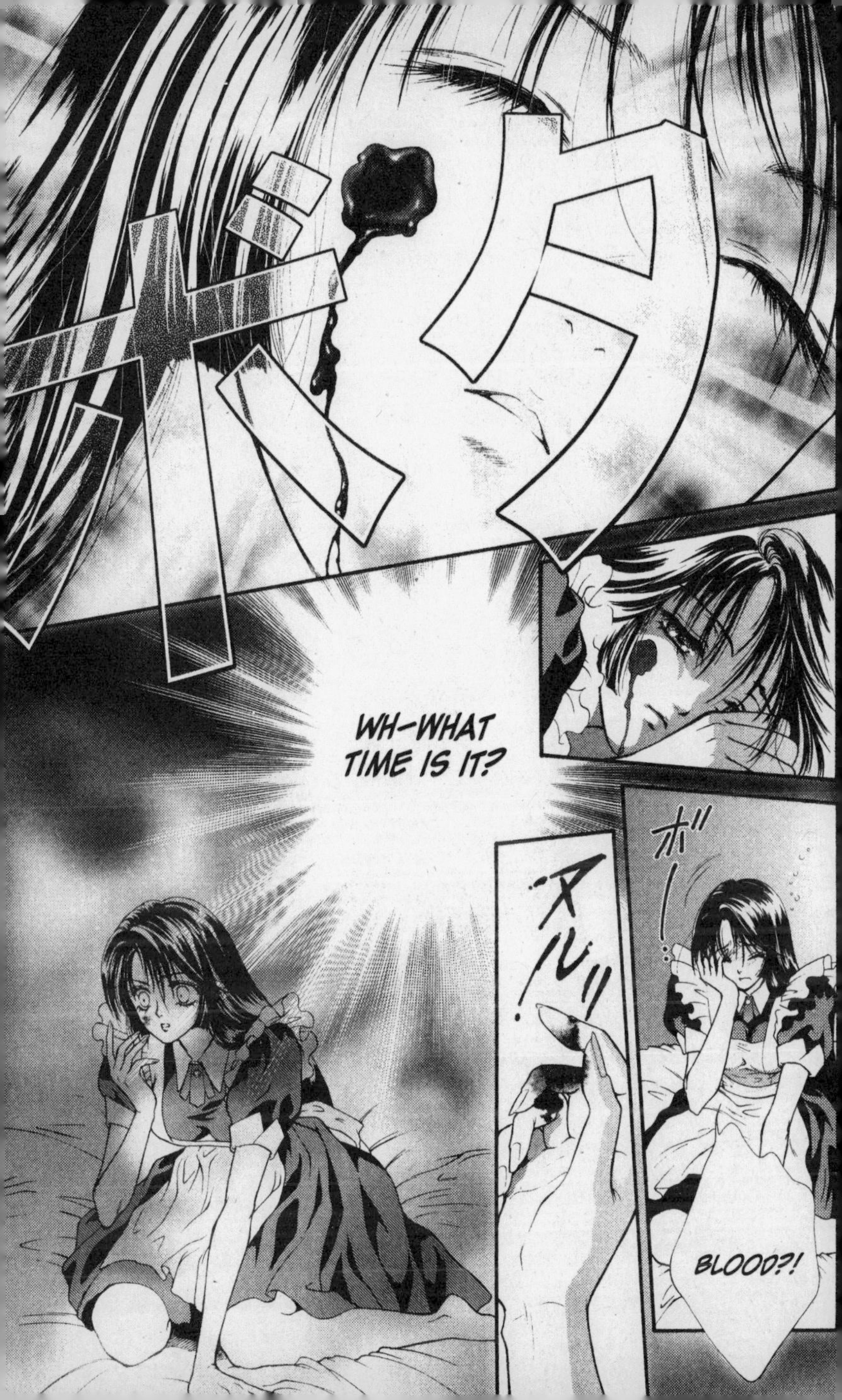
WH-WHAT TIME IS IT?
ボー…
ヌル!!
BLOOD?!

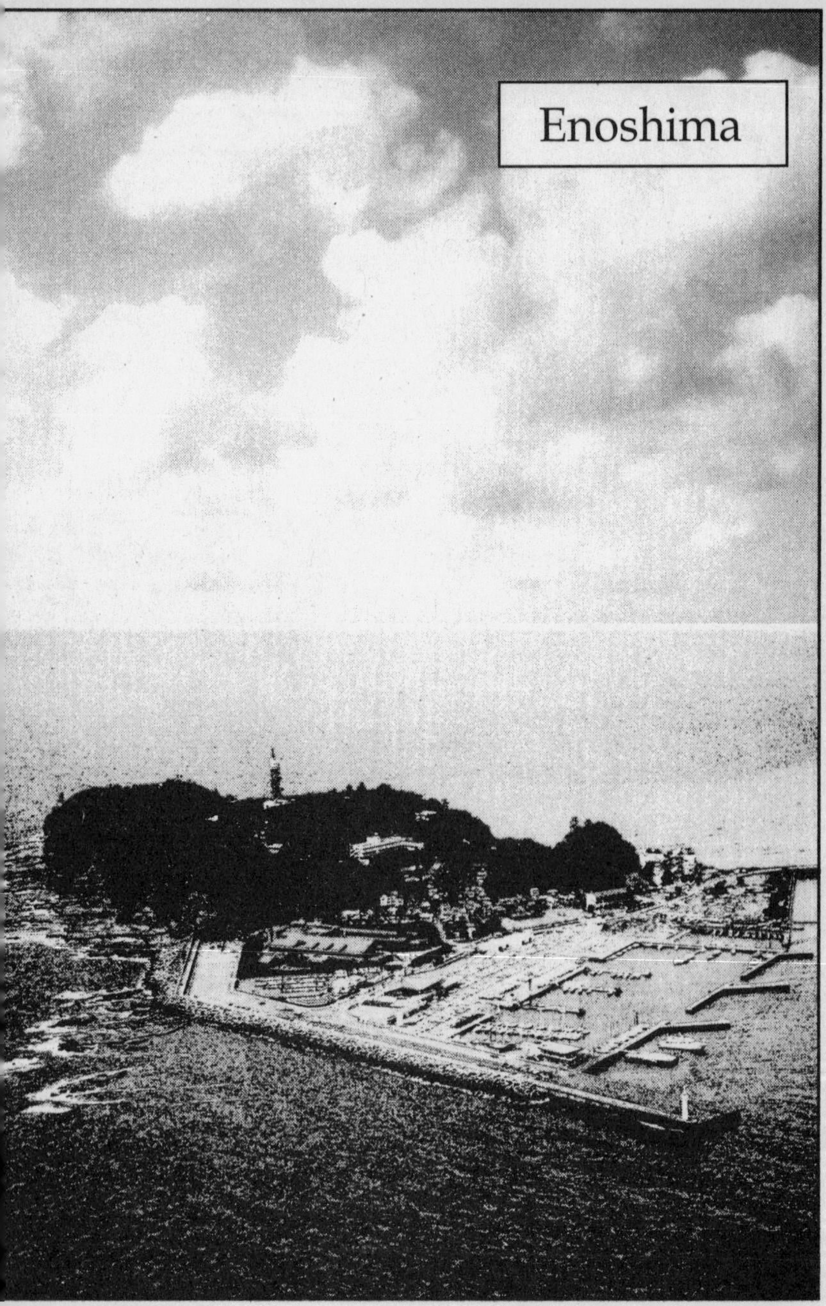
Enoshima

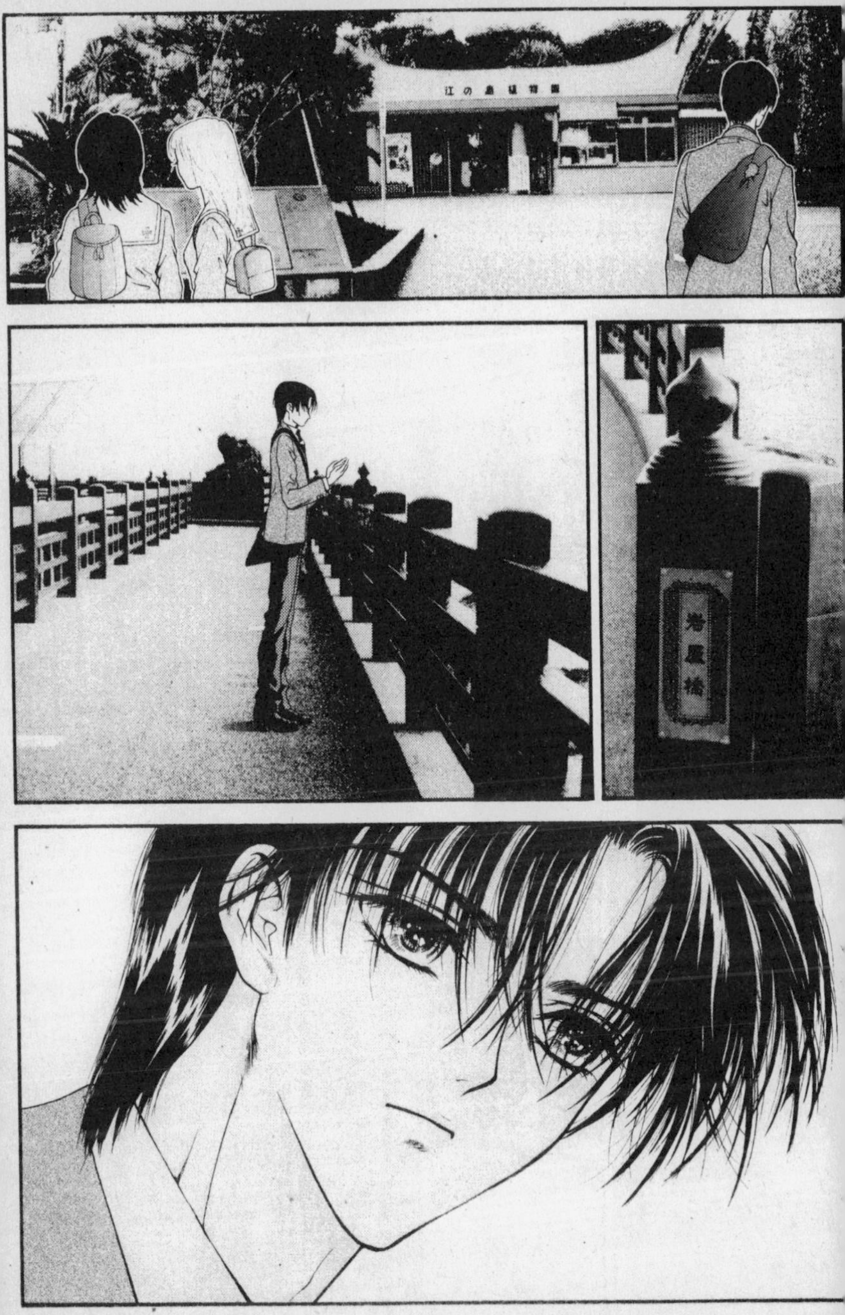
江の島植物園

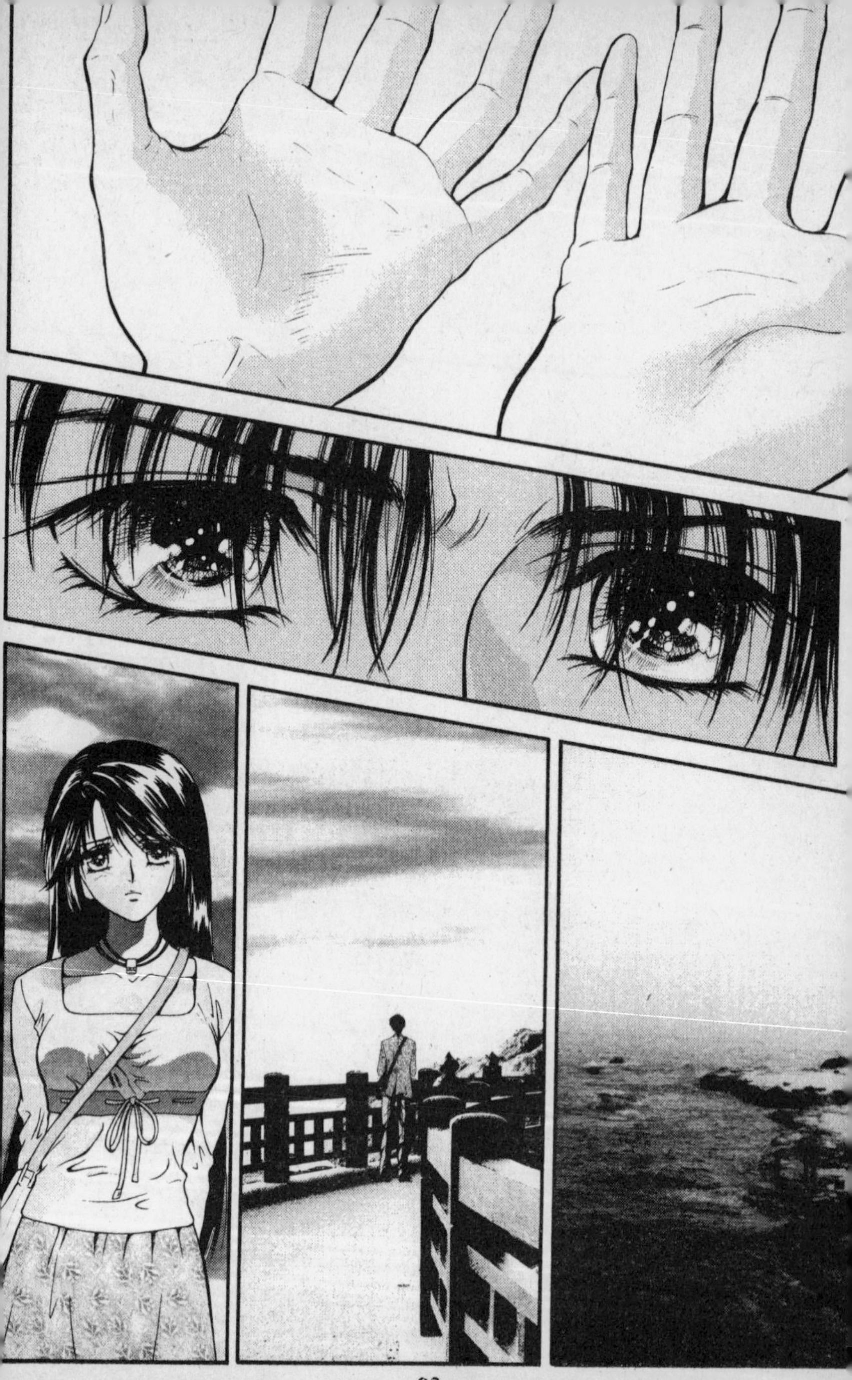

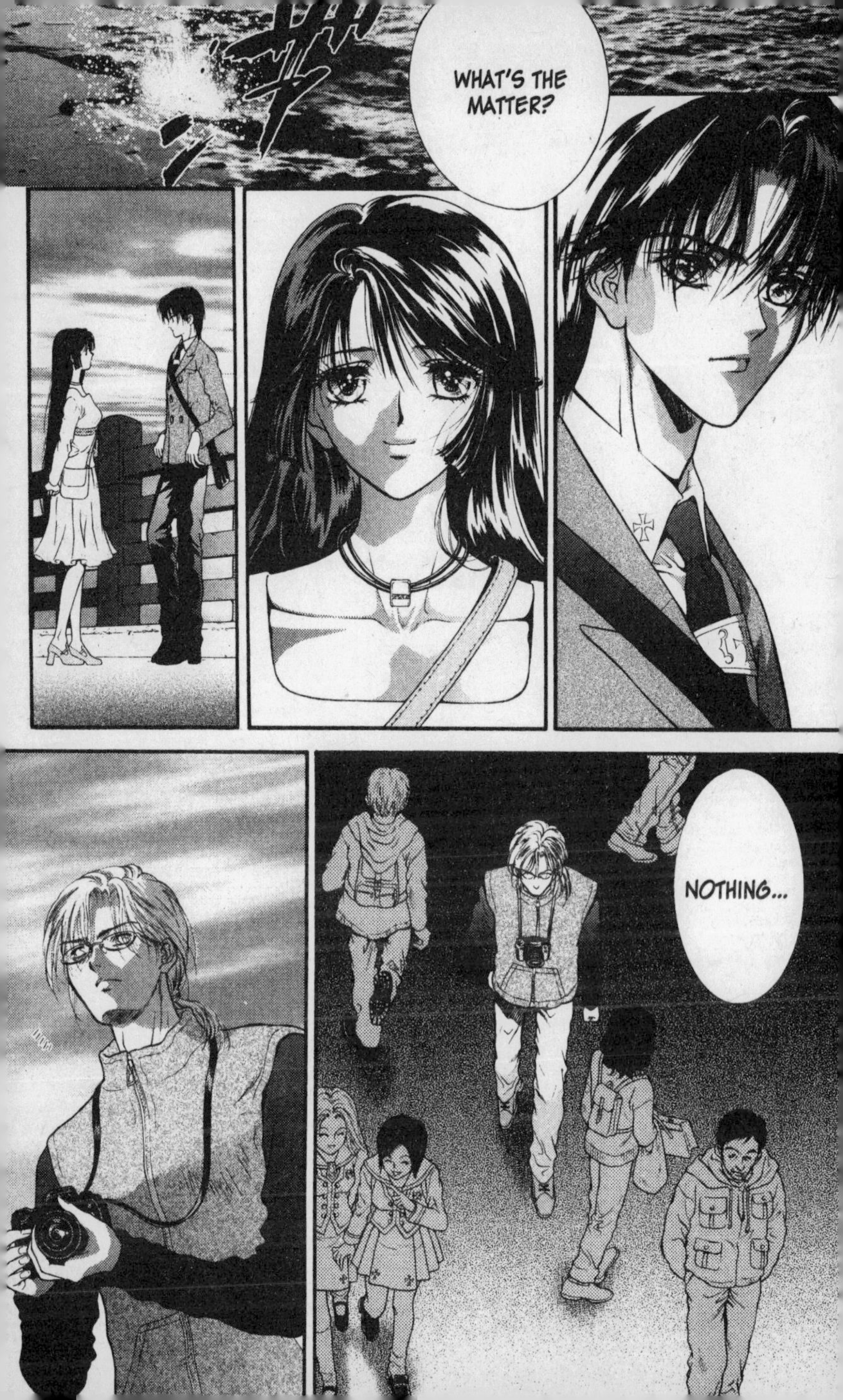
WHAT'S THE MATTER?
NOTHING...

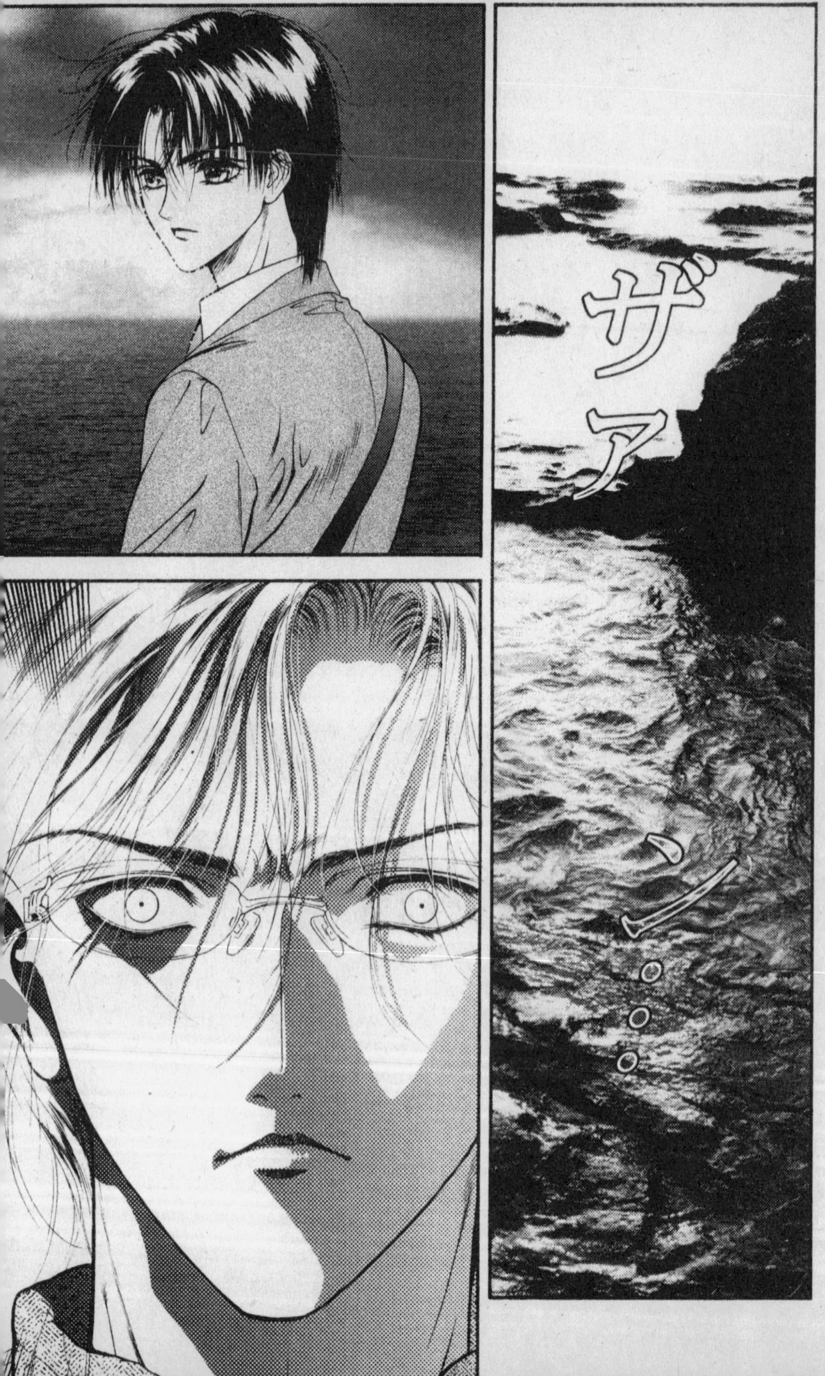
ザアーン…

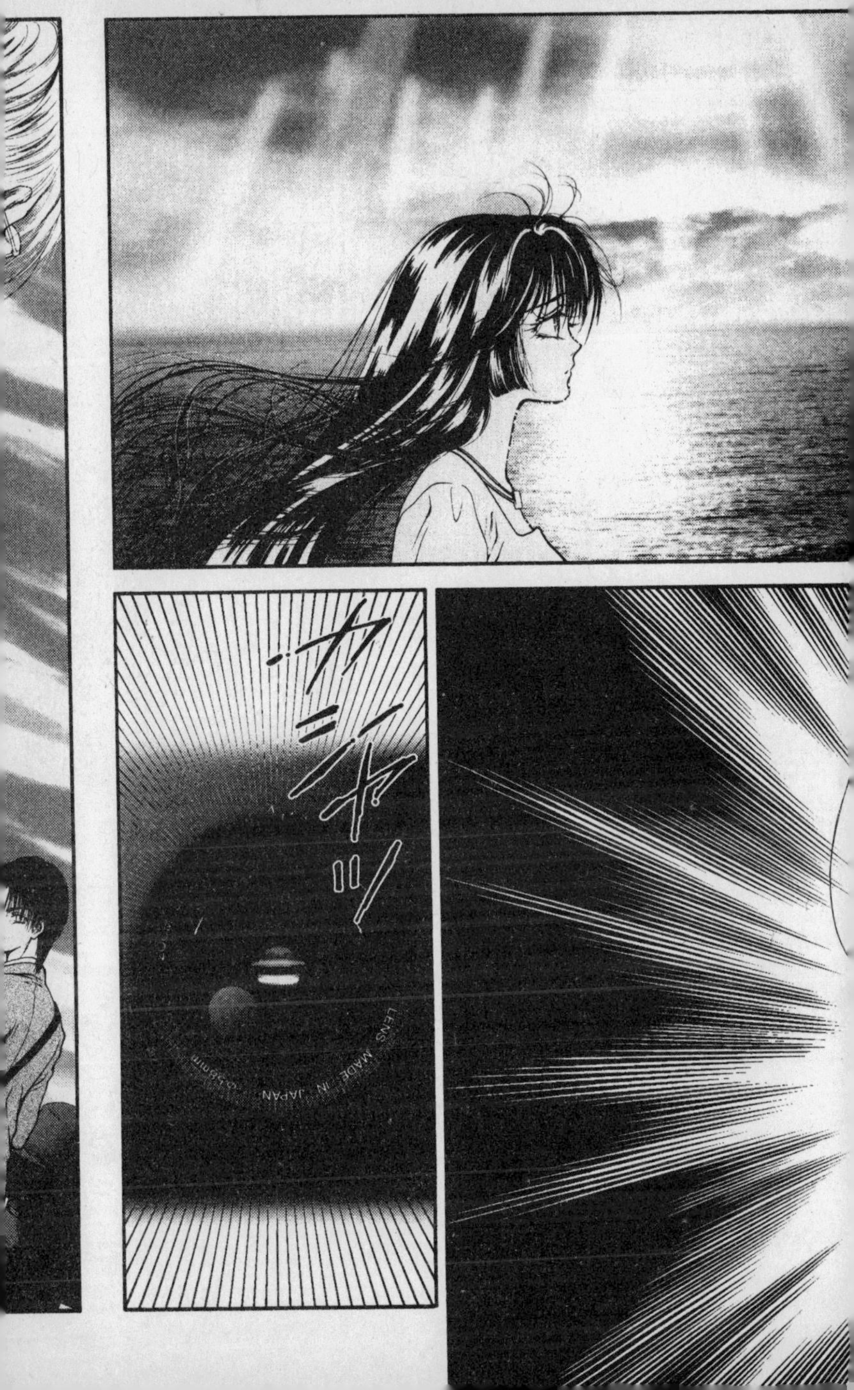
カシャ!!
LENS MADE IN JAPAN

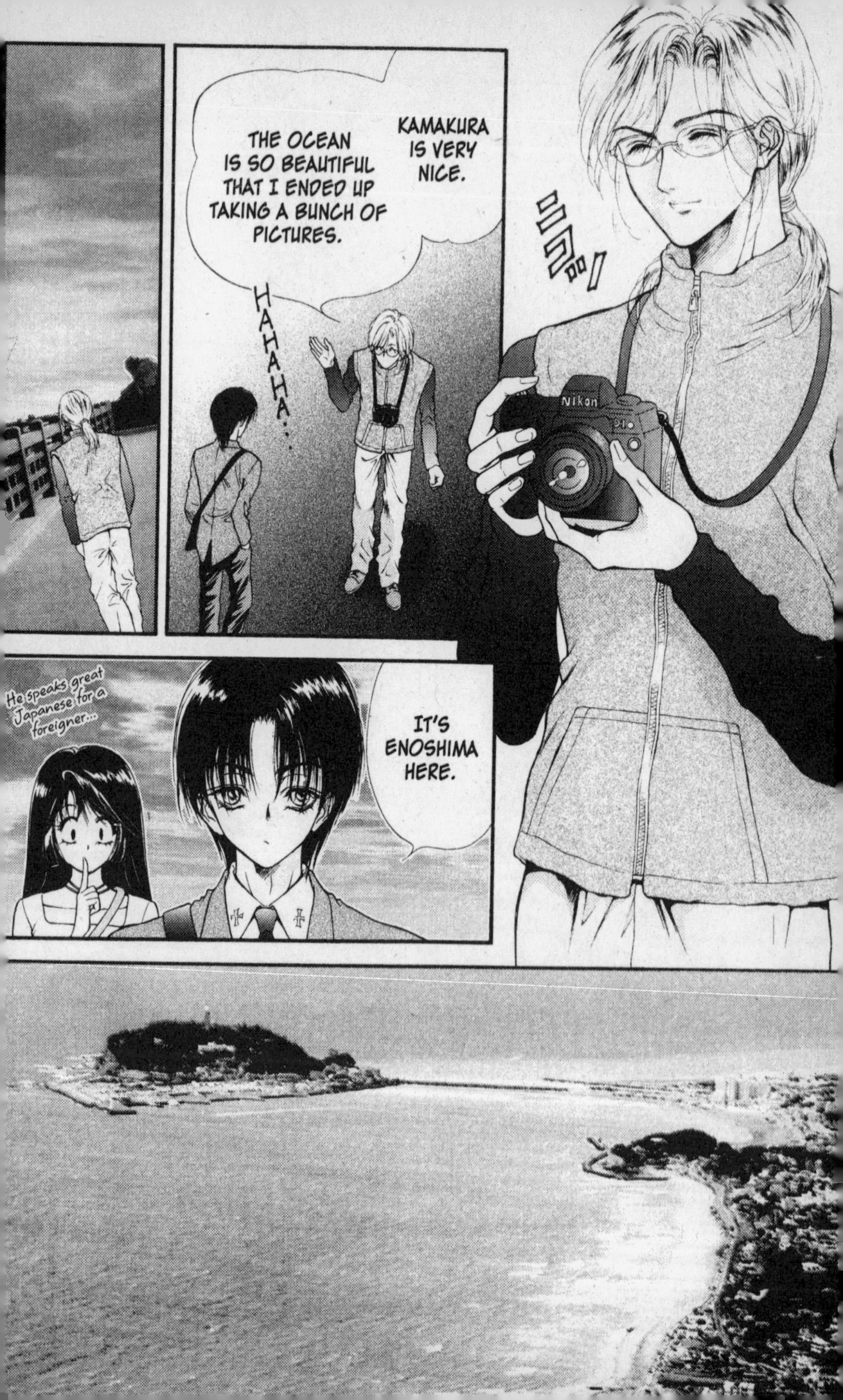
ニコッ
KAMAKURA IS VERY NICE.
THE OCEAN IS SO BEAUTIFUL THAT I ENDED UP TAKING A BUNCH OF PICTURES.
HAHAHA...
IT'S ENOSHIMA HERE.
He speaks great Japanese for a foreigner...

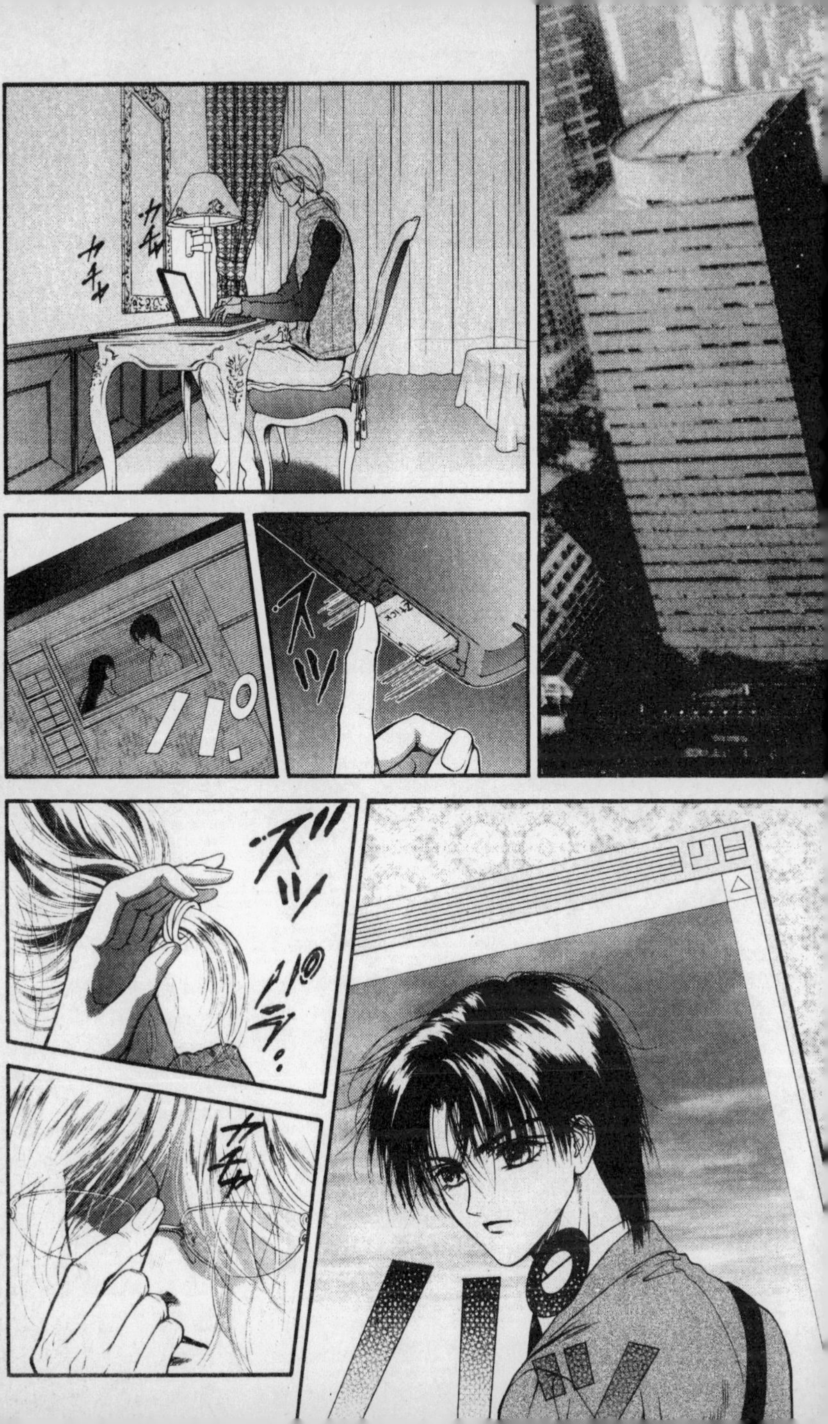
カチャ
カチャ
ズッ
パ。
パッ
ズッ
パラ。
カチャ

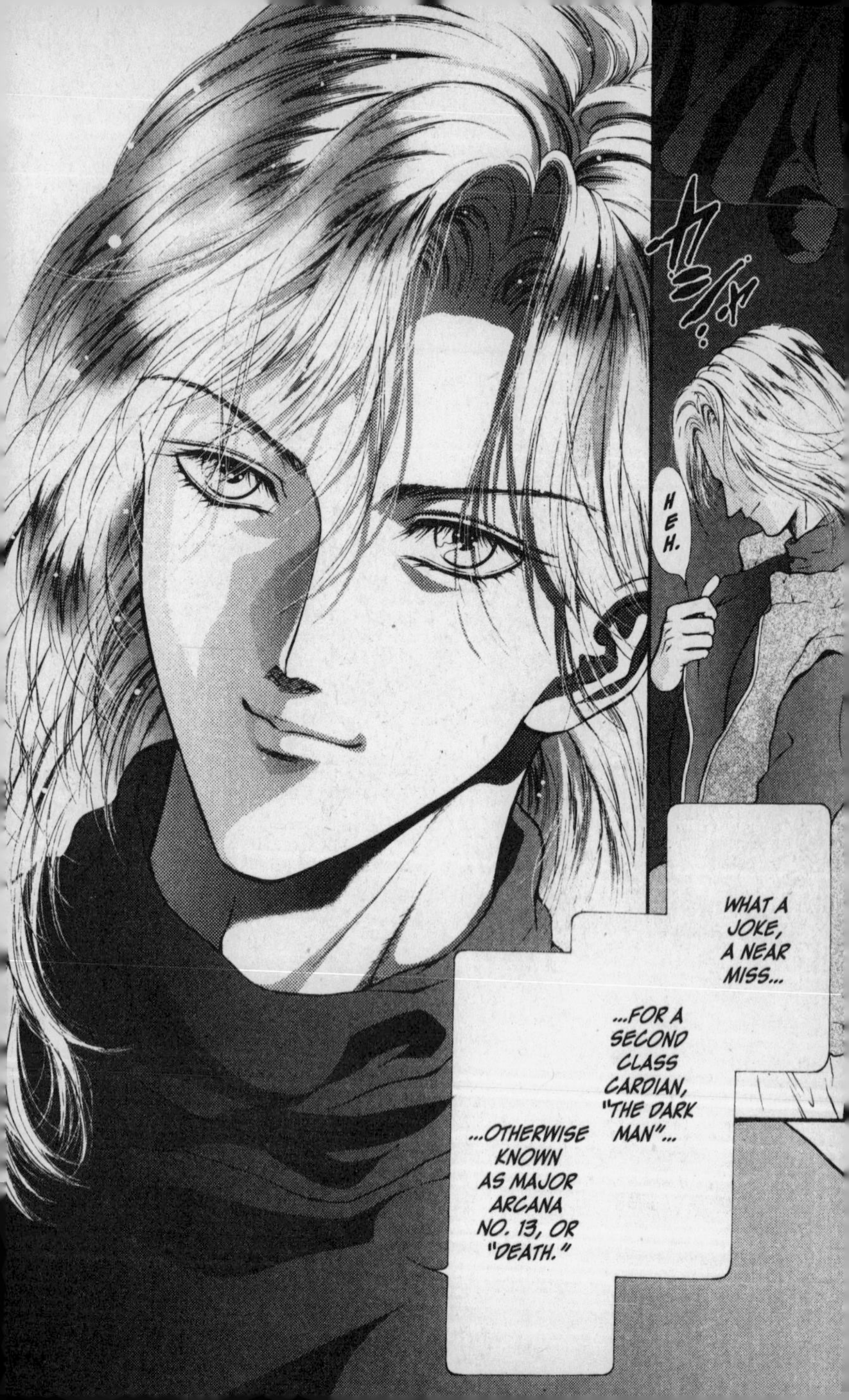
HEH.
WHAT A JOKE, A NEAR MISS...
...FOR A SECOND CLASS CARDIAN, "THE DARK MAN"...
...OTHERWISE KNOWN AS MAJOR ARCANA NO. 13, OR "DEATH."

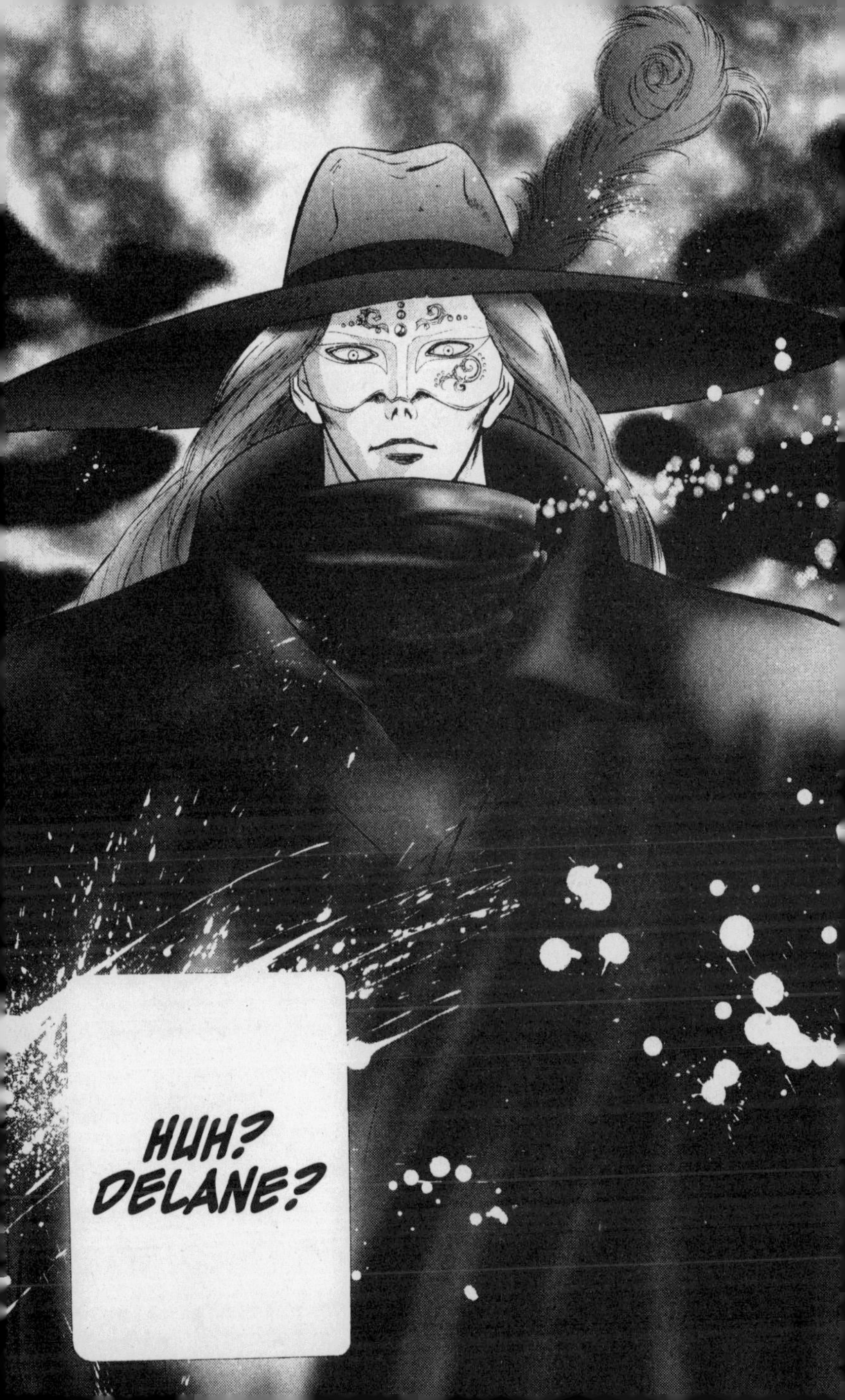
HUH? DELANE?

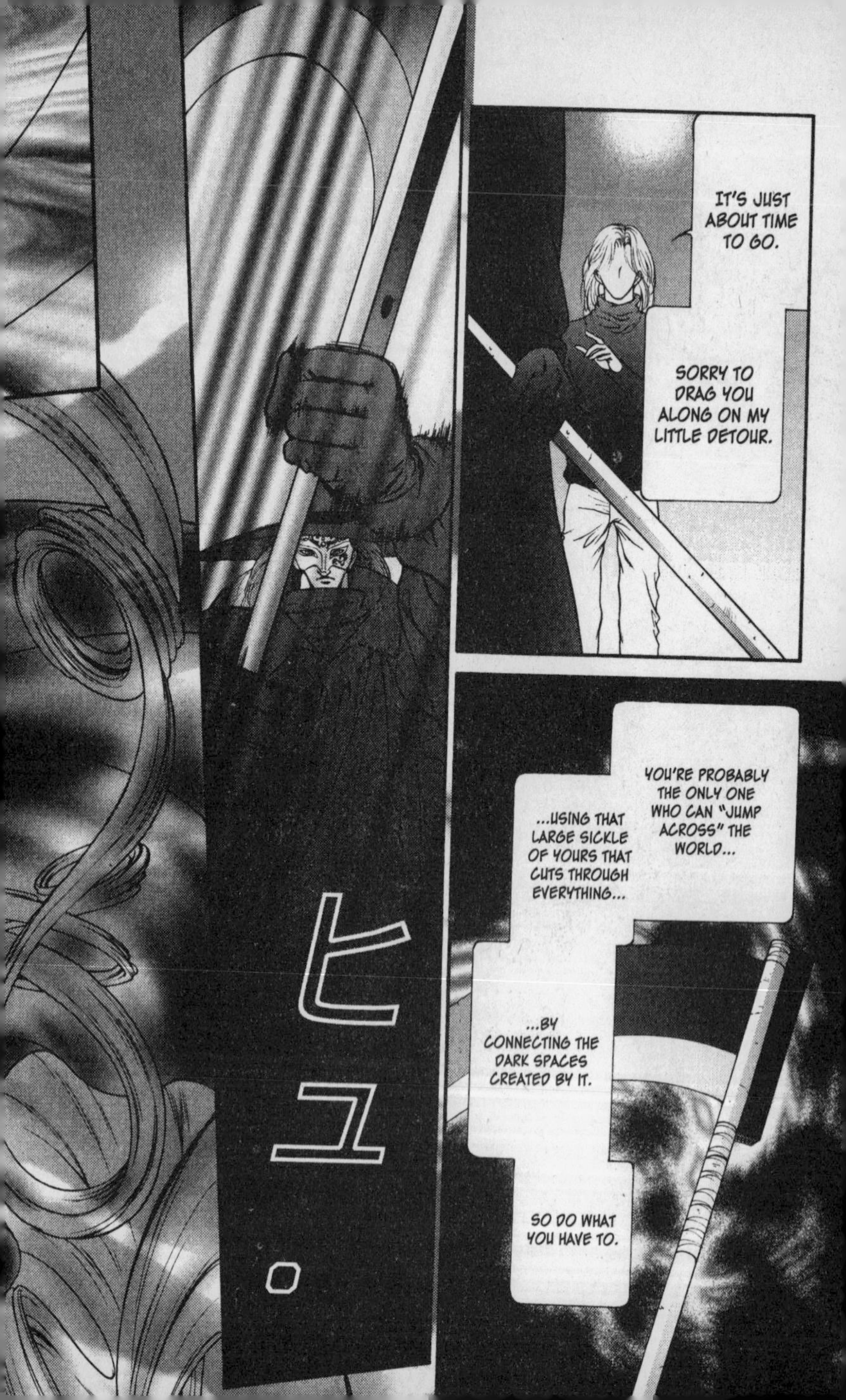
IT'S JUST ABOUT TIME TO GO.
SORRY TO DRAG YOU ALONG ON MY LITTLE DETOUR.
YOU'RE PROBABLY THE ONLY ONE WHO CAN "JUMP ACROSS" THE WORLD...
...USING THAT LARGE SICKLE OF YOURS THAT CUTS THROUGH EVERYTHING...
...BY CONNECTING THE DARK SPACES CREATED BY IT.
SO DO WHAT YOU HAVE TO.
ヒュ

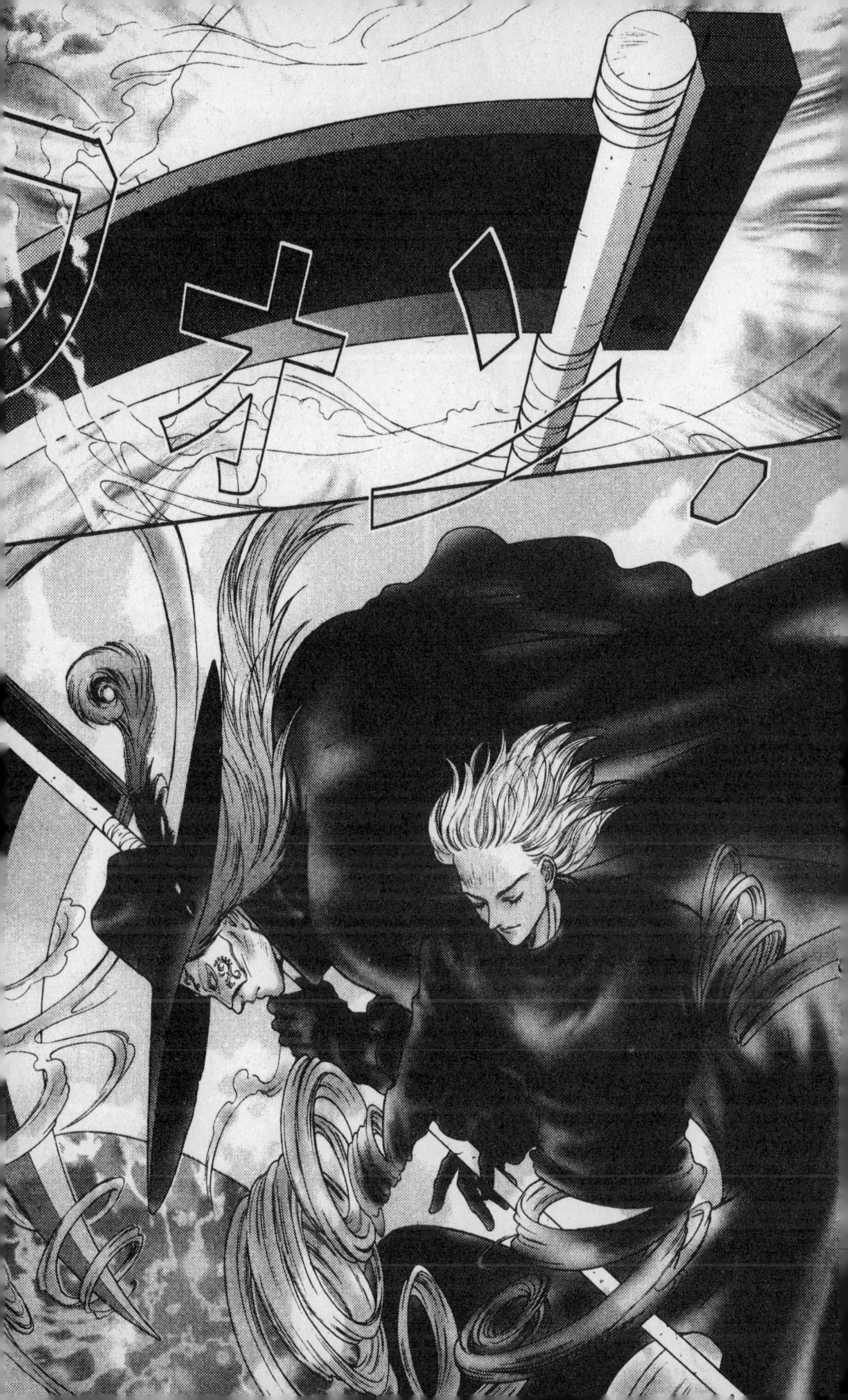
ウオン

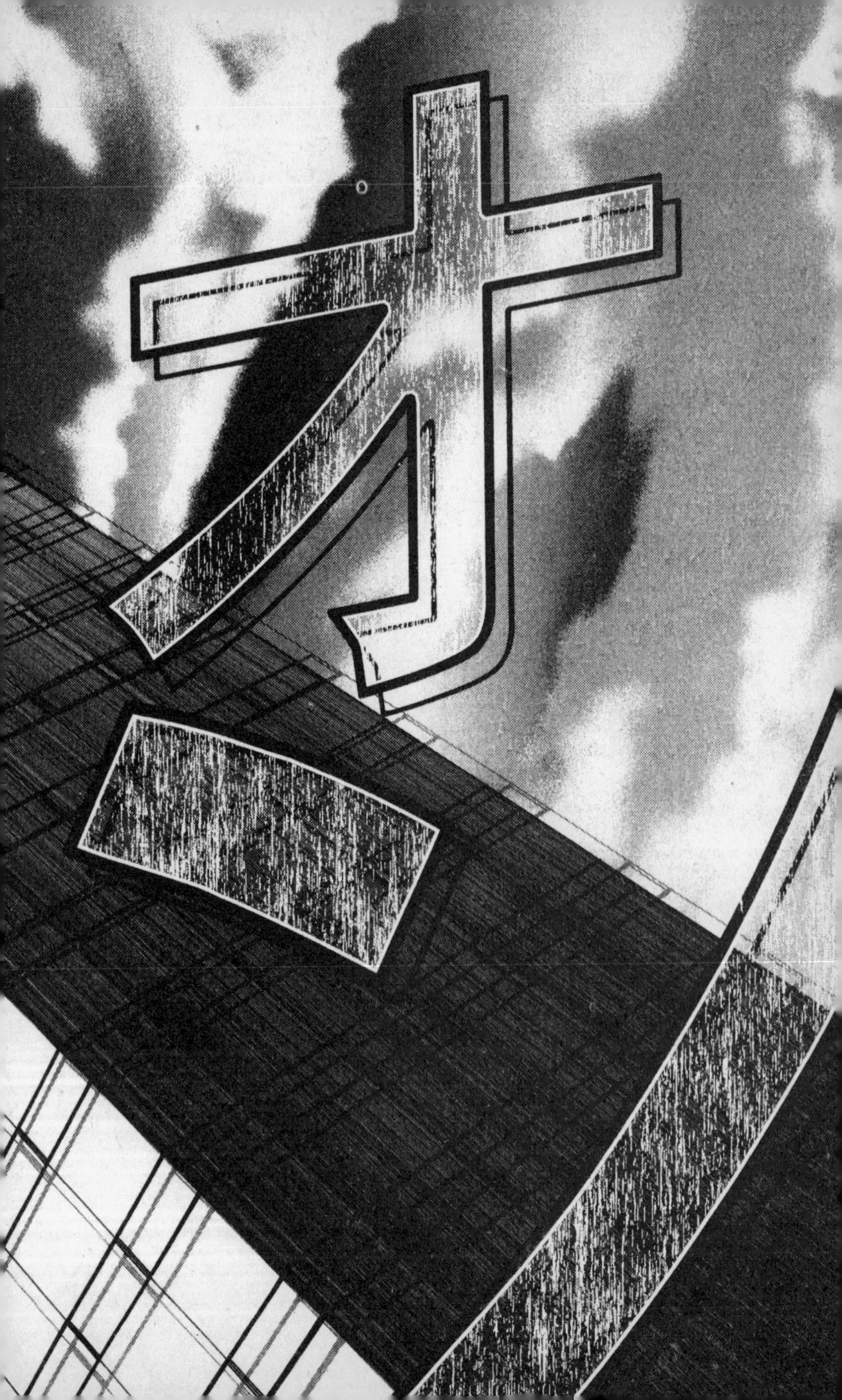
オー

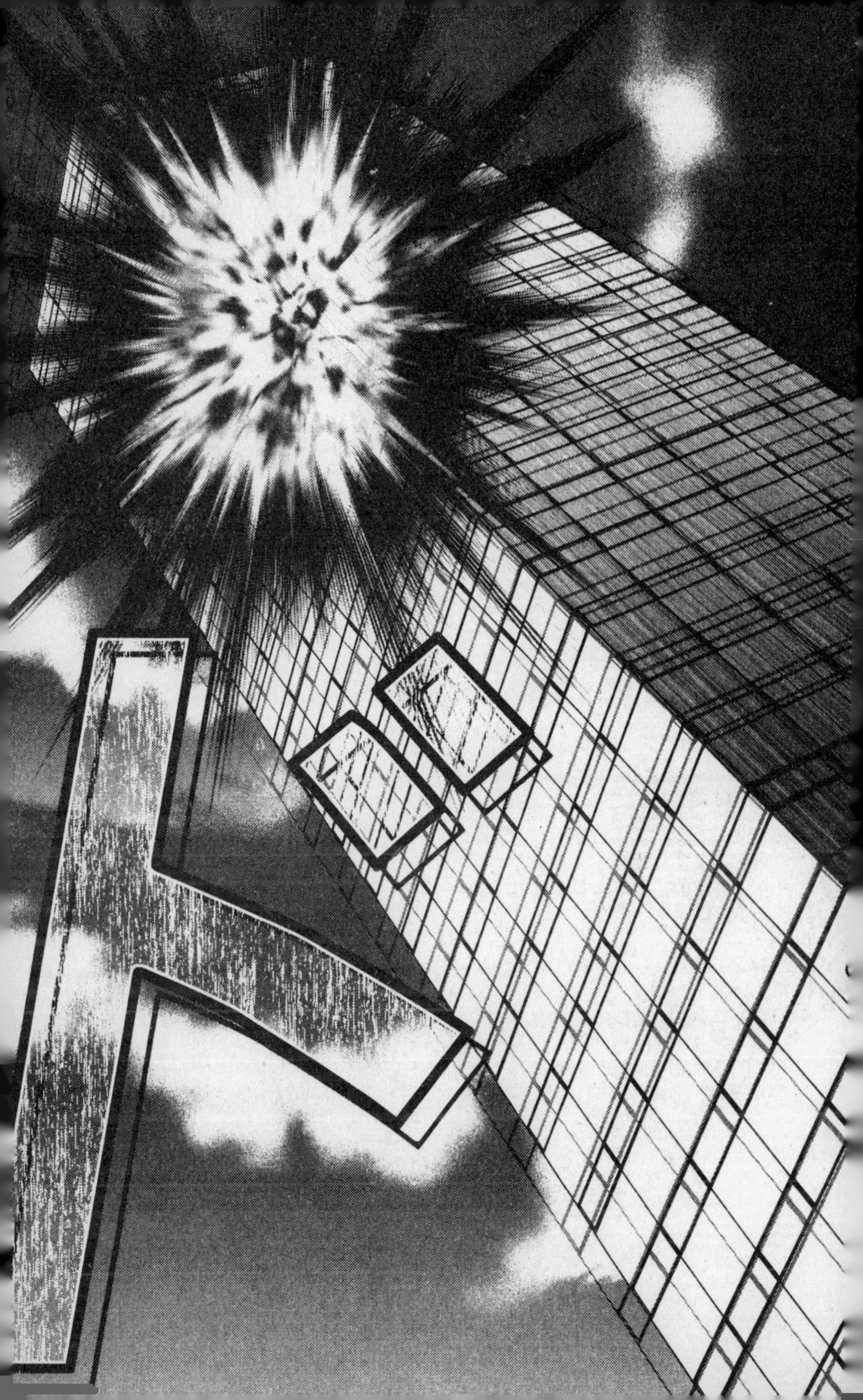
ド

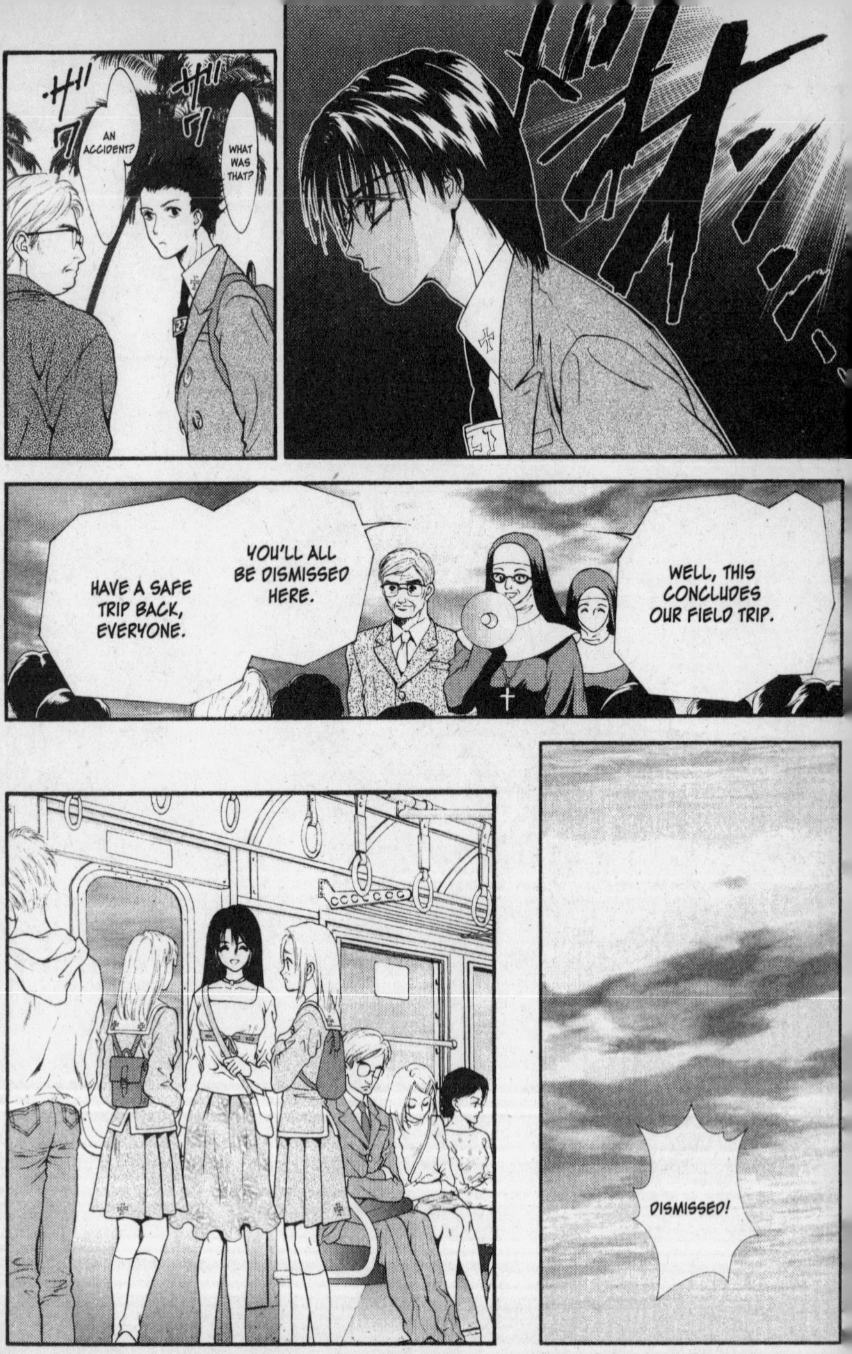
WHAT WAS THAT?
AN ACCIDENT?
WELL, THIS CONCLUDES OUR FIELD TRIP.
YOU'LL ALL BE DISMISSED HERE.
HAVE A SAFE TRIP BACK, EVERYONE.
DISMISSED!

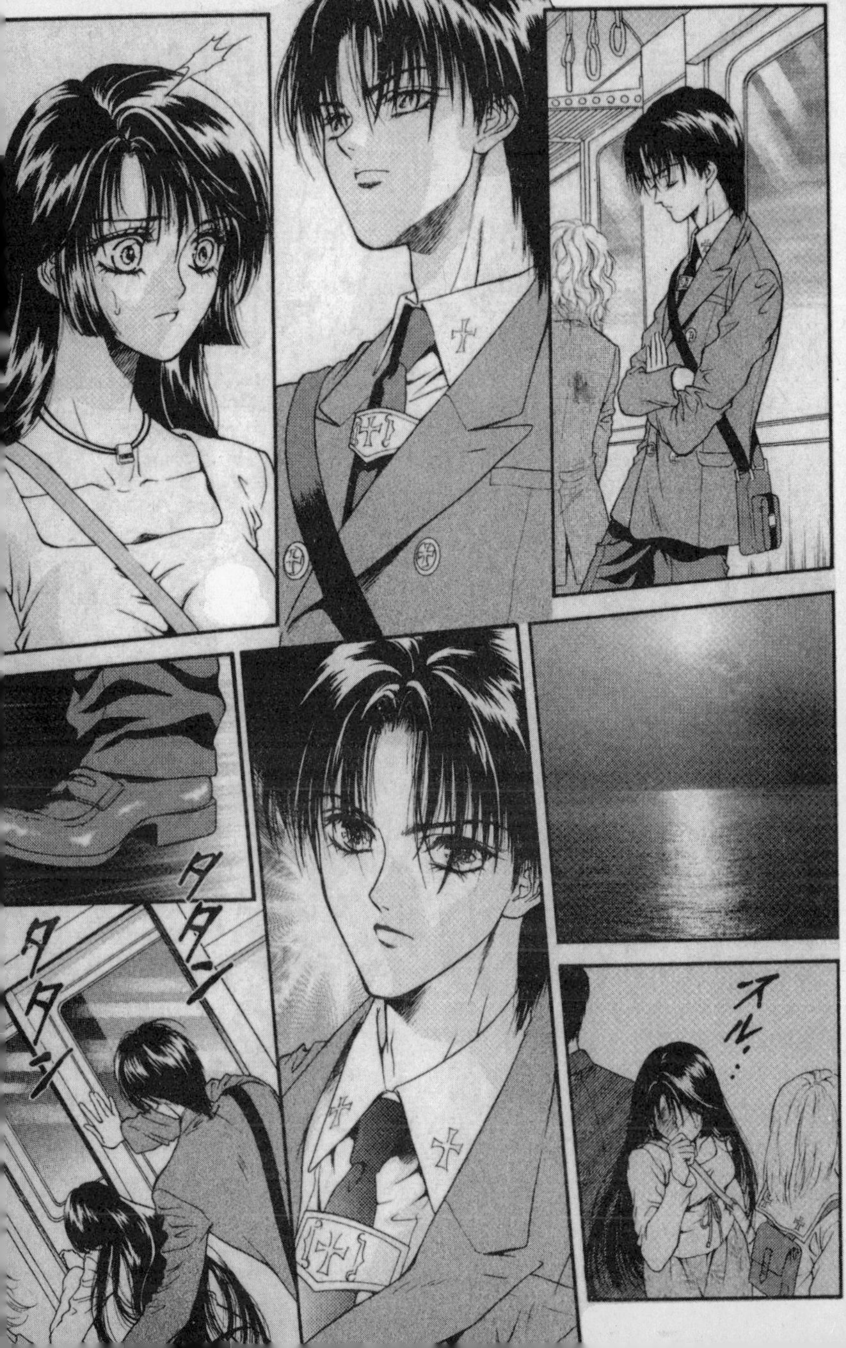
スル…
タタン
タタン

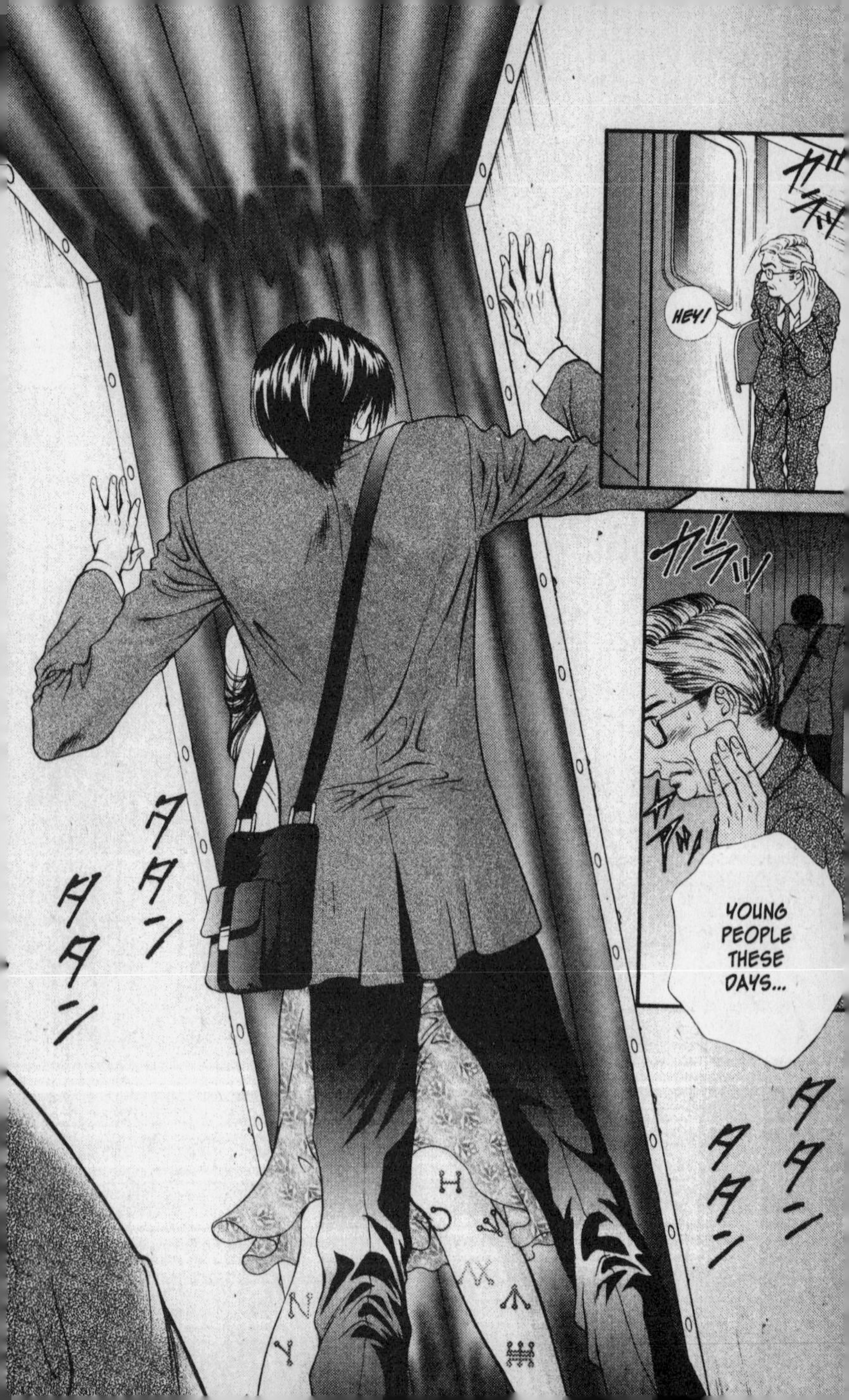
ガラッ
HEY!
ガラッ
YOUNG PEOPLE THESE DAYS...
タタン タタン
タタン タタン

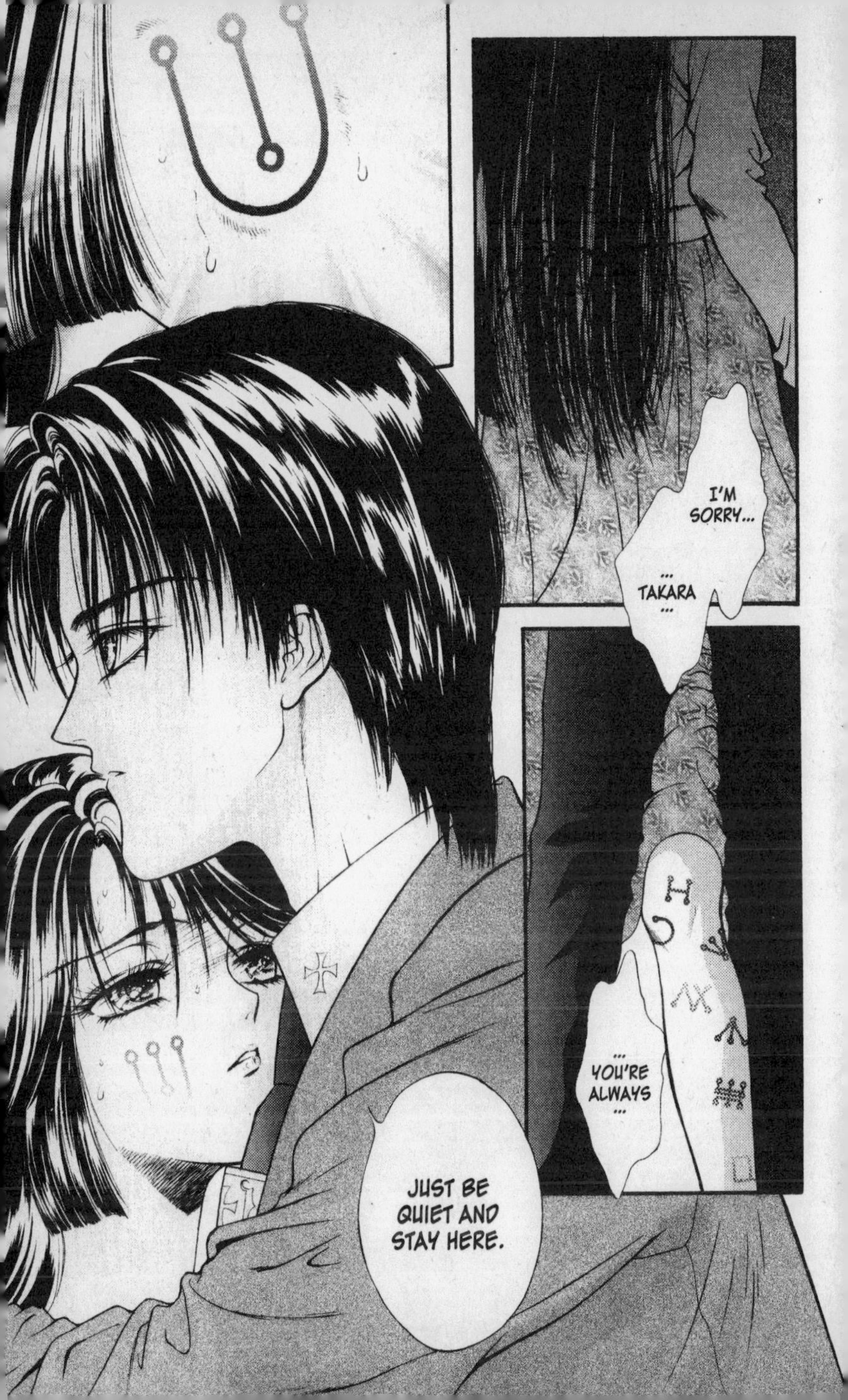
I'M SORRY...
...TAKARA...
...YOU'RE ALWAYS...
JUST BE QUIET AND STAY HERE.

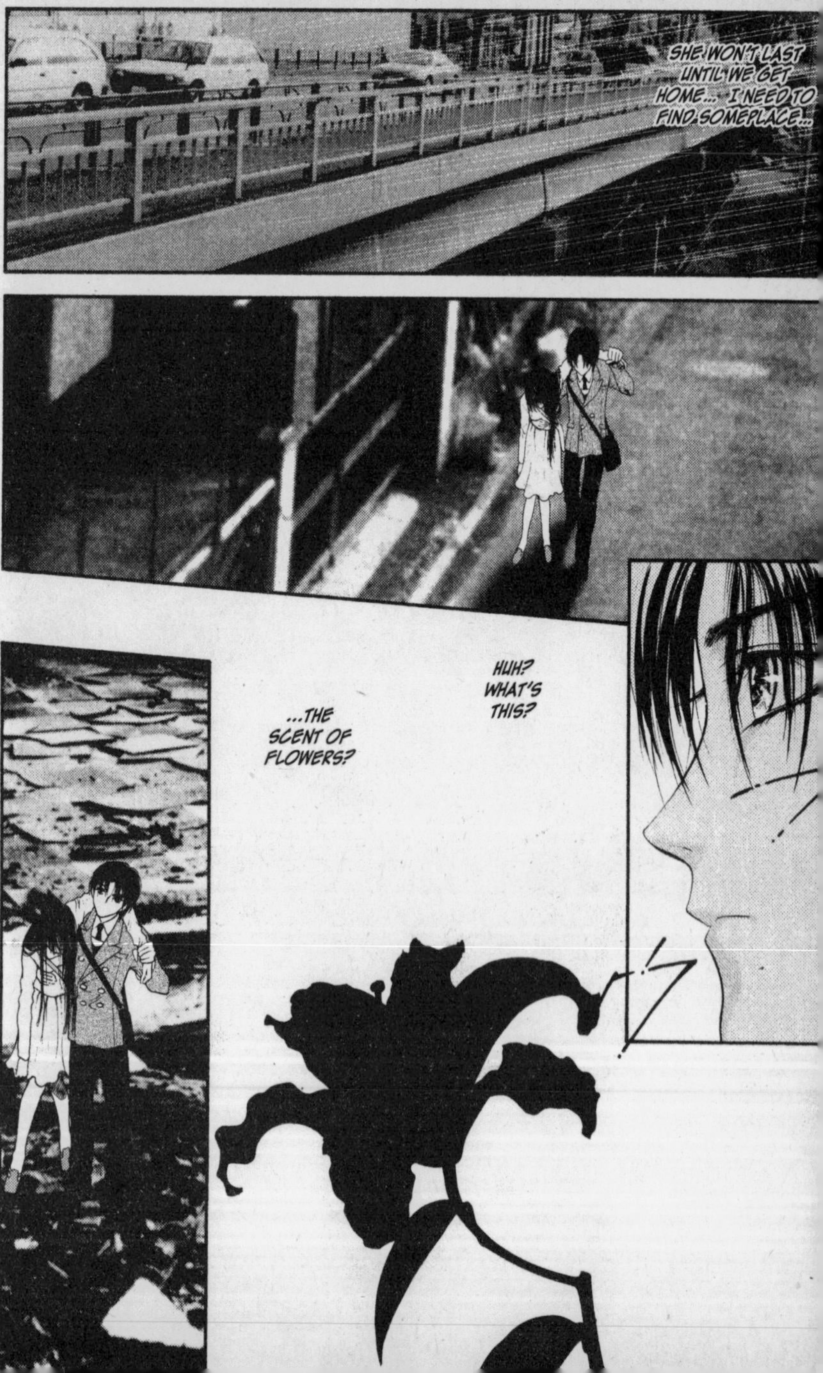
SHE WON'T LAST UNTIL WE GET HOME... I NEED TO FIND SOMEPLACE...
HUH? WHAT'S THIS?
...THE SCENT OF FLOWERS?

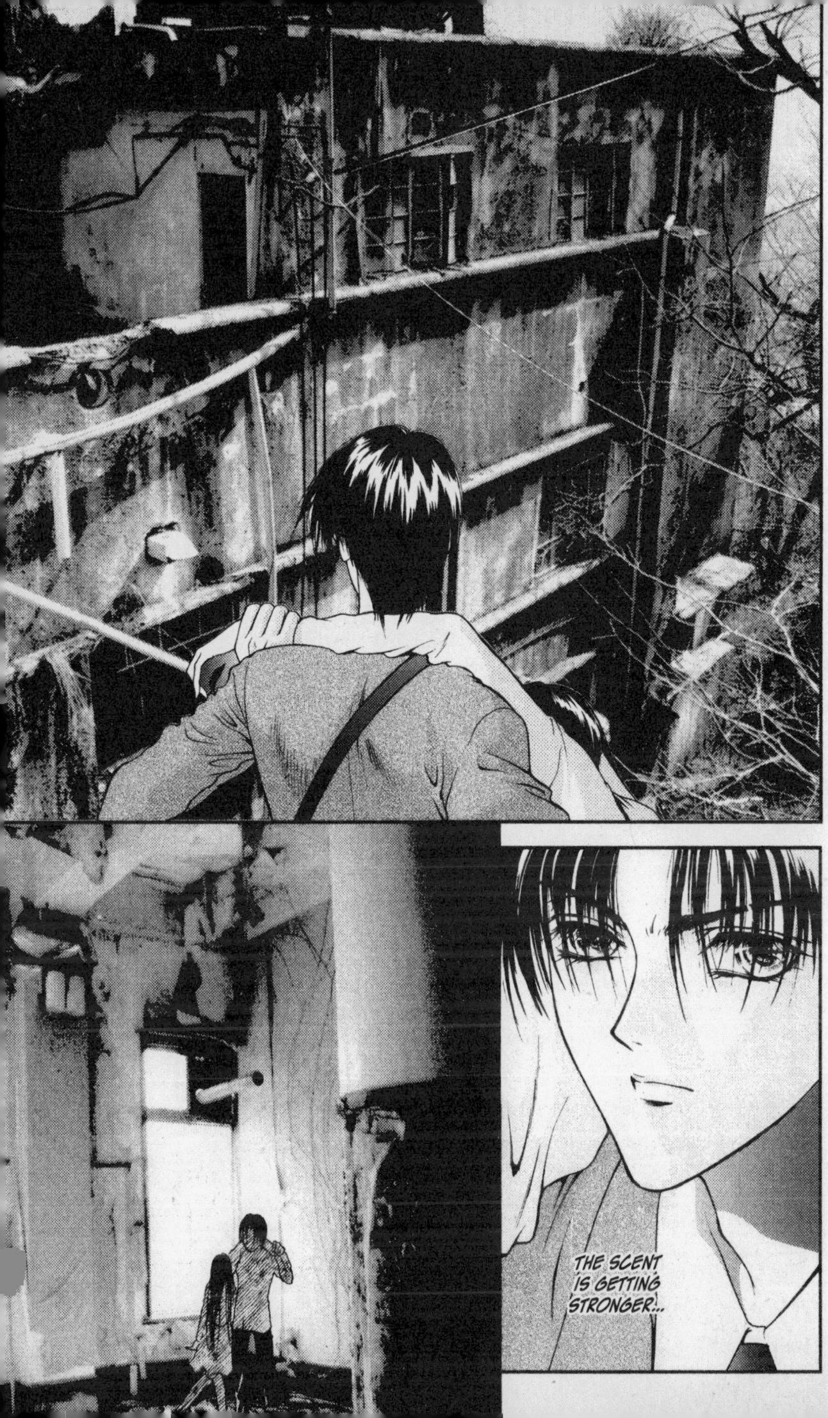
THE SCENT IS GETTING STRONGER...

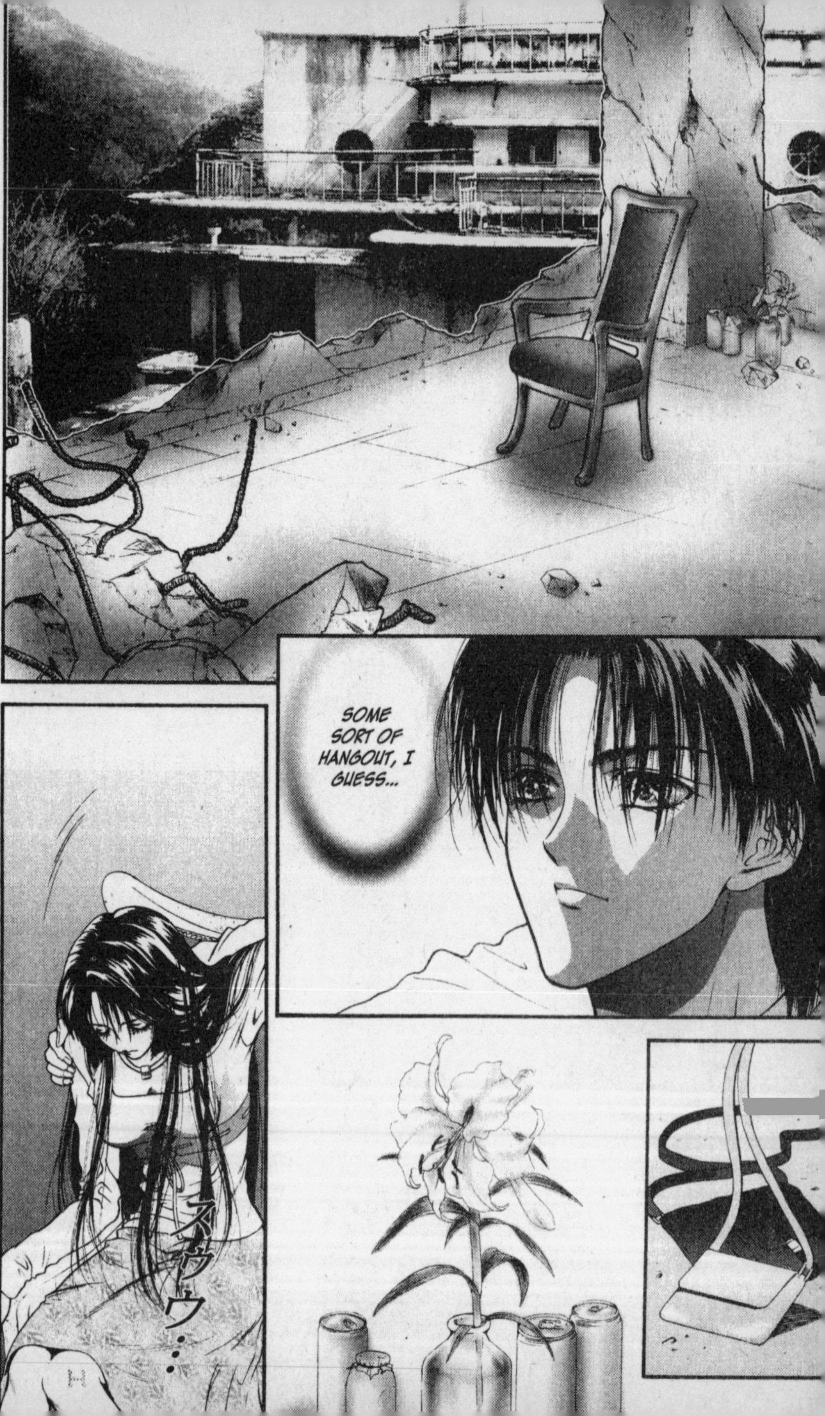
SOME SORT OF HANGOUT, I GUESS...
スゥゥウ…

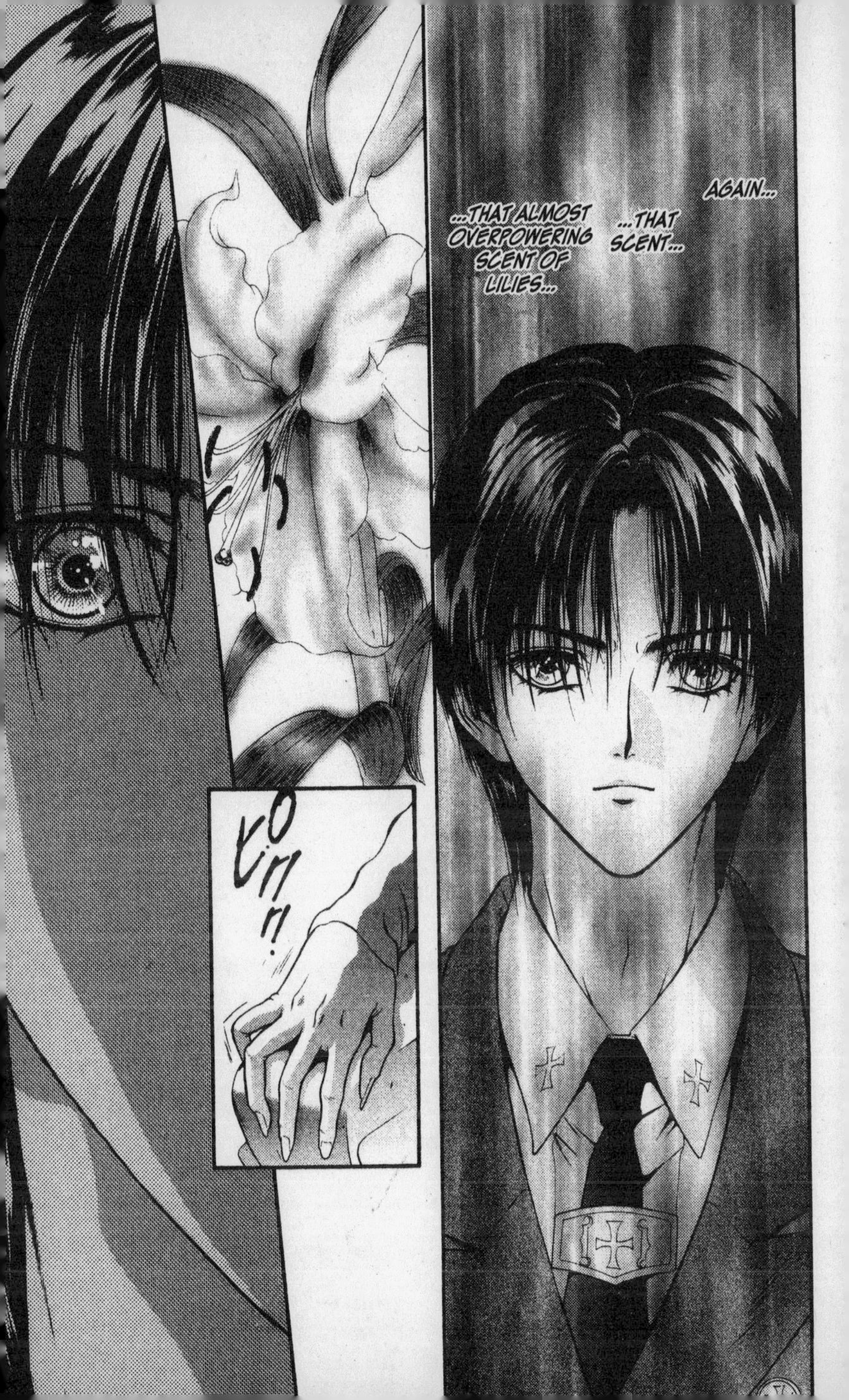
AGAIN...
...THAT SCENT...
...THAT ALMOST OVERPOWERING SCENT OF LILIES...

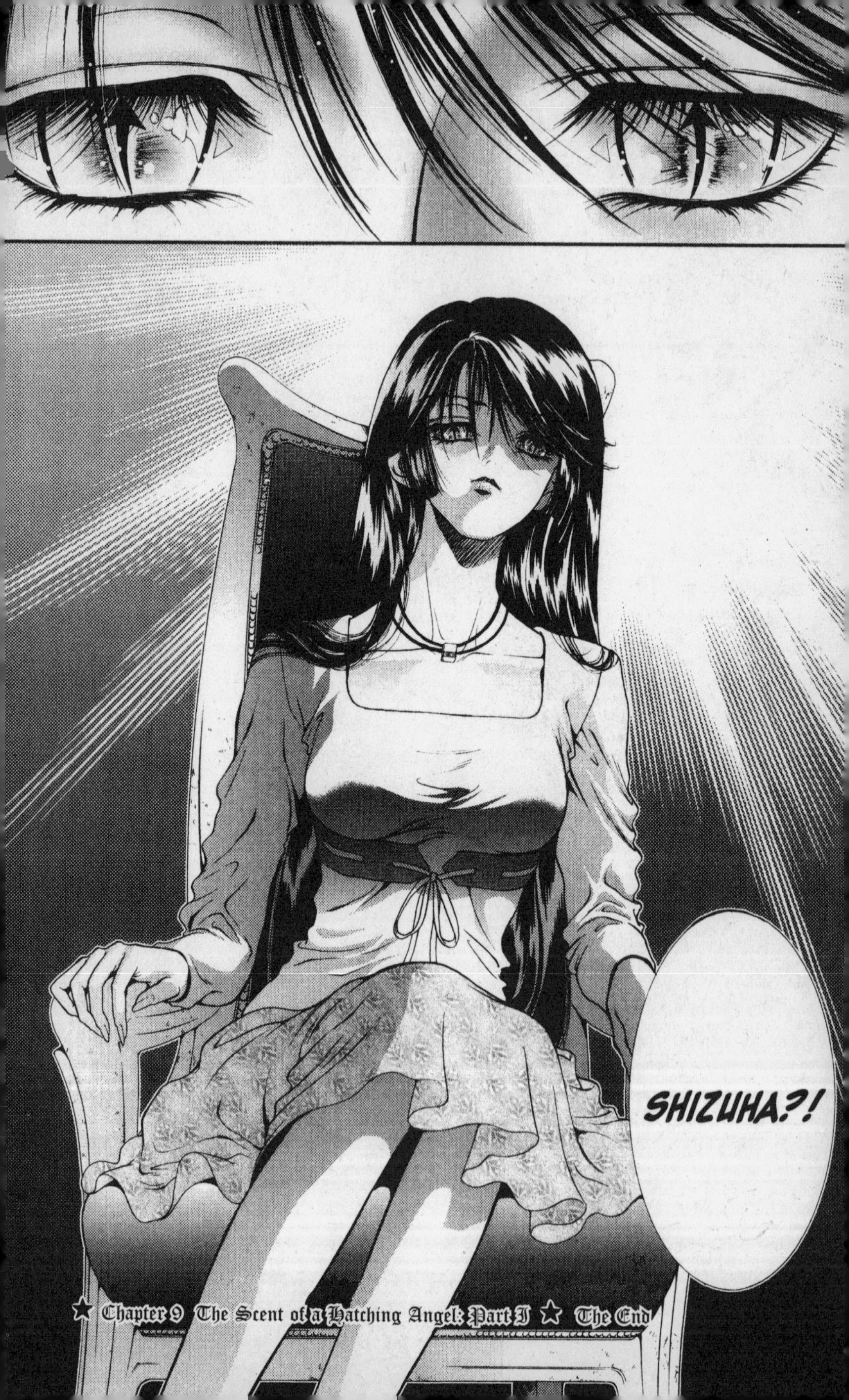
SHIZUHA?!
☆ Chapter 9 The Scent of a Hatching Angel: Part I ☆ The End

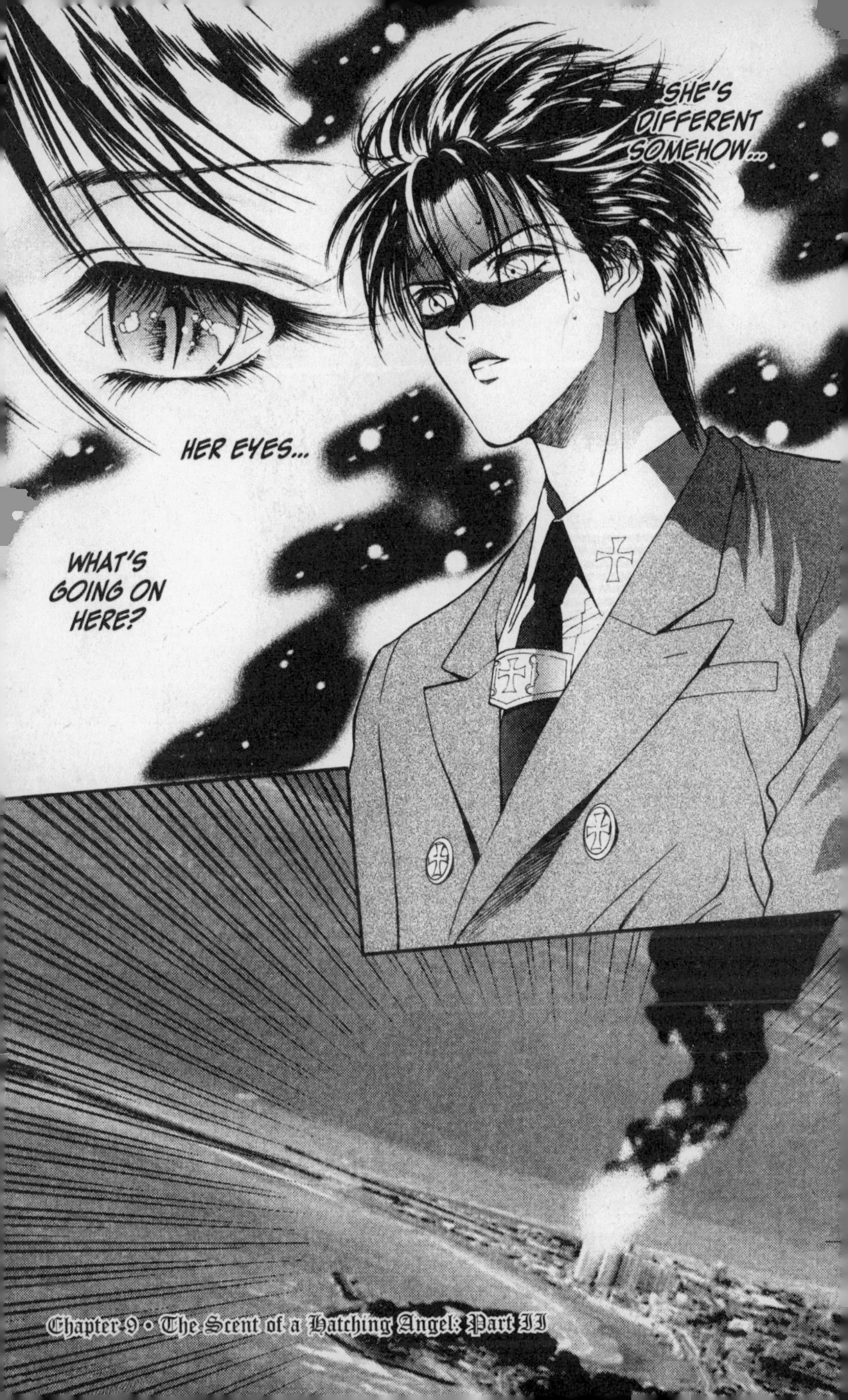
SHE'S DIFFERENT SOMEHOW...
HER EYES...
WHAT'S GOING ON HERE?

Chapter 9 • The Scent of a Hatching Angel: Part II

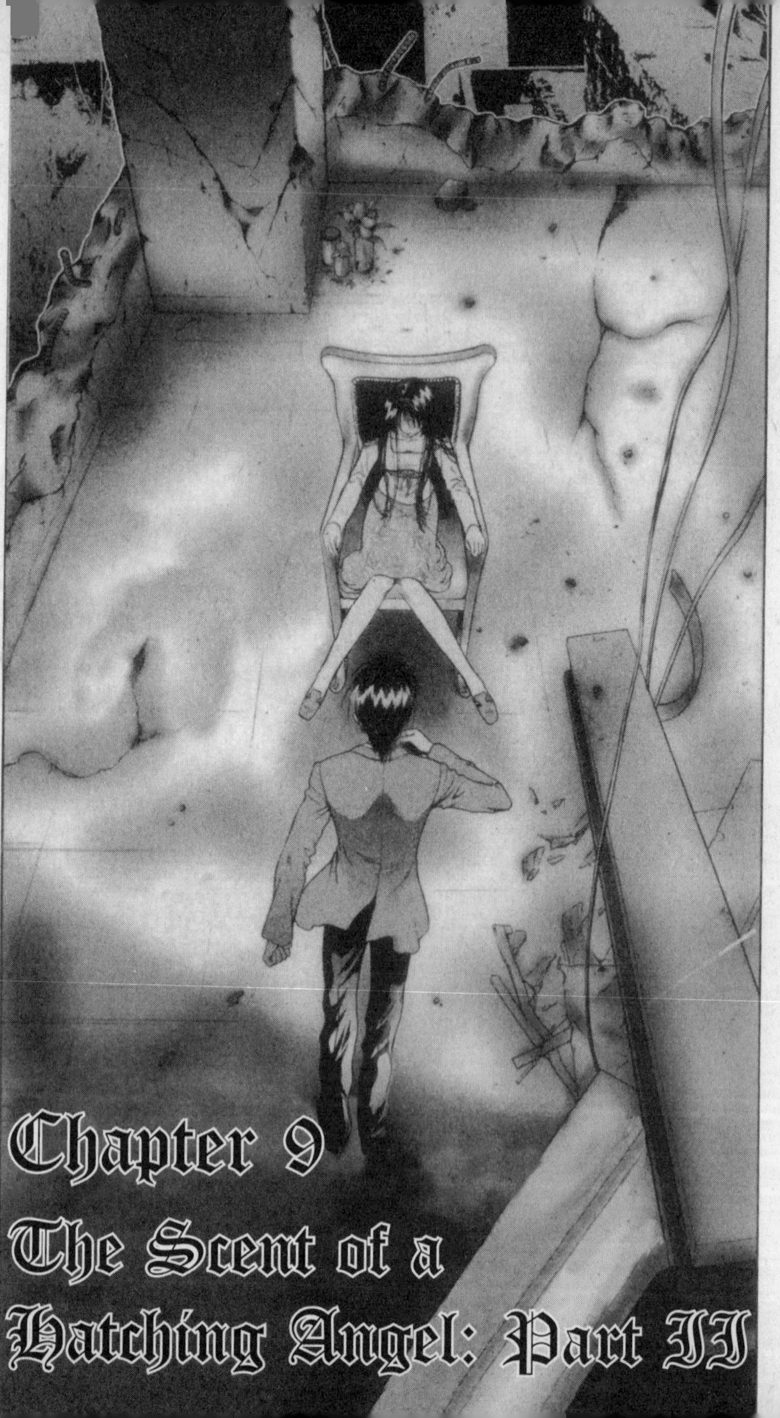
Chapter 9
The Scent of a Hatching Angel: Part II

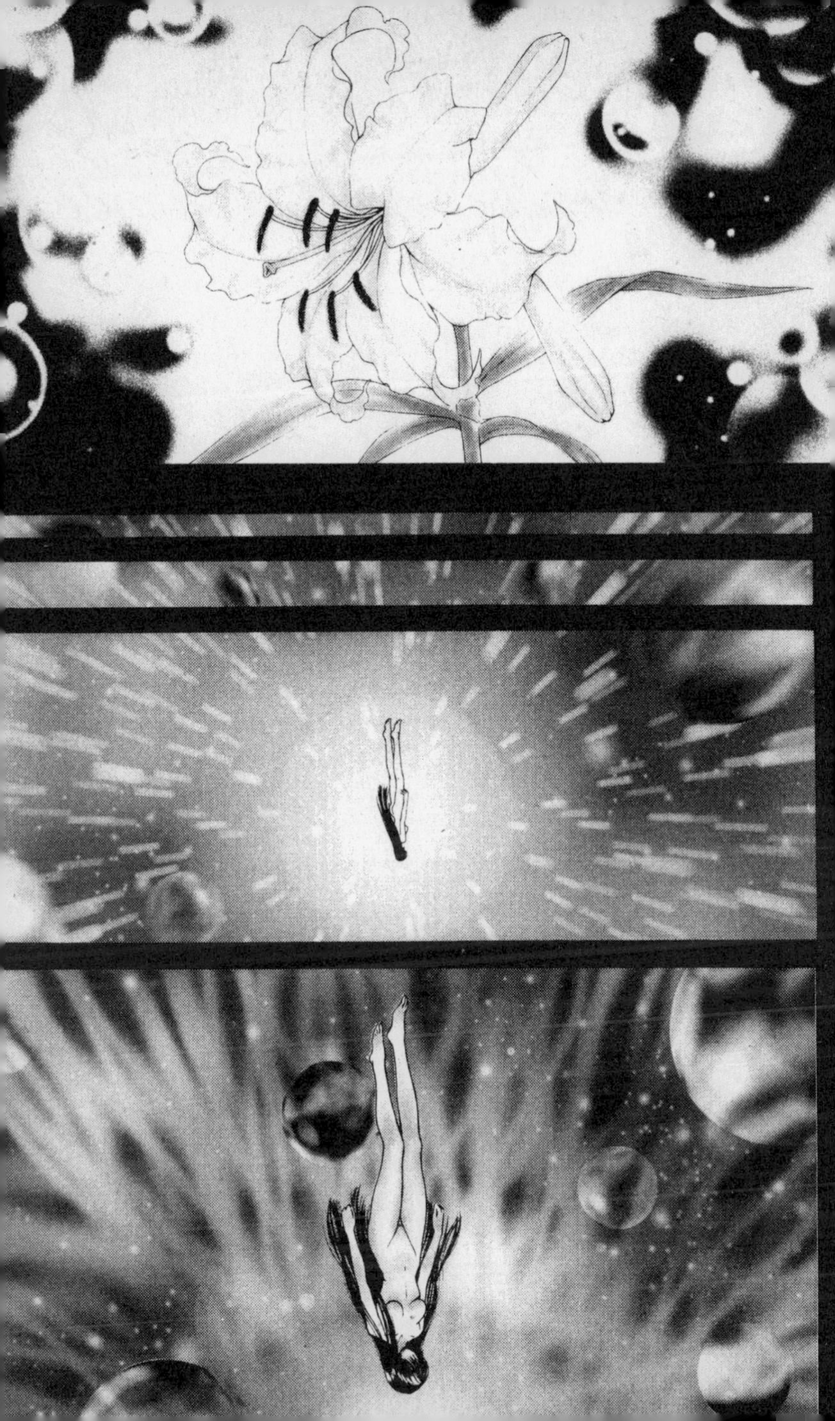

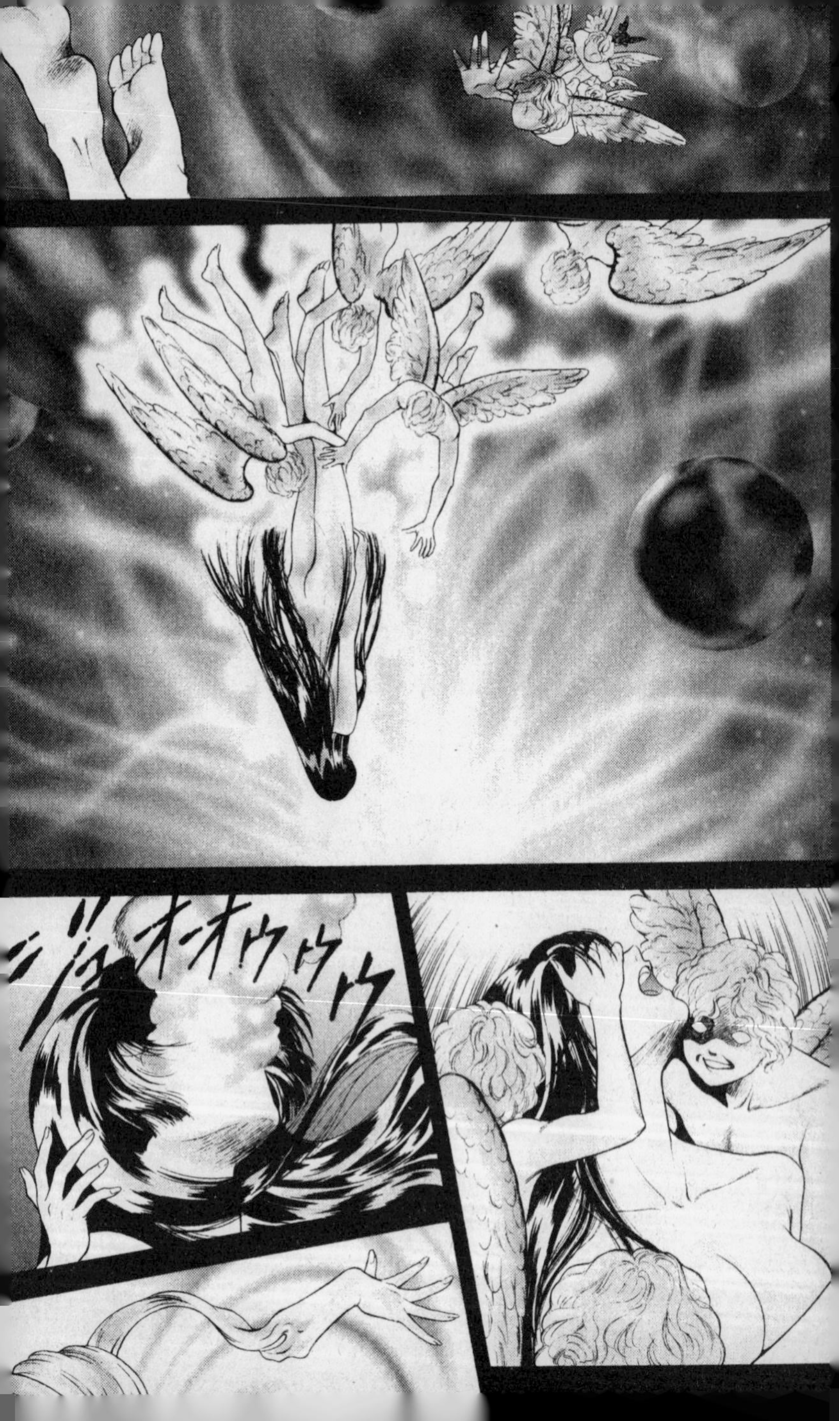
ジュオーオ!ウウウ

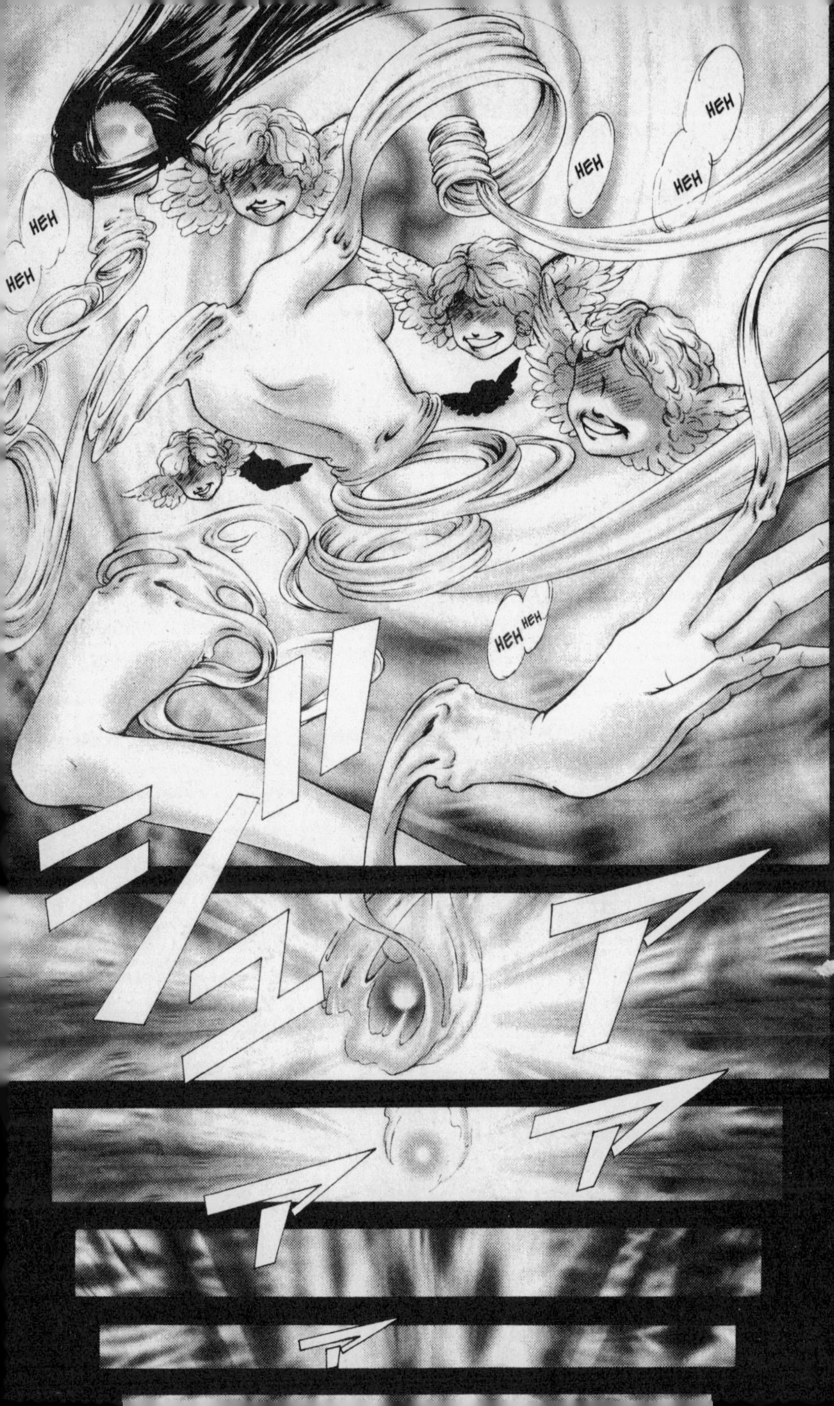
HEH
HEH
HEH
HEH
HEH
HEH HEH

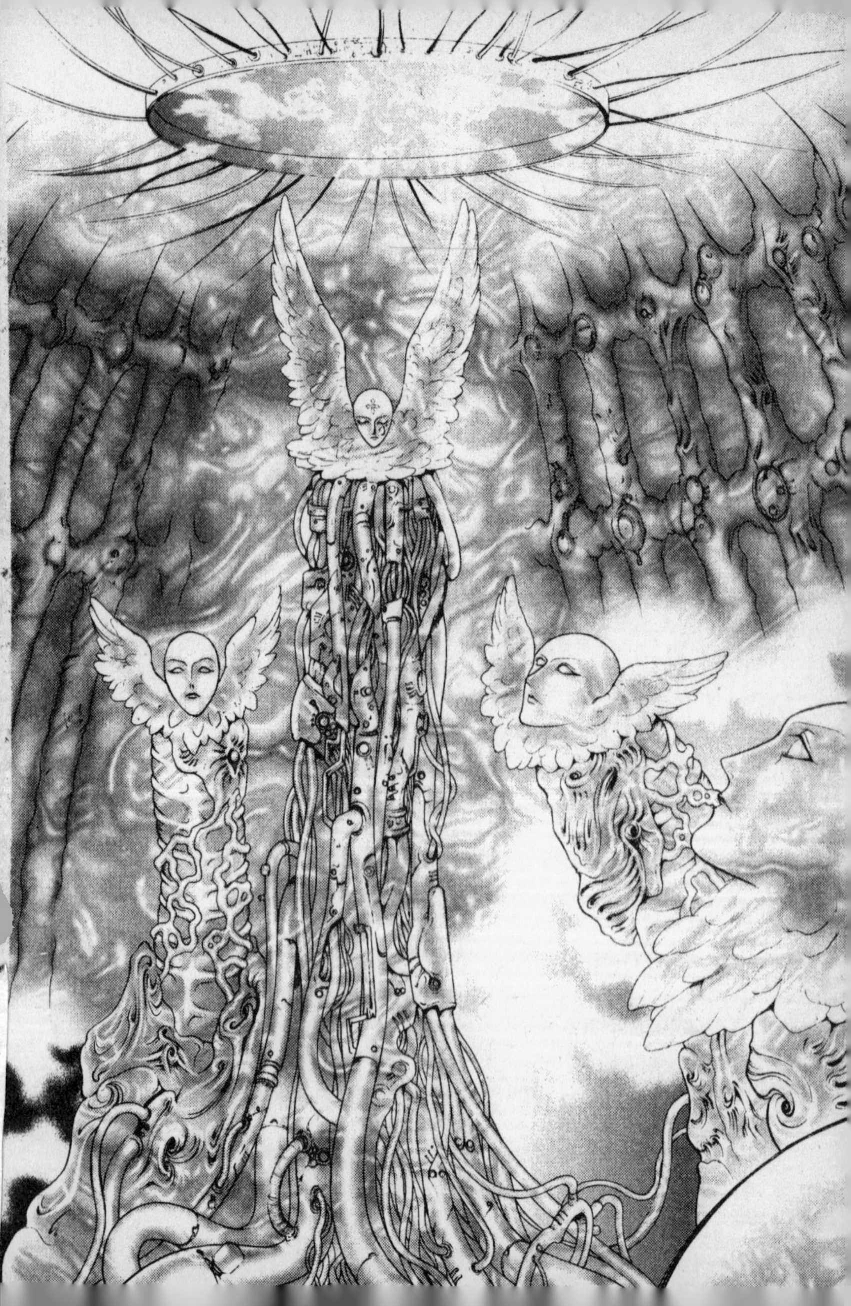

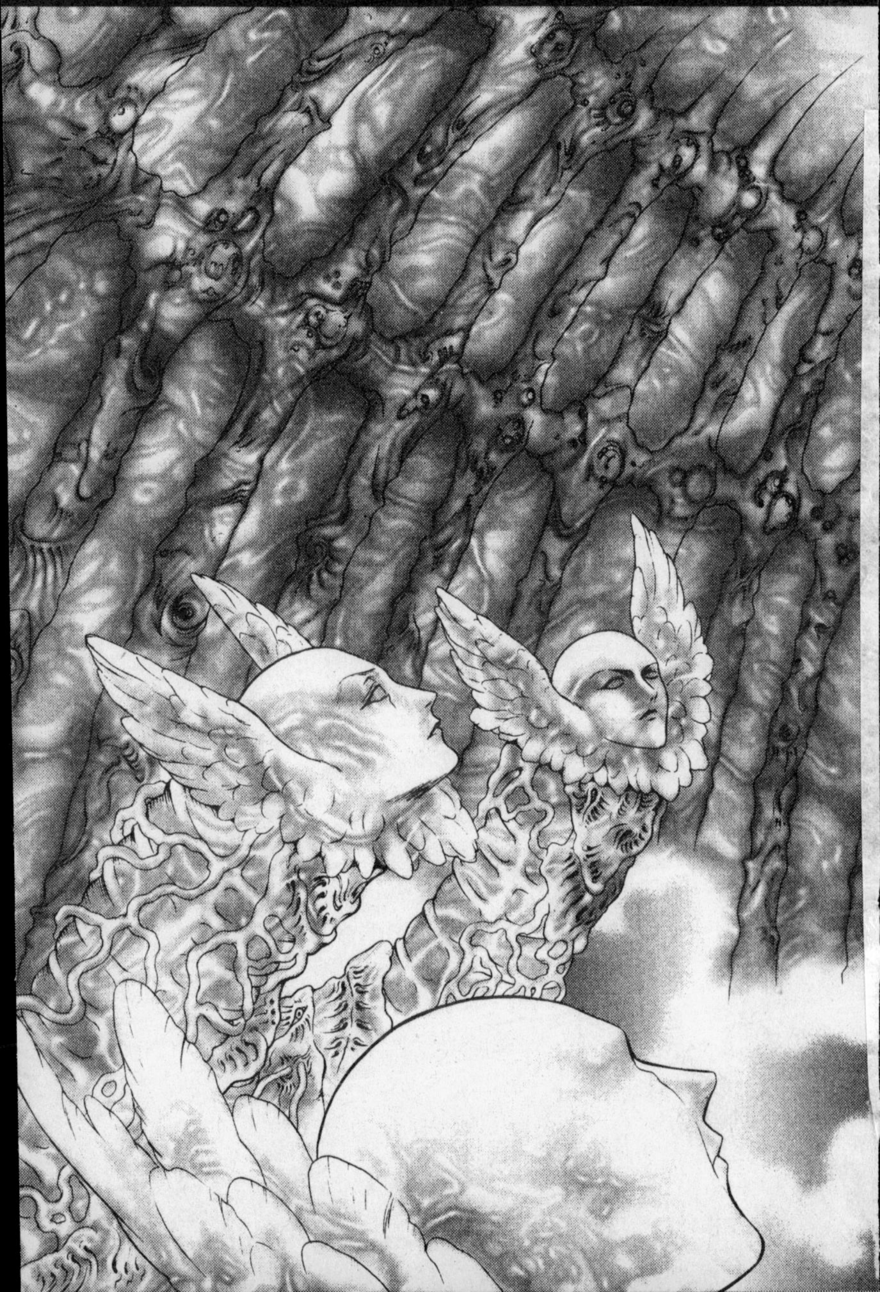

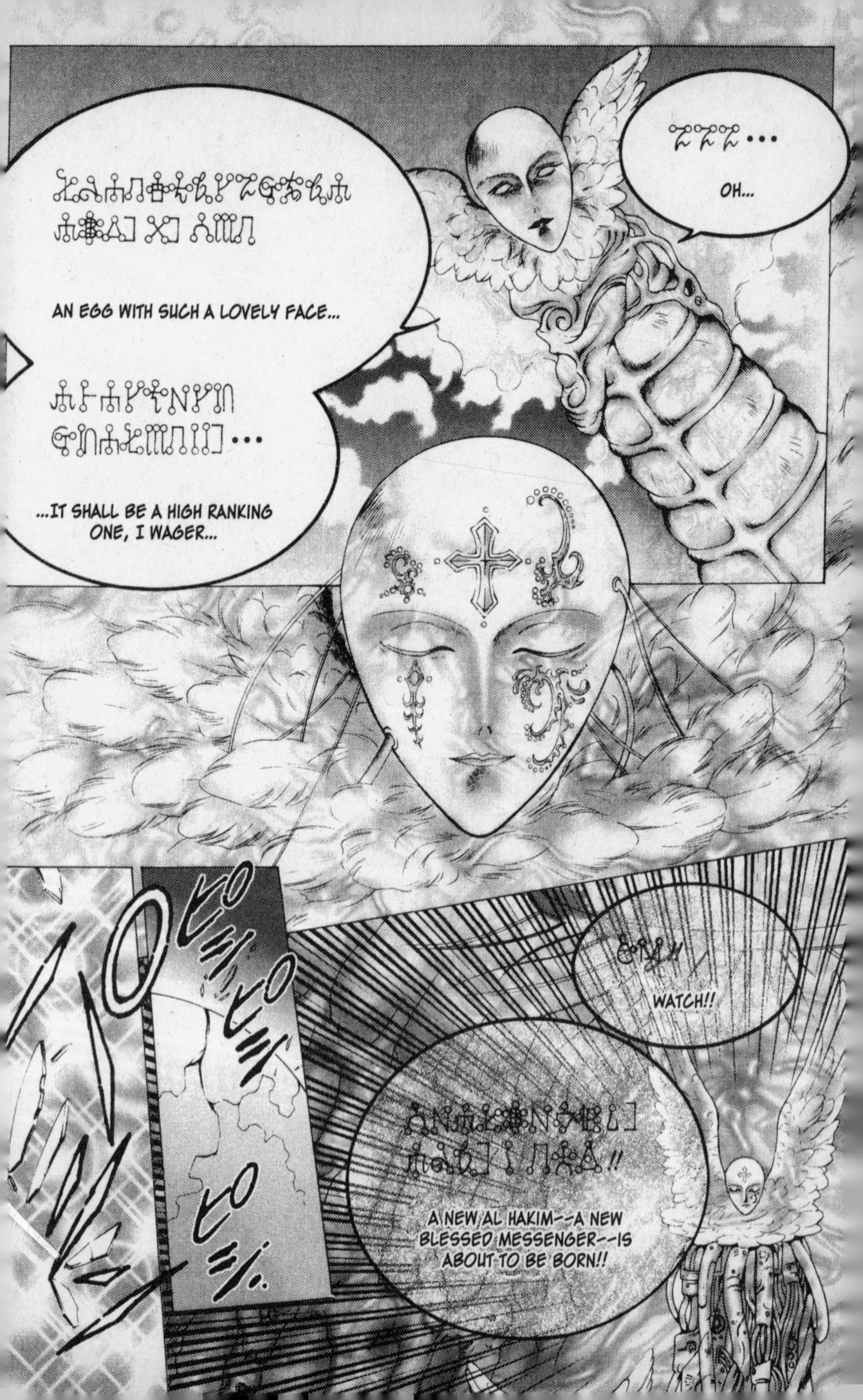
OH...
AN EGG WITH SUCH A LOVELY FACE...
...IT SHALL BE A HIGH RANKING ONE, I WAGER...
WATCH!!
A NEW AL HAKIM--A NEW BLESSED MESSENGER--IS ABOUT TO BE BORN!!

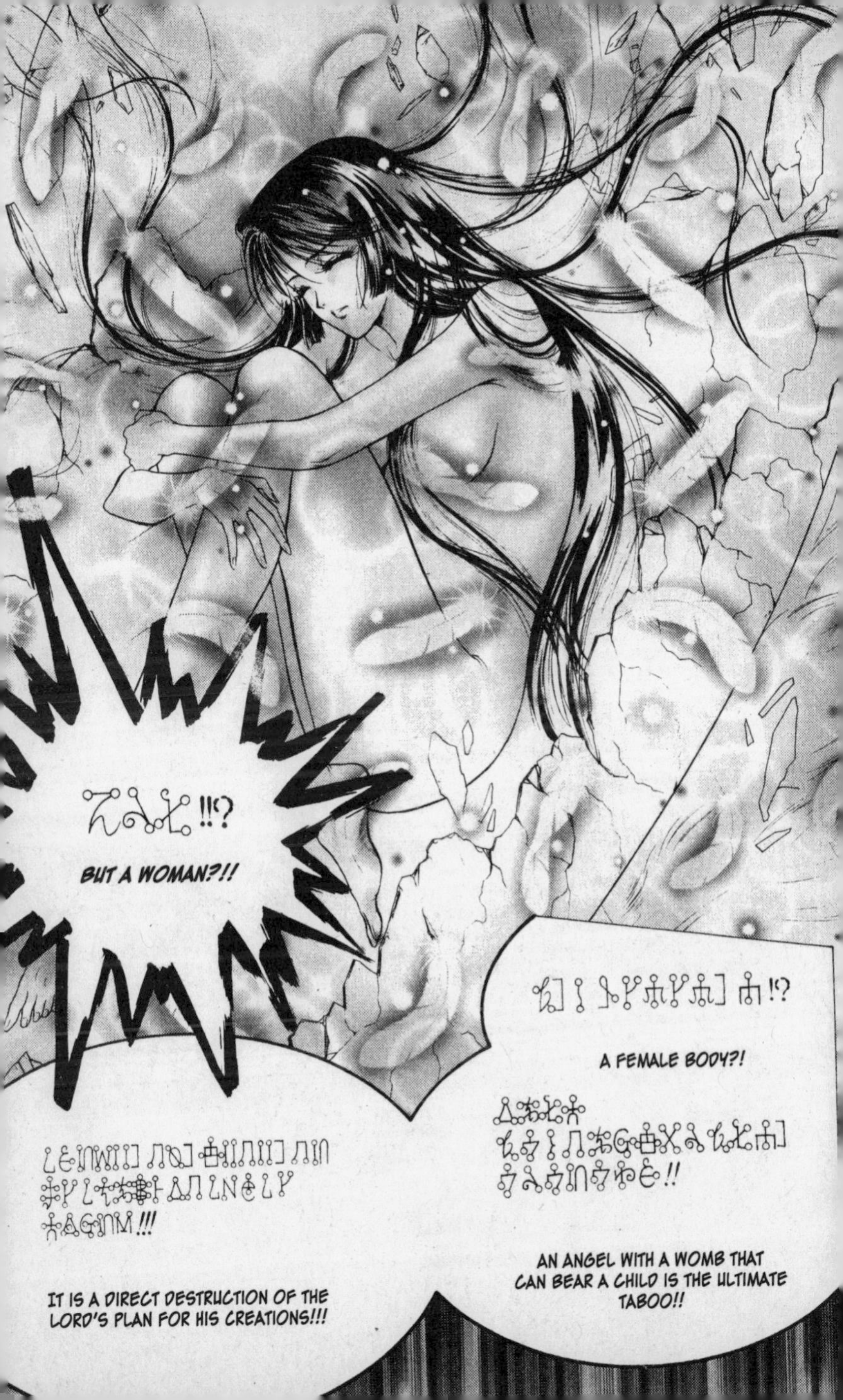
BUT A WOMAN?!!
A FEMALE BODY?!
AN ANGEL WITH A WOMB THAT CAN BEAR A CHILD IS THE ULTIMATE TABOO!!
IT IS A DIRECT DESTRUCTION OF THE LORD'S PLAN FOR HIS CREATIONS!!!

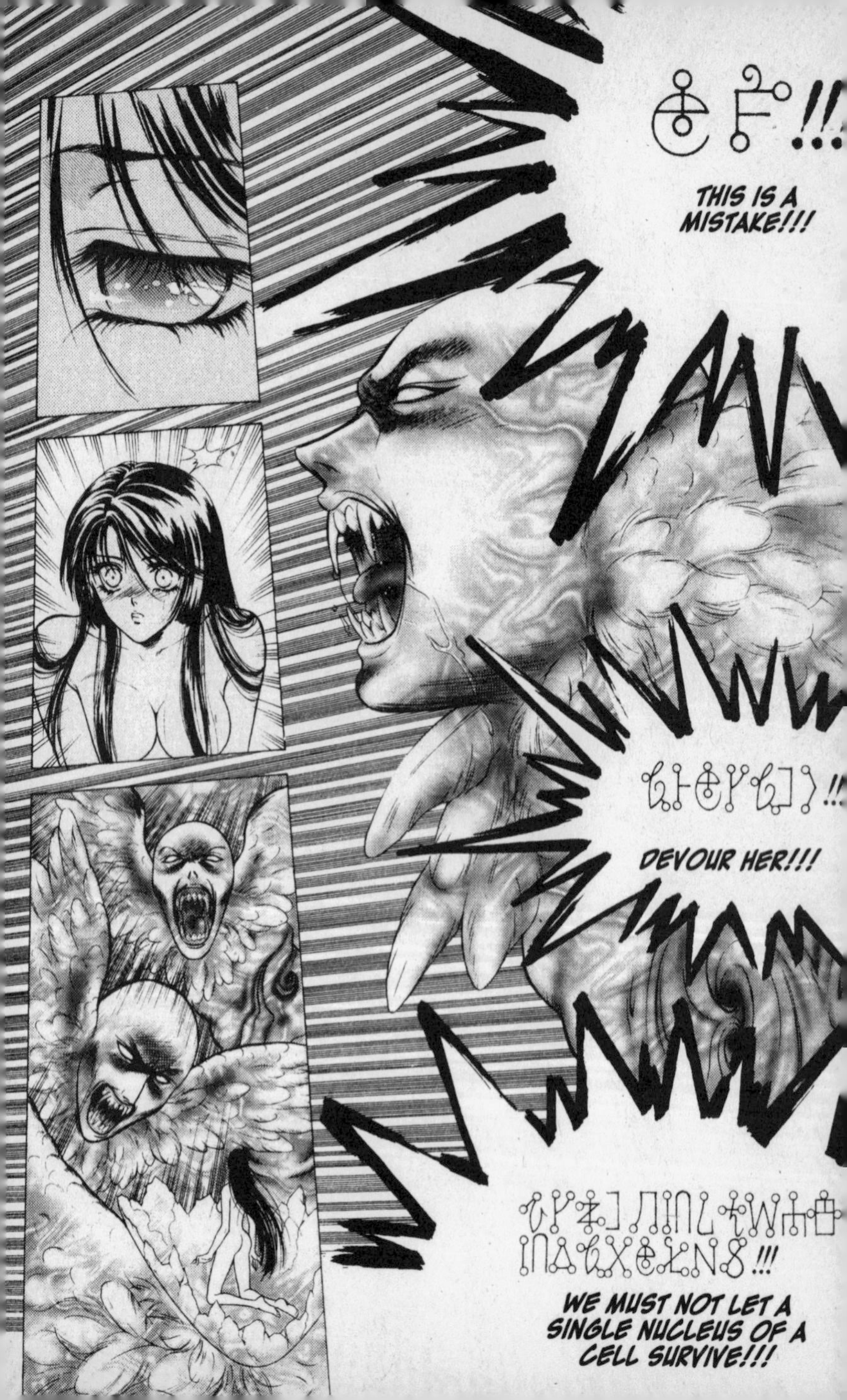
THIS IS A MISTAKE!!!
DEVOUR HER!!!
WE MUST NOT LET A SINGLE NUCLEUS OF A CELL SURVIVE!!!

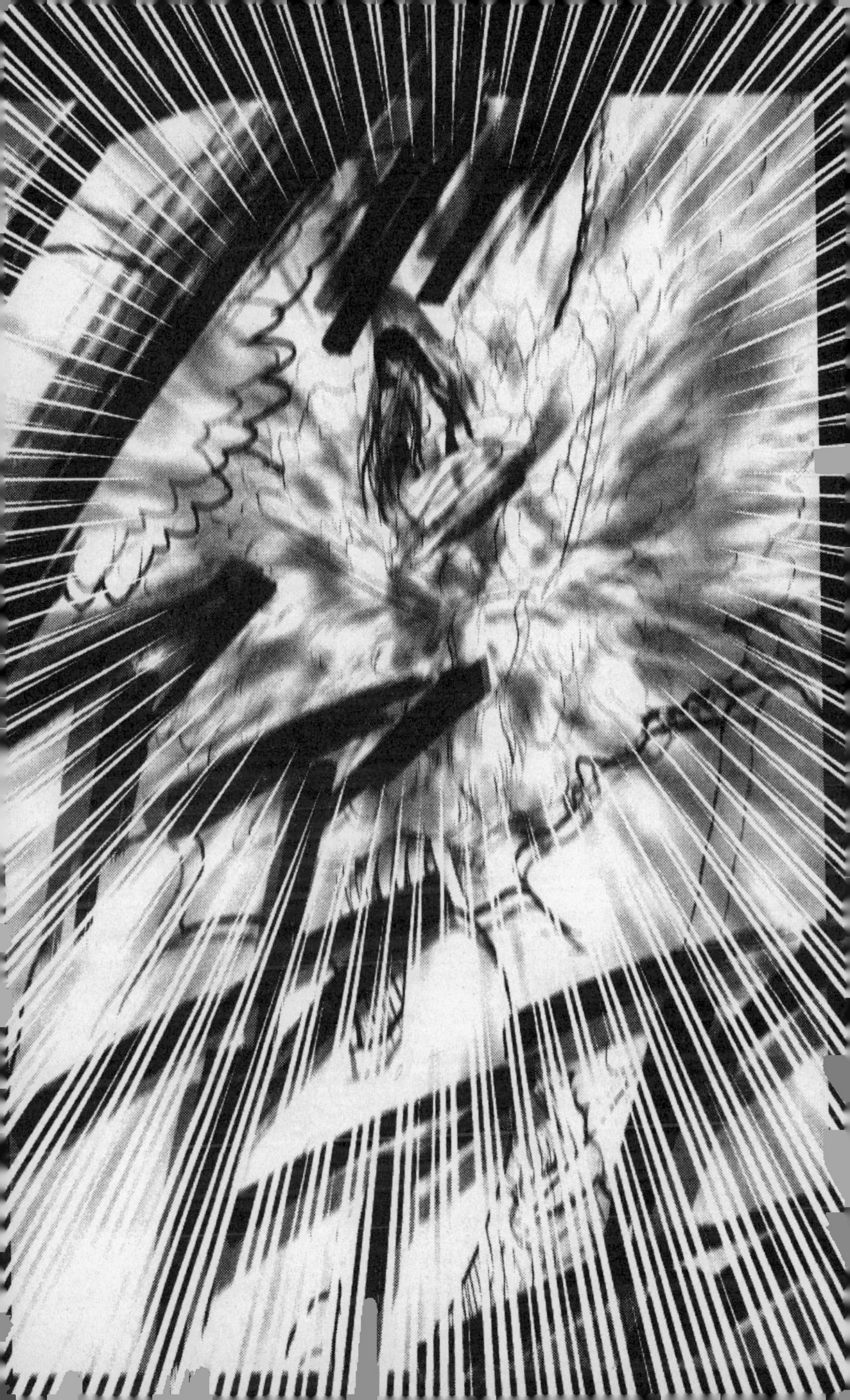

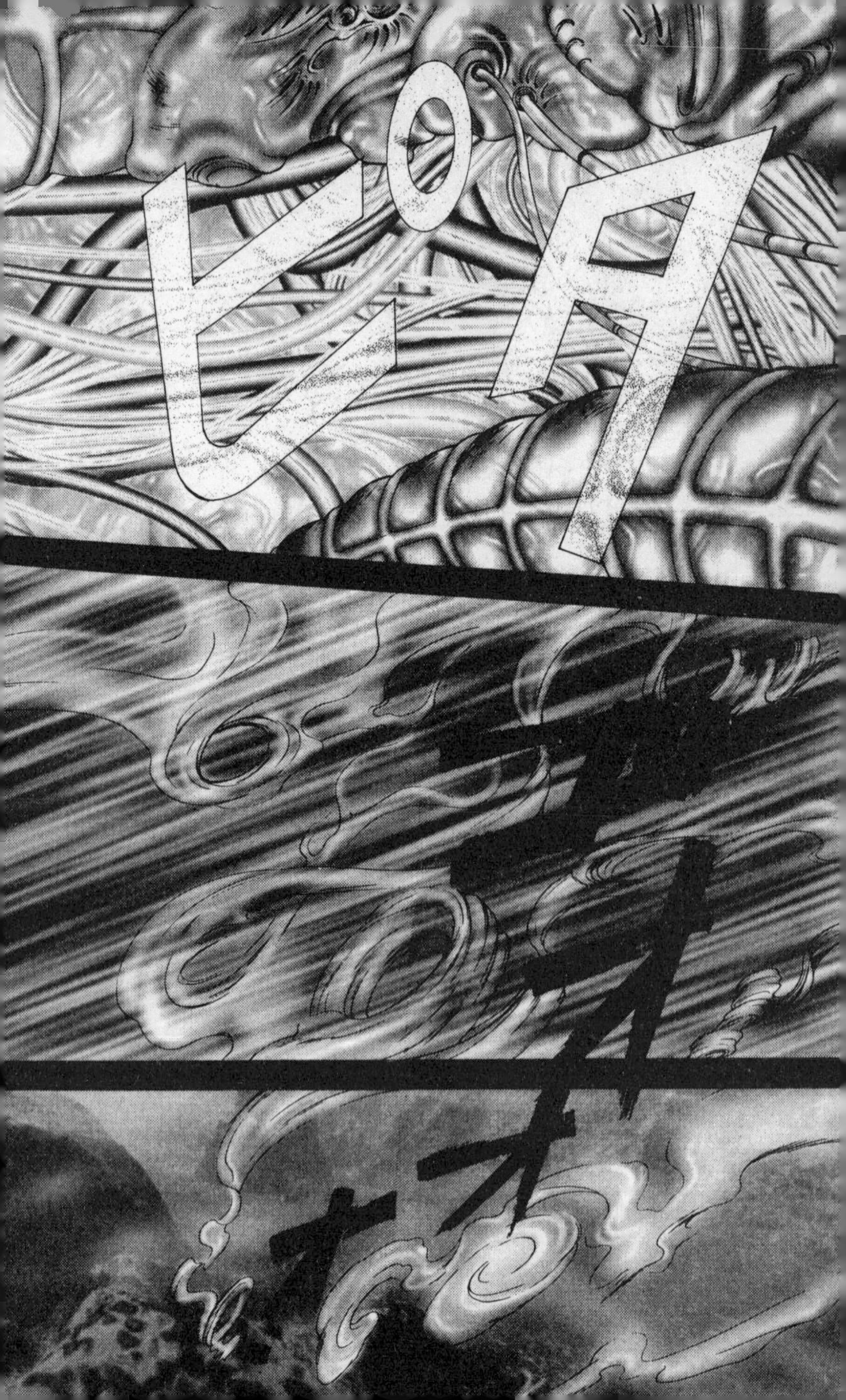
ピタ

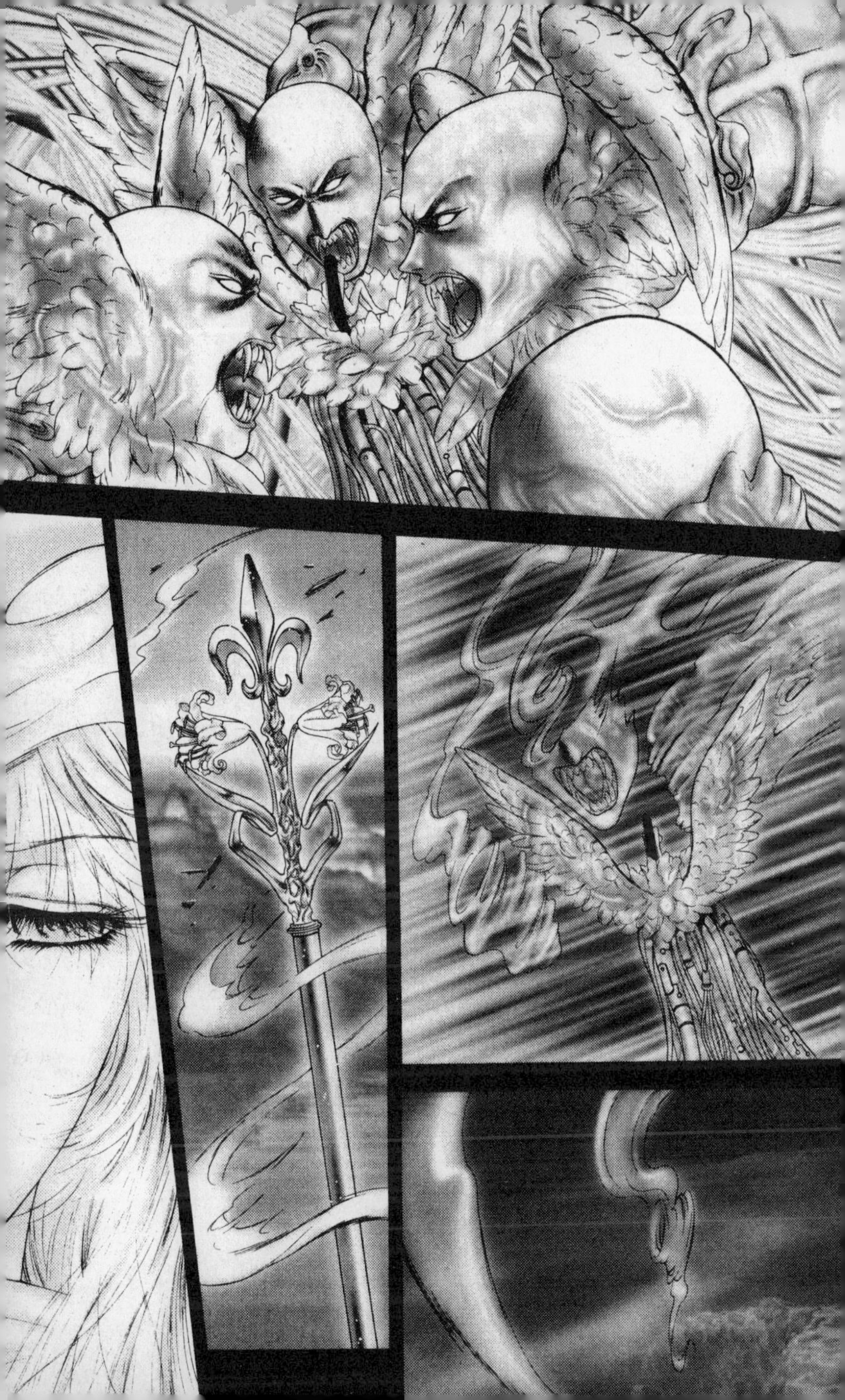

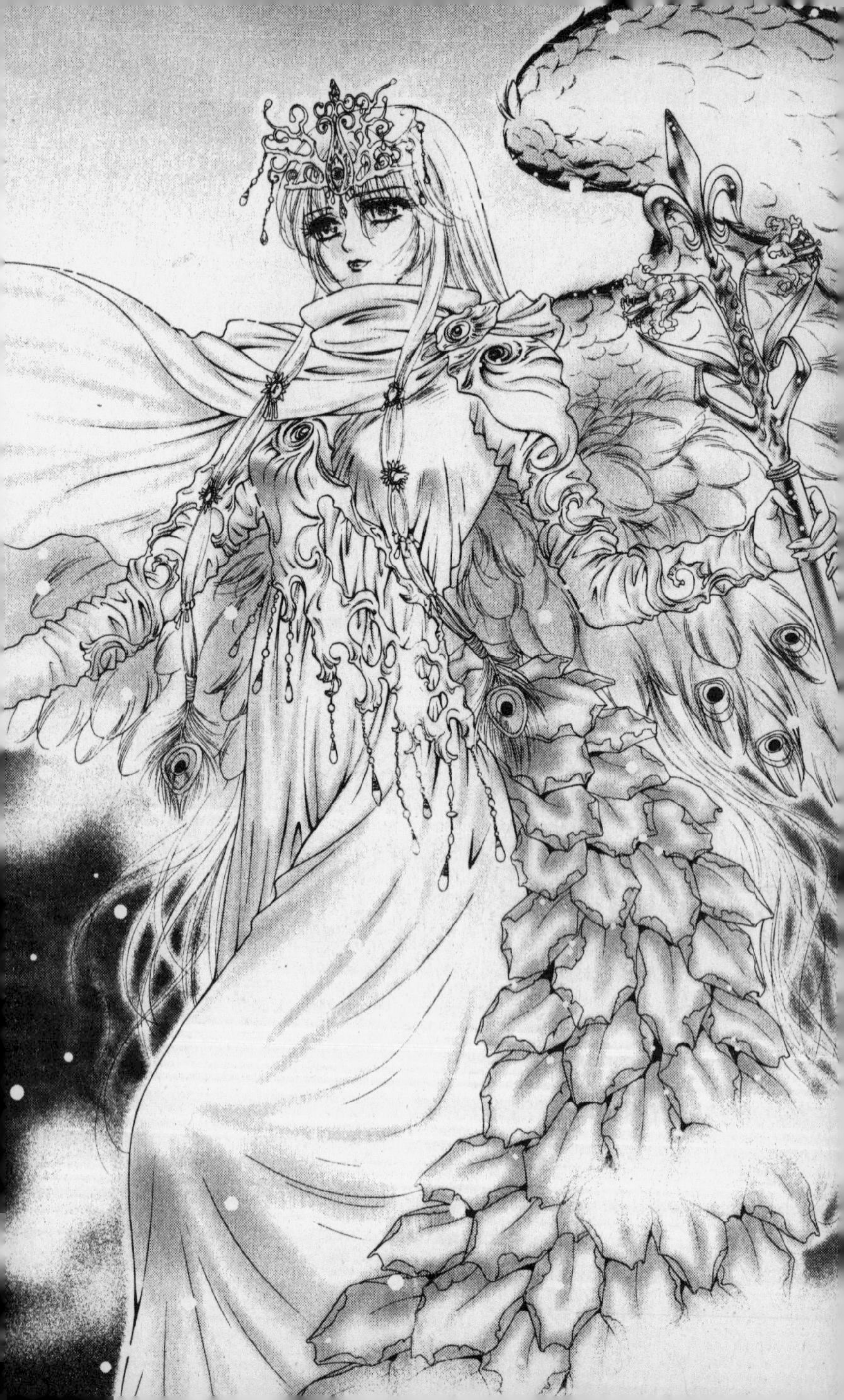

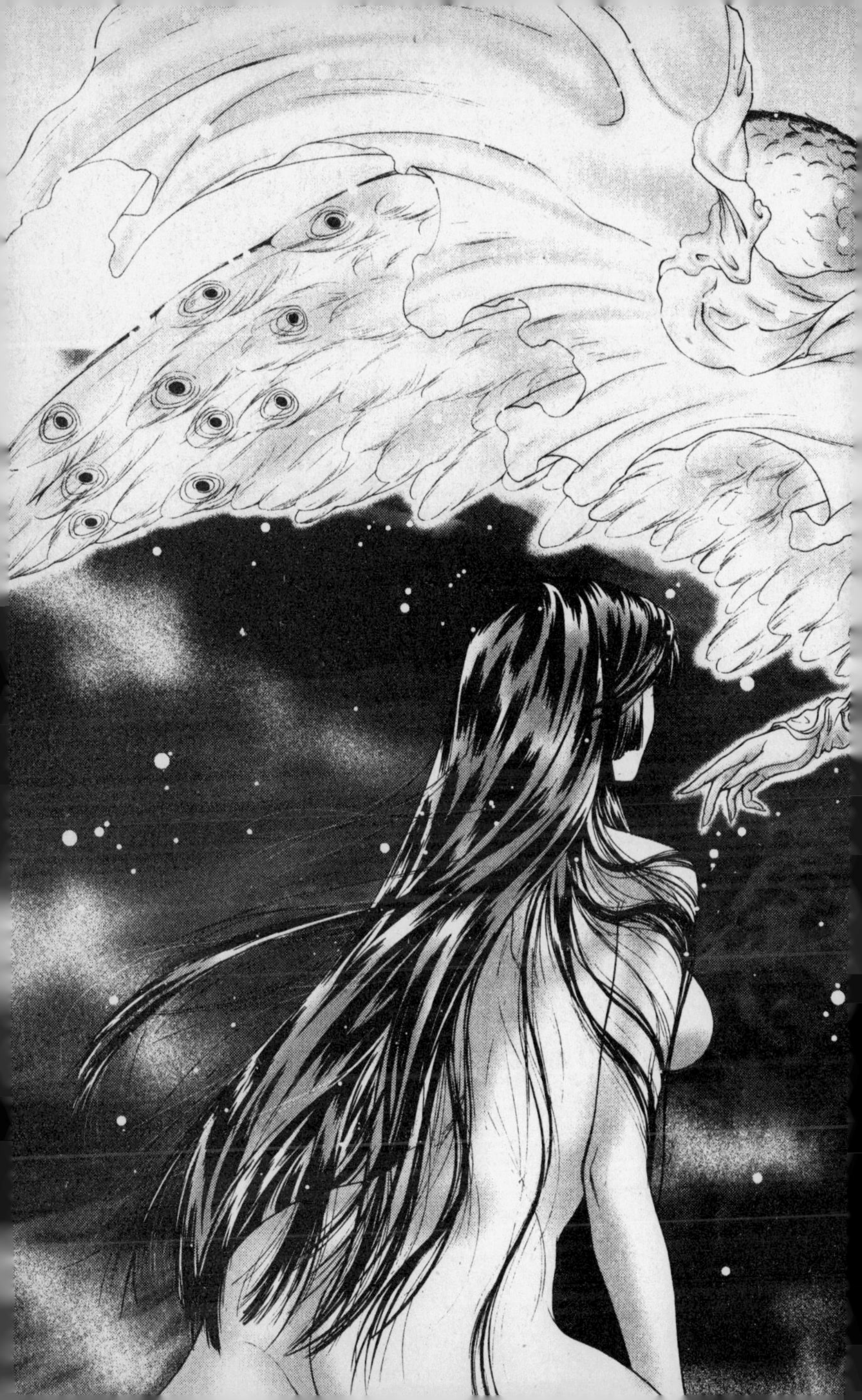

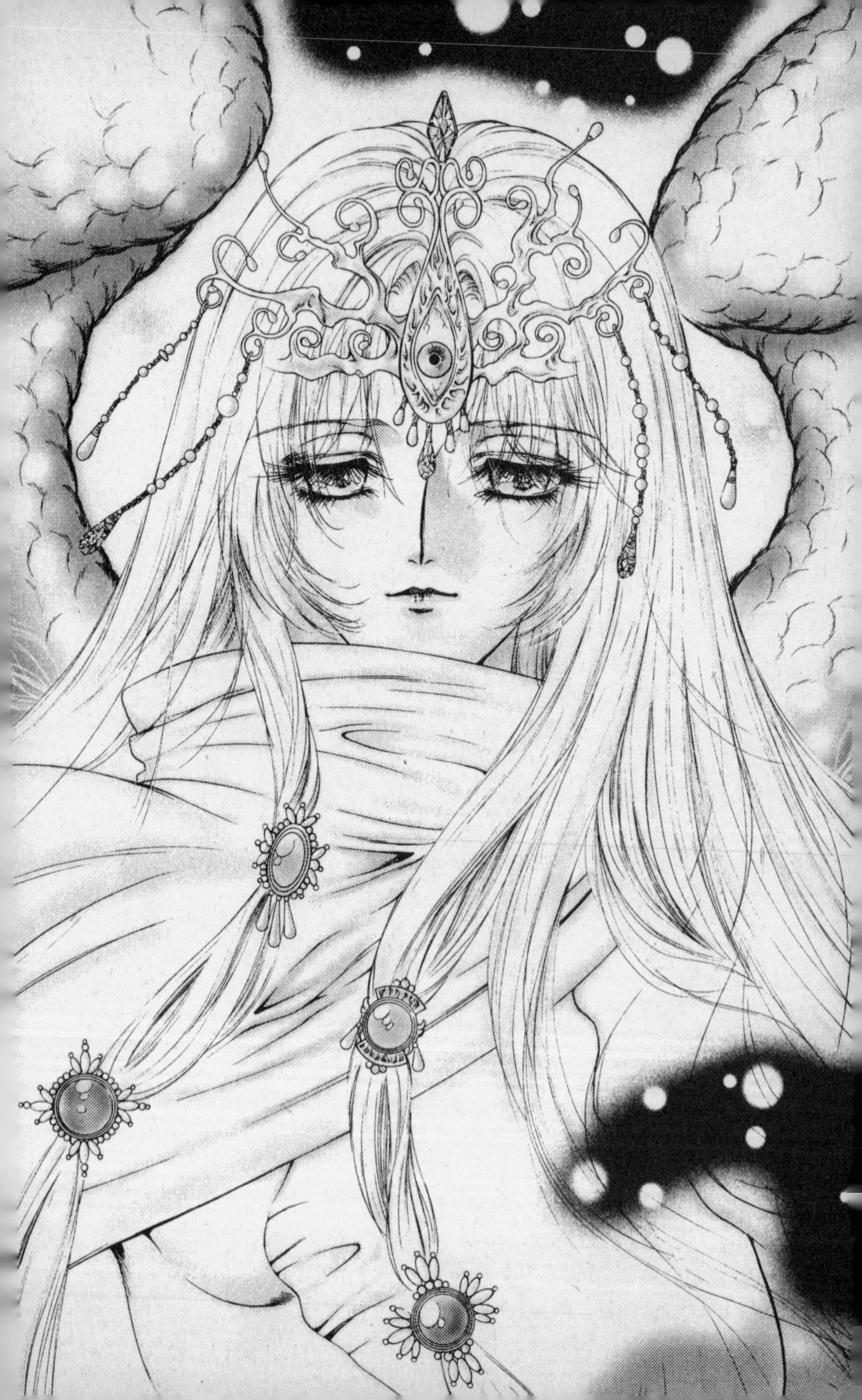

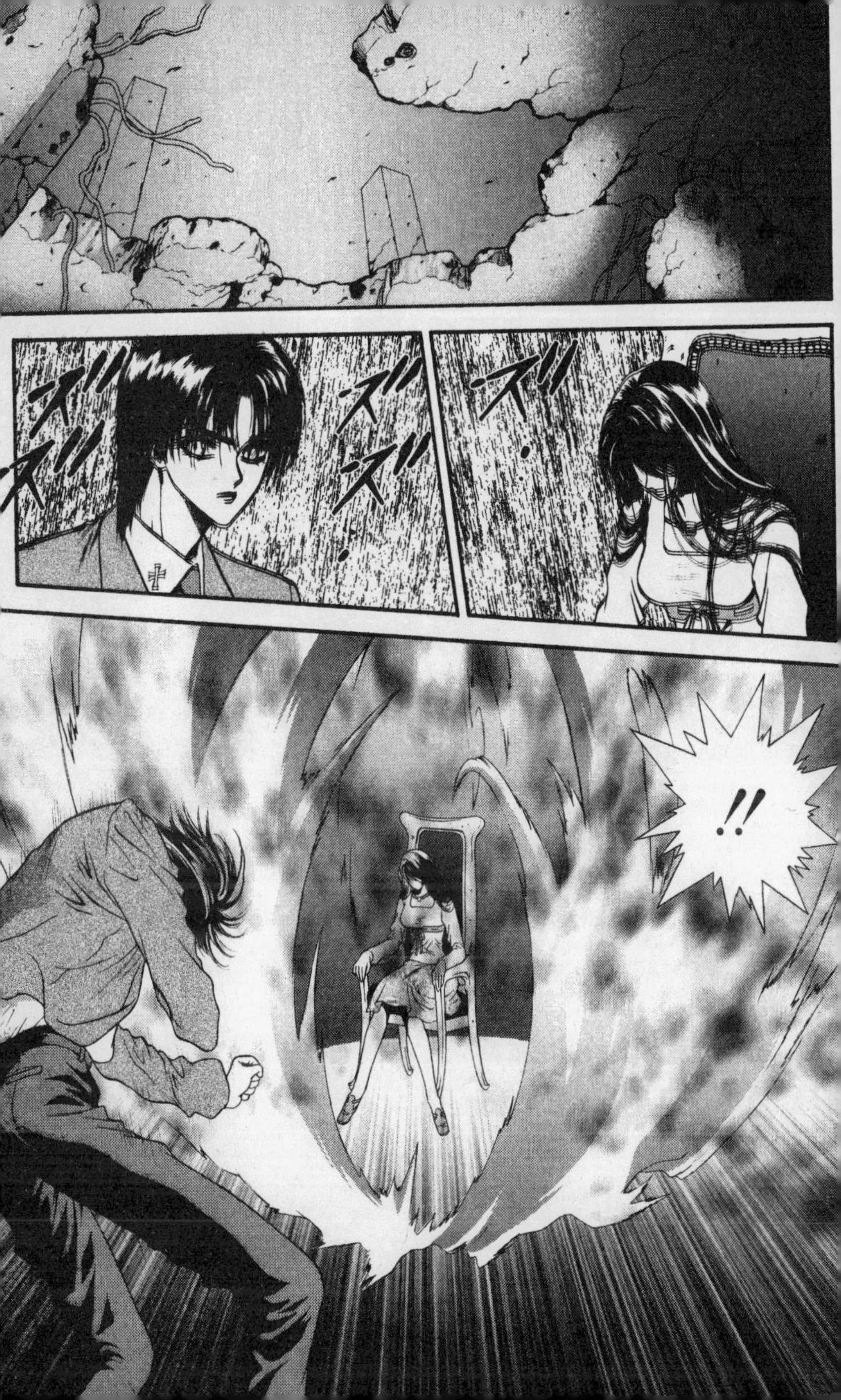

ズ!! ・
ズ!! ズ!!
ズ!! ズ!! ・
!!

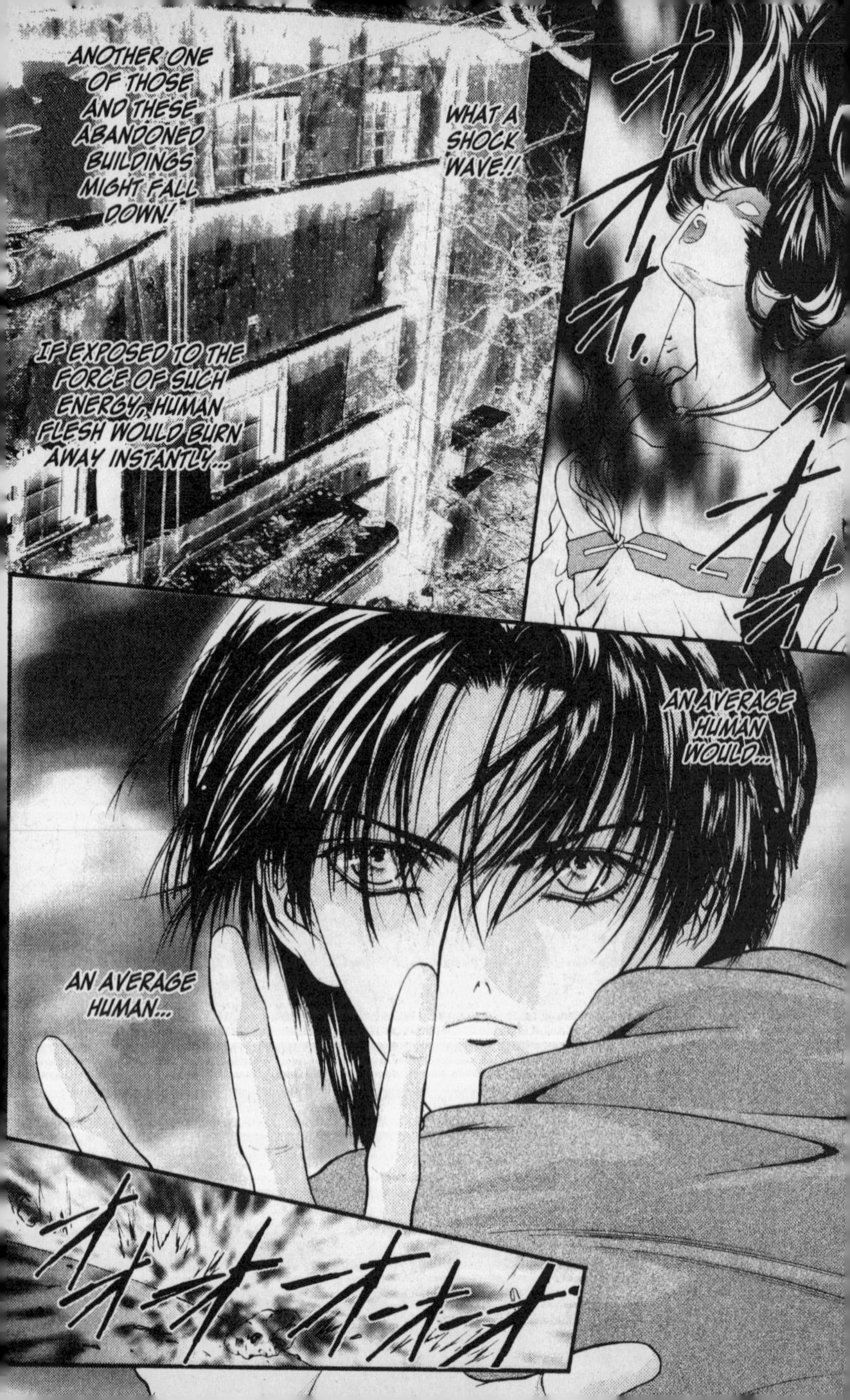
WHAT A SHOCK WAVE!!
ANOTHER ONE OF THOSE AND THESE ABANDONED BUILDINGS MIGHT FALL DOWN!
IF EXPOSED TO THE FORCE OF SUCH ENERGY, HUMAN FLESH WOULD BURN AWAY INSTANTLY...
AN AVERAGE HUMAN WOULD...
AN AVERAGE HUMAN...

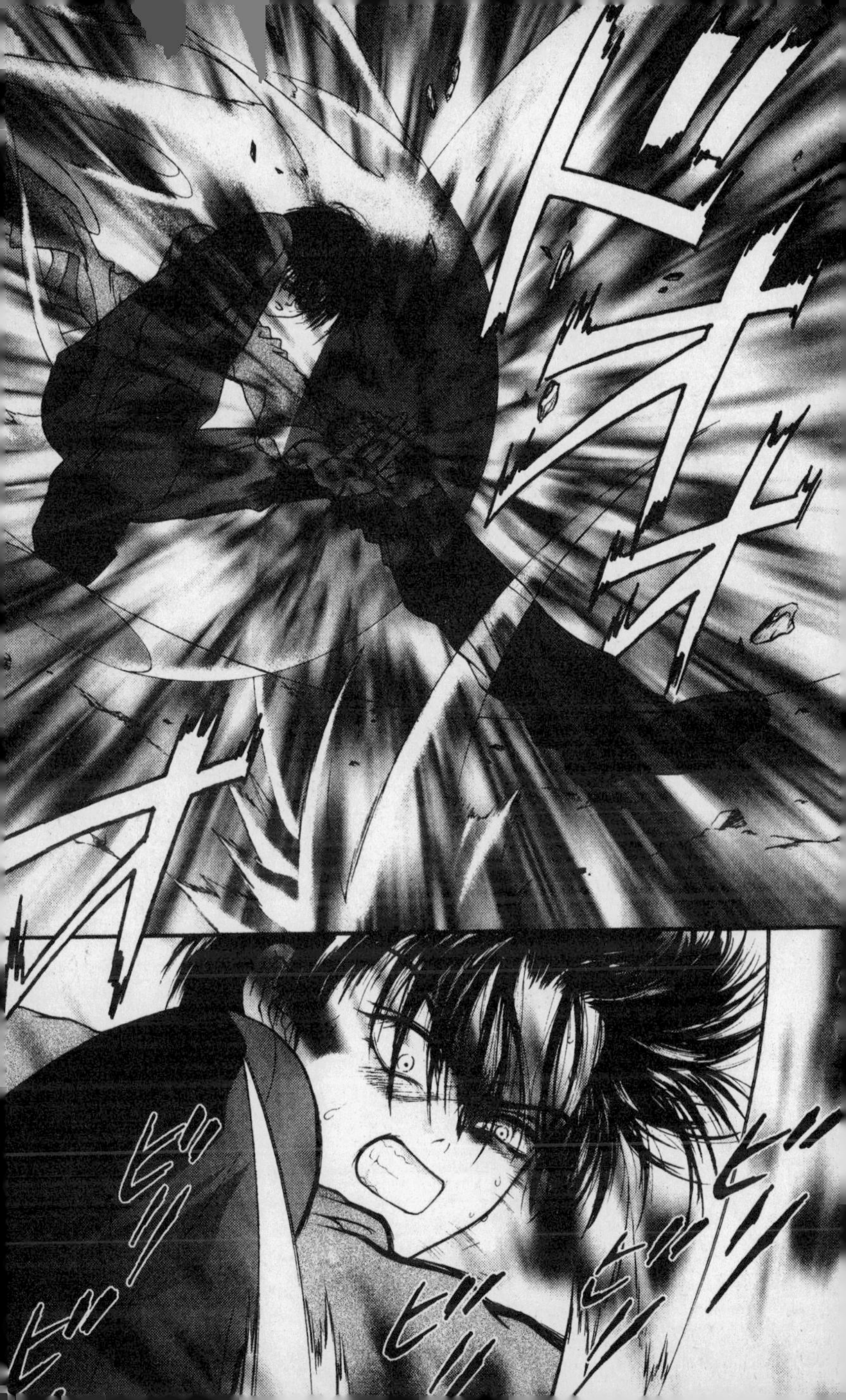

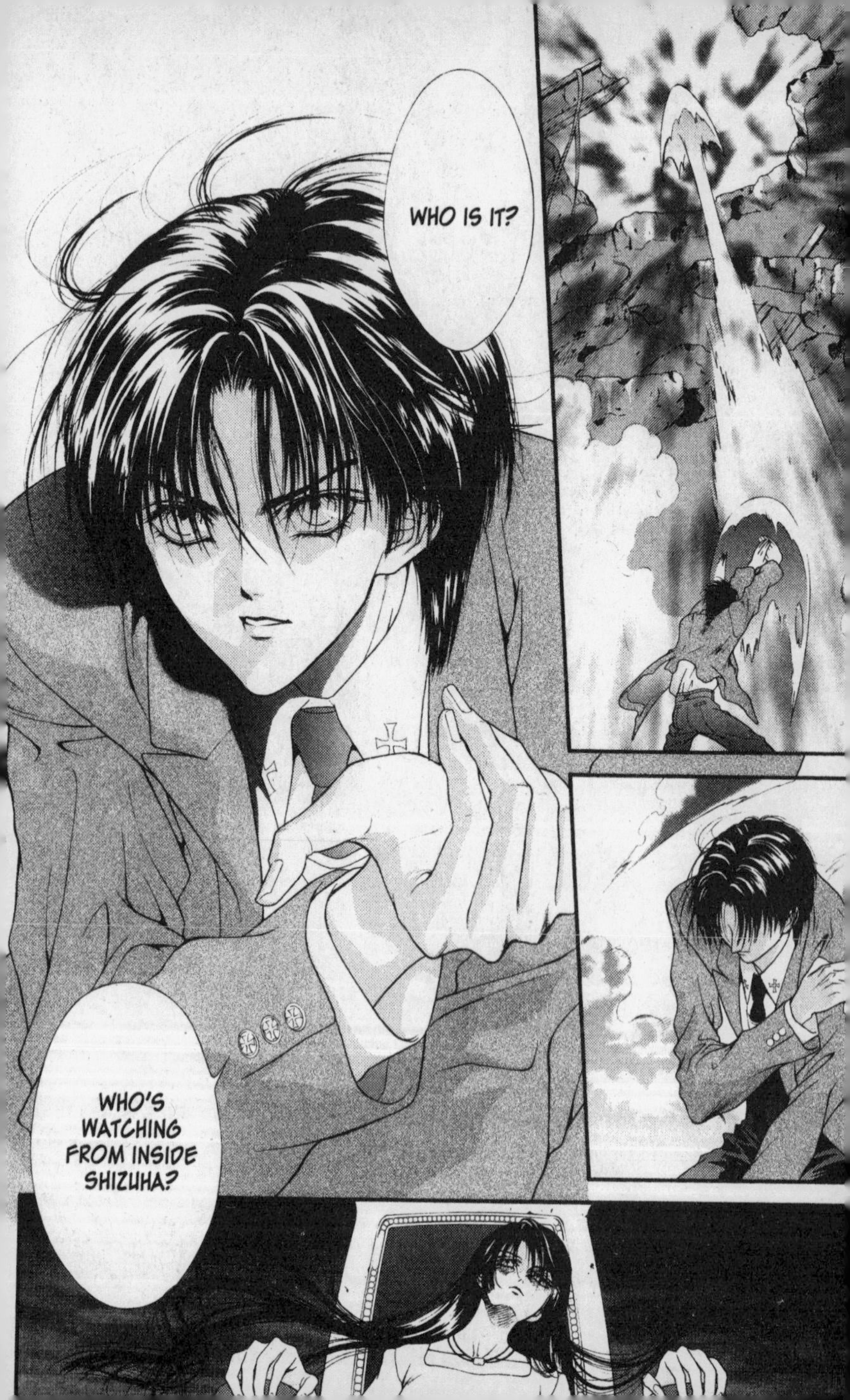
WHO IS IT?
WHO'S WATCHING FROM INSIDE SHIZUHA?

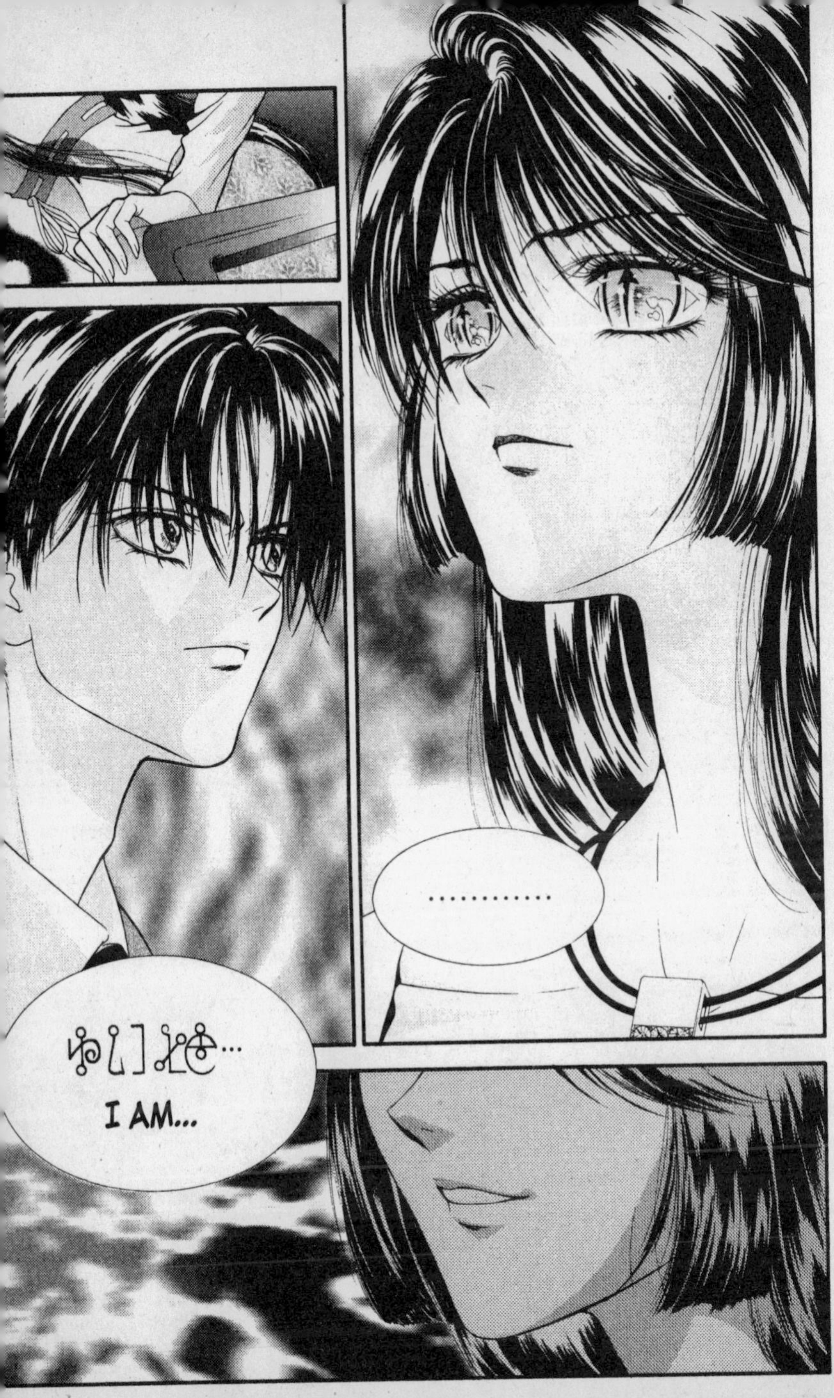
....
I AM...

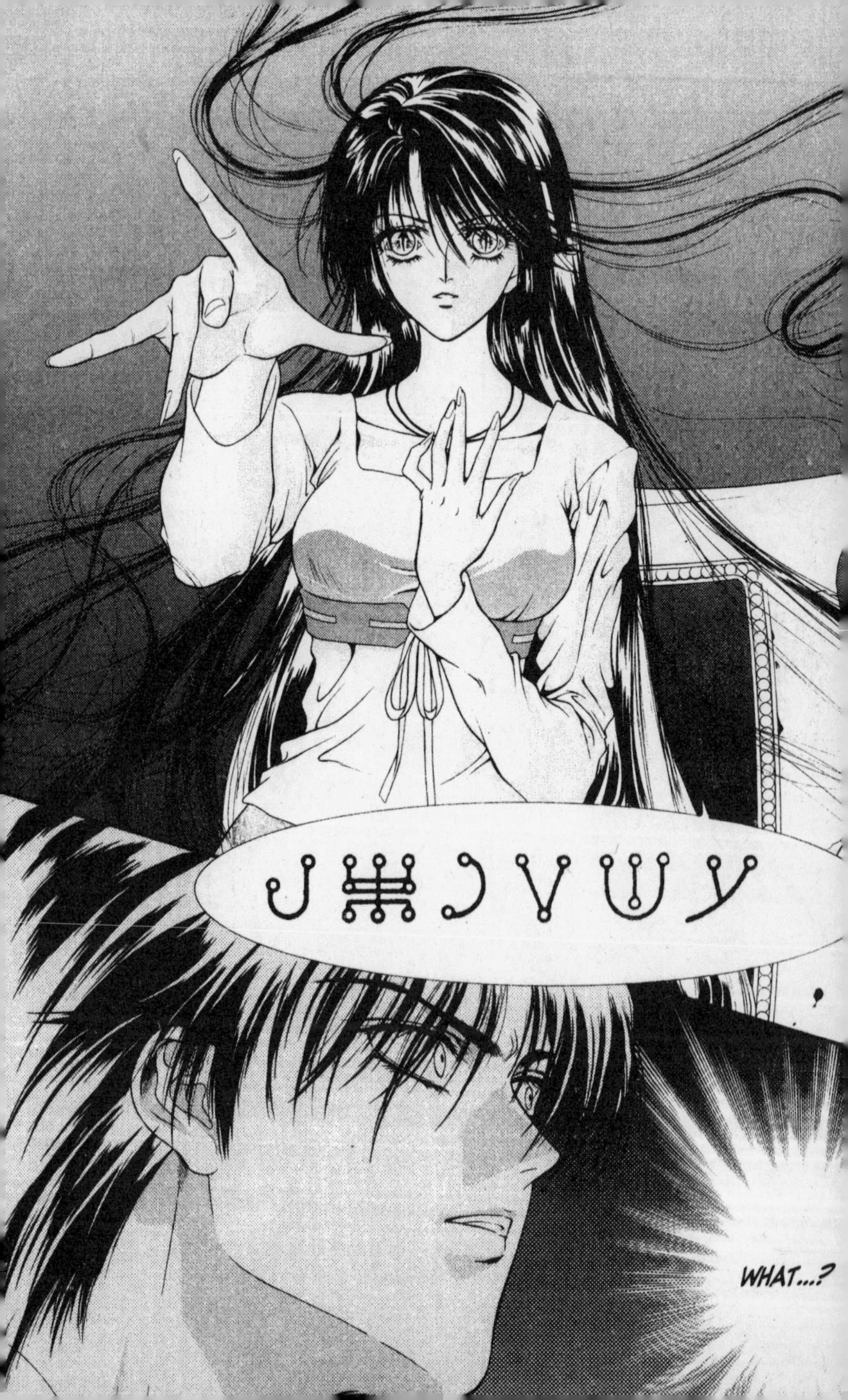
WHAT...?

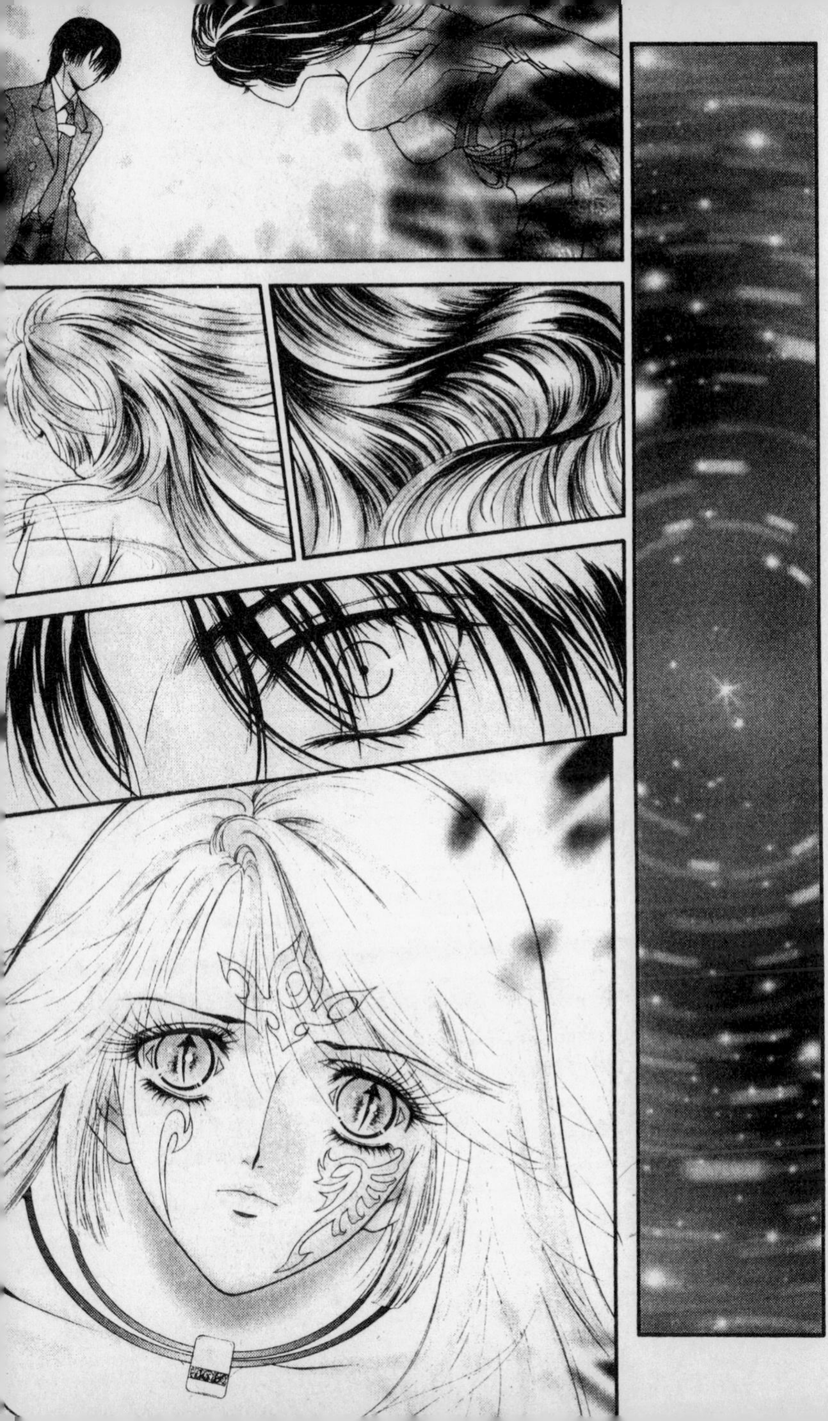

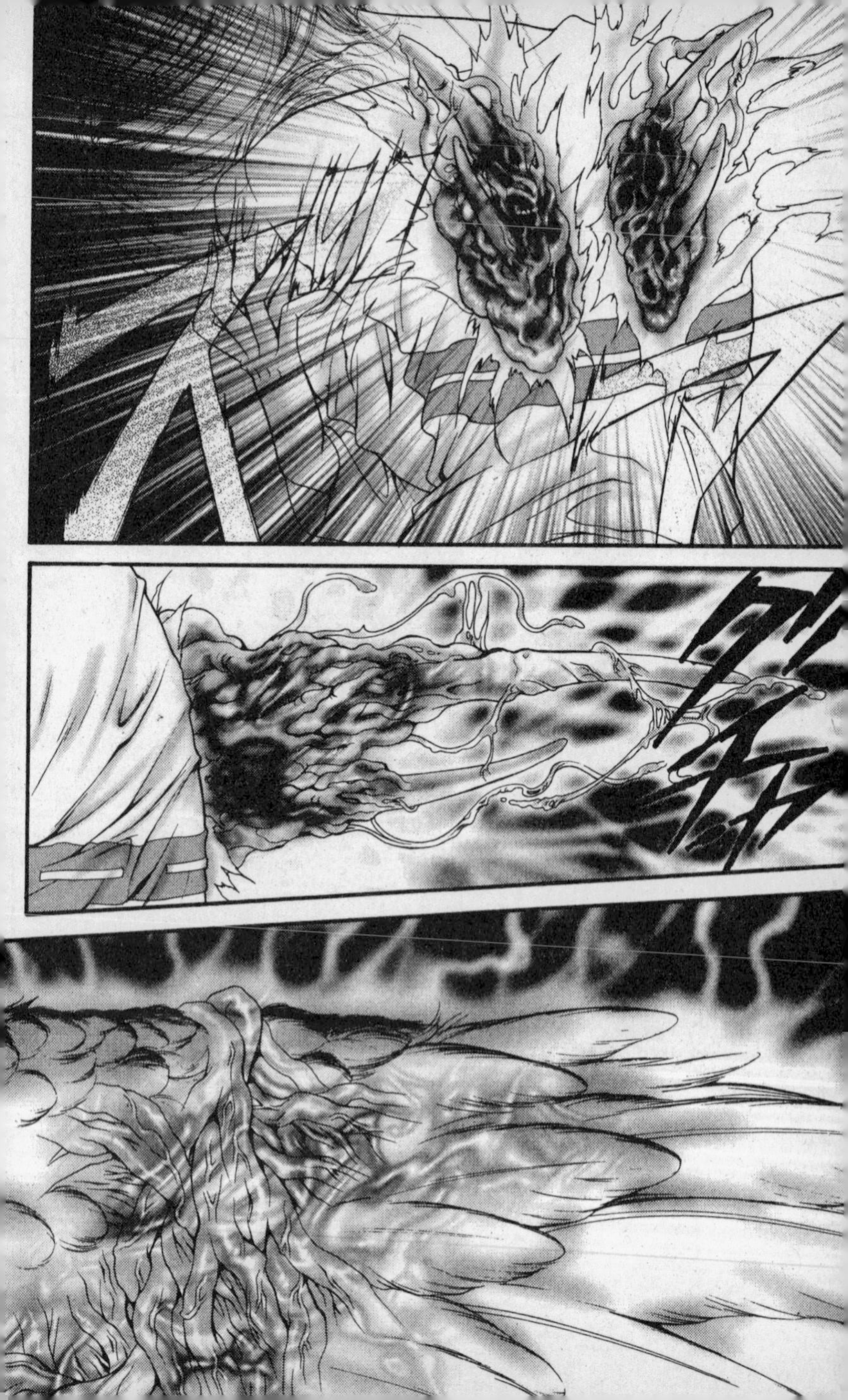

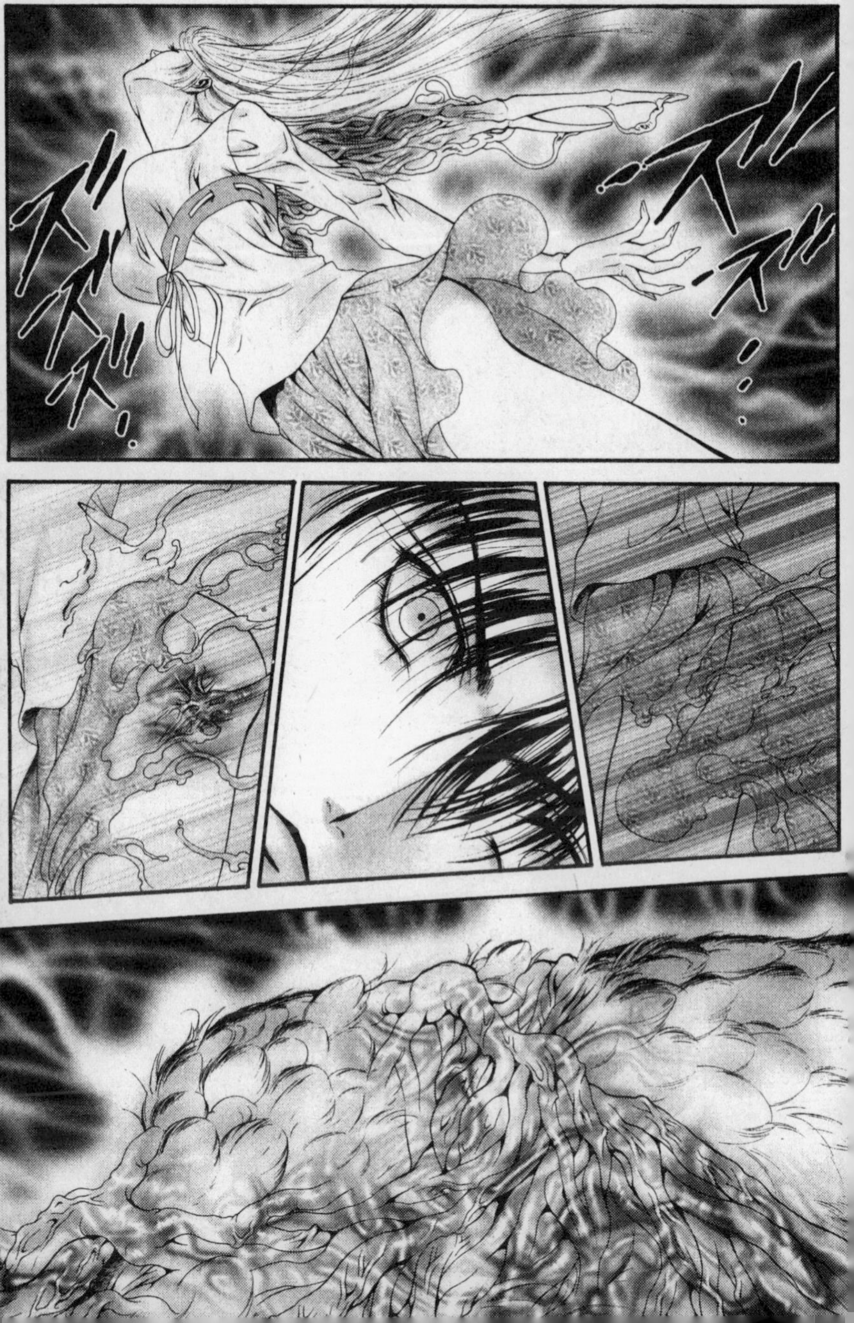
ズズズ…
ズズズ…

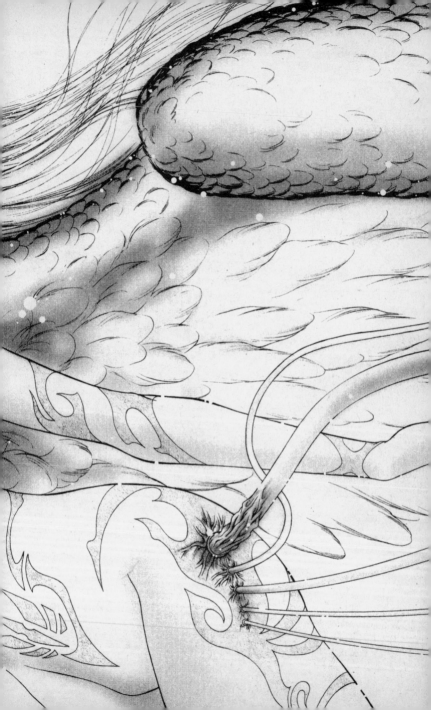

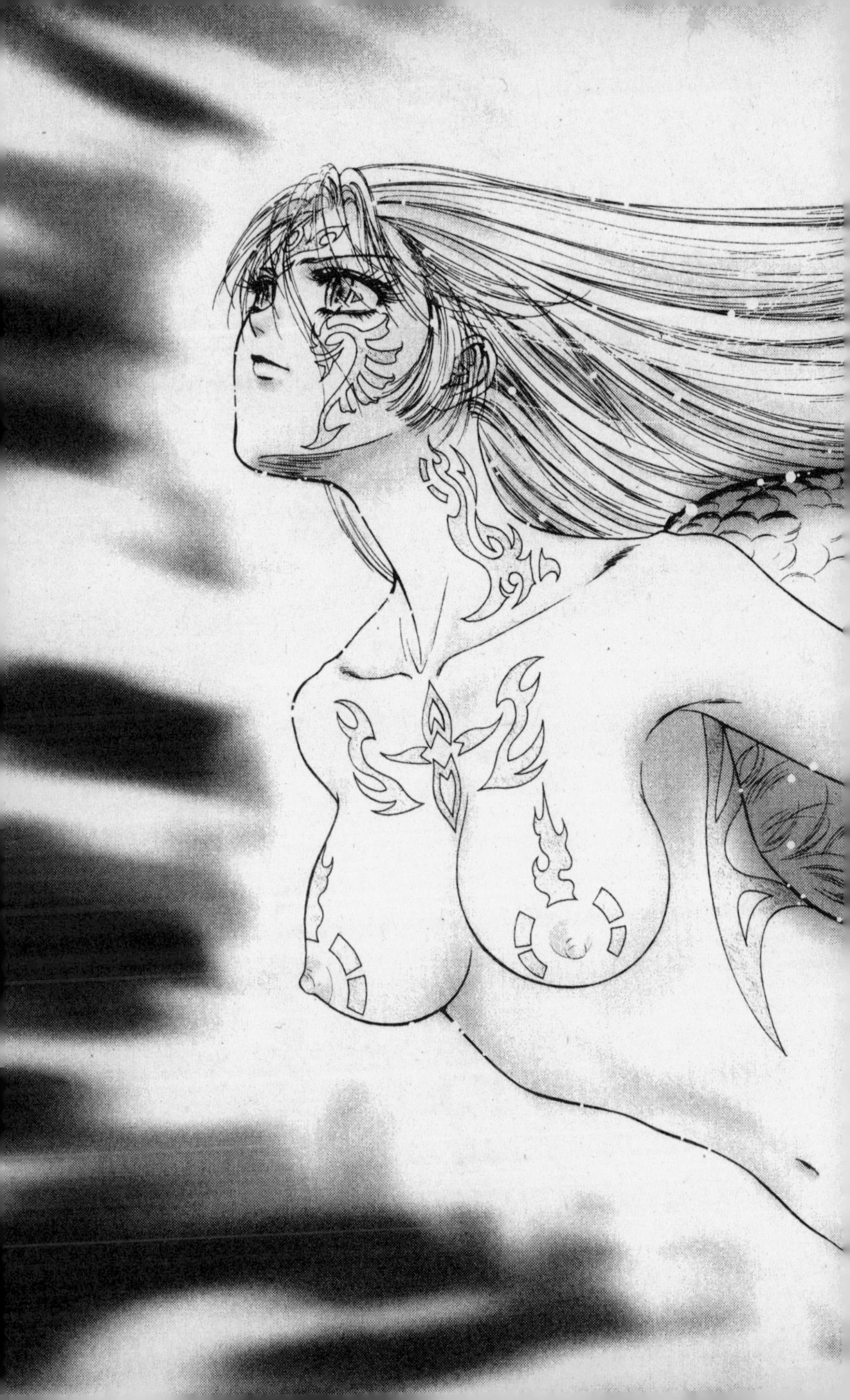

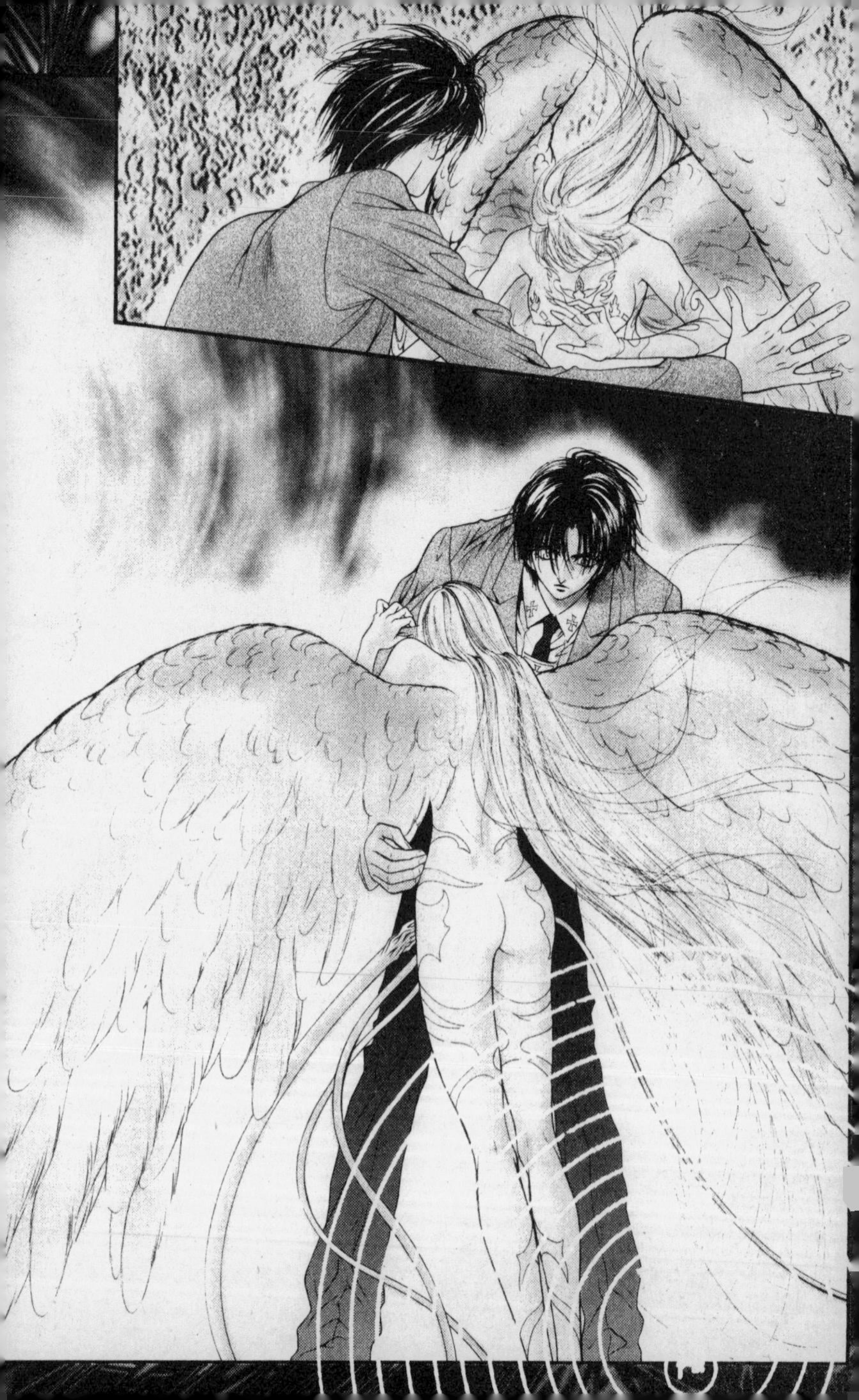

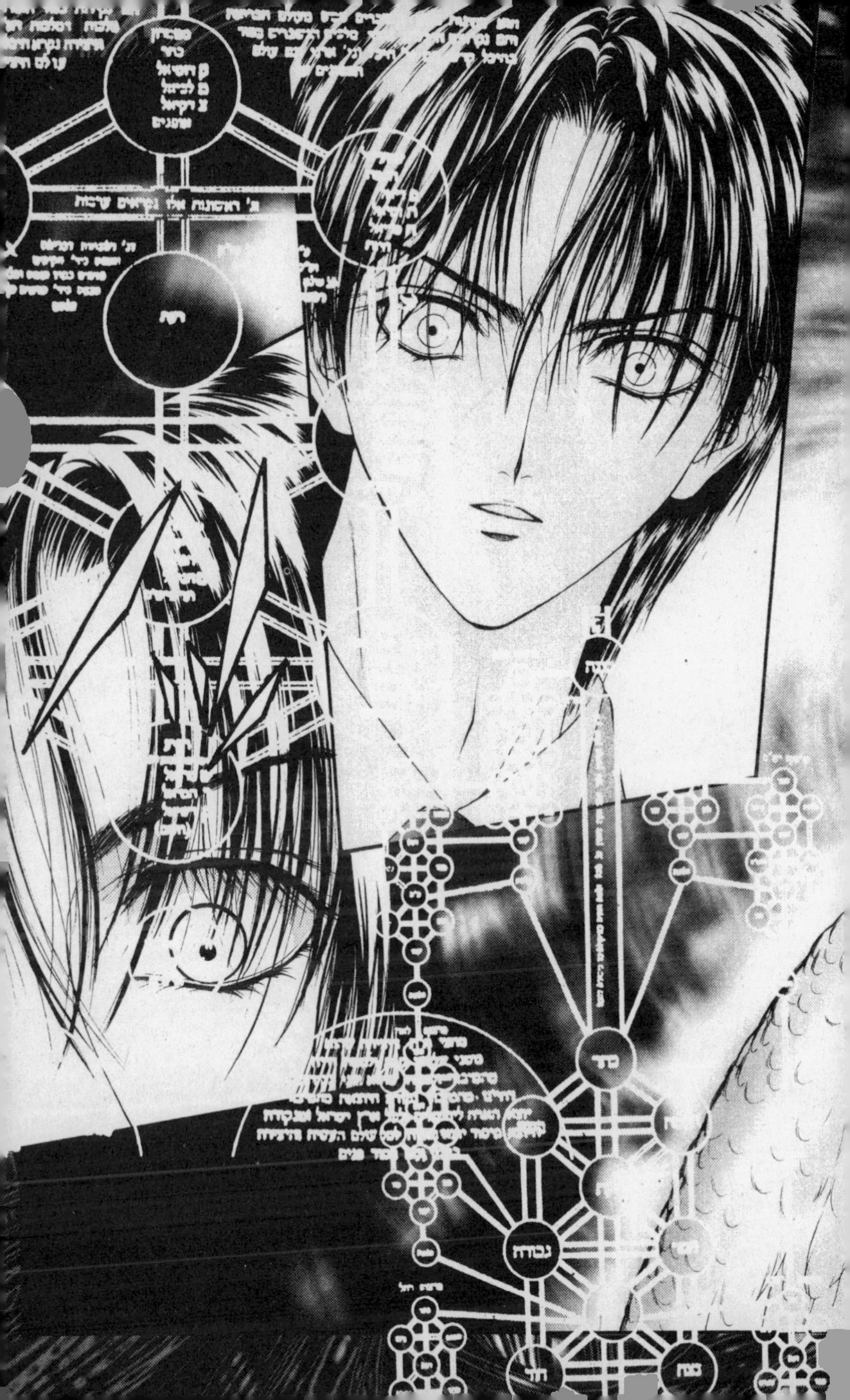
גבורה

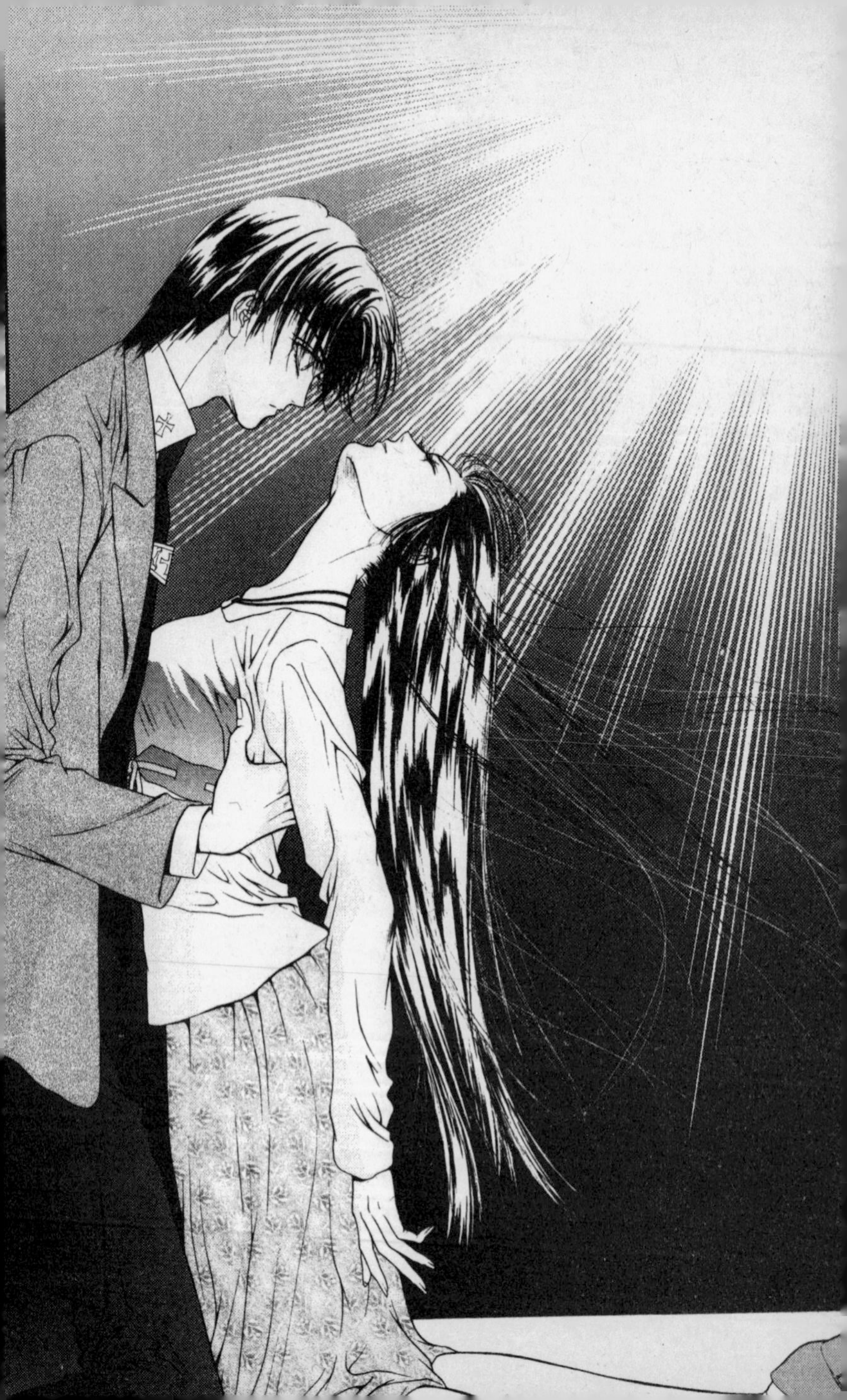

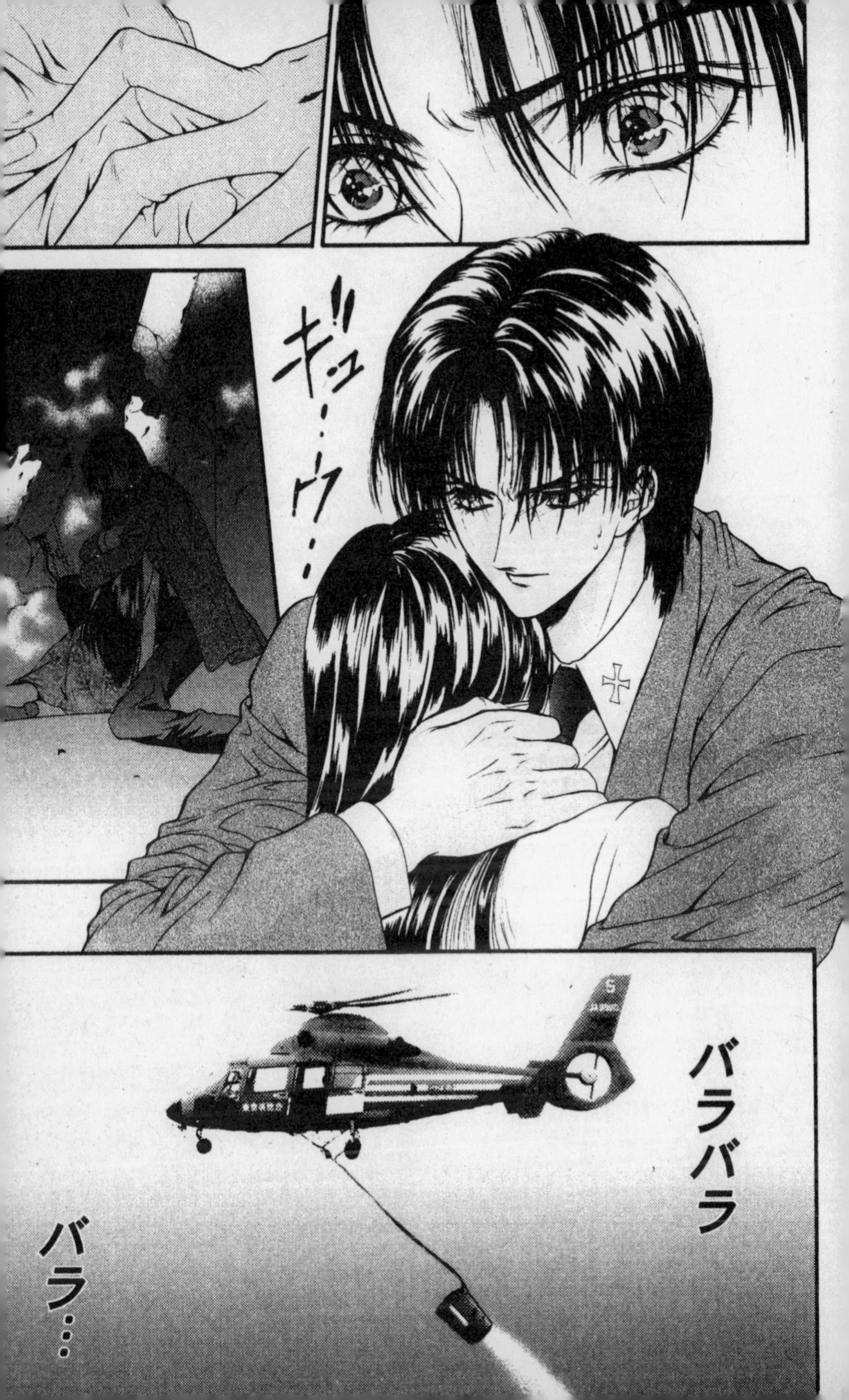
ギュ…ウ…!!
バラバラ
バラ…

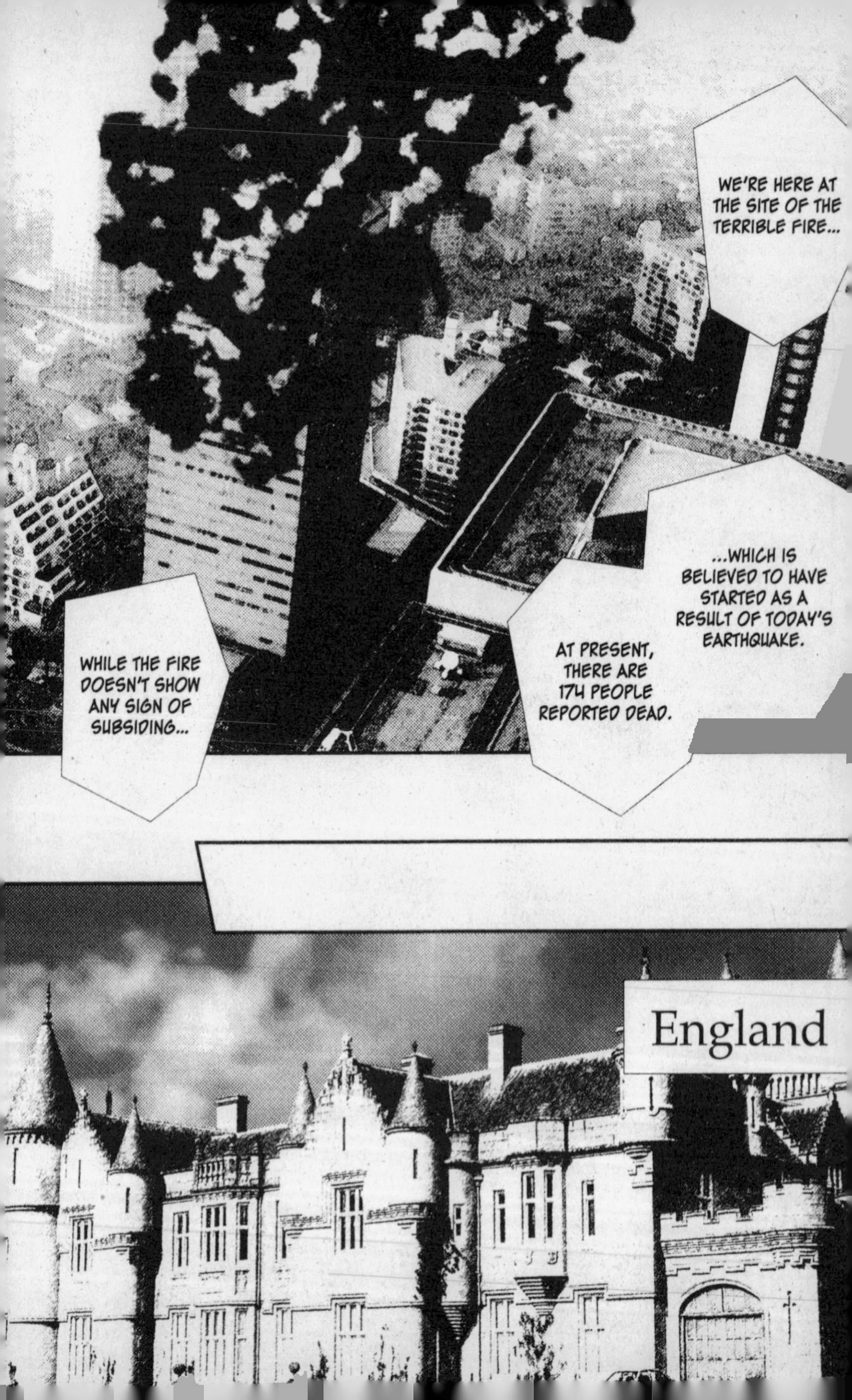
WE'RE HERE AT THE SITE OF THE TERRIBLE FIRE...
...WHICH IS BELIEVED TO HAVE STARTED AS A RESULT OF TODAY'S EARTHQUAKE.
AT PRESENT, THERE ARE 174 PEOPLE REPORTED DEAD.
WHILE THE FIRE DOESN'T SHOW ANY SIGN OF SUBSIDING...
England

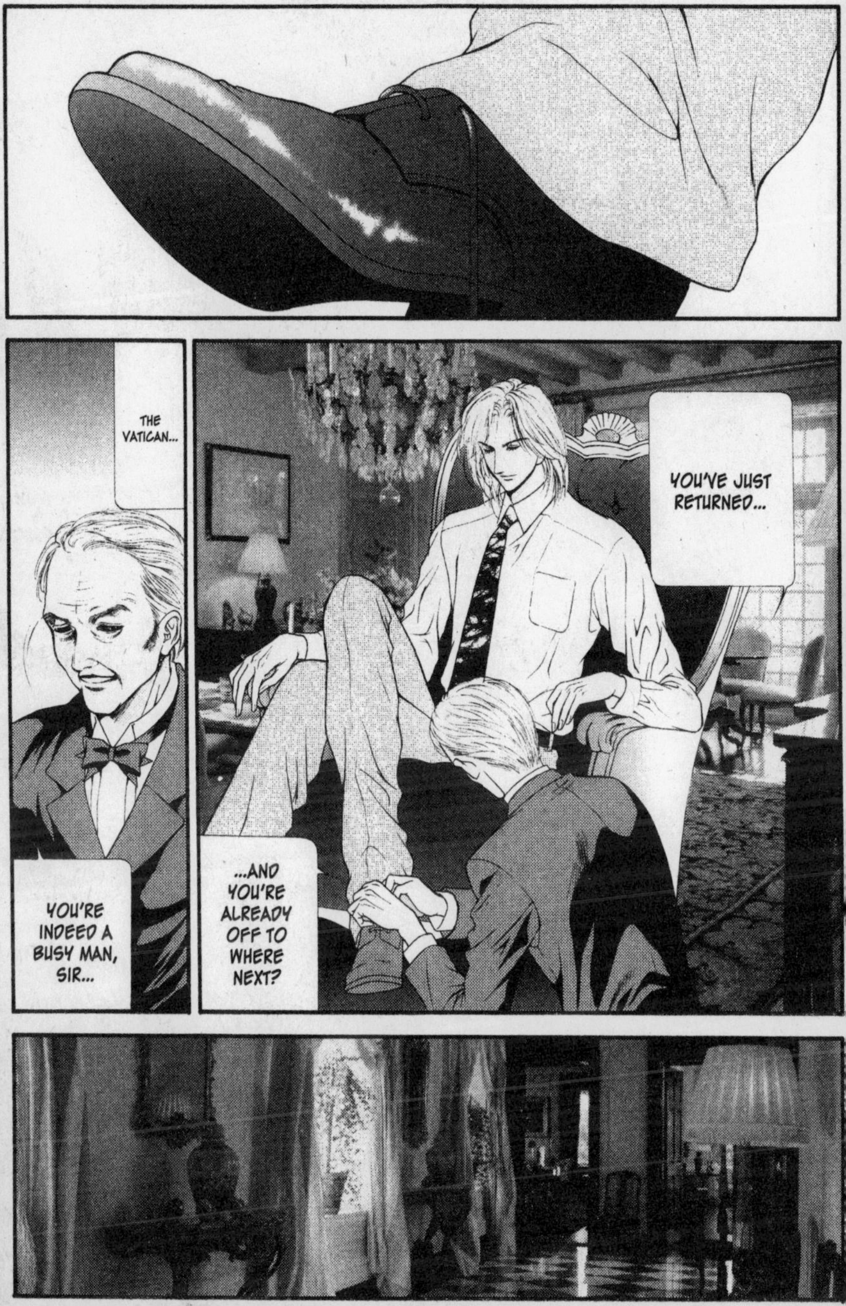
YOU'VE JUST RETURNED...
...AND YOU'RE ALREADY OFF TO WHERE NEXT?
THE VATICAN...
YOU'RE INDEED A BUSY MAN, SIR...

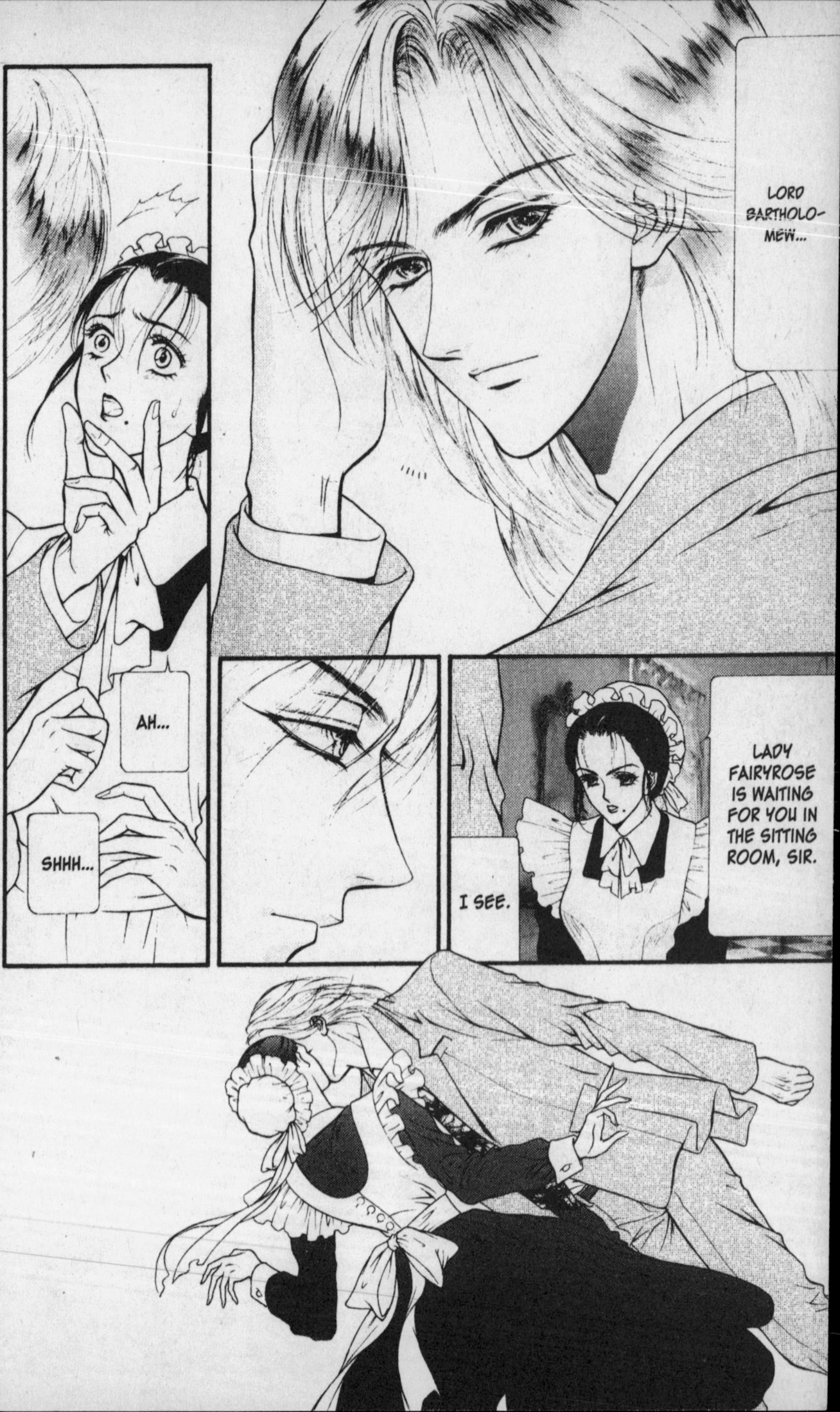
LORD BARTHOLO-MEW...
LADY FAIRYROSE IS WAITING FOR YOU IN THE SITTING ROOM, SIR.
I SEE.
AH...
SHHH...

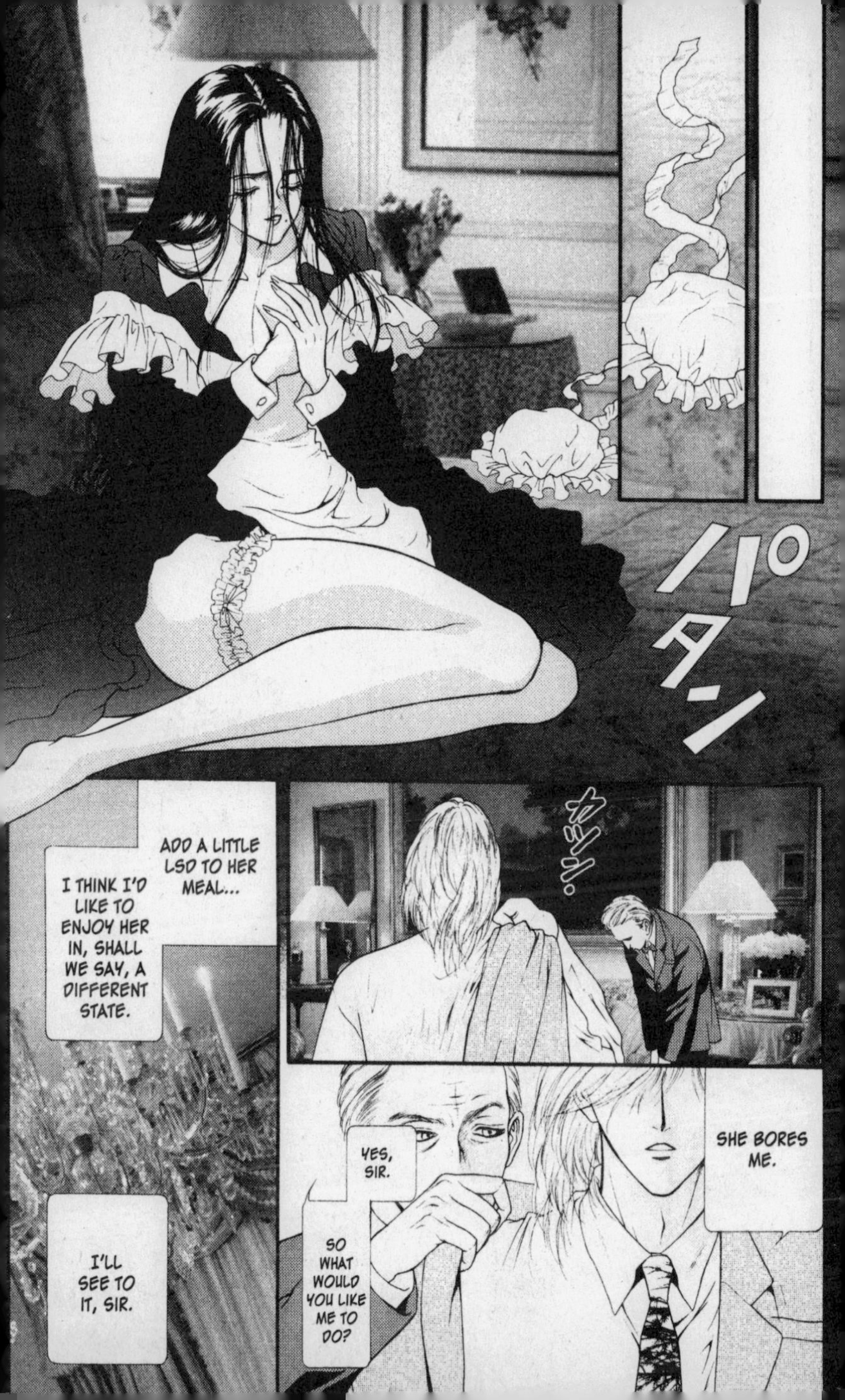
パタン
カツン。
SHE BORES ME.
YES, SIR.
SO WHAT WOULD YOU LIKE ME TO DO?
ADD A LITTLE LSD TO HER MEAL...
I THINK I'D LIKE TO ENJOY HER IN, SHALL WE SAY, A DIFFERENT STATE.
I'LL SEE TO IT, SIR.

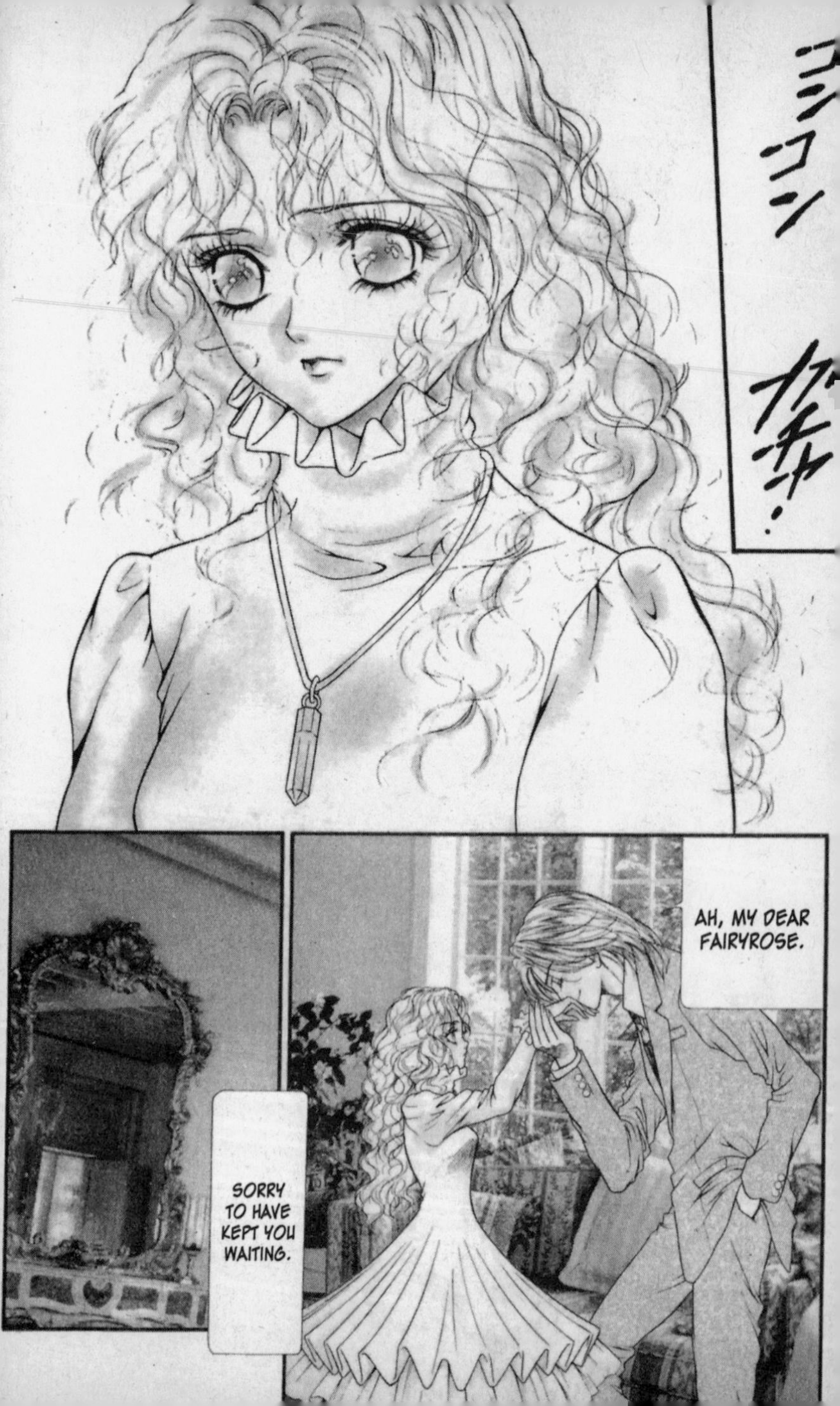
コンコン
ガチャッ!
AH, MY DEAR FAIRYROSE.
SORRY TO HAVE KEPT YOU WAITING.

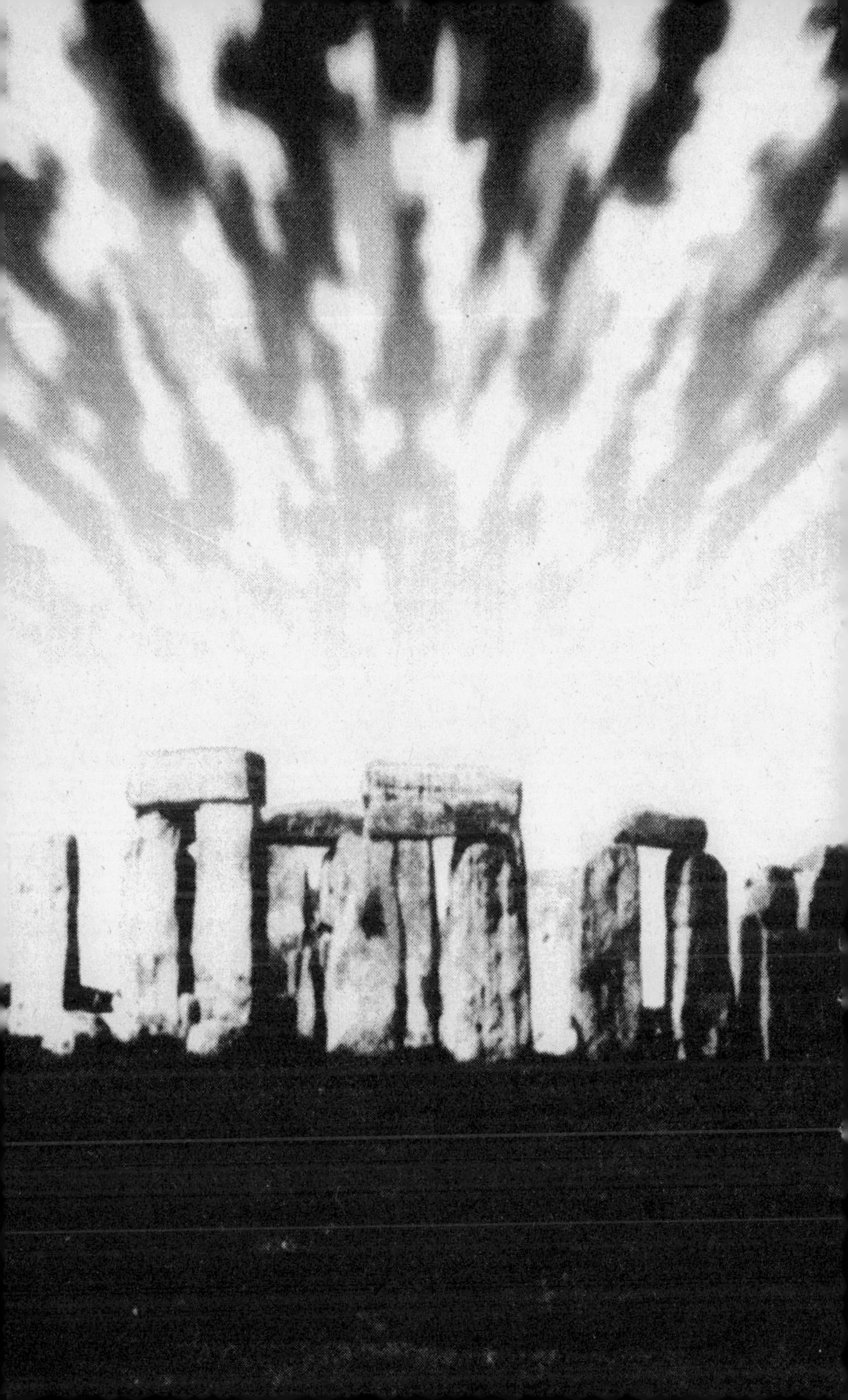

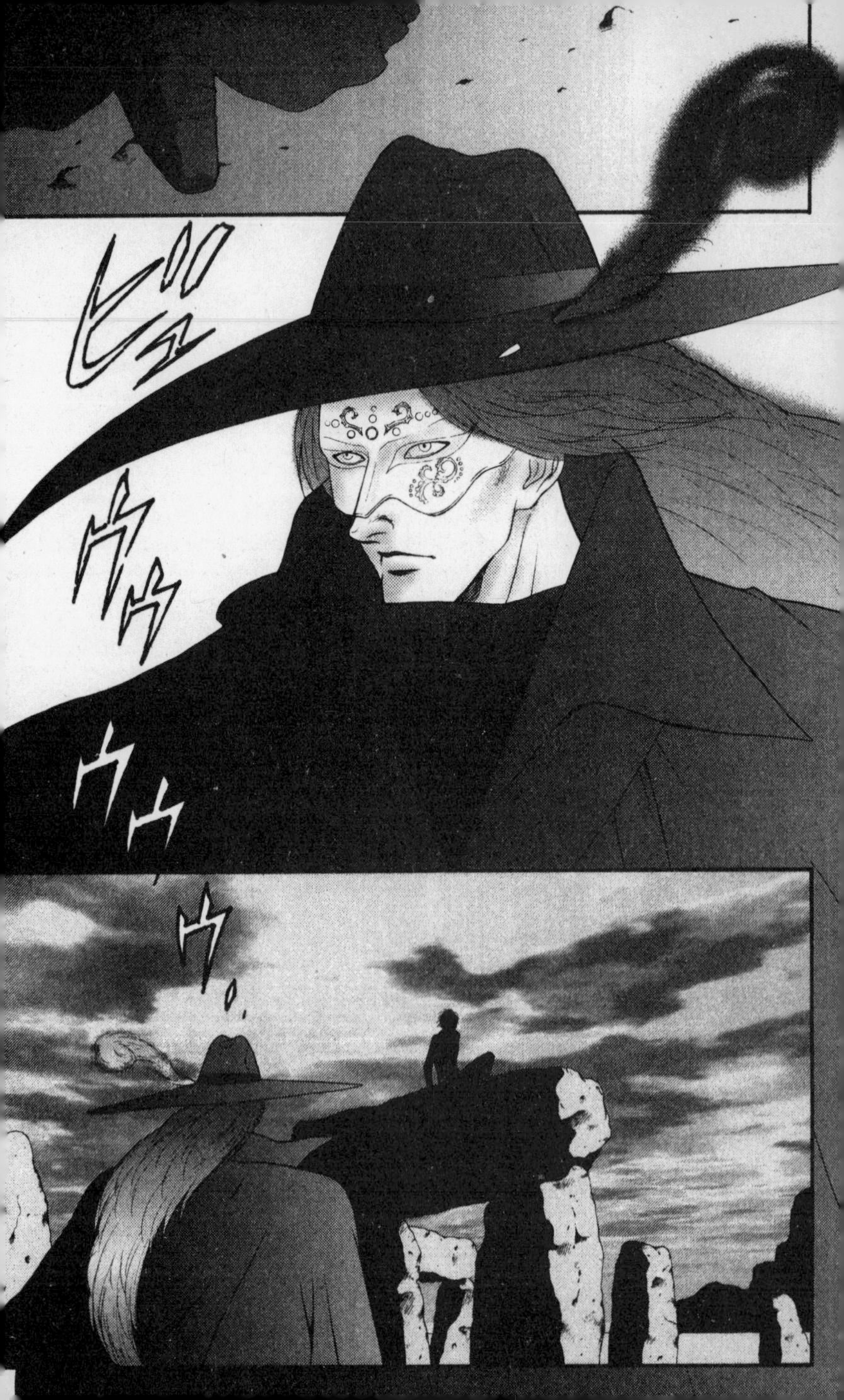
ビュ
ウゥ
ウゥ
ウ、、

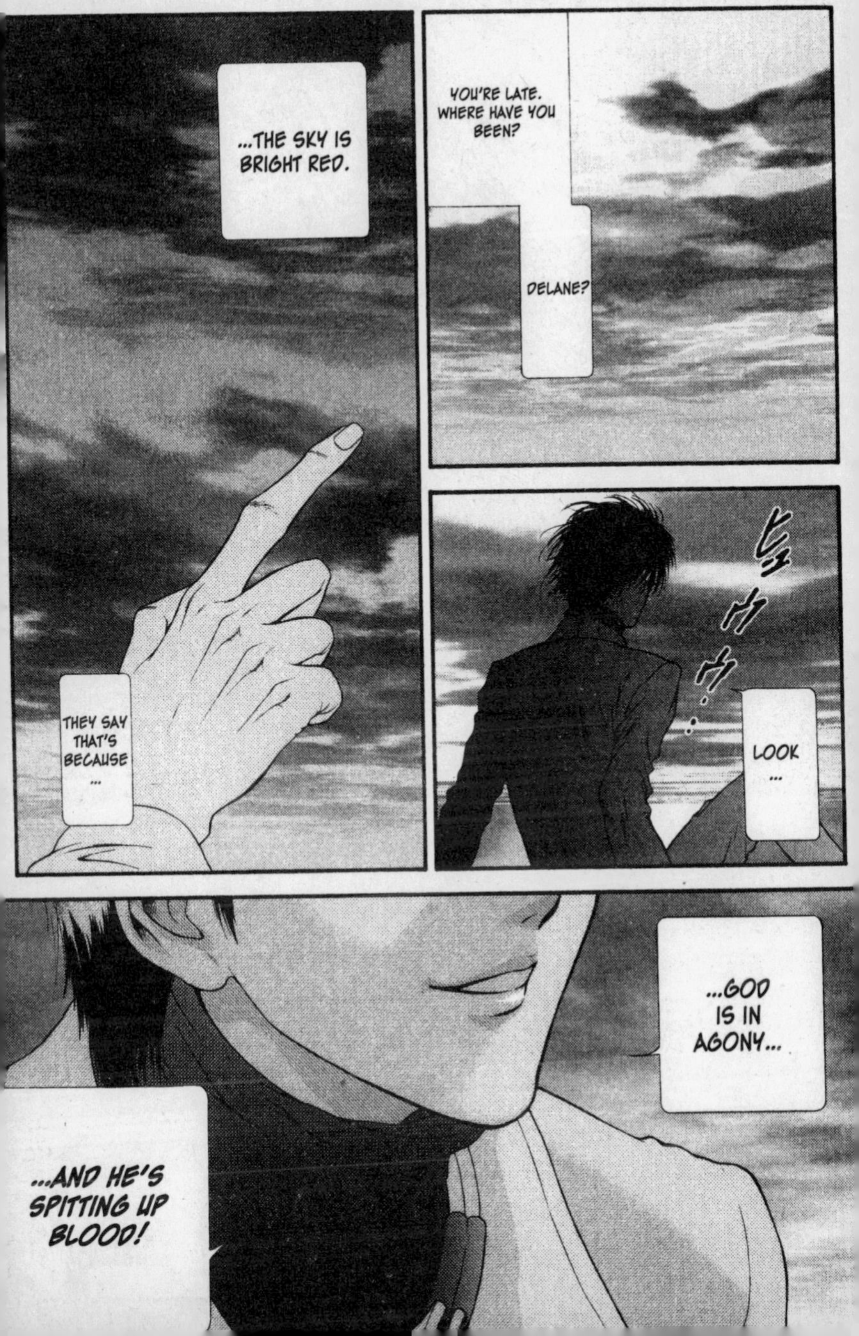
YOU'RE LATE. WHERE HAVE YOU BEEN?
DELANE?
LOOK...
...THE SKY IS BRIGHT RED.
THEY SAY THAT'S BECAUSE...
...GOD IS IN AGONY...
...AND HE'S SPITTING UP BLOOD!

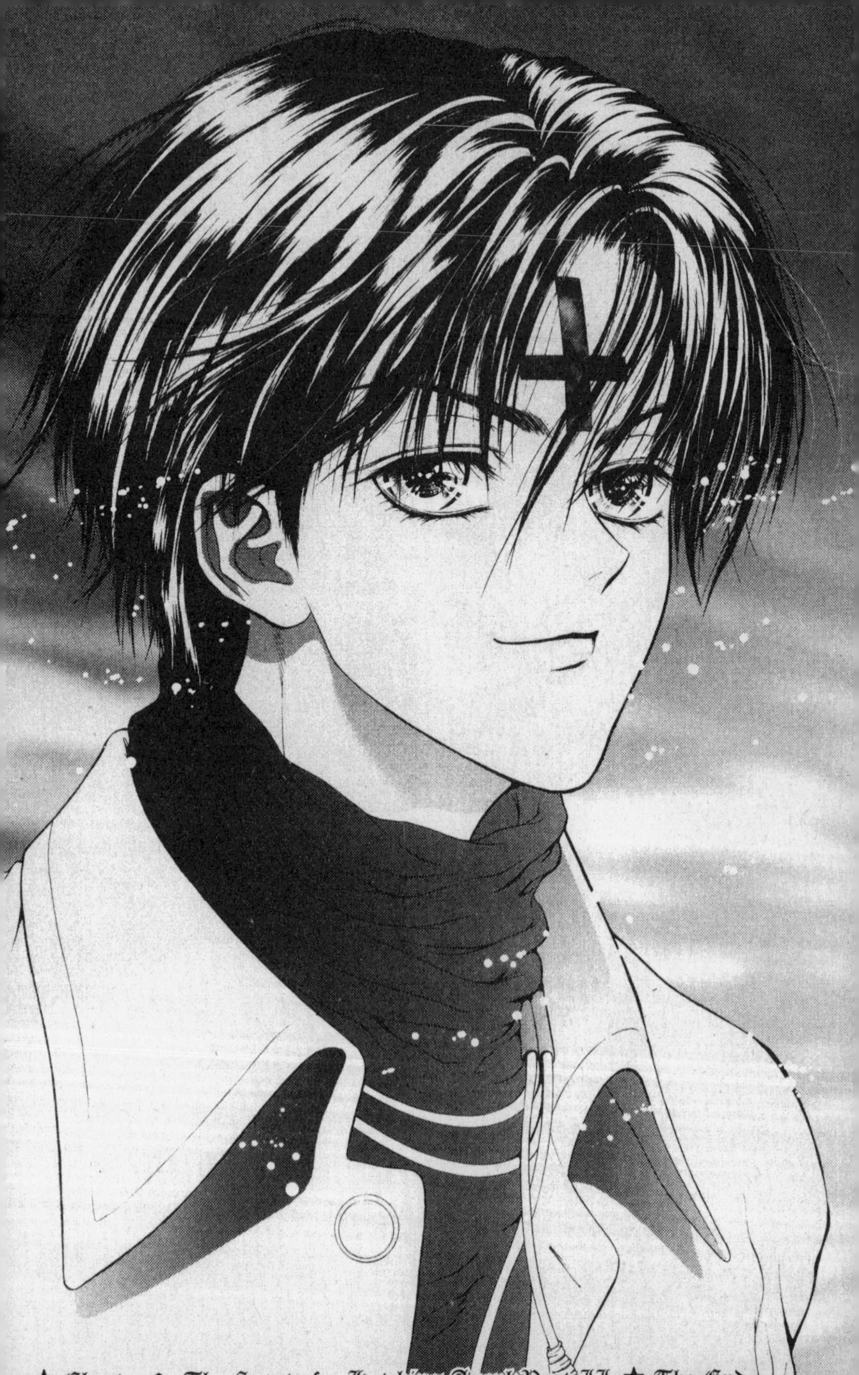

★ Chapter 9 The Scent of a Hatching Angel: Part II ★ The End

Chapter 10 The Visible Hole, The Invisible Hole

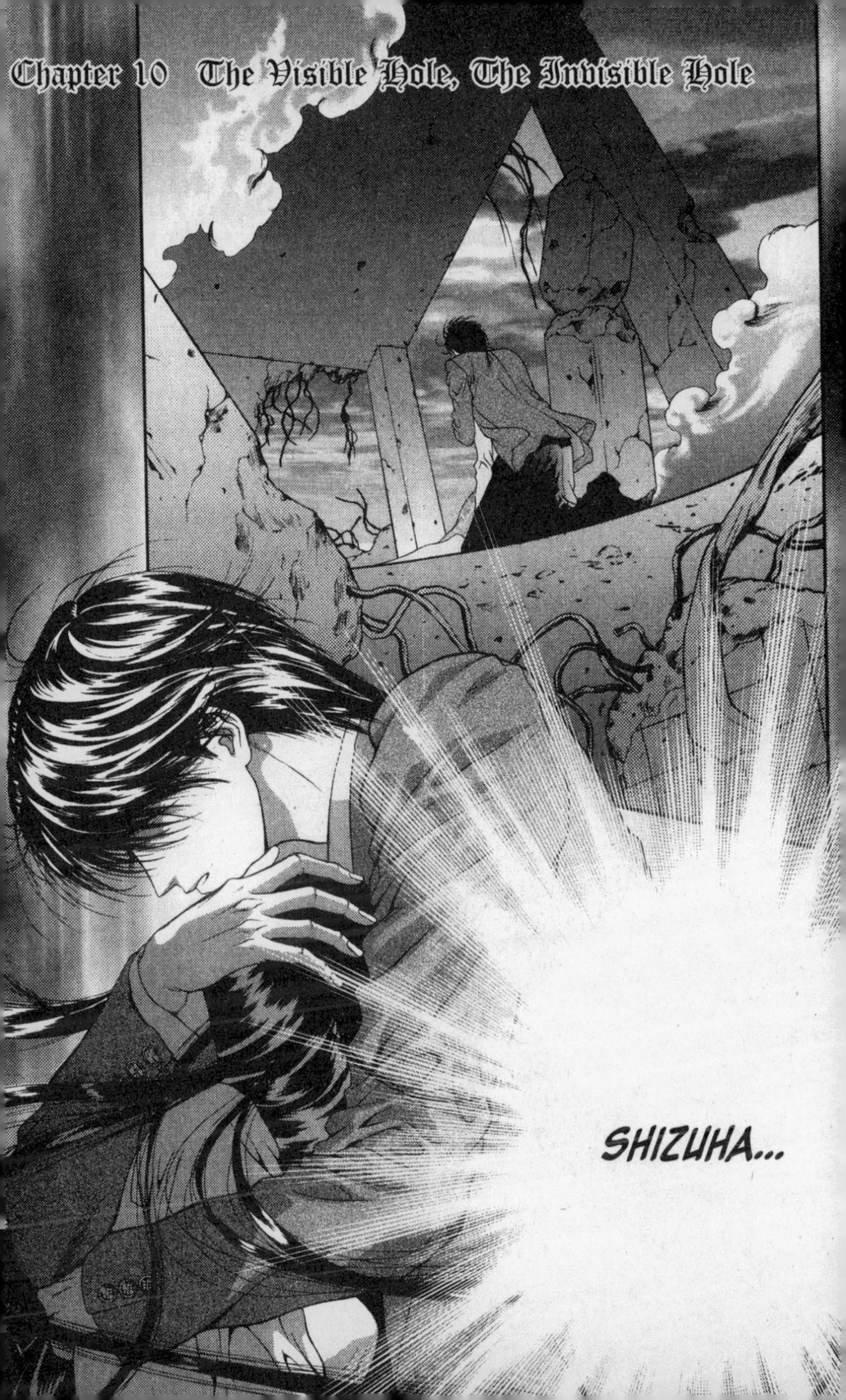
SHIZUHA...

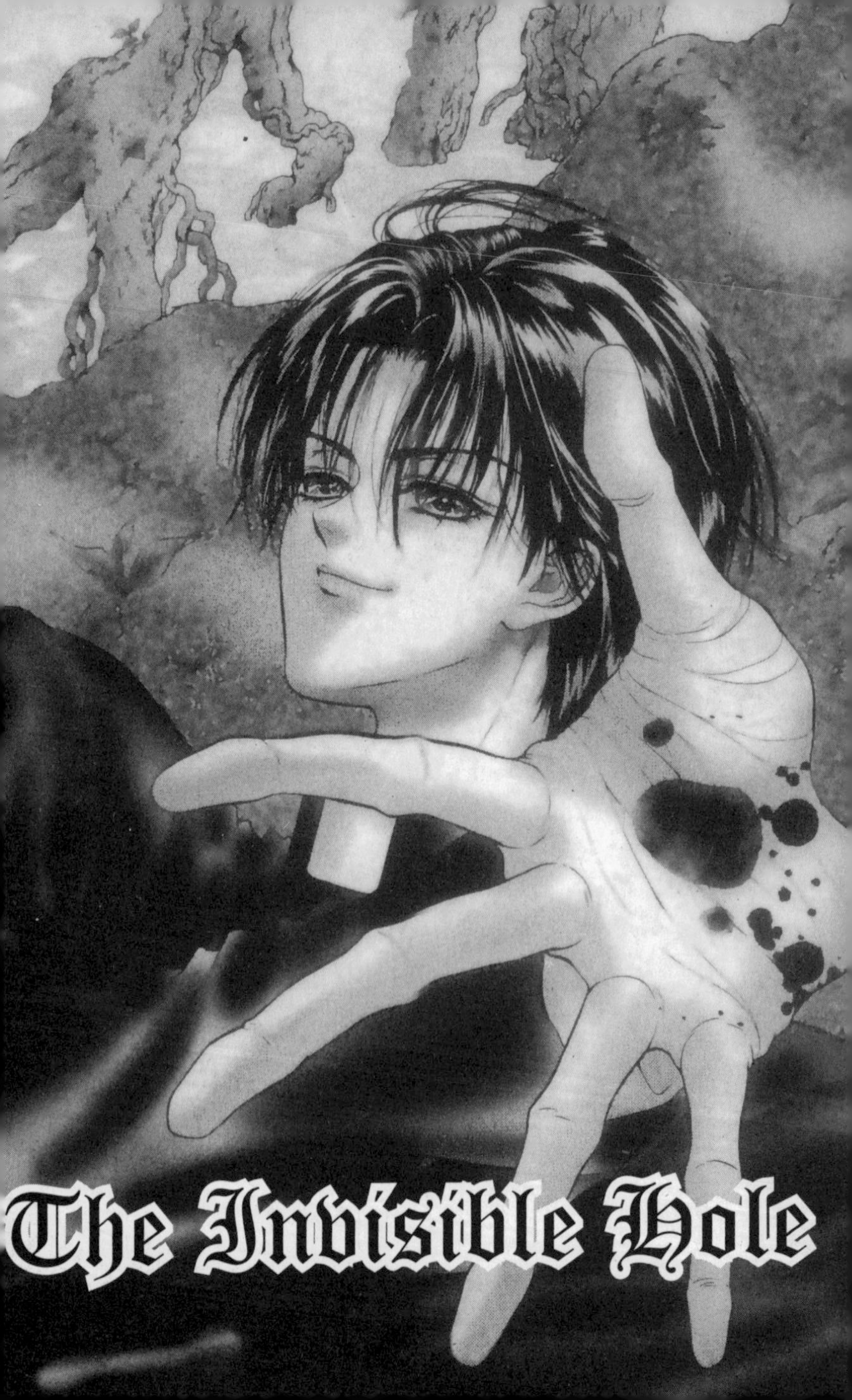
The Invisible Hole

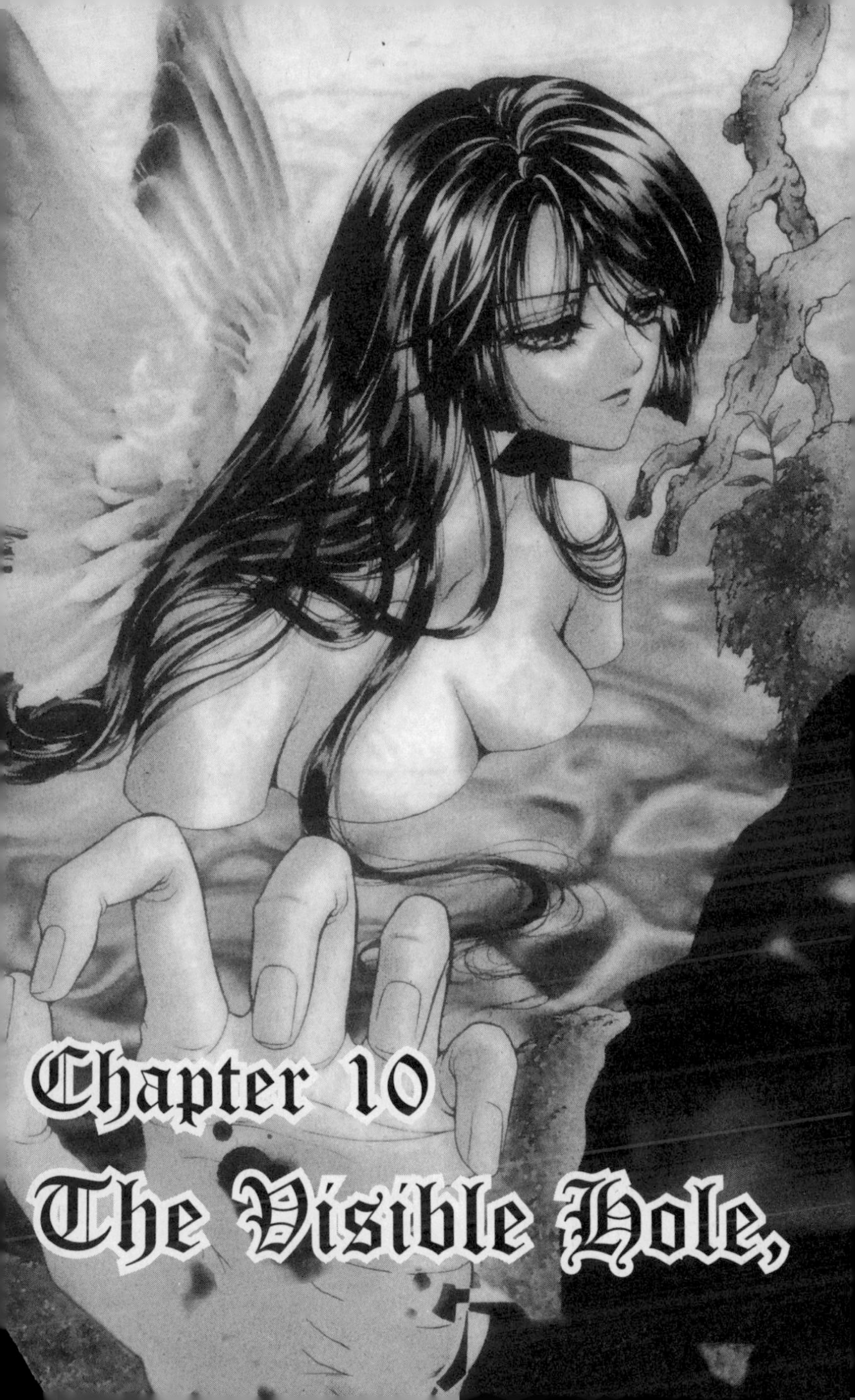
Chapter 10
The Visible Hole,

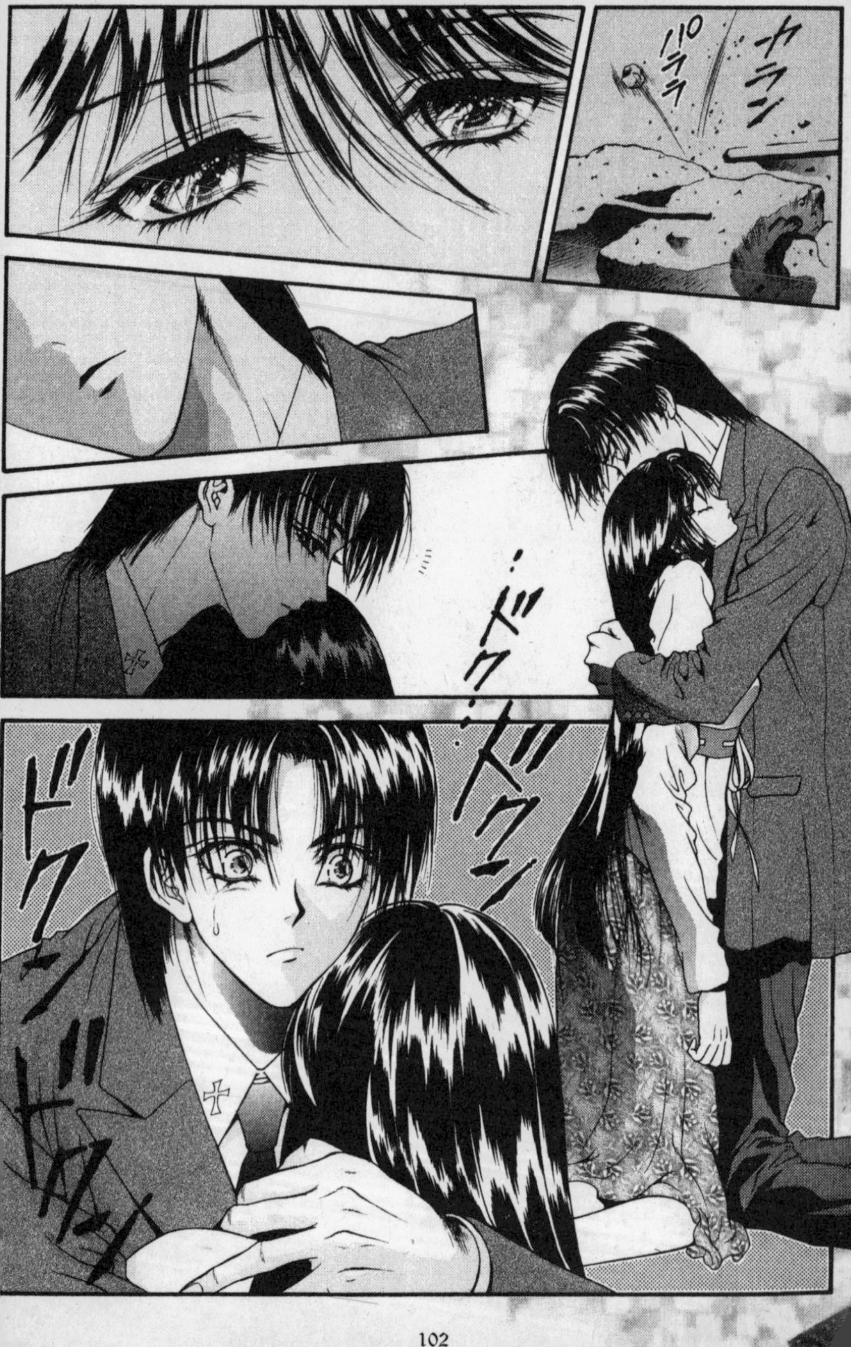
カラン
パララ
……
…ドク…ドクン
ドクッ
ドクッ

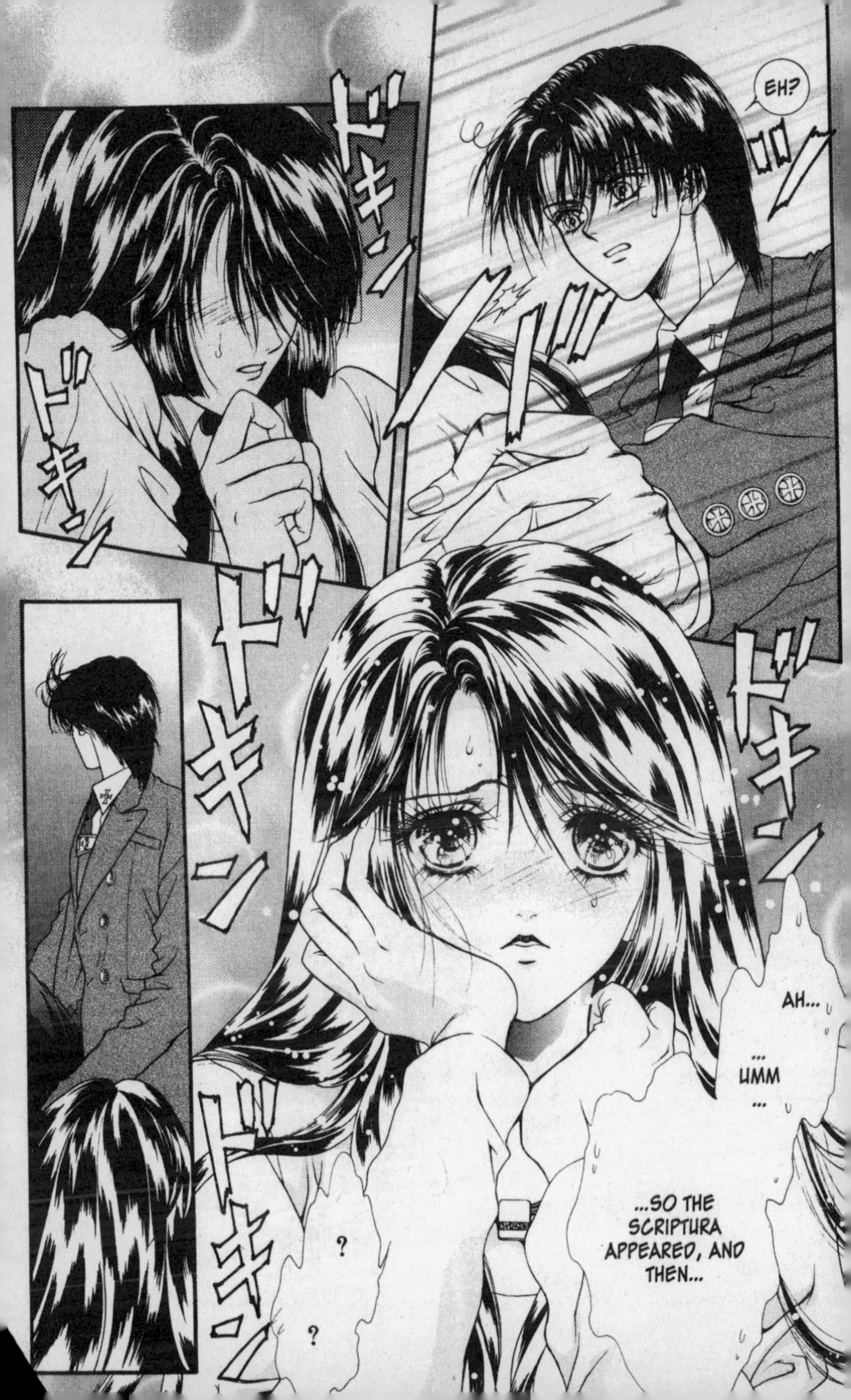

EH?
ドキン
ドキン
ドキン
AH...
... UMM ...
...SO THE SCRIPTURA APPEARED, AND THEN...
ドキン
ドキン
?
?

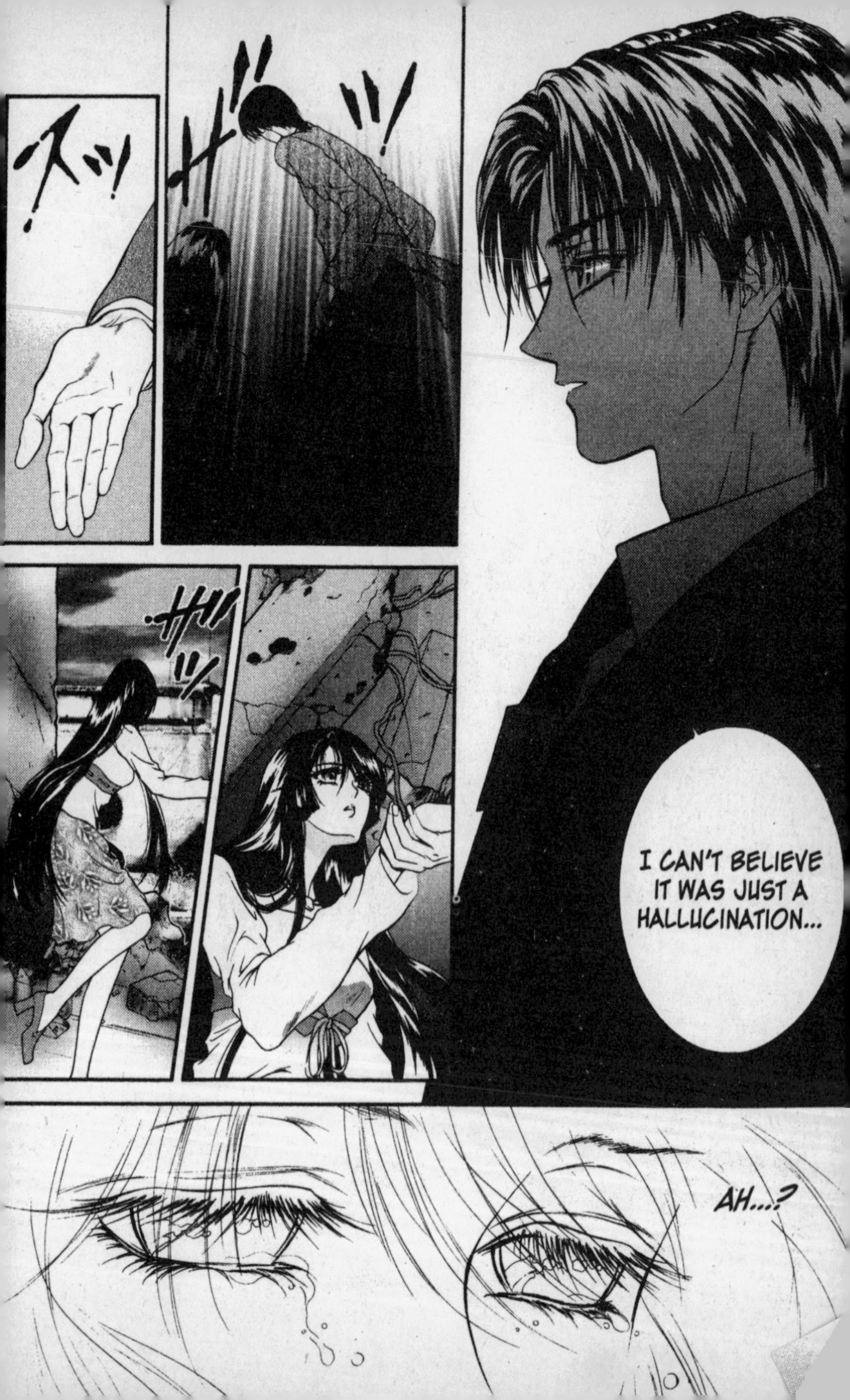

I CAN'T BELIEVE IT WAS JUST A HALLUCINATION...
ザッ!!
スッ!
ザッ
AH...?

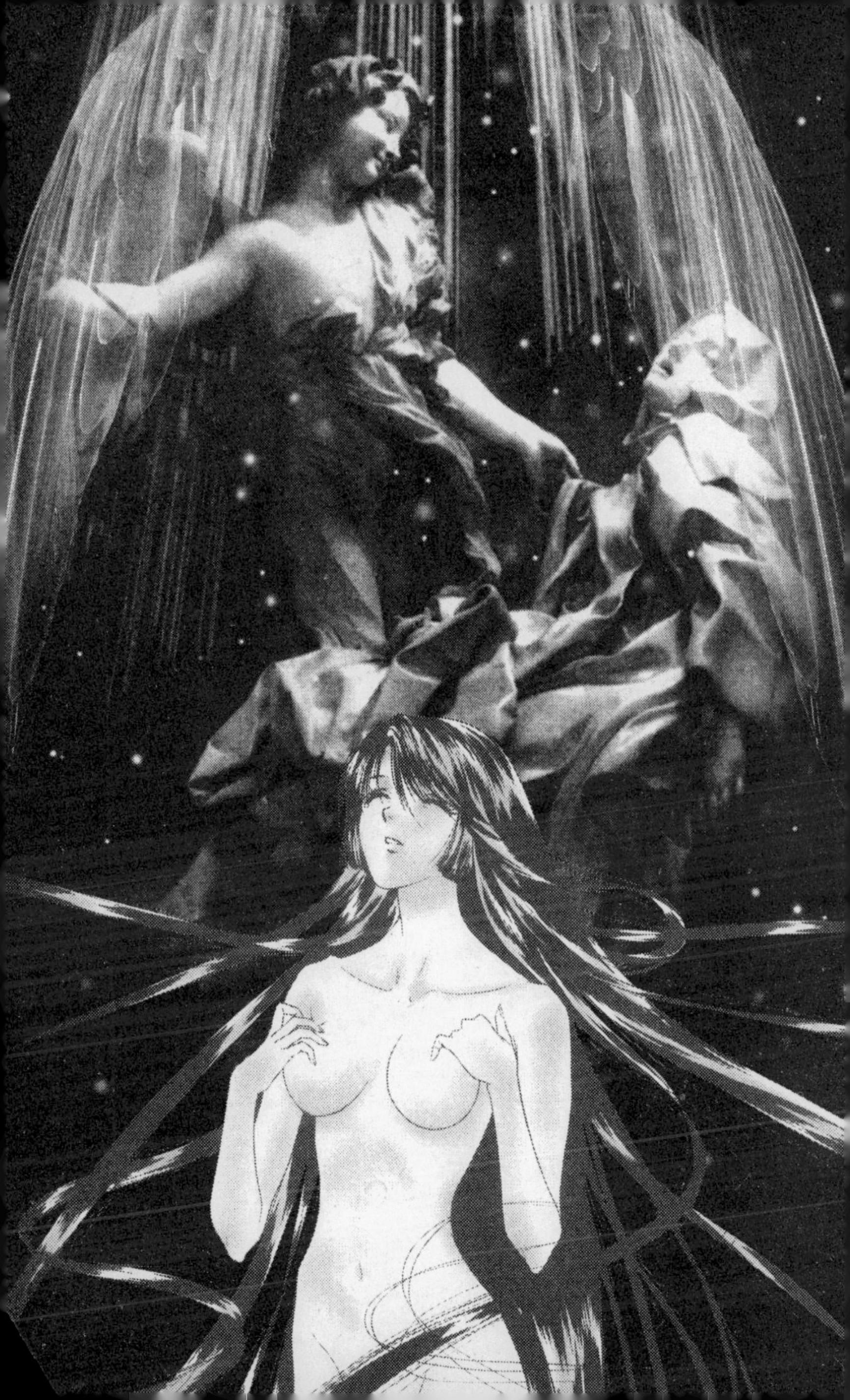

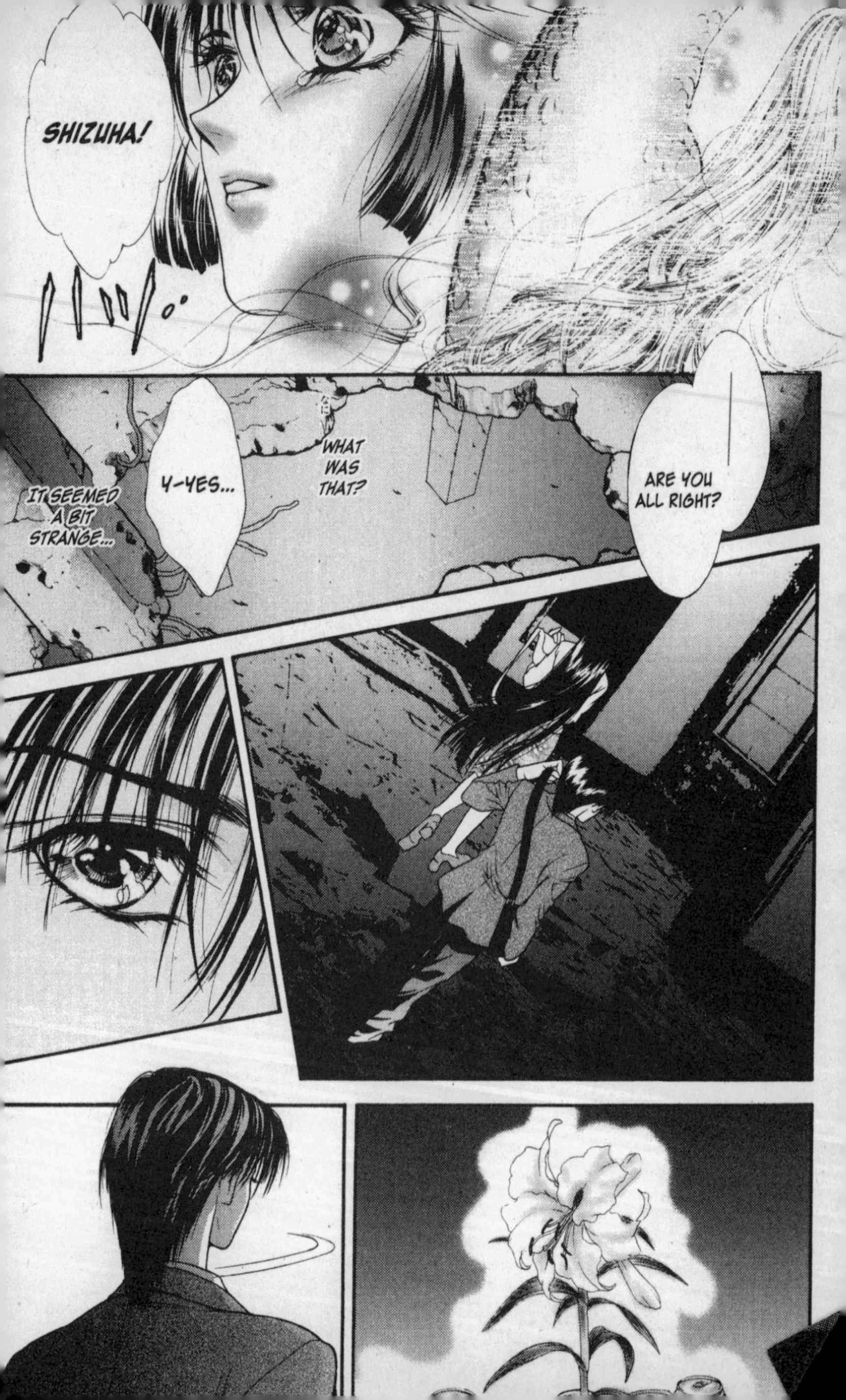
SHIZUHA!
ARE YOU ALL RIGHT?
WHAT WAS THAT?
Y-YES...
IT SEEMED A BIT STRANGE...

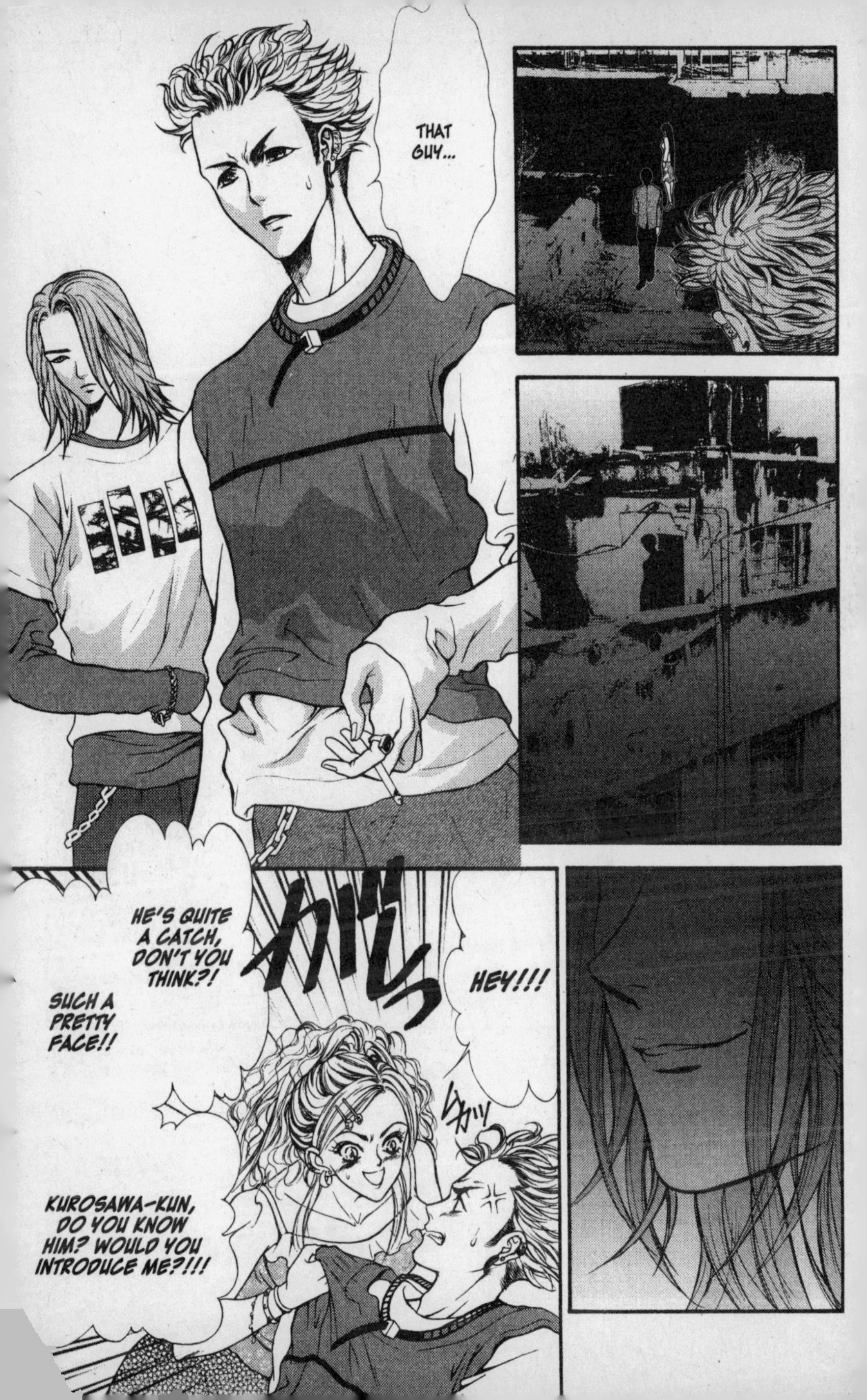
THAT GUY...
HEY!!!
HE'S QUITE A CATCH, DON'T YOU THINK?!
SUCH A PRETTY FACE!!
KUROSAWA-KUN, DO YOU KNOW HIM? WOULD YOU INTRODUCE ME?!!!

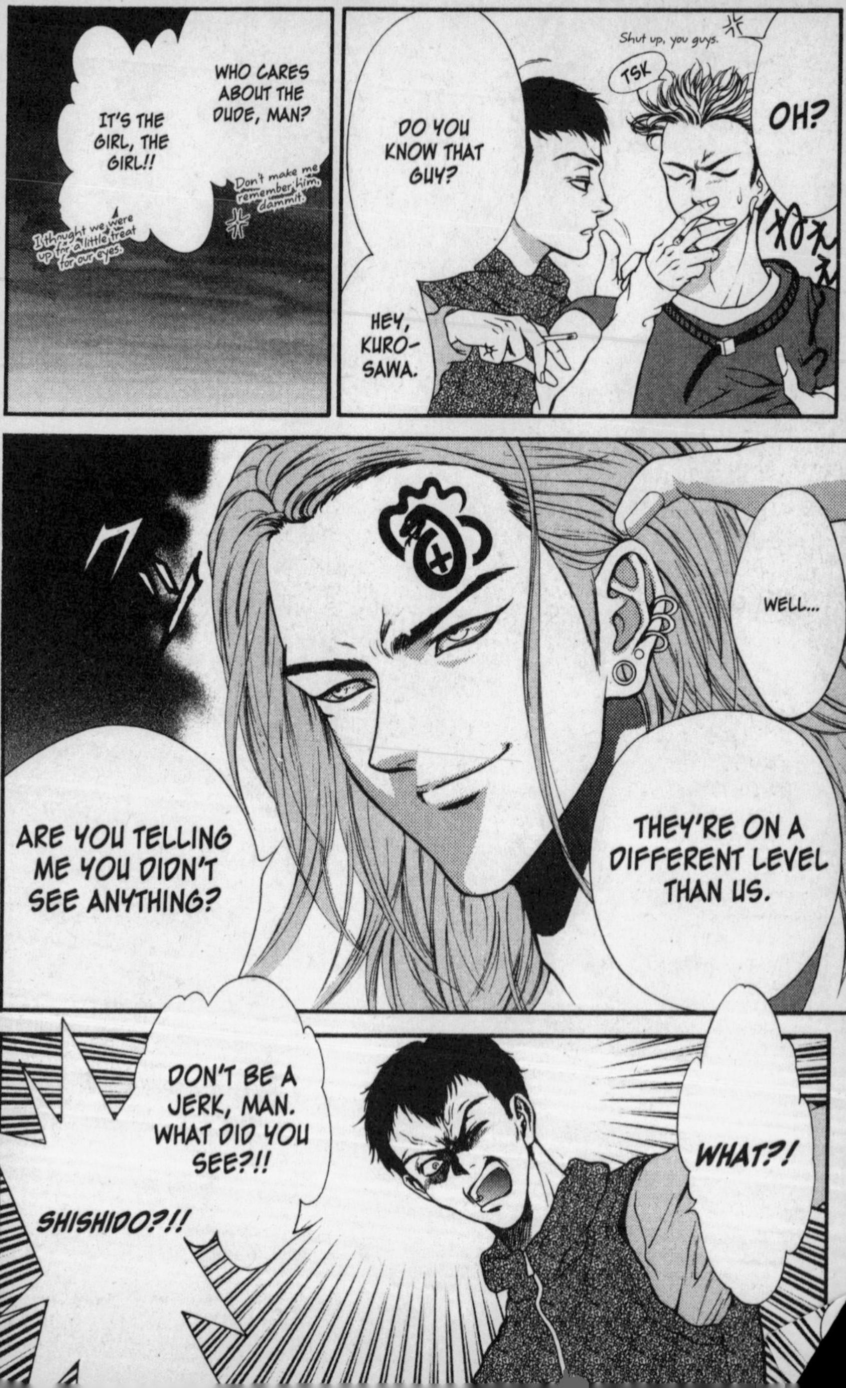

Shut up, you guys.
OH?
TSK
DO YOU KNOW THAT GUY?
HEY, KURO-SAWA.
WHO CARES ABOUT THE DUDE, MAN?
Don't make me remember him, dammit.
IT'S THE GIRL, THE GIRL!!
I thought we were up for a little treat for our eyes.
WELL...
THEY'RE ON A DIFFERENT LEVEL THAN US.
ARE YOU TELLING ME YOU DIDN'T SEE ANYTHING?
WHAT?!
DON'T BE A JERK, MAN. WHAT DID YOU SEE?!!
SHISHIDO?!!

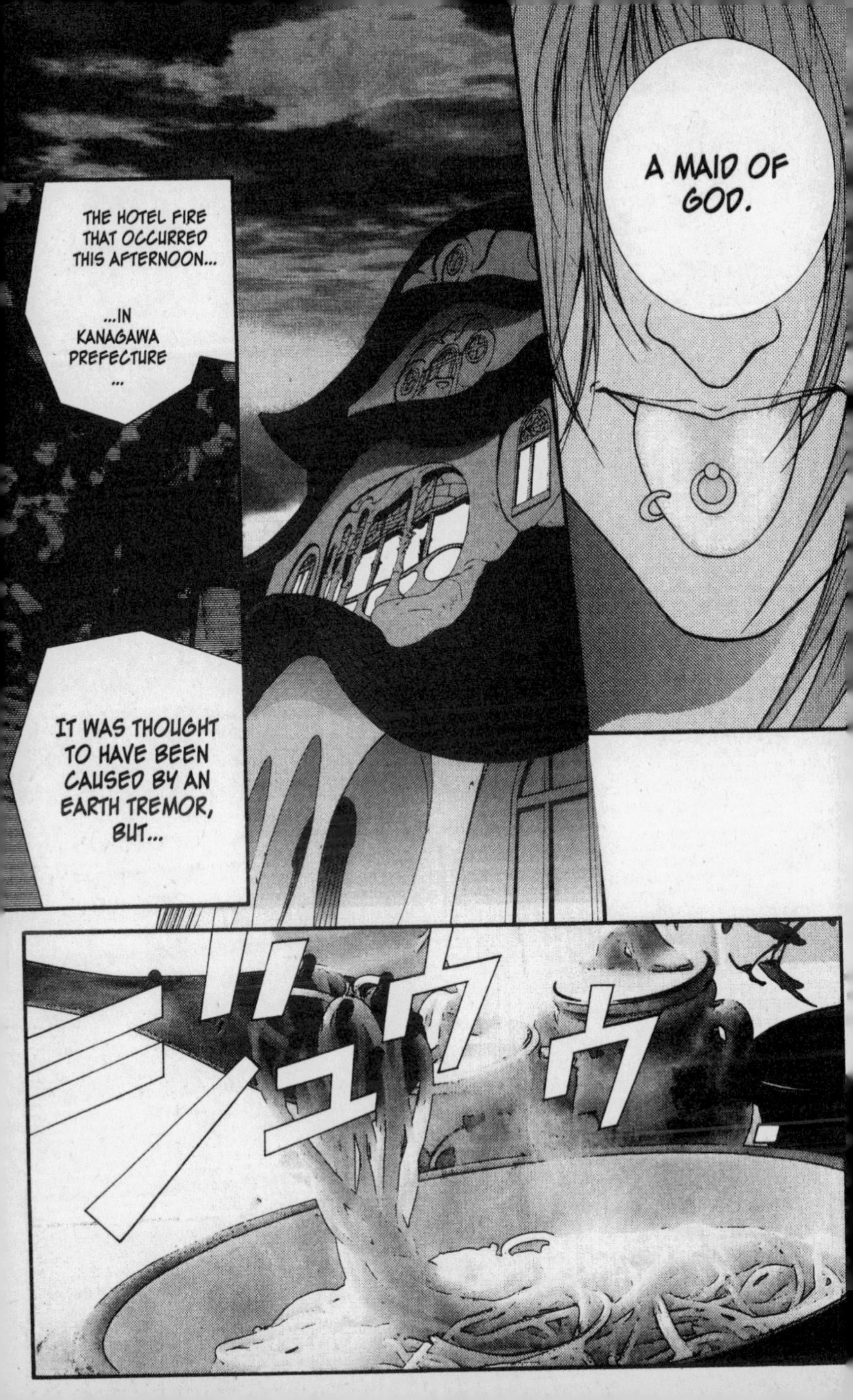
A MAID OF GOD.
THE HOTEL FIRE THAT OCCURRED THIS AFTERNOON...
...IN KANAGAWA PREFECTURE ...
IT WAS THOUGHT TO HAVE BEEN CAUSED BY AN EARTH TREMOR, BUT...
ジュウウ.

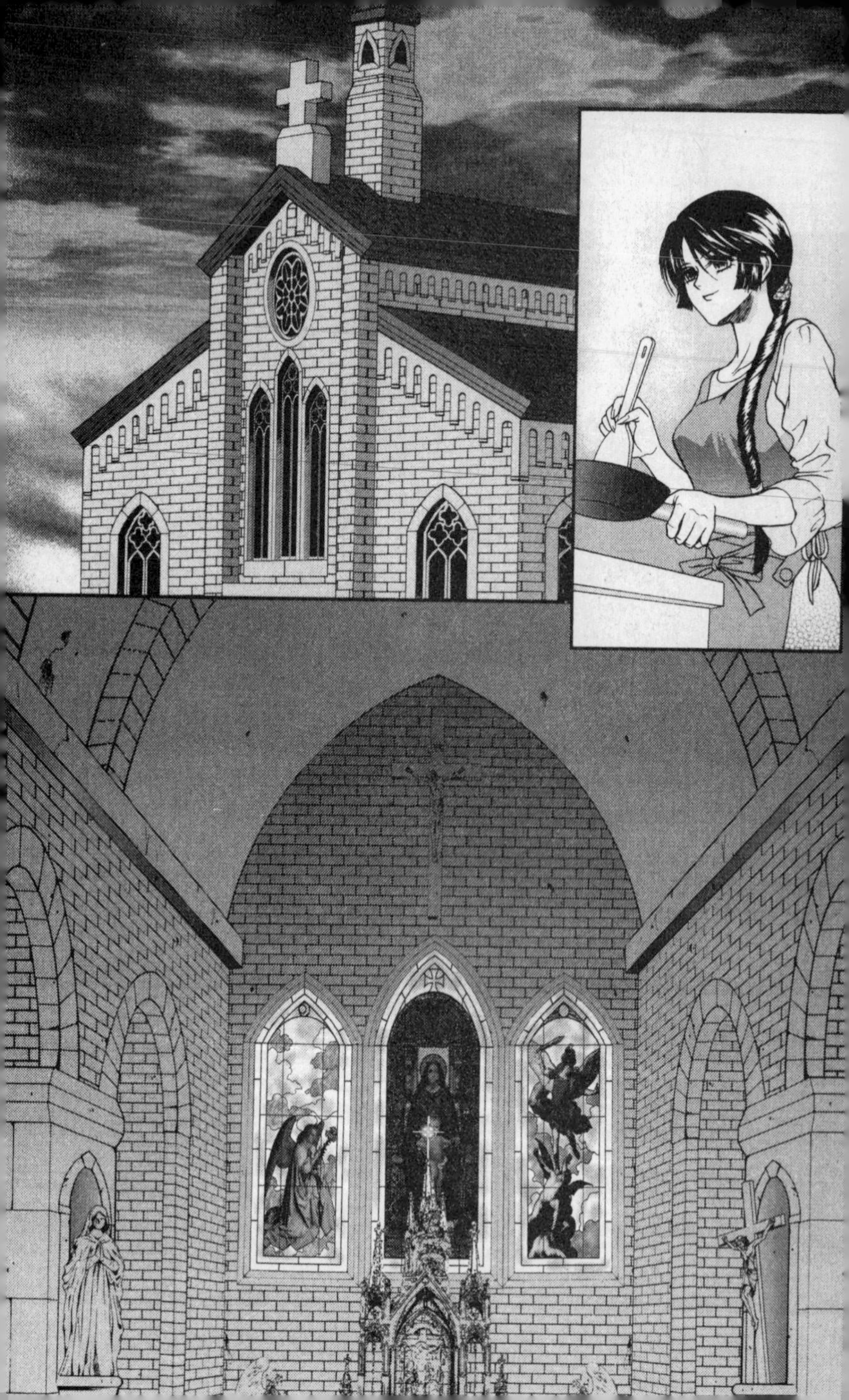

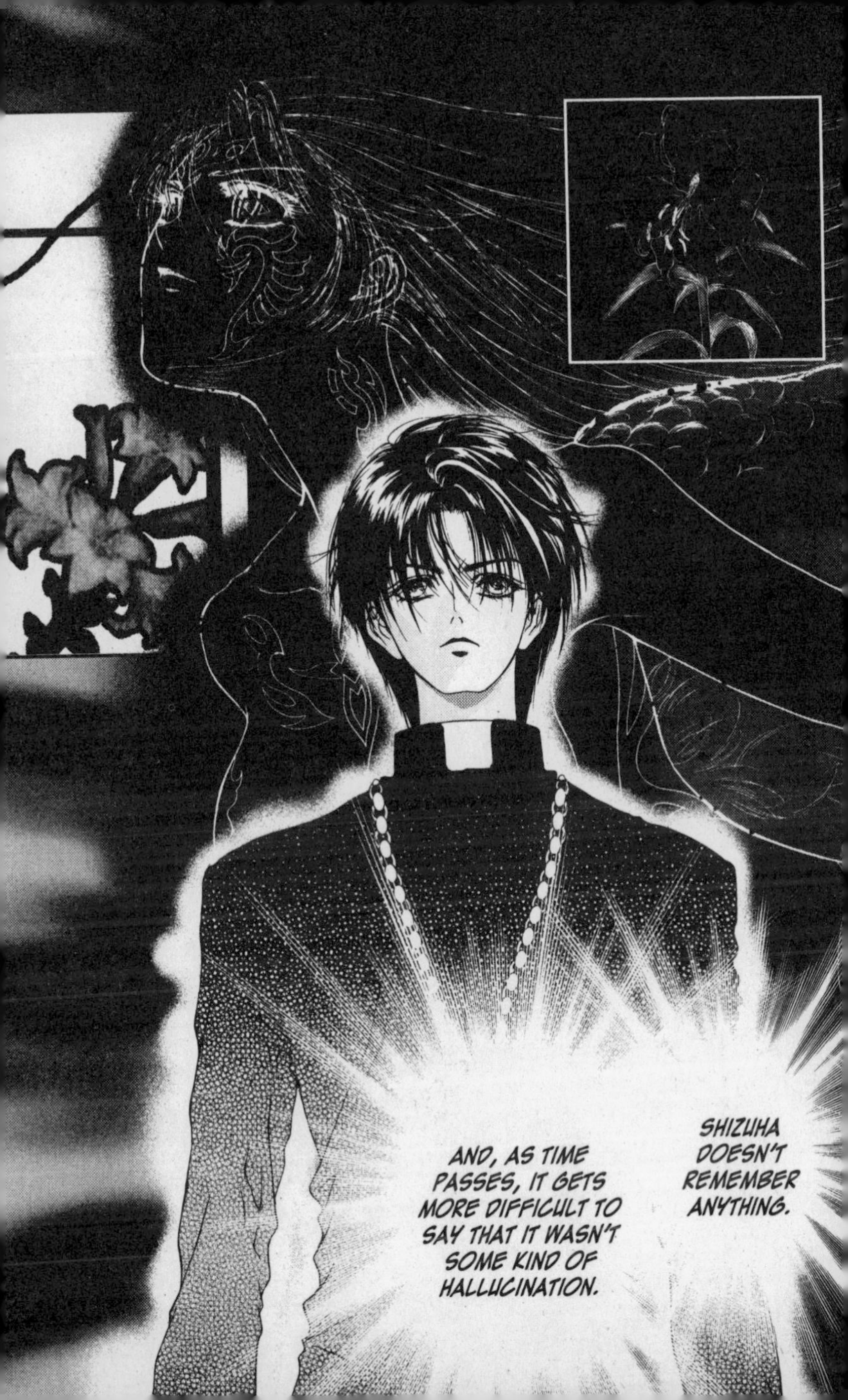
SHIZUHA DOESN'T REMEMBER ANYTHING.
AND, AS TIME PASSES, IT GETS MORE DIFFICULT TO SAY THAT IT WASN'T SOME KIND OF HALLUCINATION.

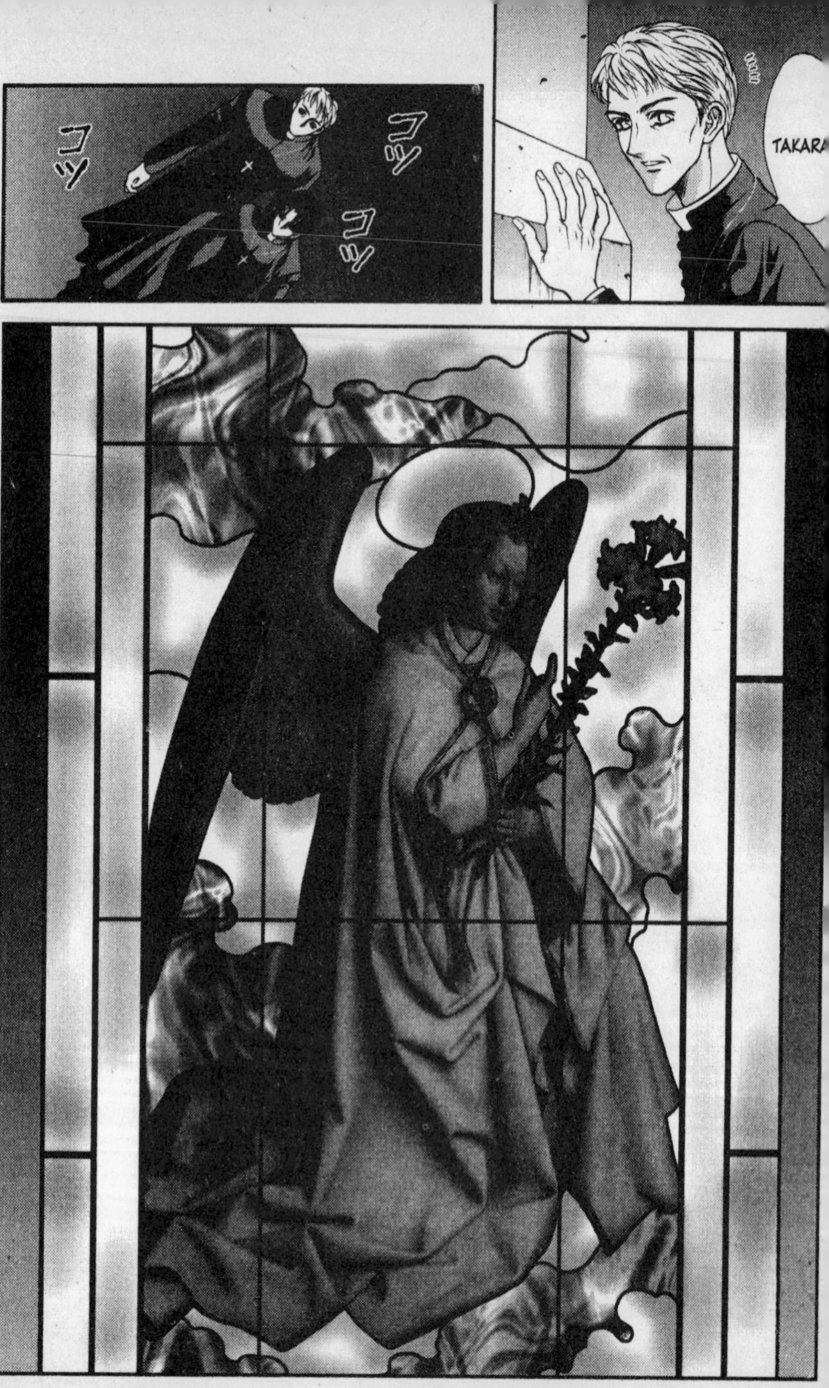
TAKARA
コツ
コツ
コツ

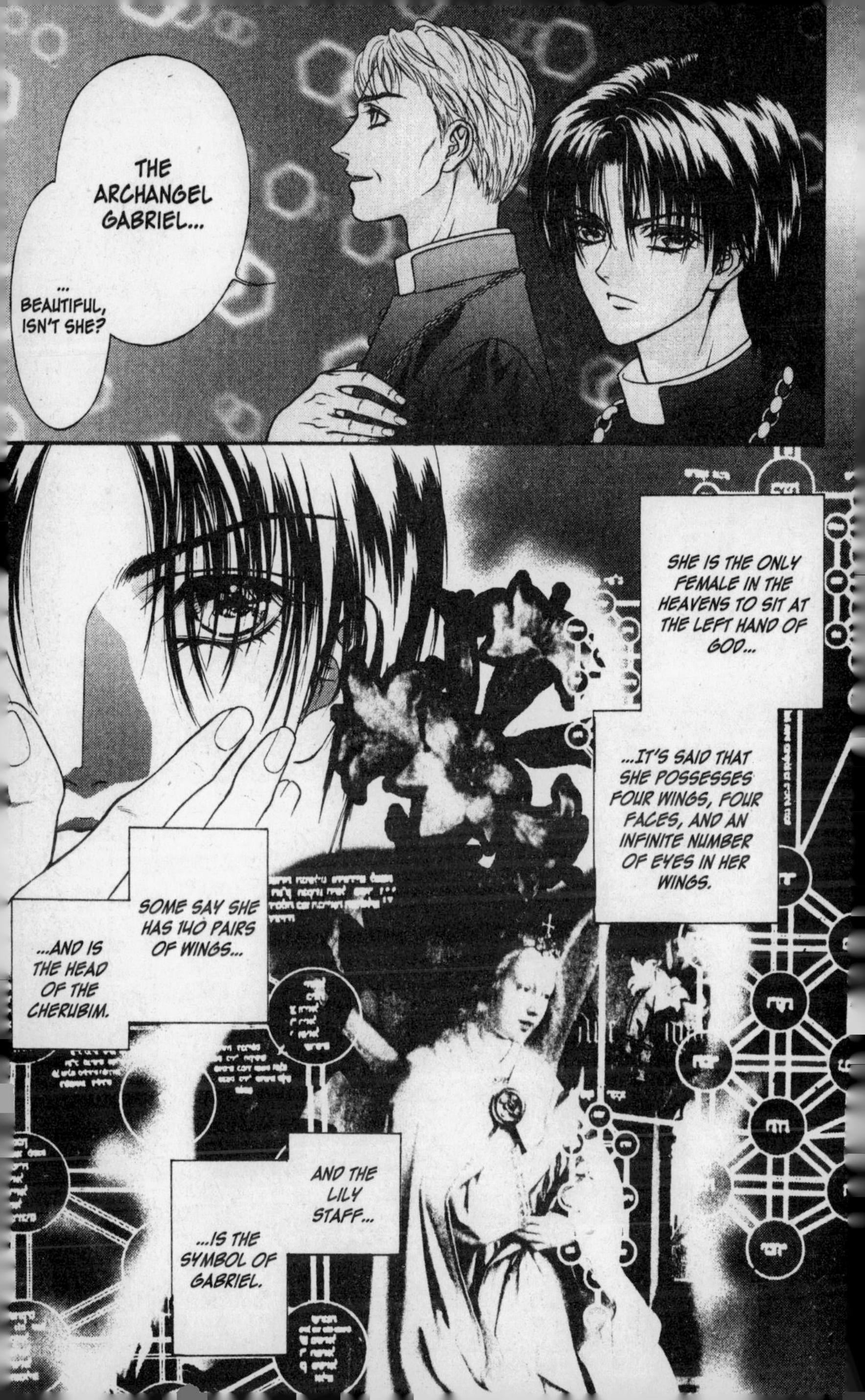
THE ARCHANGEL GABRIEL...
...BEAUTIFUL, ISN'T SHE?
SHE IS THE ONLY FEMALE IN THE HEAVENS TO SIT AT THE LEFT HAND OF GOD...
...IT'S SAID THAT SHE POSSESSES FOUR WINGS, FOUR FACES, AND AN INFINITE NUMBER OF EYES IN HER WINGS.
SOME SAY SHE HAS 140 PAIRS OF WINGS...
...AND IS THE HEAD OF THE CHERUBIM.
AND THE LILY STAFF...
...IS THE SYMBOL OF GABRIEL.

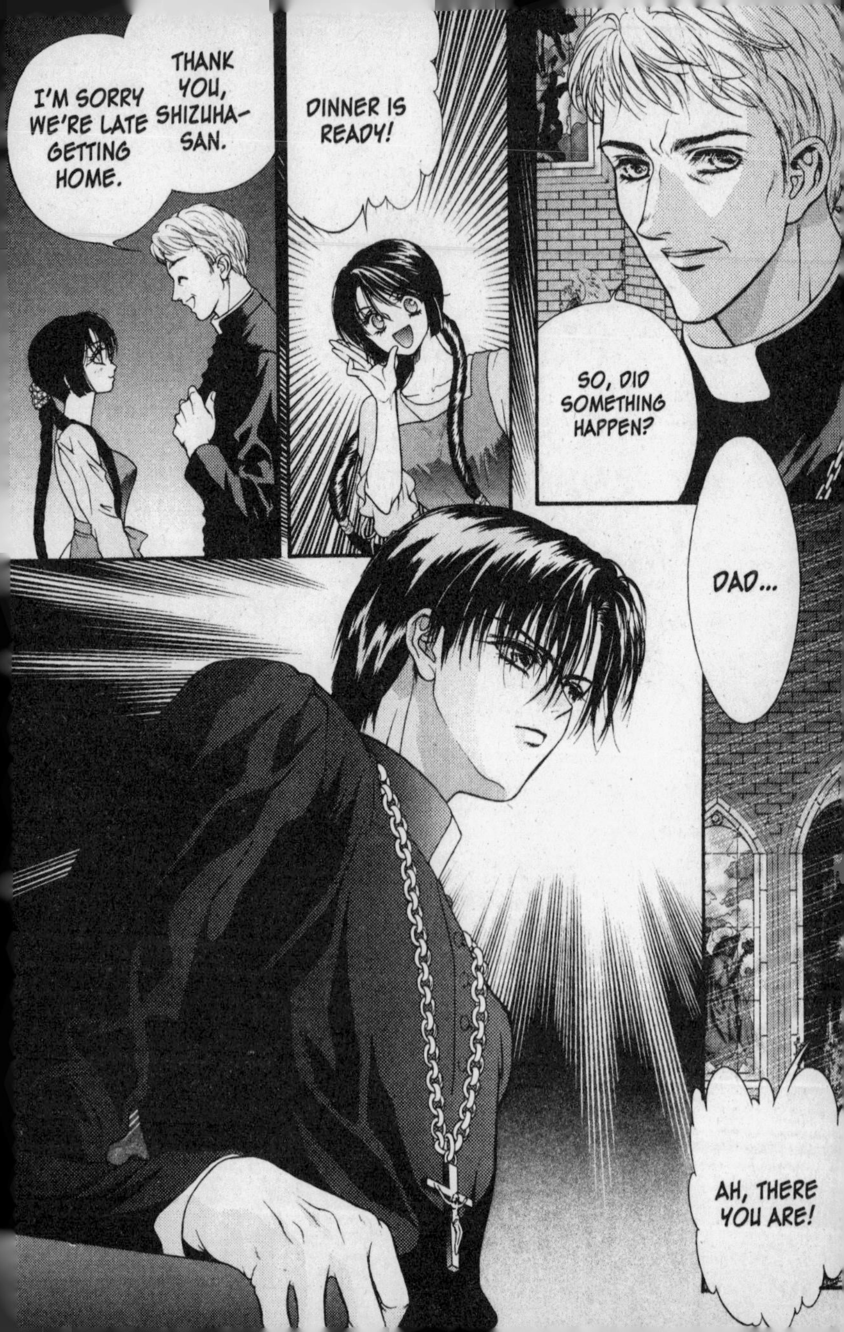
SO, DID SOMETHING HAPPEN?
DINNER IS READY!
THANK YOU, SHIZUHA-SAN.
I'M SORRY WE'RE LATE GETTING HOME.
DAD...
AH, THERE YOU ARE!

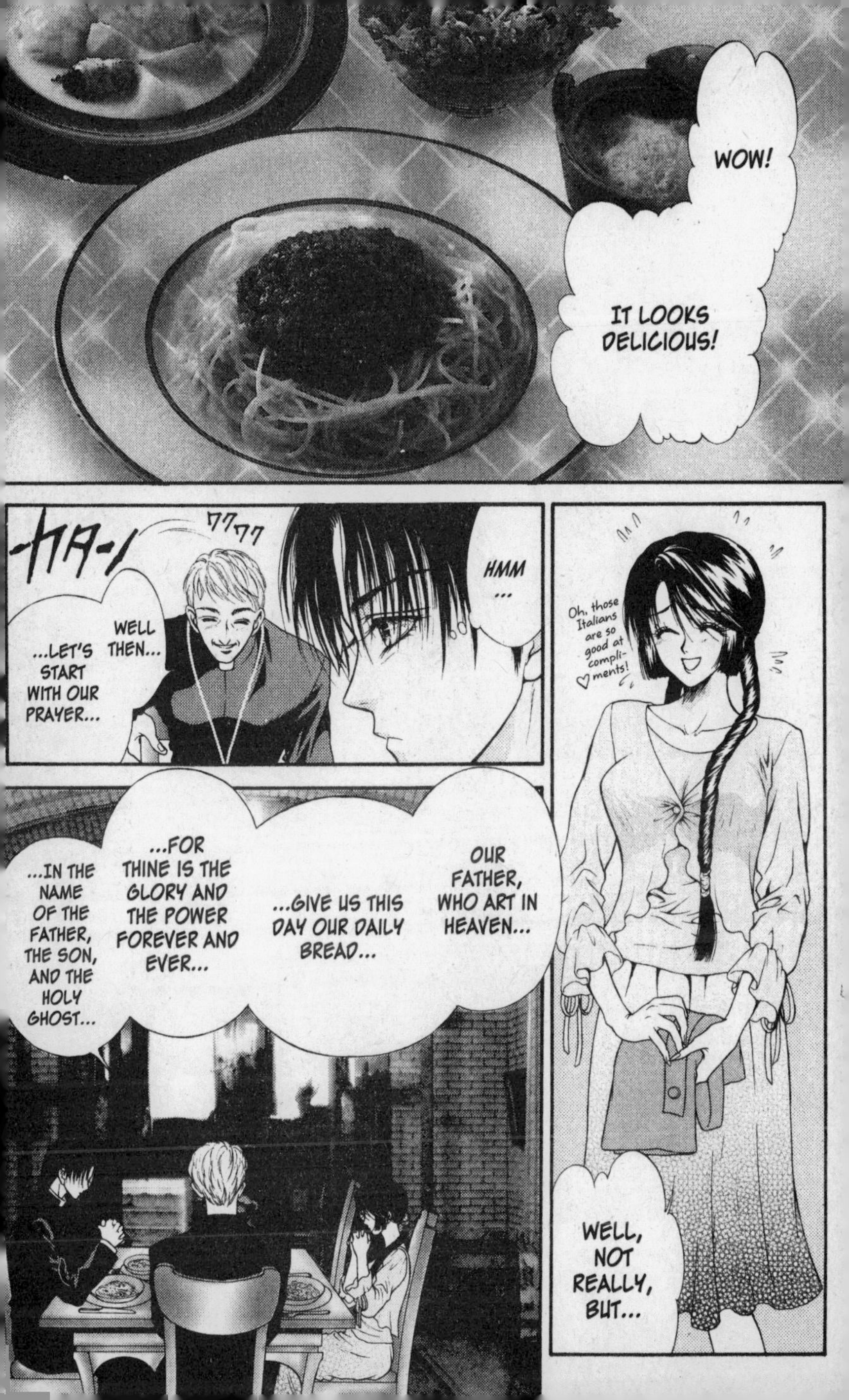
WOW!
IT LOOKS DELICIOUS!
Oh, those Italians are so good at compli- ♡ ments!
WELL, NOT REALLY, BUT...
HMM ...
WELL THEN...
...LET'S START WITH OUR PRAYER...
OUR FATHER, WHO ART IN HEAVEN...
...GIVE US THIS DAY OUR DAILY BREAD...
...FOR THINE IS THE GLORY AND THE POWER FOREVER AND EVER...
...IN THE NAME OF THE FATHER, THE SON, AND THE HOLY GHOST...

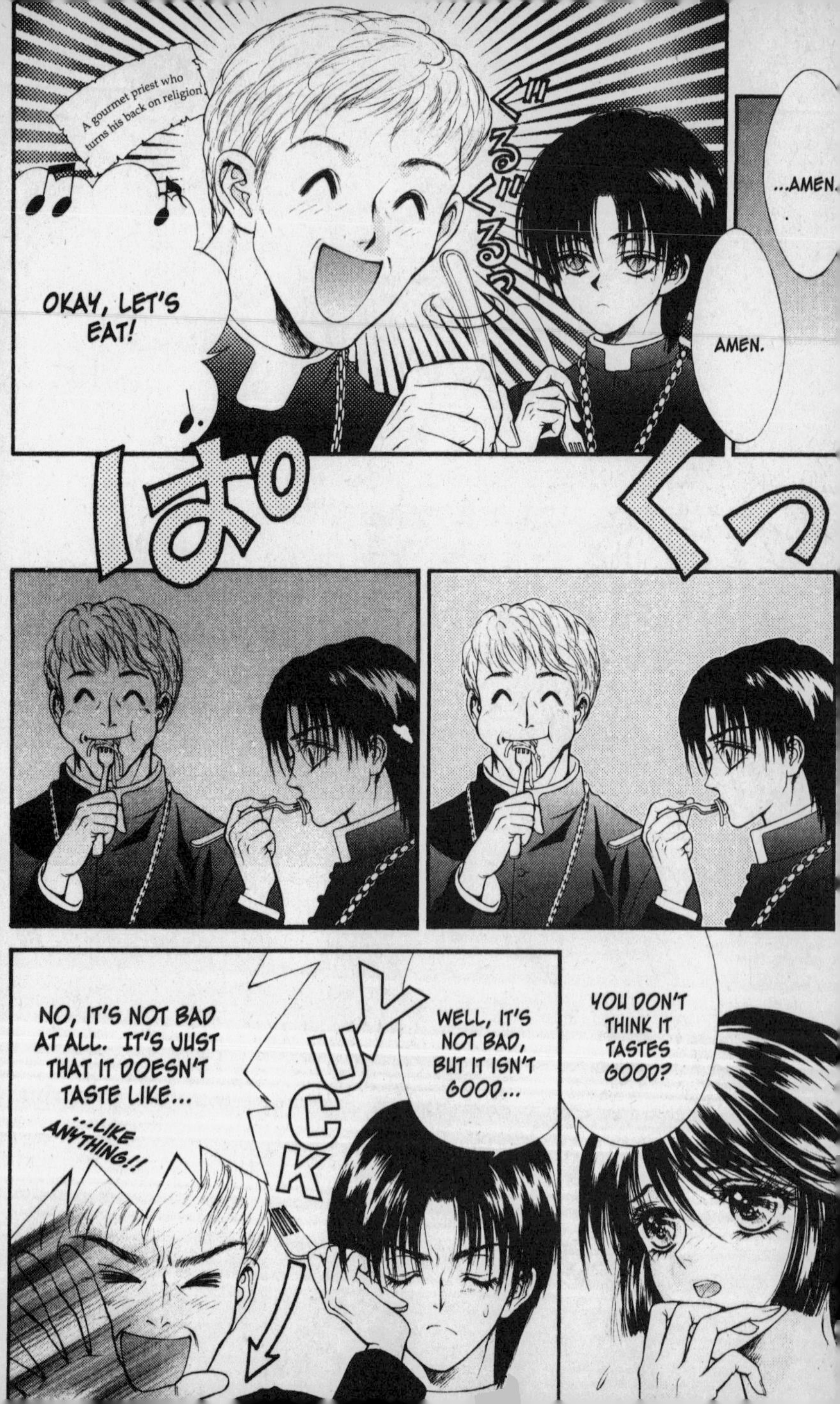
...AMEN.
AMEN.
A gourmet priest who turns his back on religion
OKAY, LET'S EAT!
ぱくっ
YOU DON'T THINK IT TASTES GOOD?
WELL, IT'S NOT BAD, BUT IT ISN'T GOOD...
YUCK
NO, IT'S NOT BAD AT ALL. IT'S JUST THAT IT DOESN'T TASTE LIKE...
...LIKE ANYTHING!!

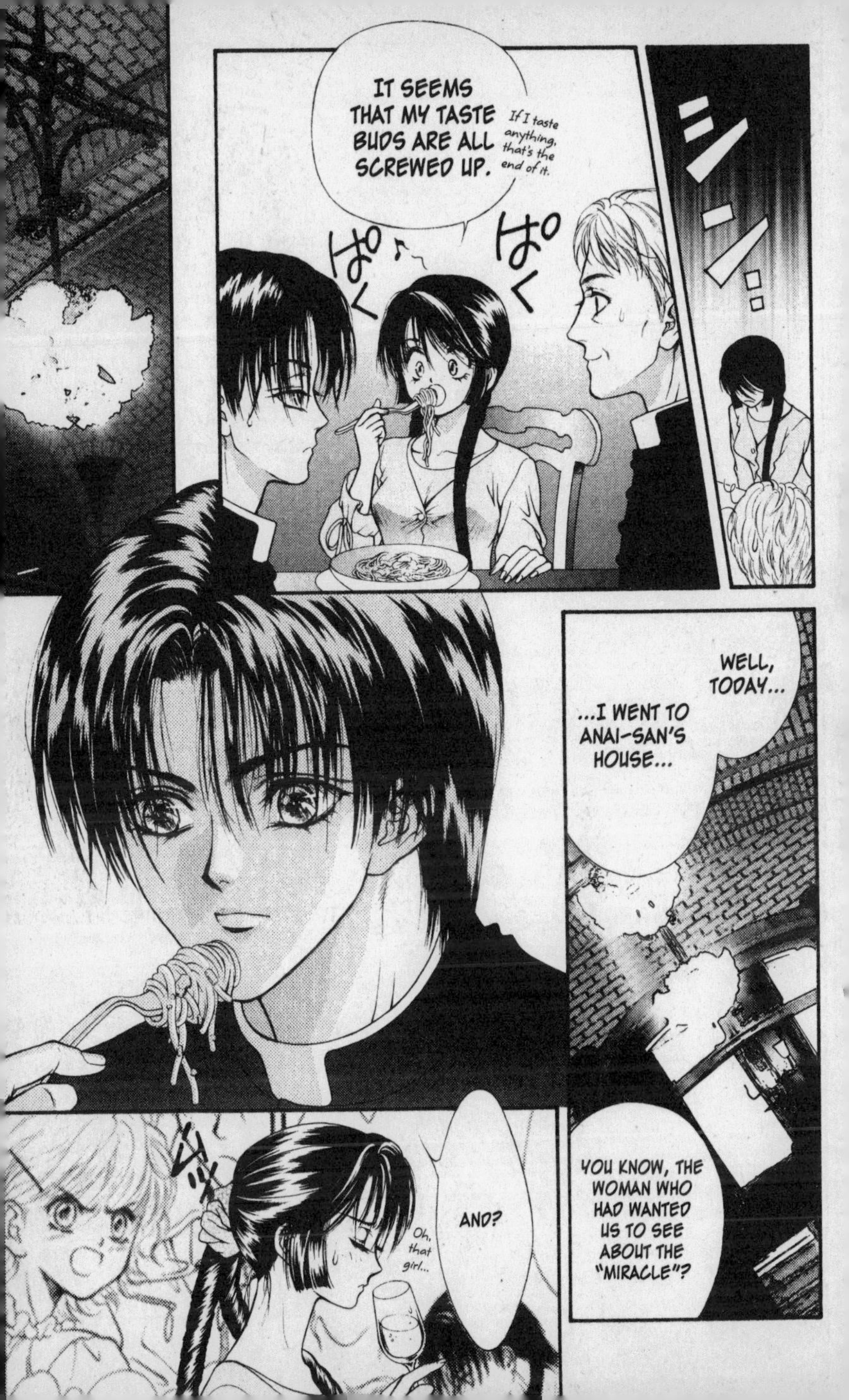

IT SEEMS THAT MY TASTE BUDS ARE ALL SCREWED UP.
If I taste anything, that's the end of it.
ぱく
ぱく
WELL, TODAY...
...I WENT TO ANAI-SAN'S HOUSE...
YOU KNOW, THE WOMAN WHO HAD WANTED US TO SEE ABOUT THE "MIRACLE"?
AND?
Oh, that girl...

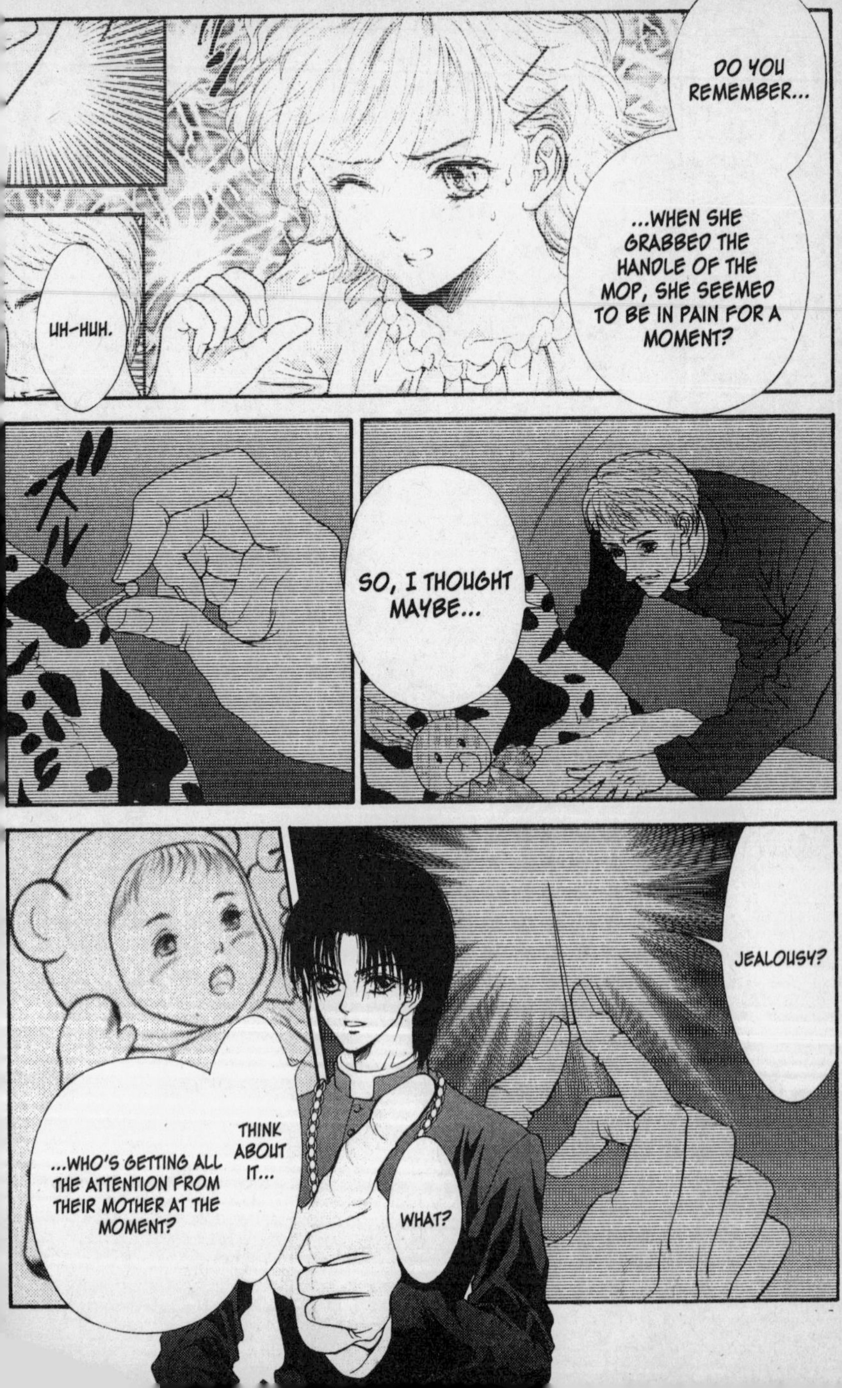
DO YOU REMEMBER...
...WHEN SHE GRABBED THE HANDLE OF THE MOP, SHE SEEMED TO BE IN PAIN FOR A MOMENT?
UH-HUH.
SO, I THOUGHT MAYBE...
JEALOUSY?
WHAT?
THINK ABOUT IT...
...WHO'S GETTING ALL THE ATTENTION FROM THEIR MOTHER AT THE MOMENT?

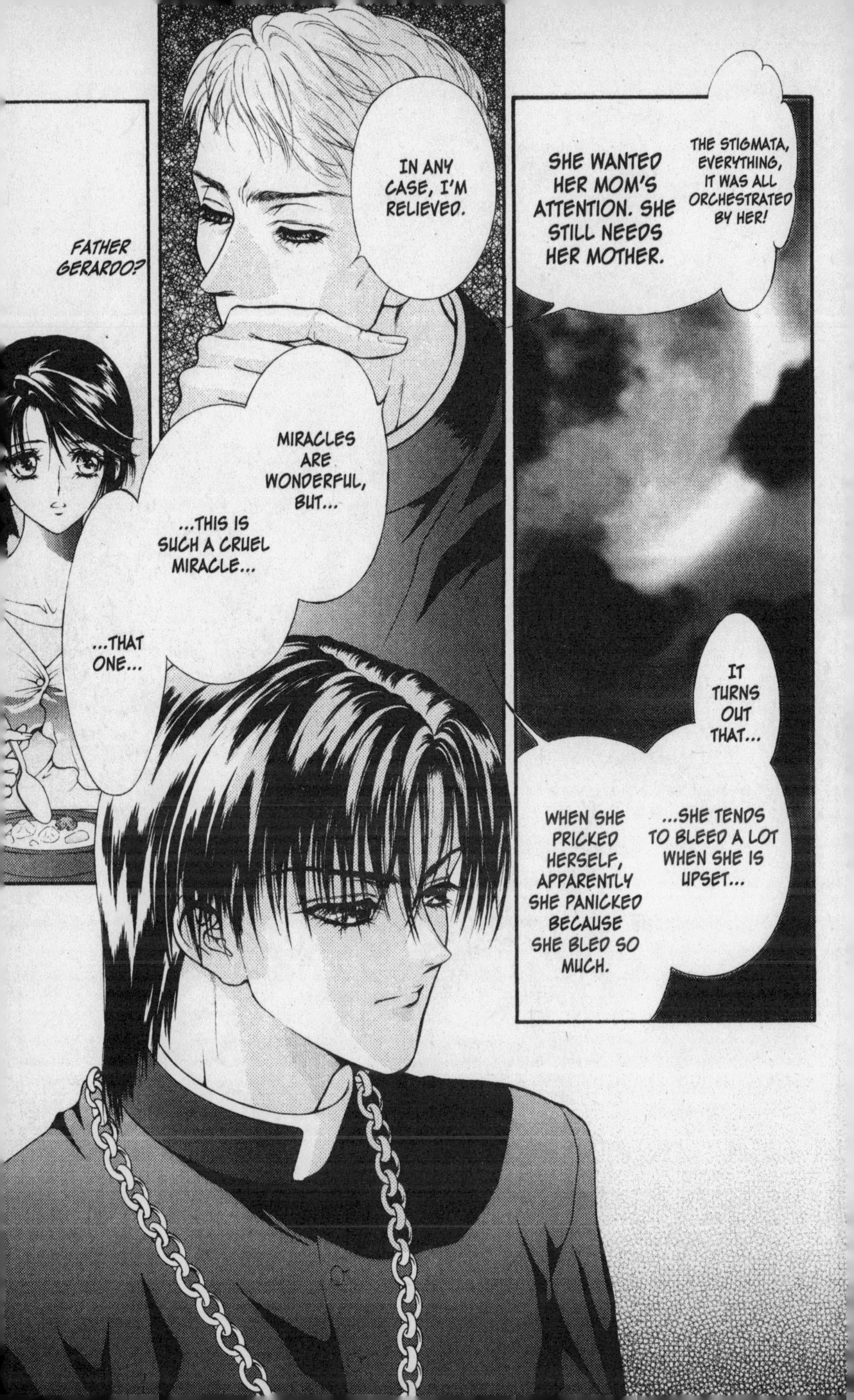
THE STIGMATA, EVERYTHING, IT WAS ALL ORCHESTRATED BY HER!
SHE WANTED HER MOM'S ATTENTION. SHE STILL NEEDS HER MOTHER.
IT TURNS OUT THAT...
...SHE TENDS TO BLEED A LOT WHEN SHE IS UPSET...
WHEN SHE PRICKED HERSELF, APPARENTLY SHE PANICKED BECAUSE SHE BLED SO MUCH.
IN ANY CASE, I'M RELIEVED.
MIRACLES ARE WONDERFUL, BUT...
...THIS IS SUCH A CRUEL MIRACLE...
...THAT ONE...
FATHER GERARDO?

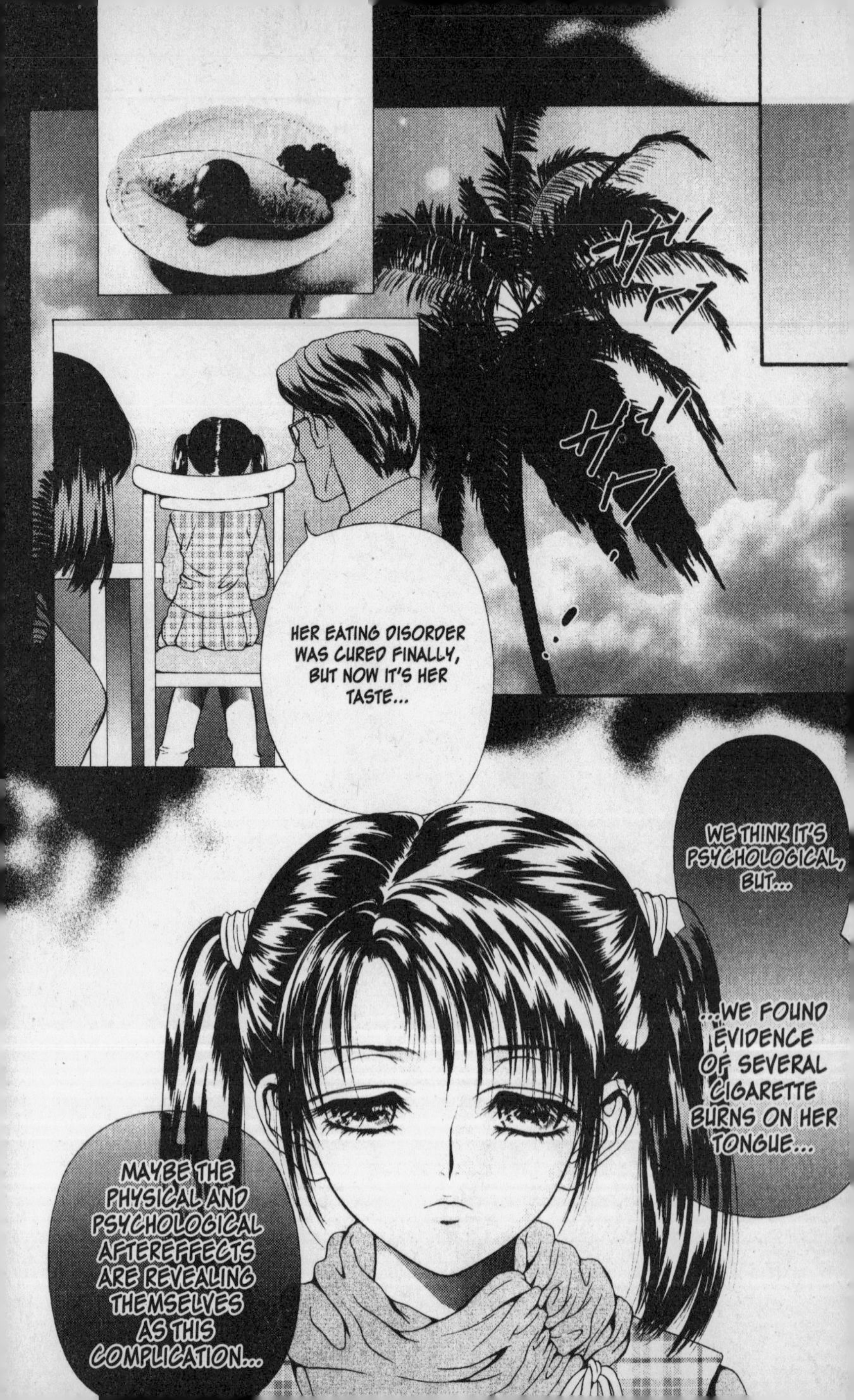
HER EATING DISORDER WAS CURED FINALLY, BUT NOW IT'S HER TASTE...
WE THINK IT'S PSYCHOLOGICAL, BUT...
...WE FOUND EVIDENCE OF SEVERAL CIGARETTE BURNS ON HER TONGUE...
MAYBE THE PHYSICAL AND PSYCHOLOGICAL AFTEREFFECTS ARE REVEALING THEMSELVES AS THIS COMPLICATION...

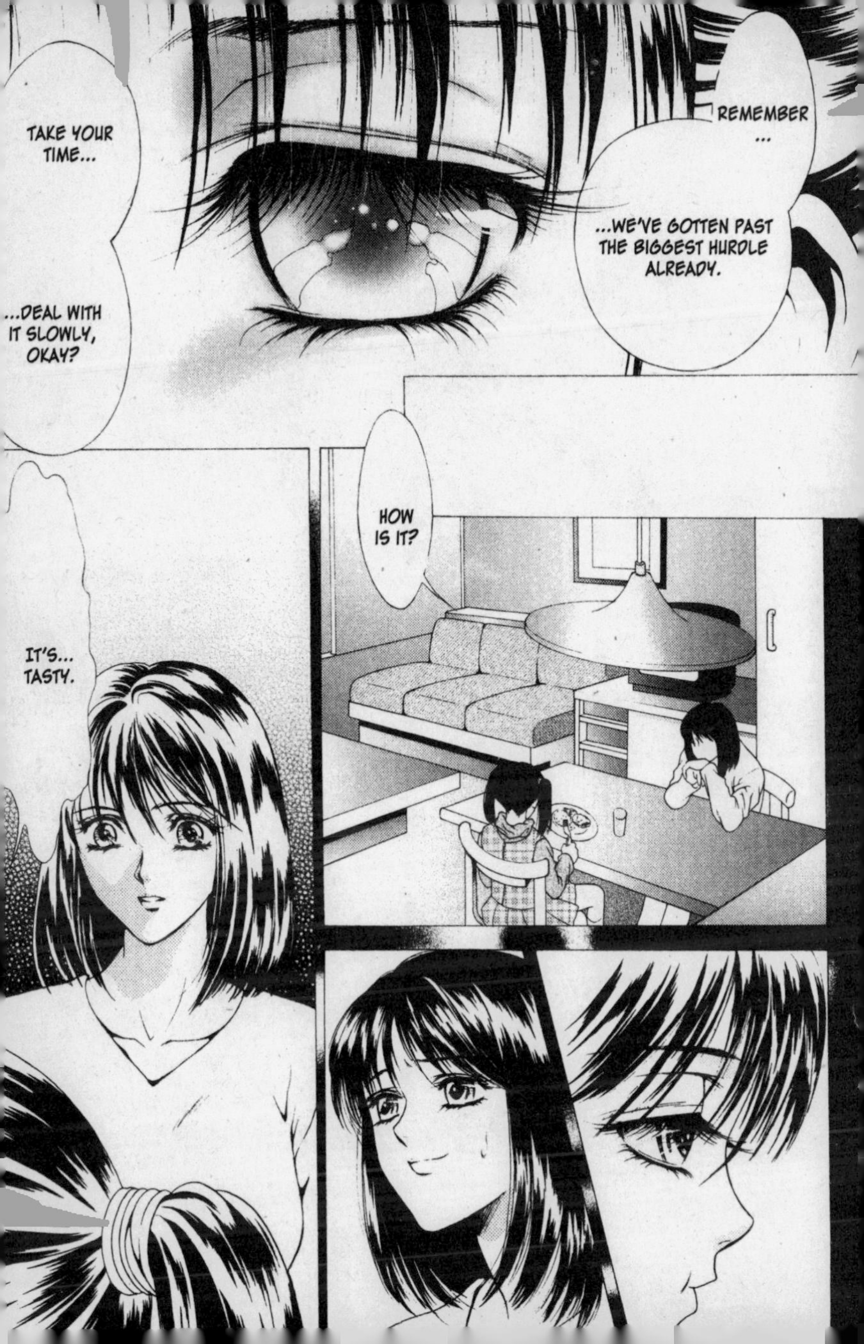
REMEMBER ...
...WE'VE GOTTEN PAST THE BIGGEST HURDLE ALREADY.
TAKE YOUR TIME...
...DEAL WITH IT SLOWLY, OKAY?
HOW IS IT?
IT'S... TASTY.

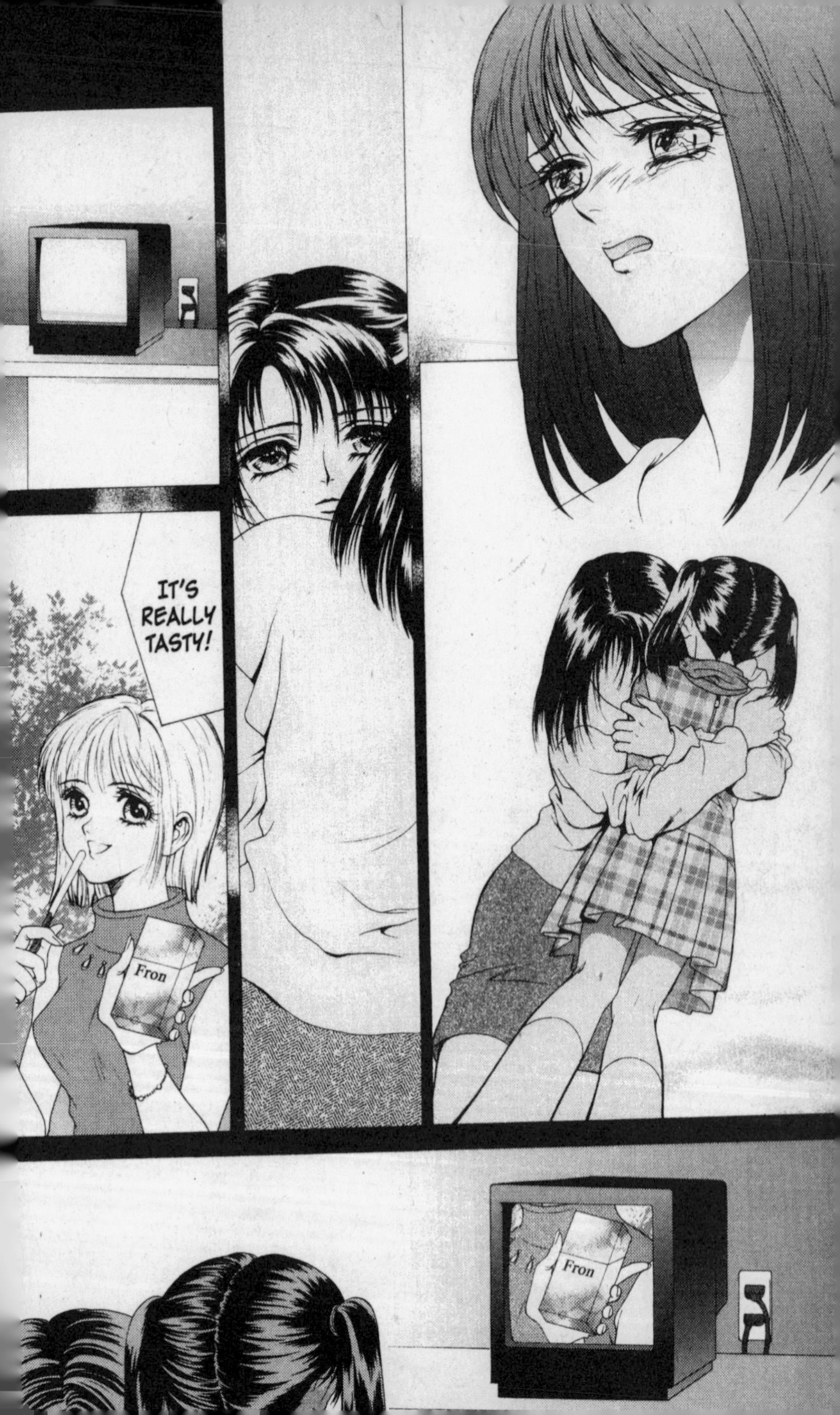
IT'S REALLY TASTY!
Fron
Fron

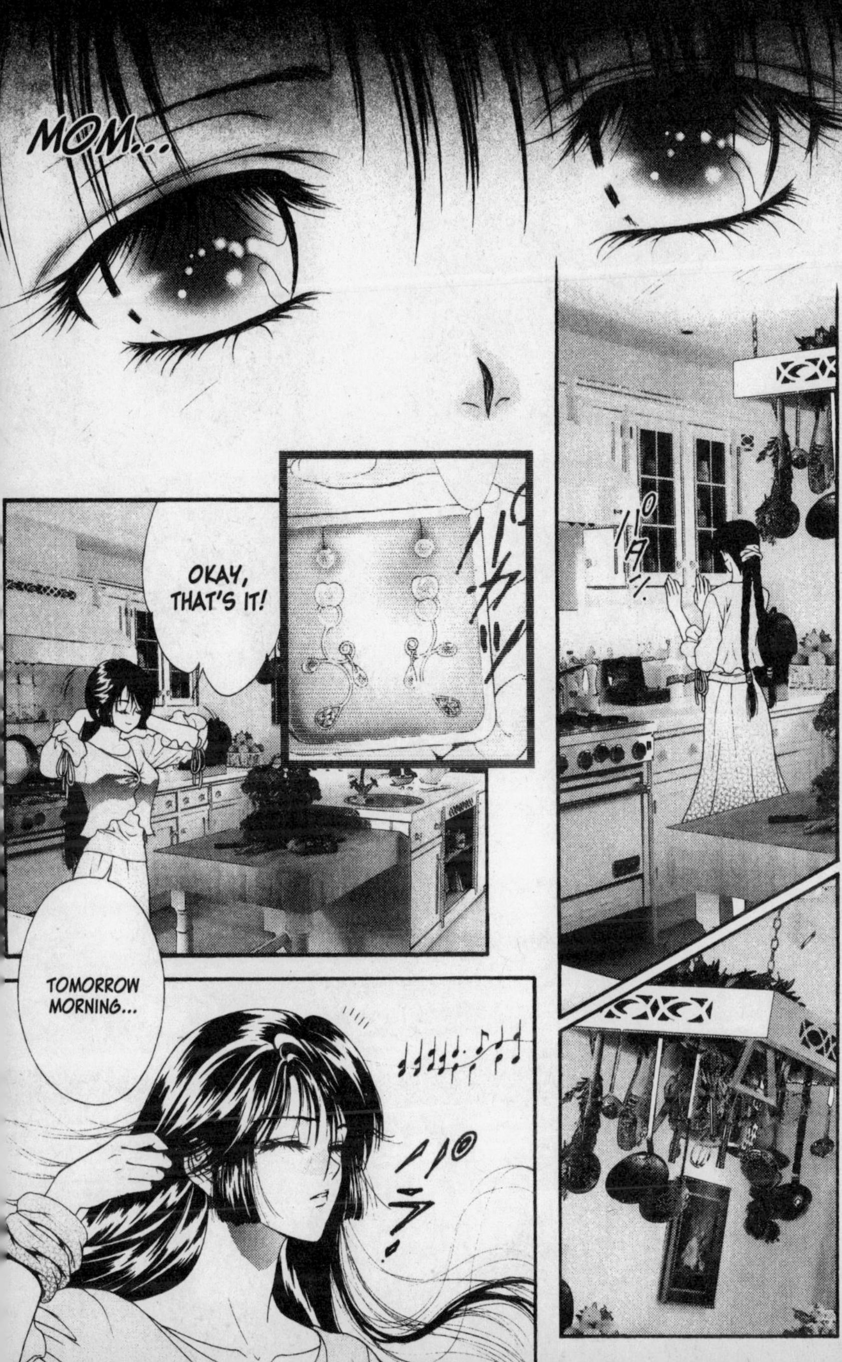
MOM...
OKAY, THAT'S IT!
TOMORROW MORNING...

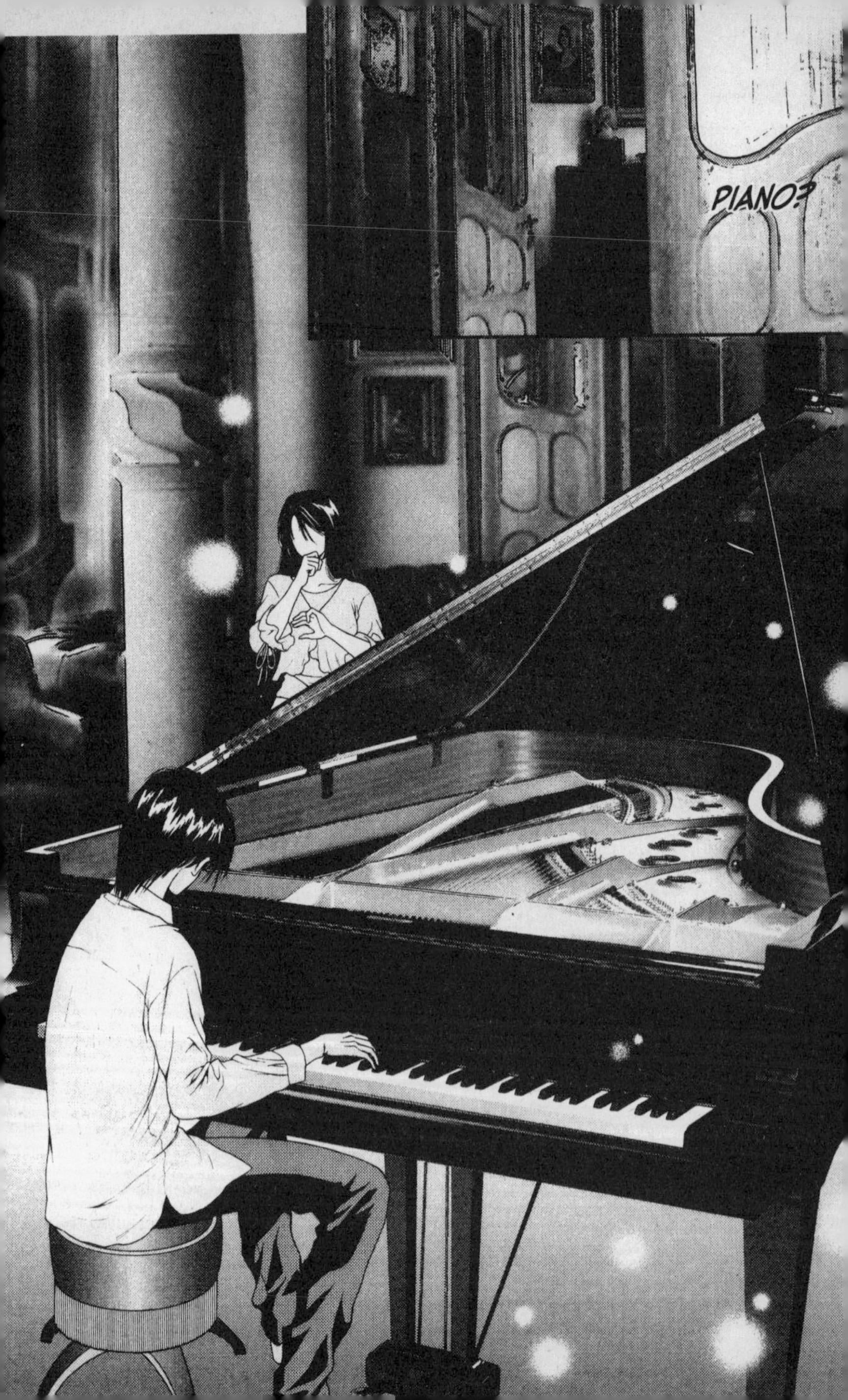
PIANO?

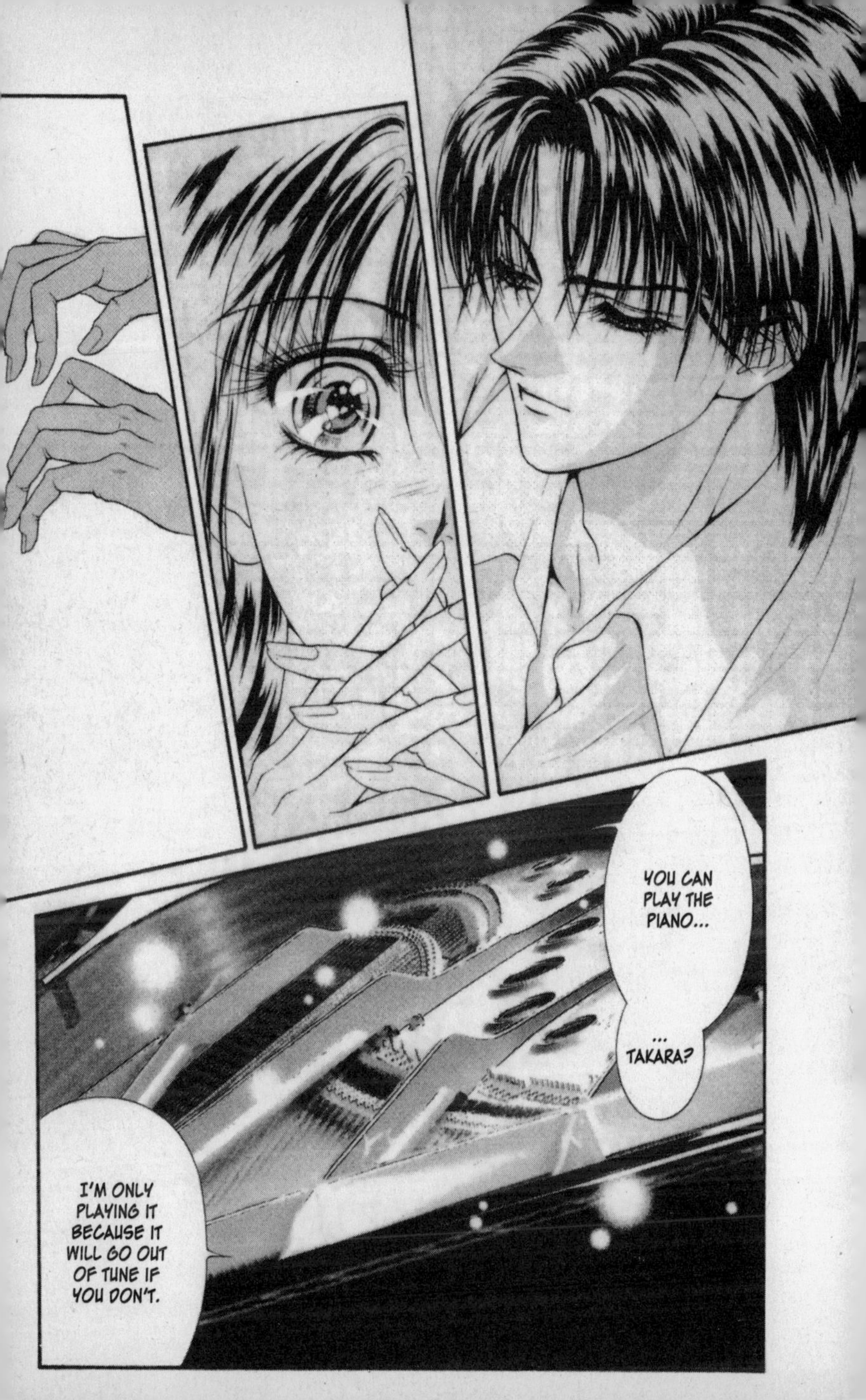
YOU CAN PLAY THE PIANO...
... TAKARA?
I'M ONLY PLAYING IT BECAUSE IT WILL GO OUT OF TUNE IF YOU DON'T.

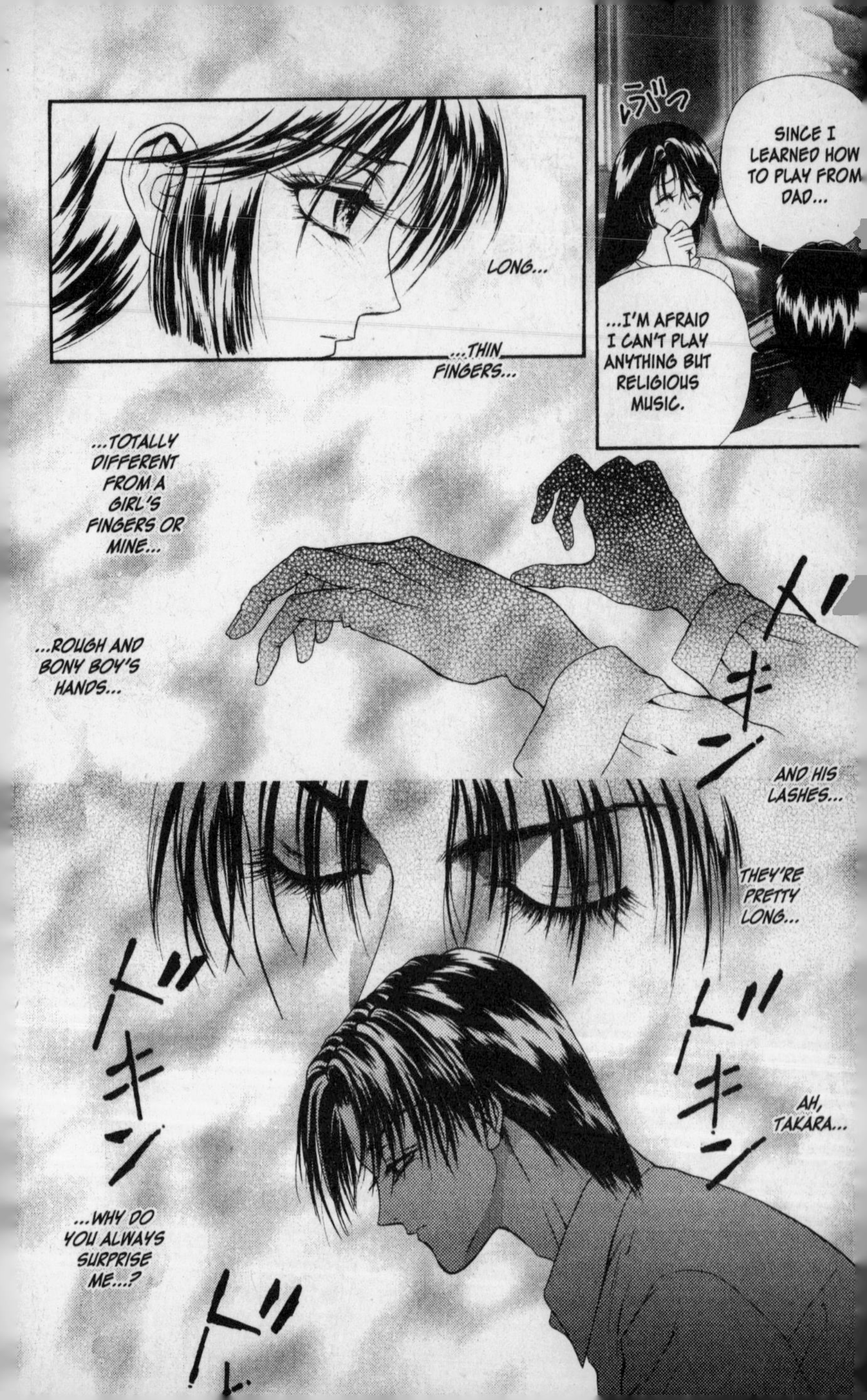
SINCE I LEARNED HOW TO PLAY FROM DAD...
...I'M AFRAID I CAN'T PLAY ANYTHING BUT RELIGIOUS MUSIC.
LONG...
...THIN FINGERS...
...TOTALLY DIFFERENT FROM A GIRL'S FINGERS OR MINE...
...ROUGH AND BONY BOY'S HANDS...
AND HIS LASHES...
THEY'RE PRETTY LONG...
AH, TAKARA...
...WHY DO YOU ALWAYS SURPRISE ME...?

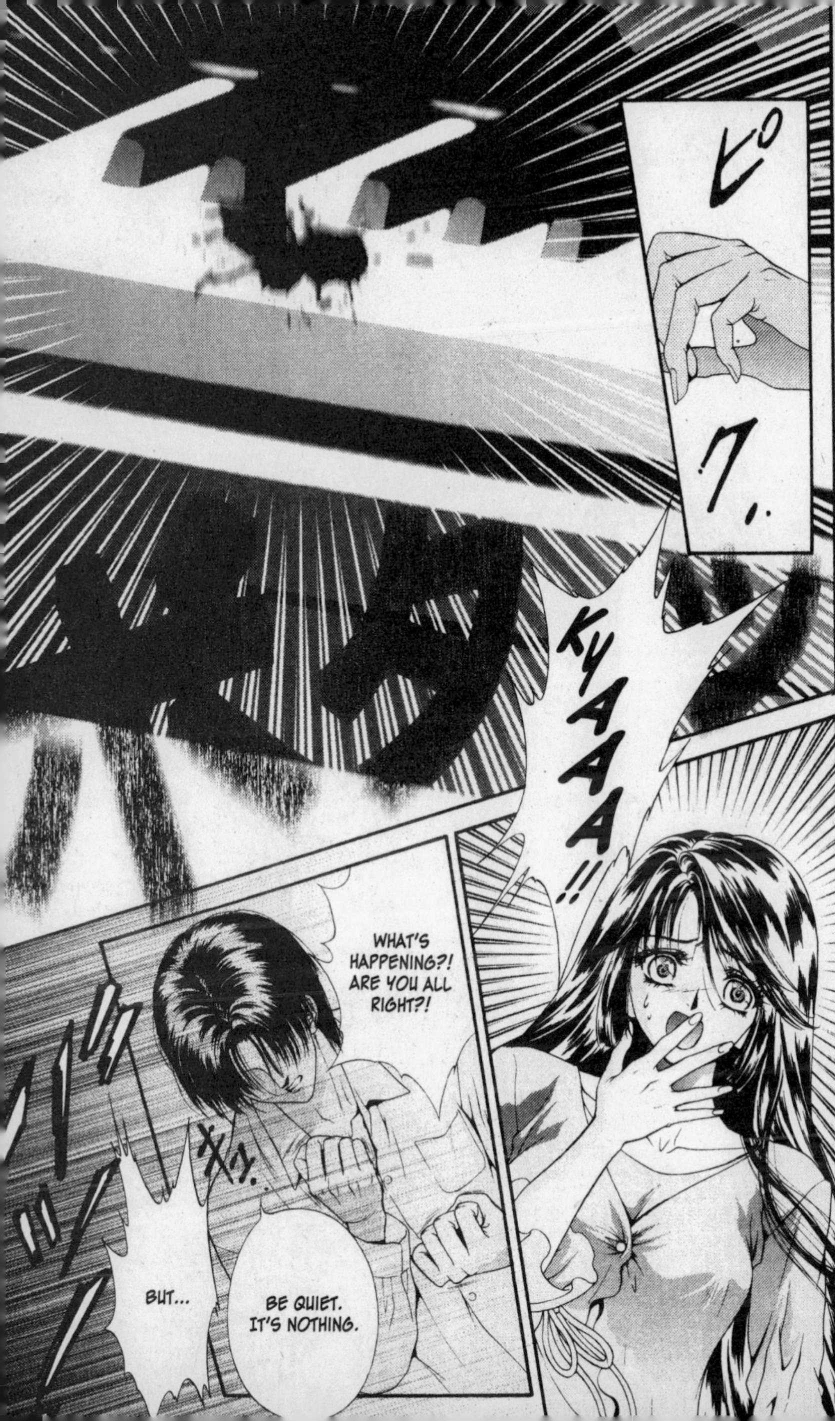
ピク..
KYAAAA!!
WHAT'S HAPPENING?! ARE YOU ALL RIGHT?!
BE QUIET. IT'S NOTHING.
BUT...

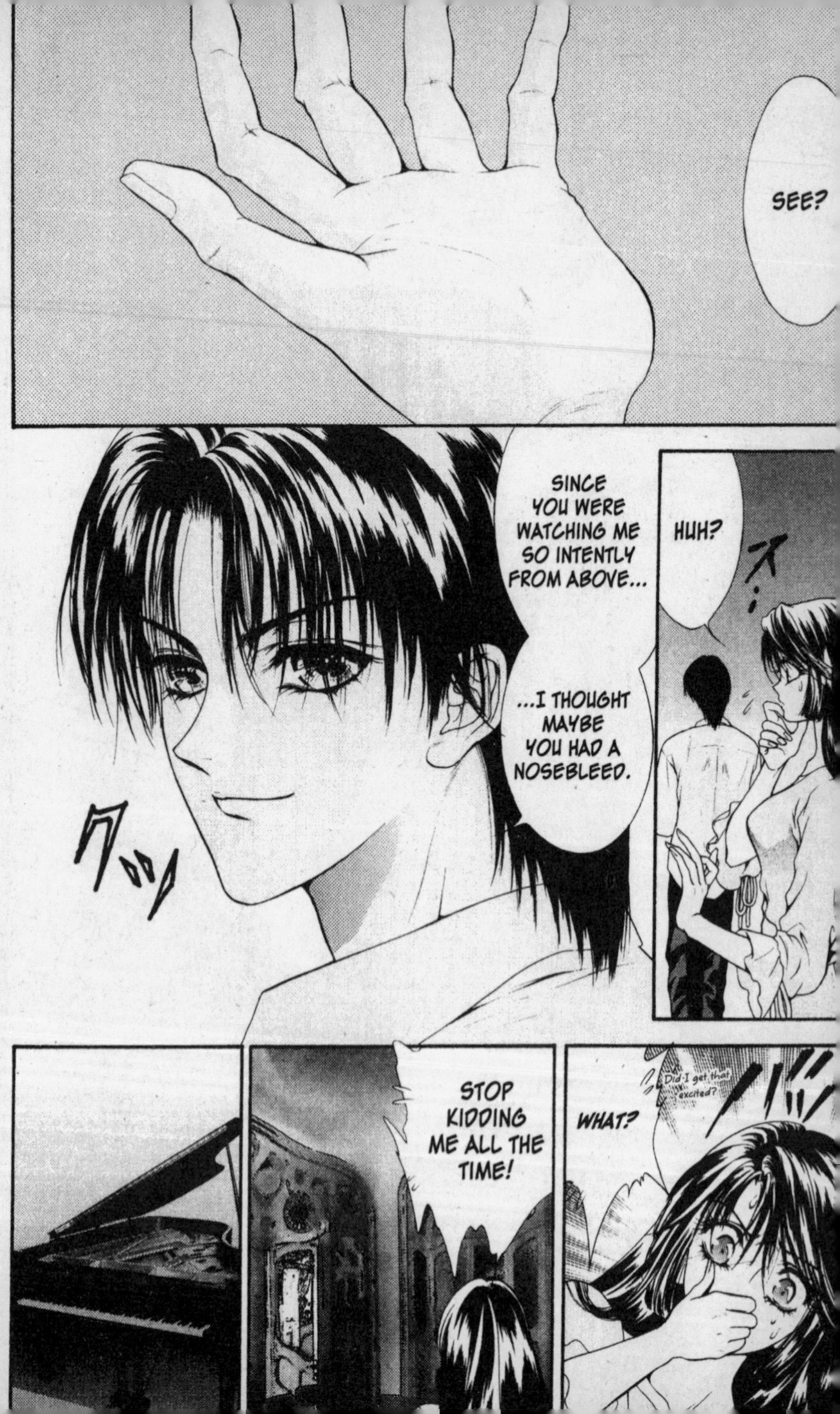
SEE?
HUH?
SINCE YOU WERE WATCHING ME SO INTENTLY FROM ABOVE...
...I THOUGHT MAYBE YOU HAD A NOSEBLEED.
Did I get that excited?
WHAT?
STOP KIDDING ME ALL THE TIME!

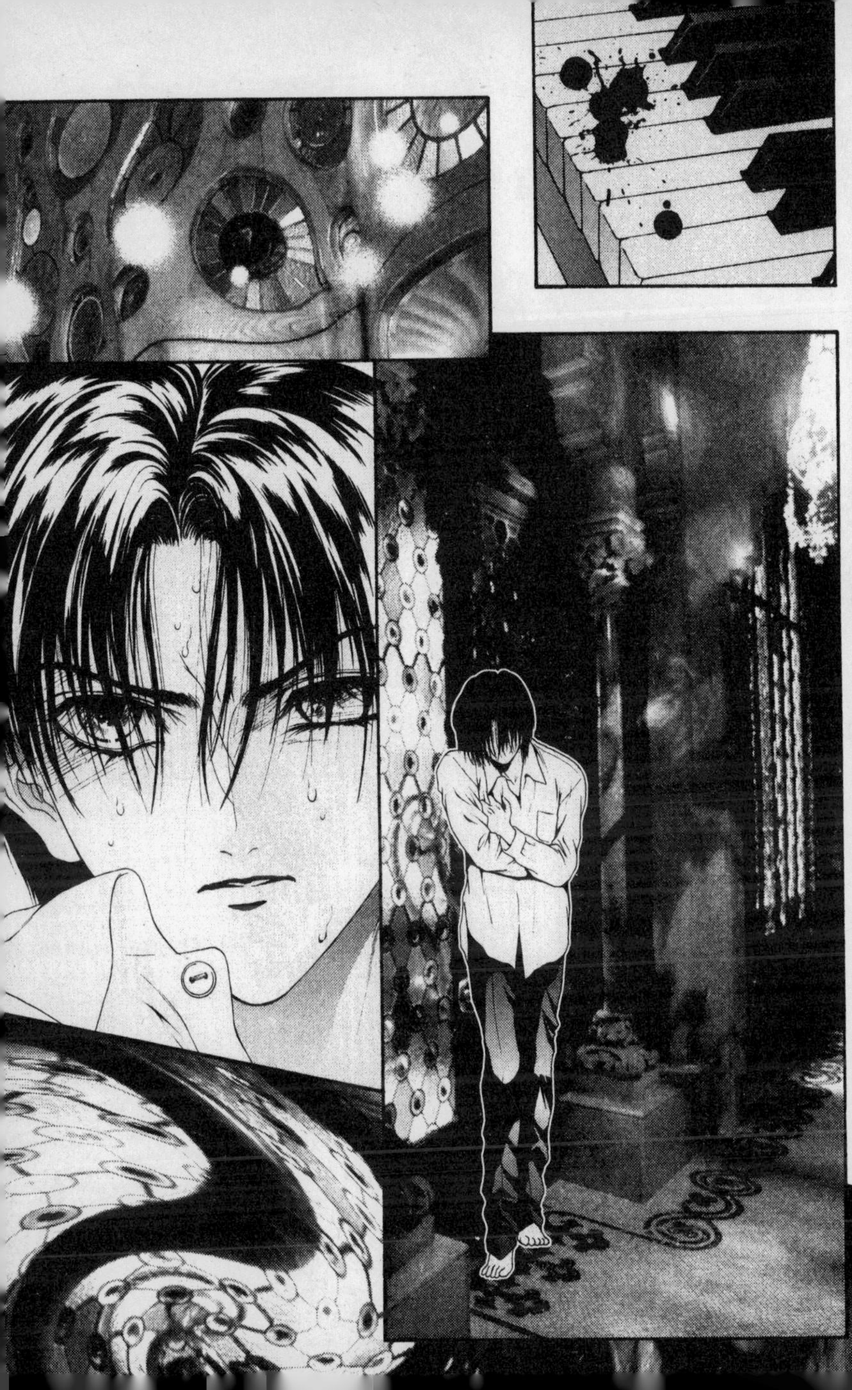

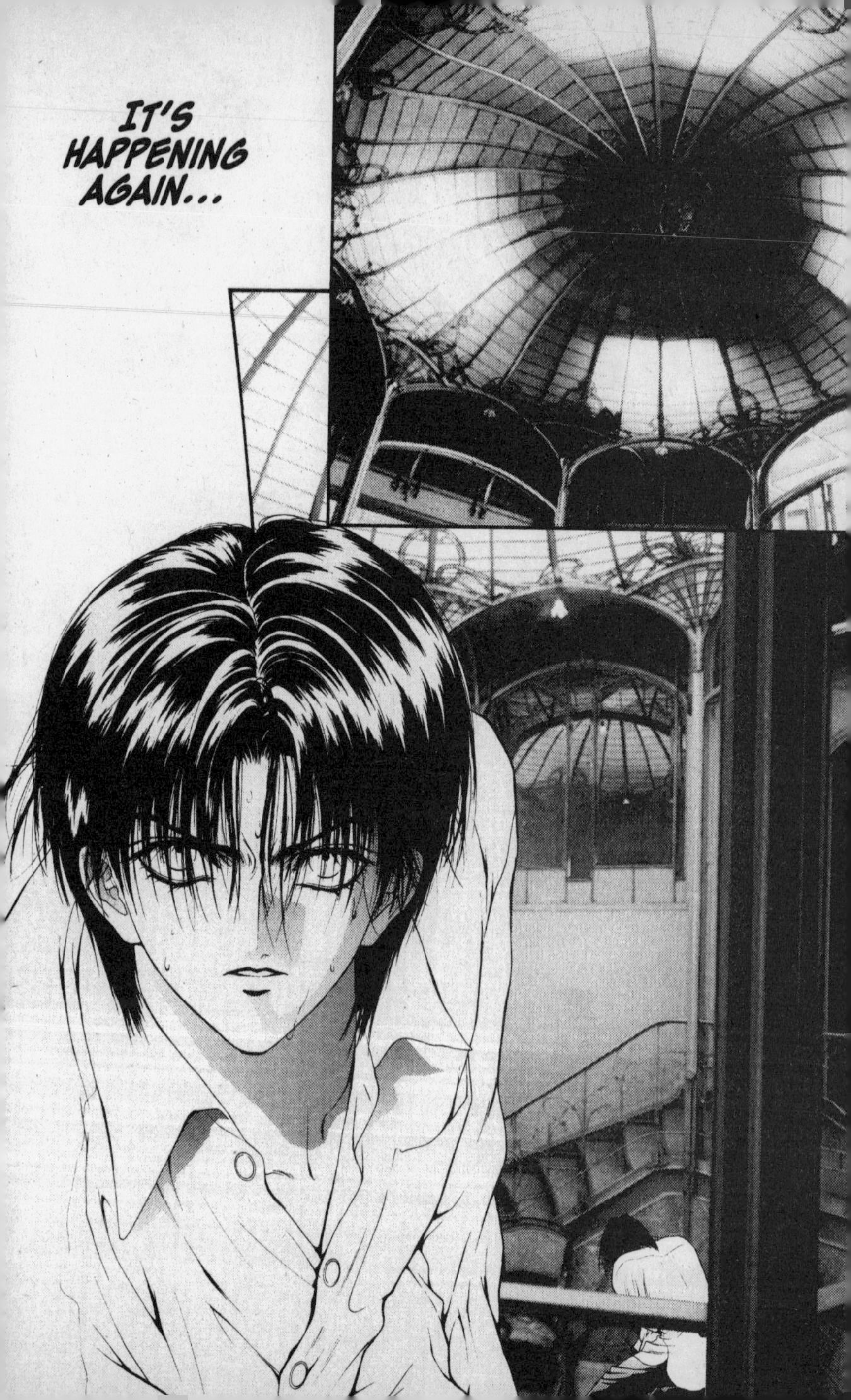
IT'S HAPPENING AGAIN...

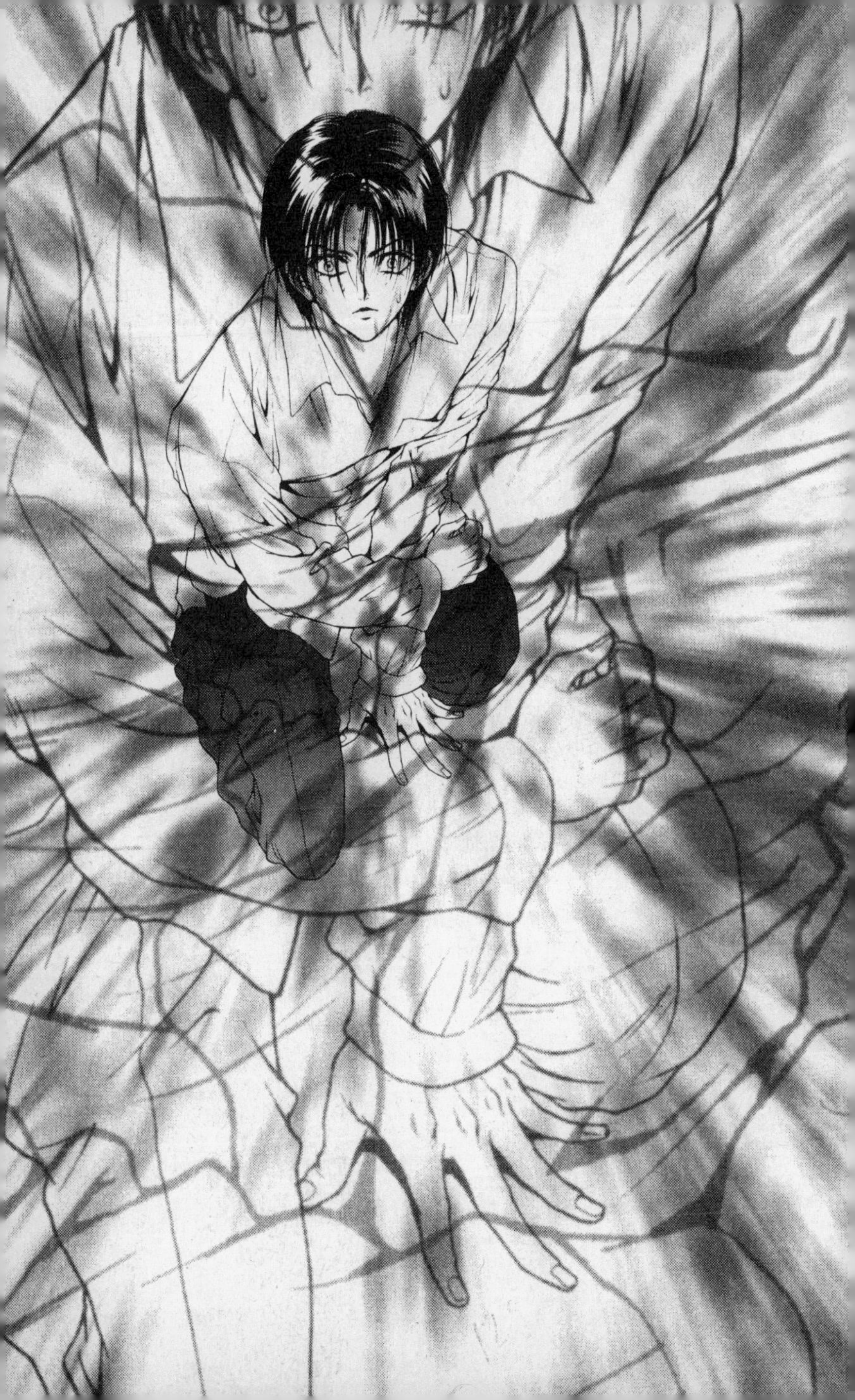

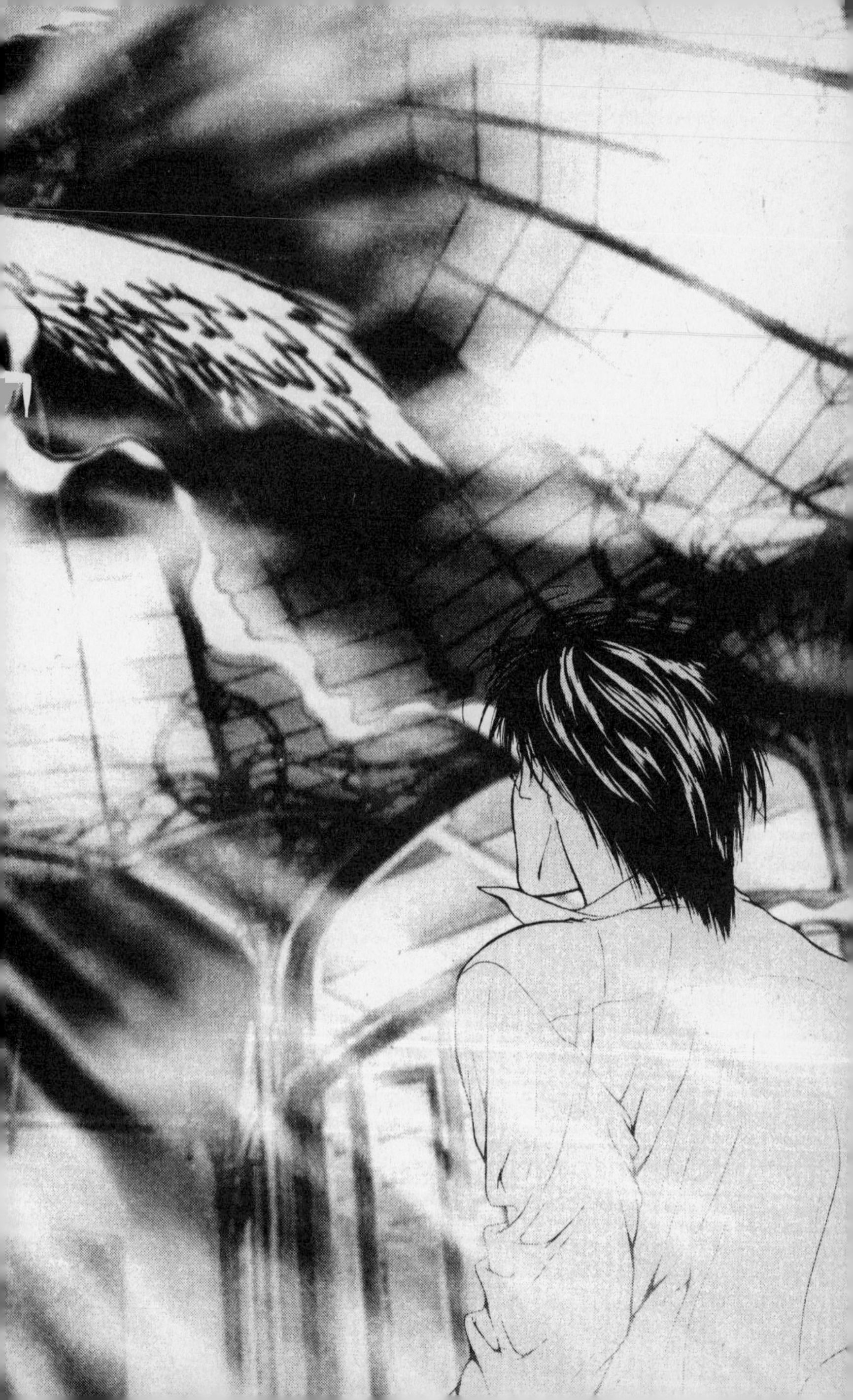

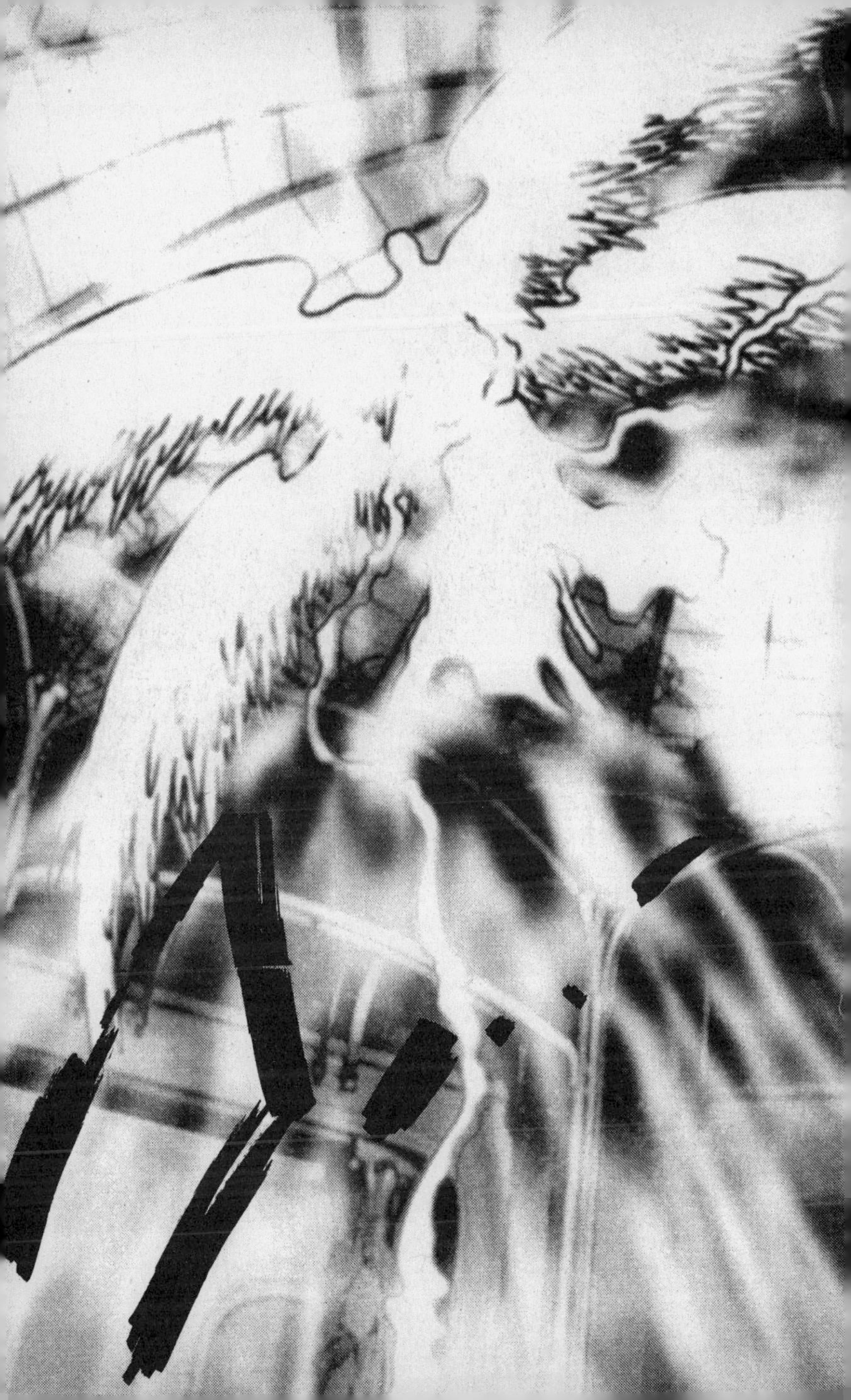

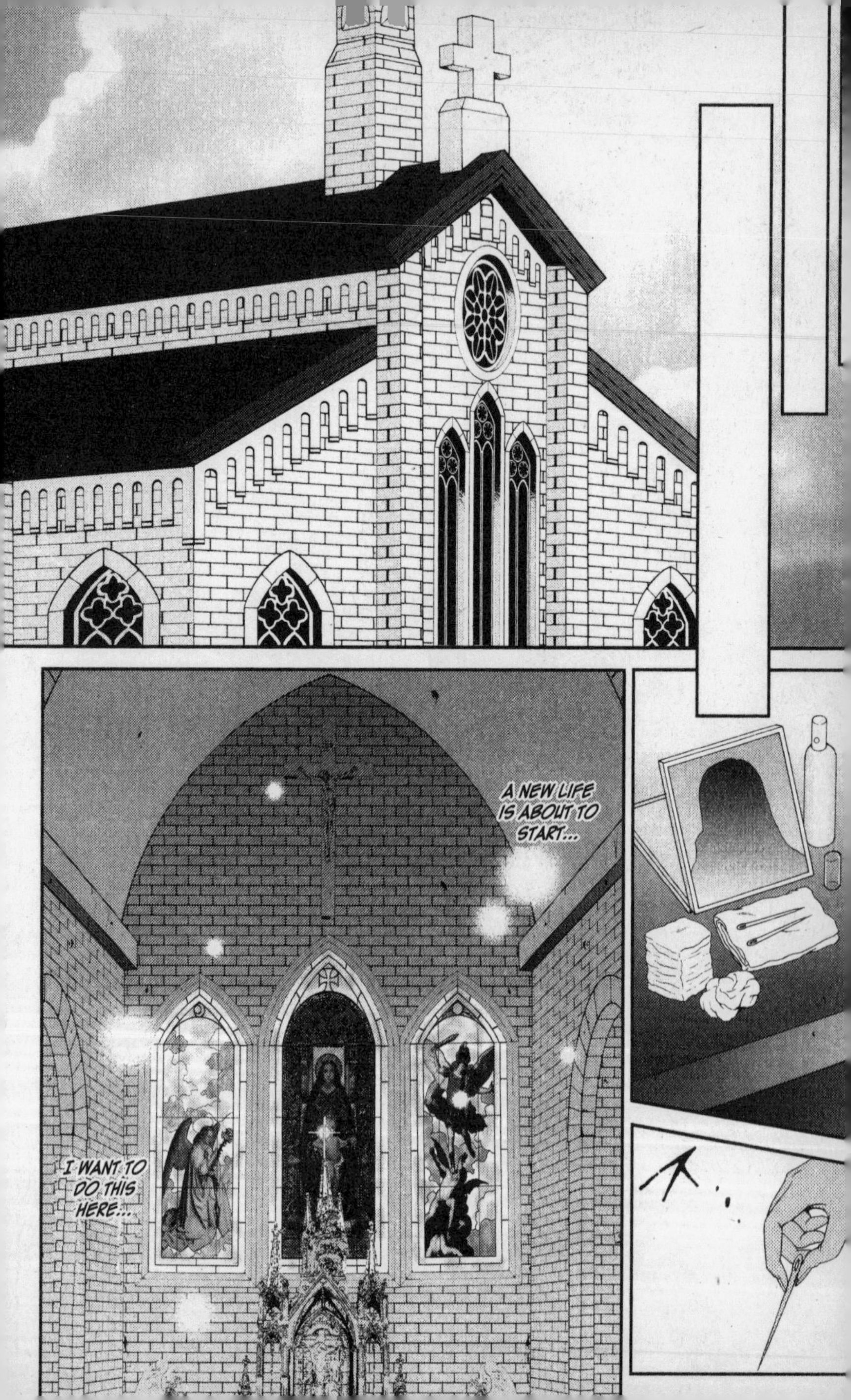
A NEW LIFE IS ABOUT TO START...
I WANT TO DO THIS HERE...

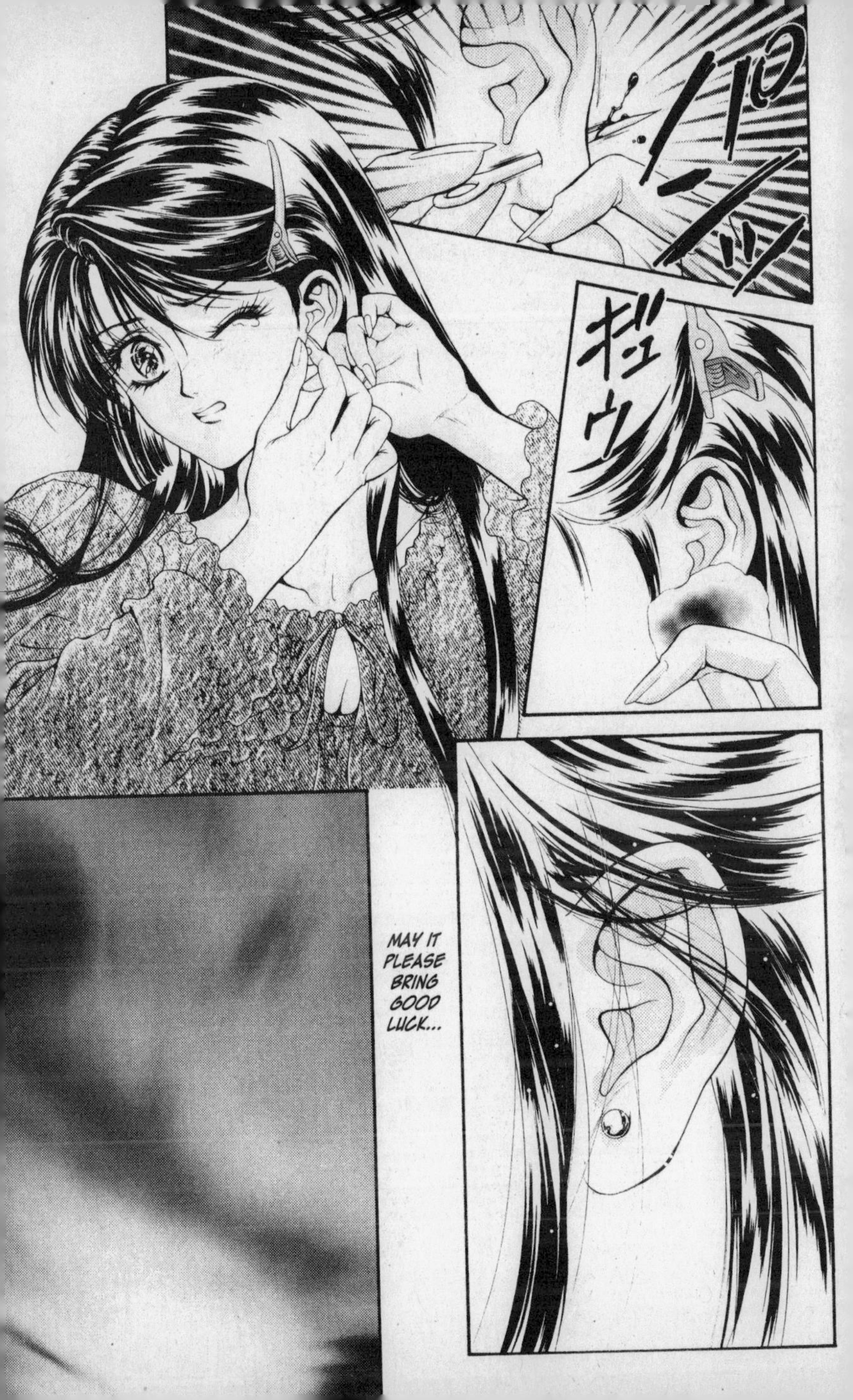
パ---ンッ
ギュウ
MAY IT PLEASE BRING GOOD LUCK...

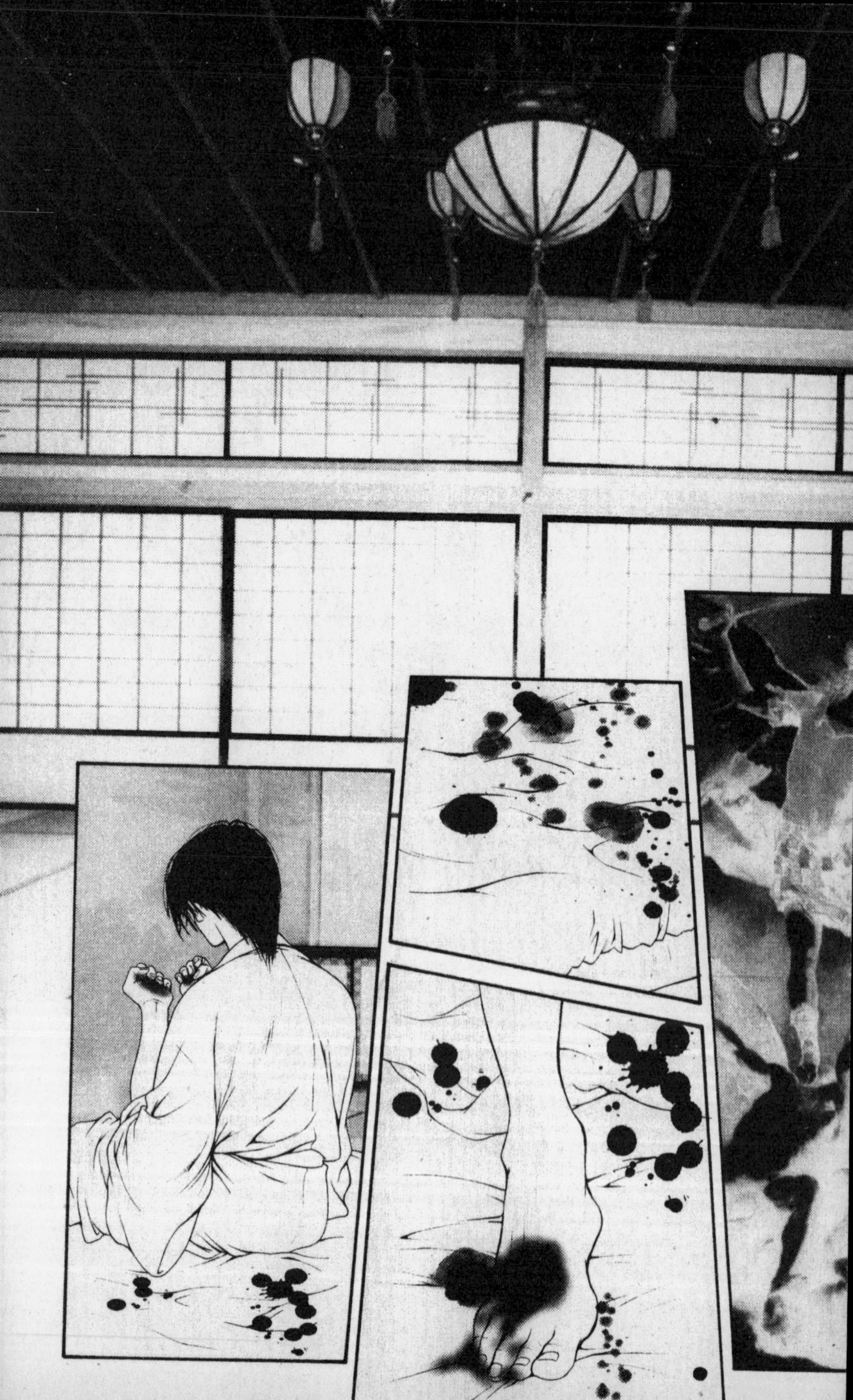

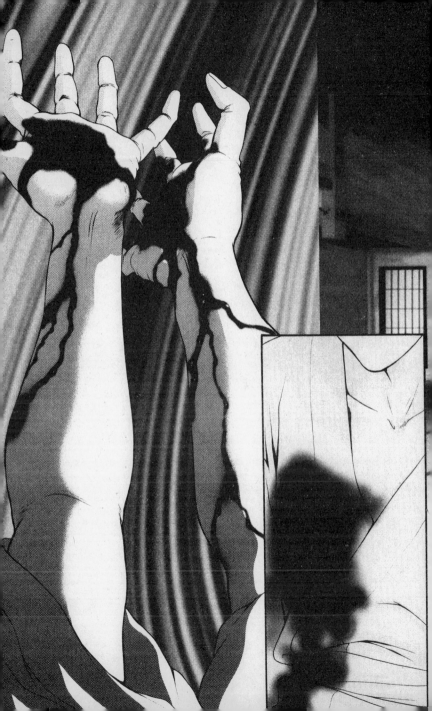

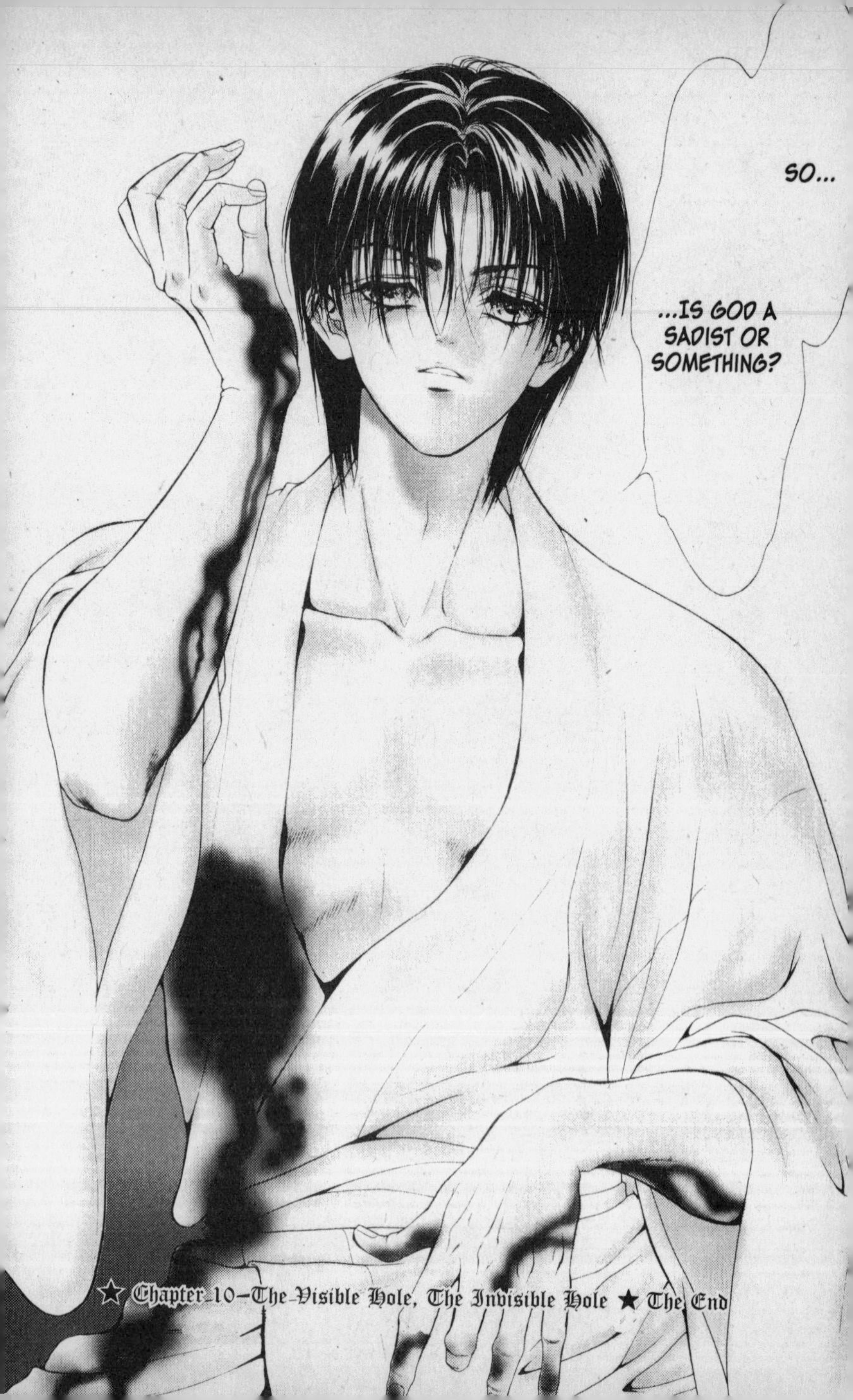
SO...
...IS GOD A SADIST OR SOMETHING?
☆ Chapter 10–The Visible Hole, The Invisible Hole ★ The End

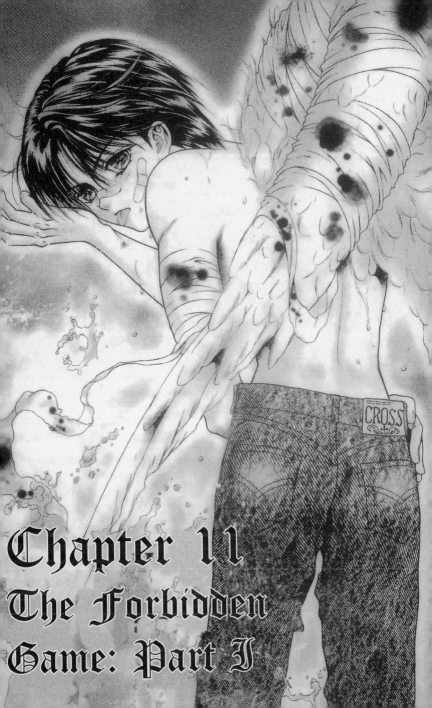

Chapter 11
The Forbidden
Game: Part I

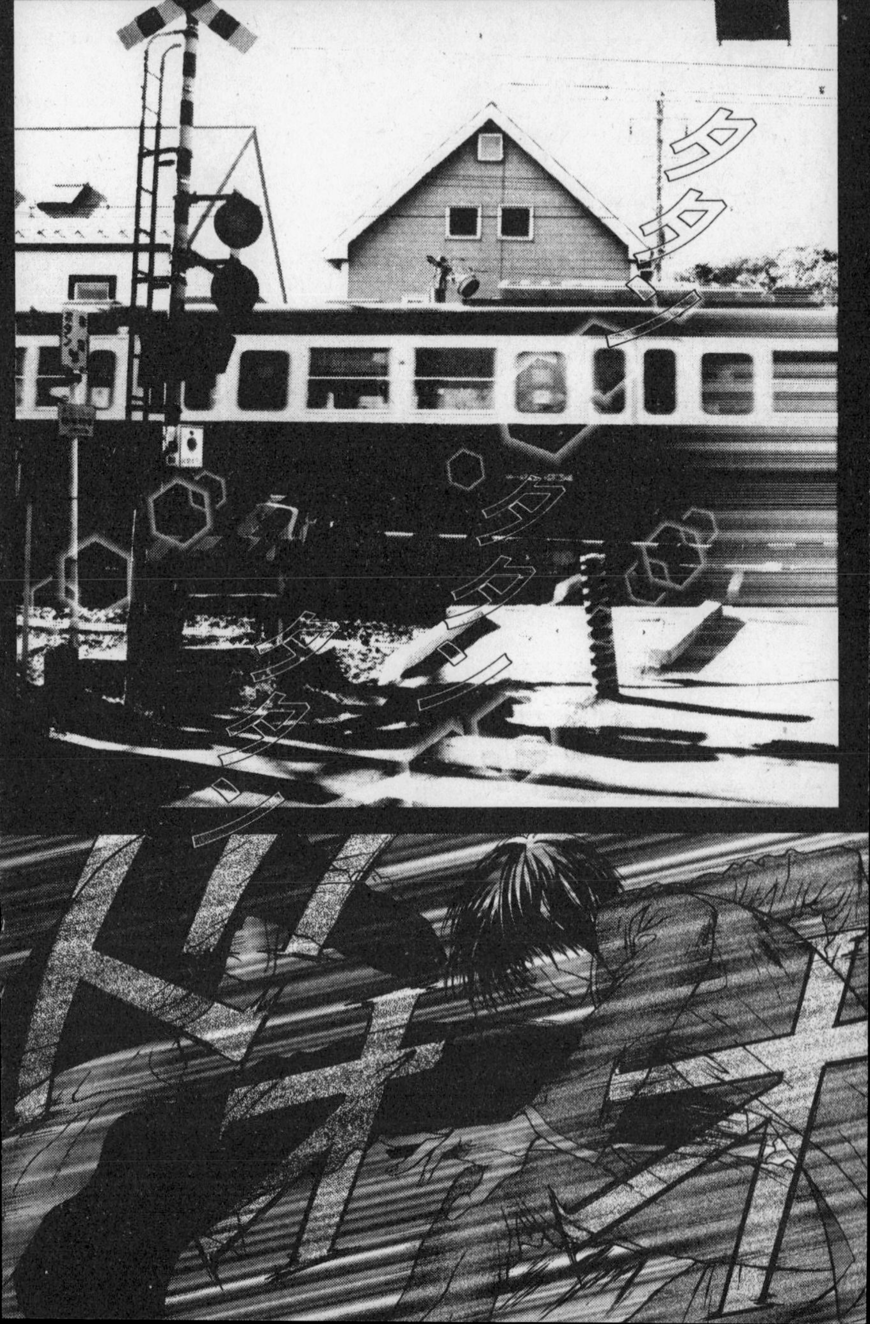
タタン
タタン
タタン

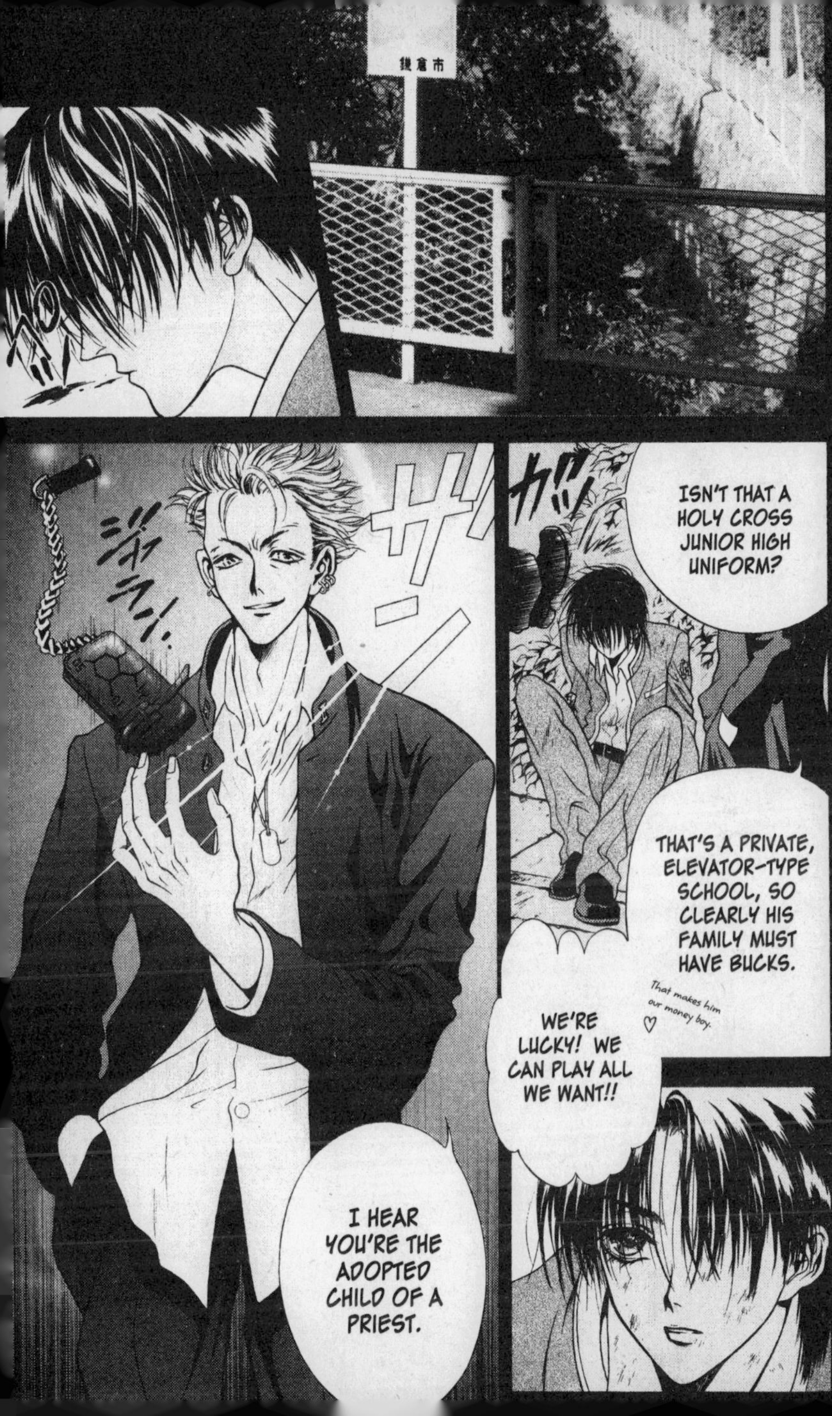
鎌倉市
ISN'T THAT A HOLY CROSS JUNIOR HIGH UNIFORM?
THAT'S A PRIVATE, ELEVATOR-TYPE SCHOOL, SO CLEARLY HIS FAMILY MUST HAVE BUCKS.
That makes him our money boy. ♡
WE'RE LUCKY! WE CAN PLAY ALL WE WANT!!
I HEAR YOU'RE THE ADOPTED CHILD OF A PRIEST.

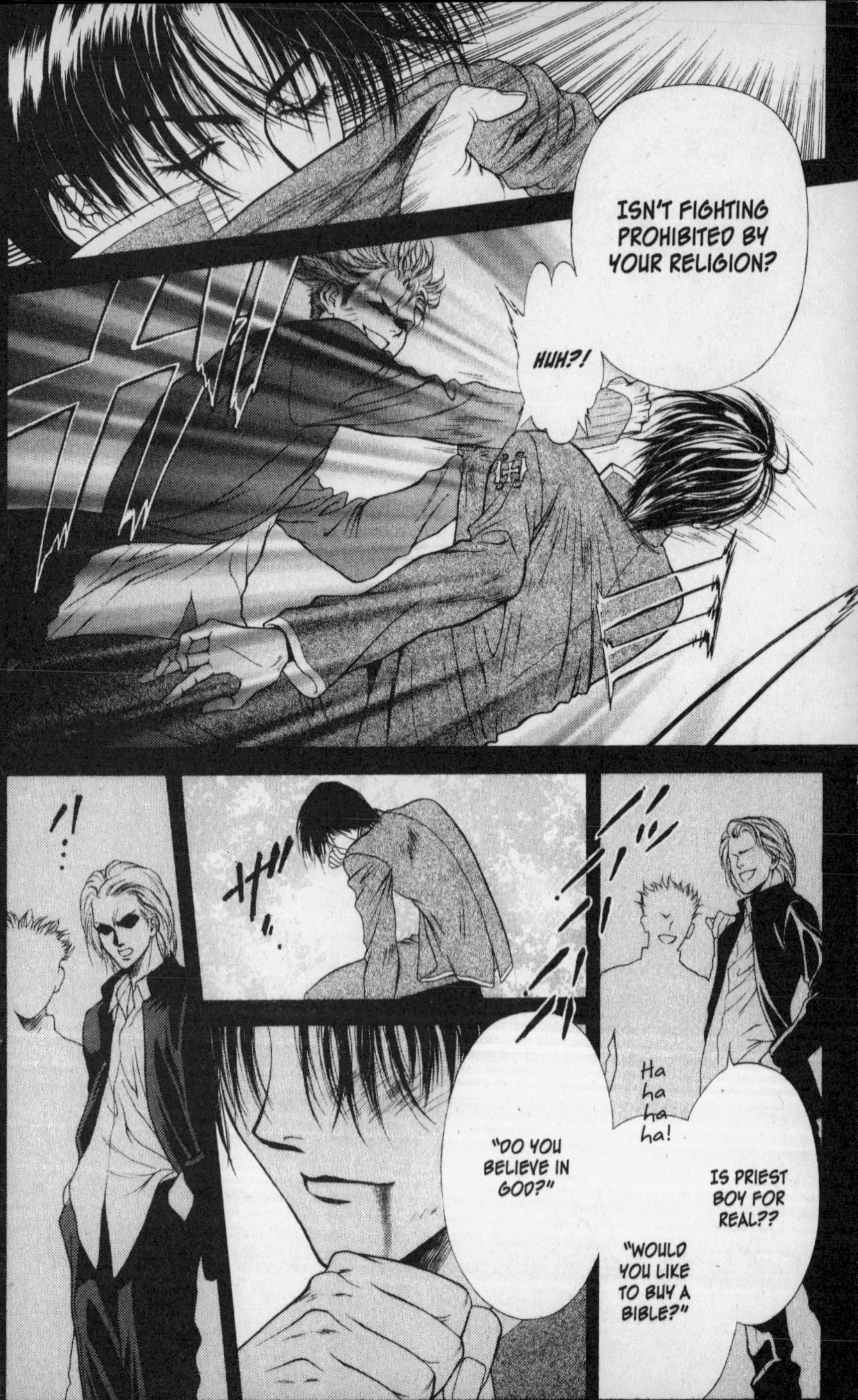

ISN'T FIGHTING PROHIBITED BY YOUR RELIGION?
HUH?!
Ha ha ha ha!
IS PRIEST BOY FOR REAL??
"WOULD YOU LIKE TO BUY A BIBLE?"
"DO YOU BELIEVE IN GOD?"
!...

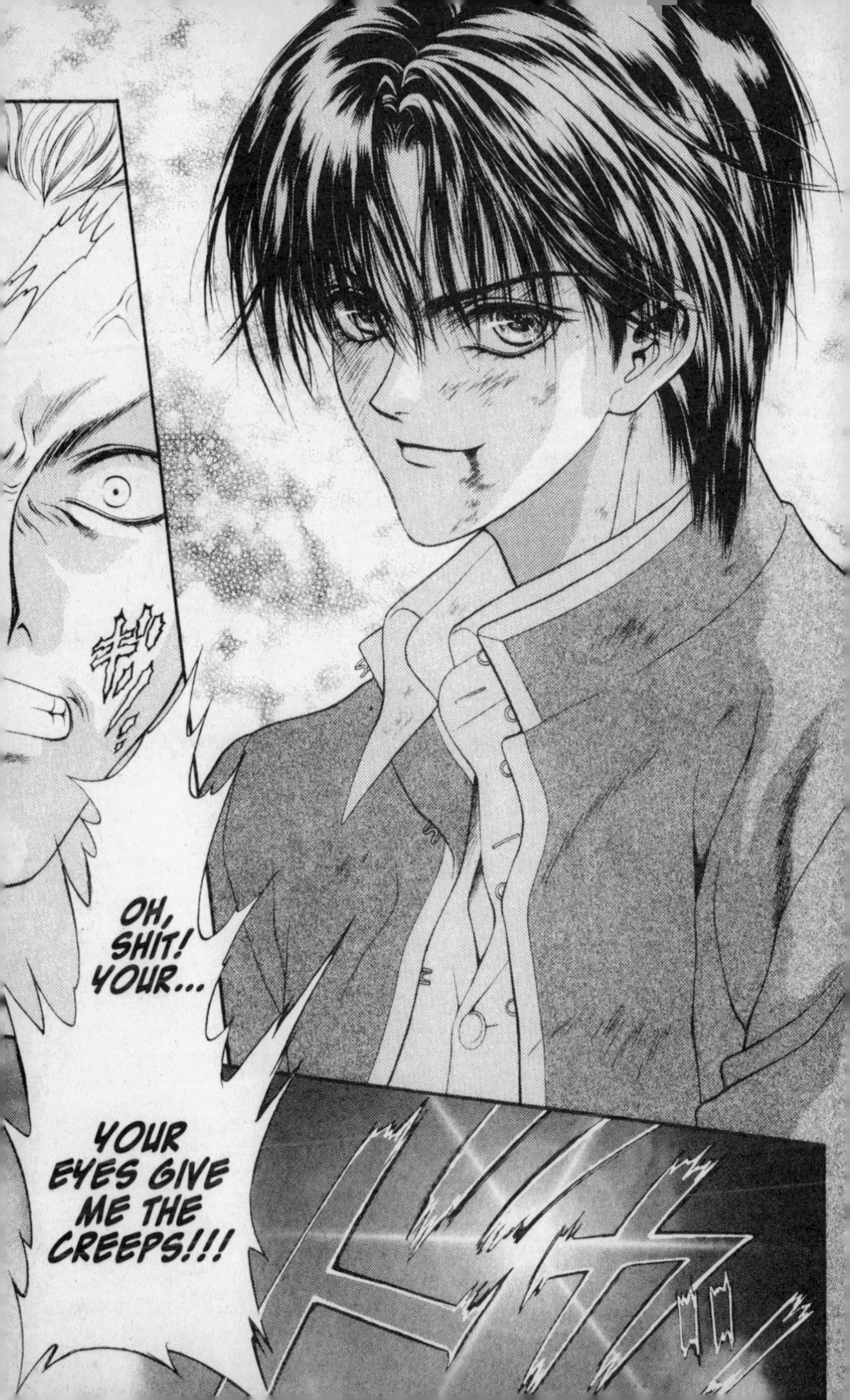
OH, SHIT! YOUR...
YOUR EYES GIVE ME THE CREEPS!!!

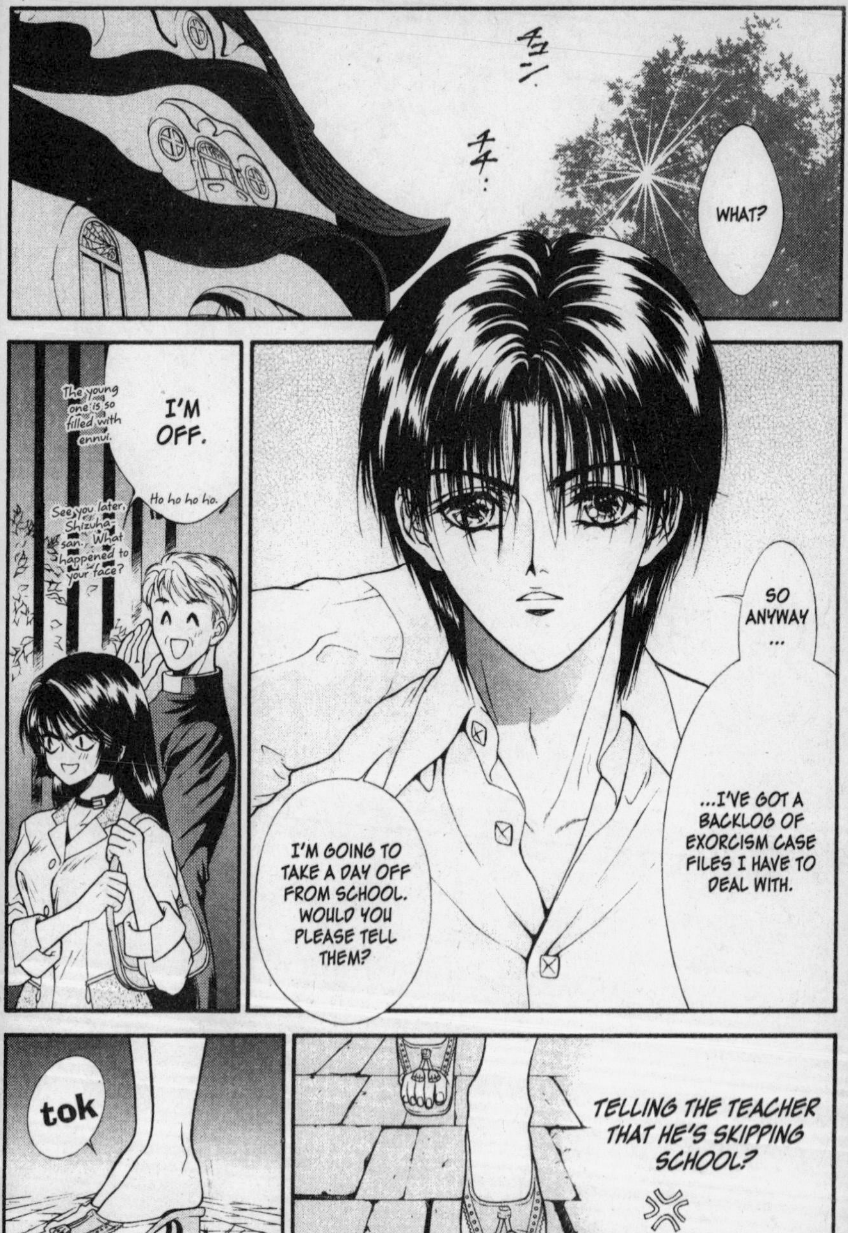
WHAT?
SO ANYWAY ...
...I'VE GOT A BACKLOG OF EXORCISM CASE FILES I HAVE TO DEAL WITH.
I'M GOING TO TAKE A DAY OFF FROM SCHOOL. WOULD YOU PLEASE TELL THEM?
I'M OFF.
Ho ho ho ho.
The young one is so filled with ennui.
See you later, Shizuha-san. What happened to your face?
TELLING THE TEACHER THAT HE'S SKIPPING SCHOOL?
tok

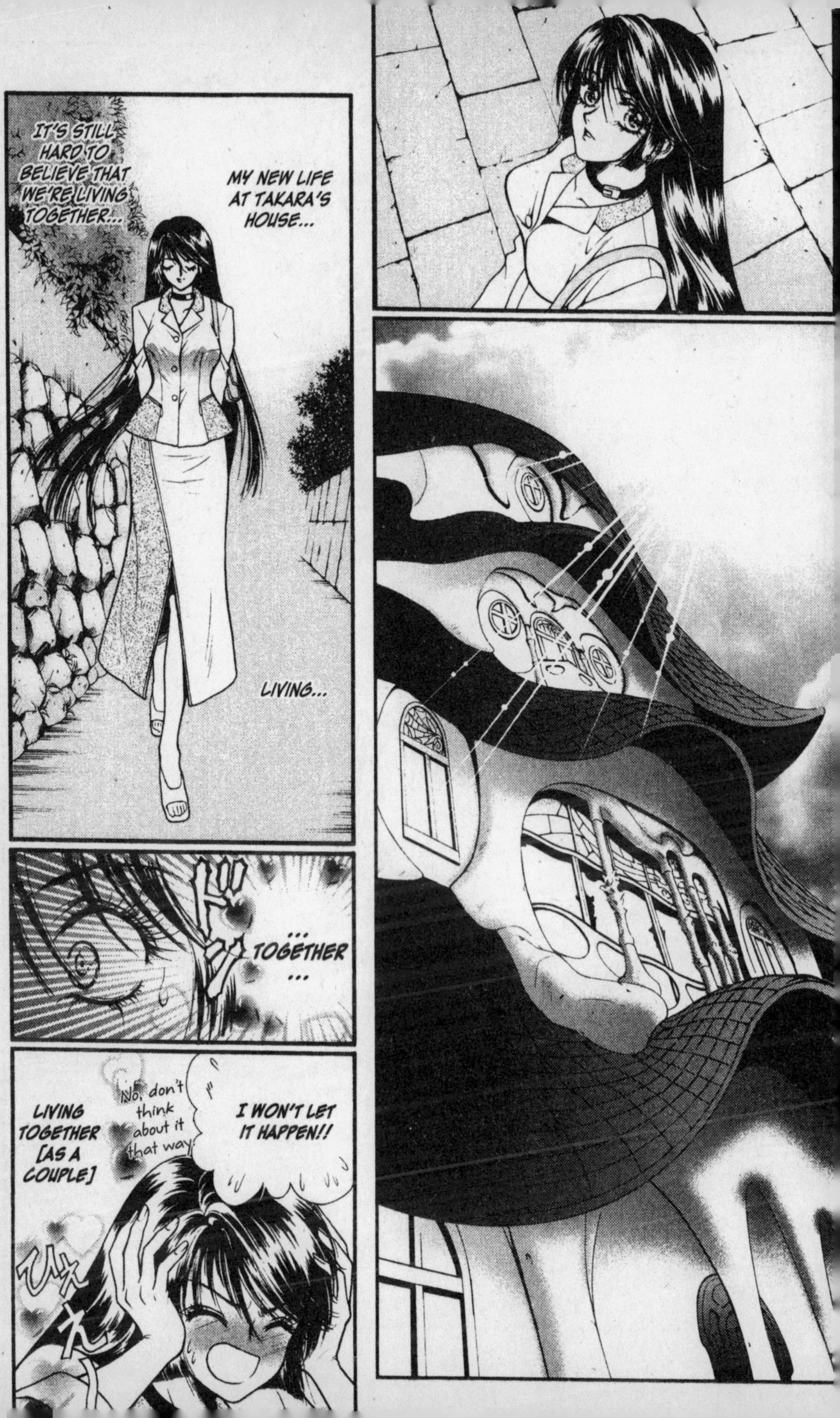
MY NEW LIFE AT TAKARA'S HOUSE...
IT'S STILL HARD TO BELIEVE THAT WE'RE LIVING TOGETHER...
LIVING...
ド!!
... TOGETHER ...
I WON'T LET IT HAPPEN!!
No, don't think about it that way
LIVING TOGETHER [AS A COUPLE]

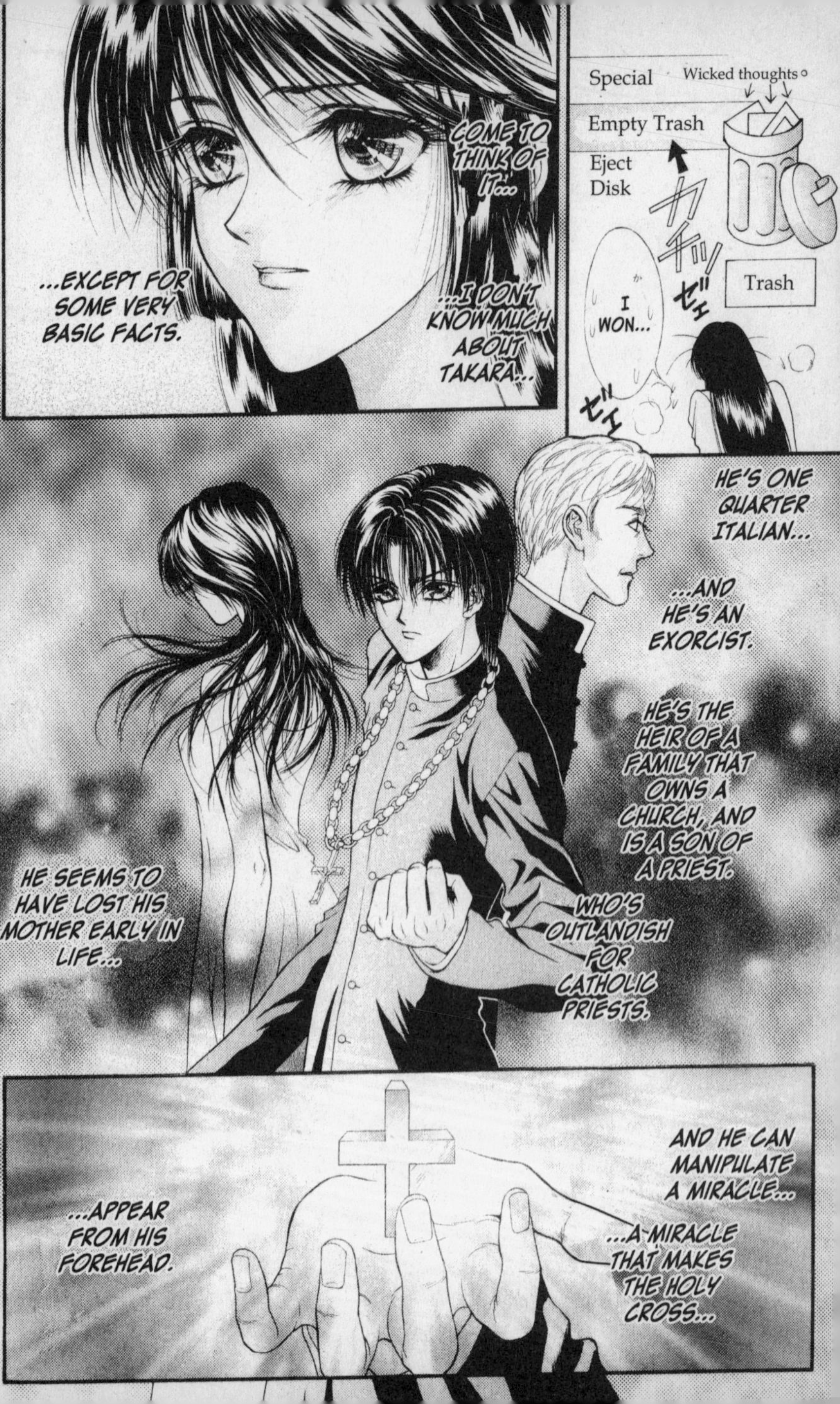

Special
Wicked thoughts
Empty Trash
Eject Disk
Trash
カチッ
I WON...
ゼェ
ゼェ
COME TO THINK OF IT...
...I DON'T KNOW MUCH ABOUT TAKARA...
...EXCEPT FOR SOME VERY BASIC FACTS.
HE'S ONE QUARTER ITALIAN...
...AND HE'S AN EXORCIST.
HE'S THE HEIR OF A FAMILY THAT OWNS A CHURCH, AND IS A SON OF A PRIEST.
WHO'S OUTLANDISH FOR CATHOLIC PRIESTS.
HE SEEMS TO HAVE LOST HIS MOTHER EARLY IN LIFE...
AND HE CAN MANIPULATE A MIRACLE...
...A MIRACLE THAT MAKES THE HOLY CROSS...
...APPEAR FROM HIS FOREHEAD.

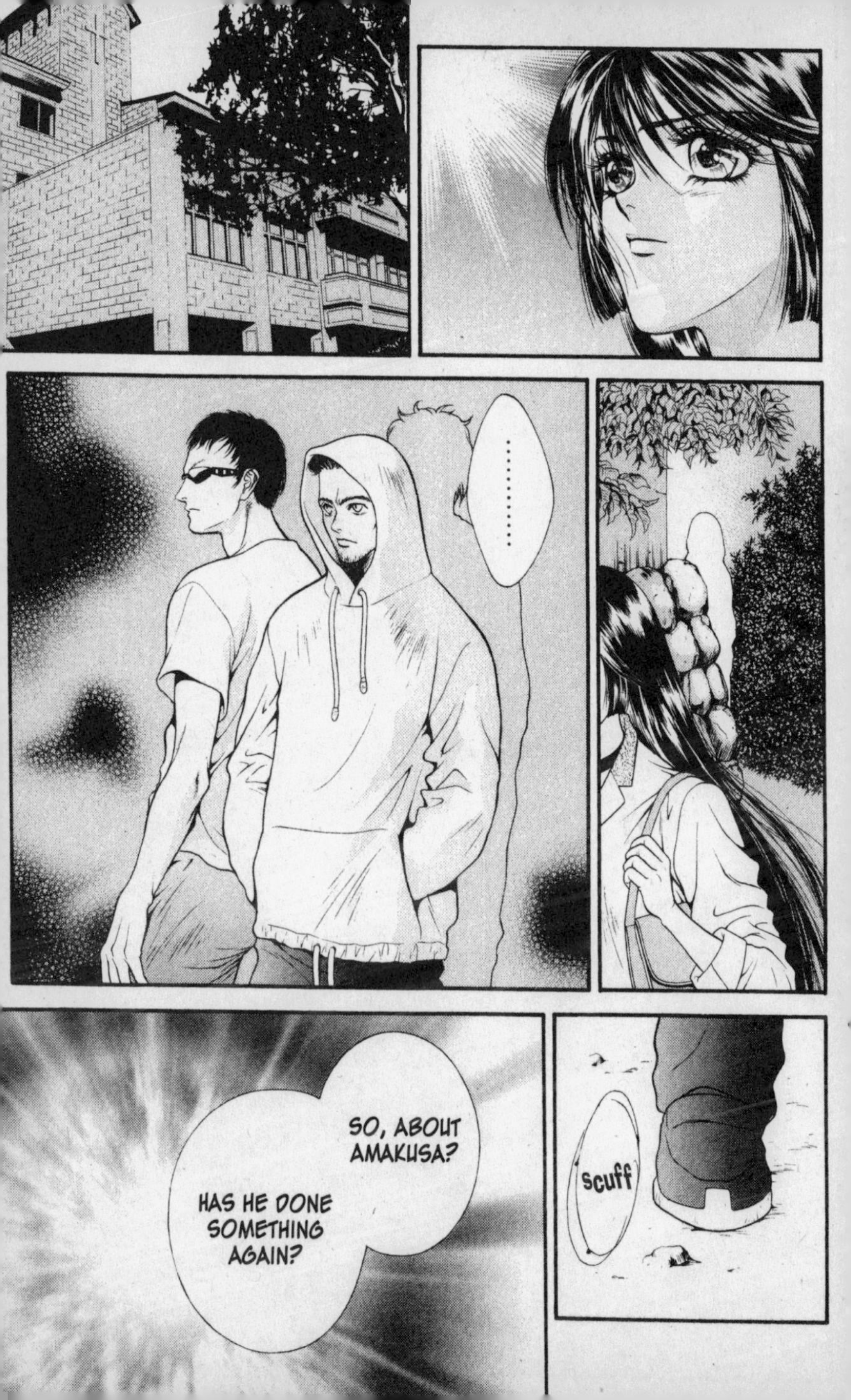
......
scuff
SO, ABOUT AMAKUSA?
HAS HE DONE SOMETHING AGAIN?

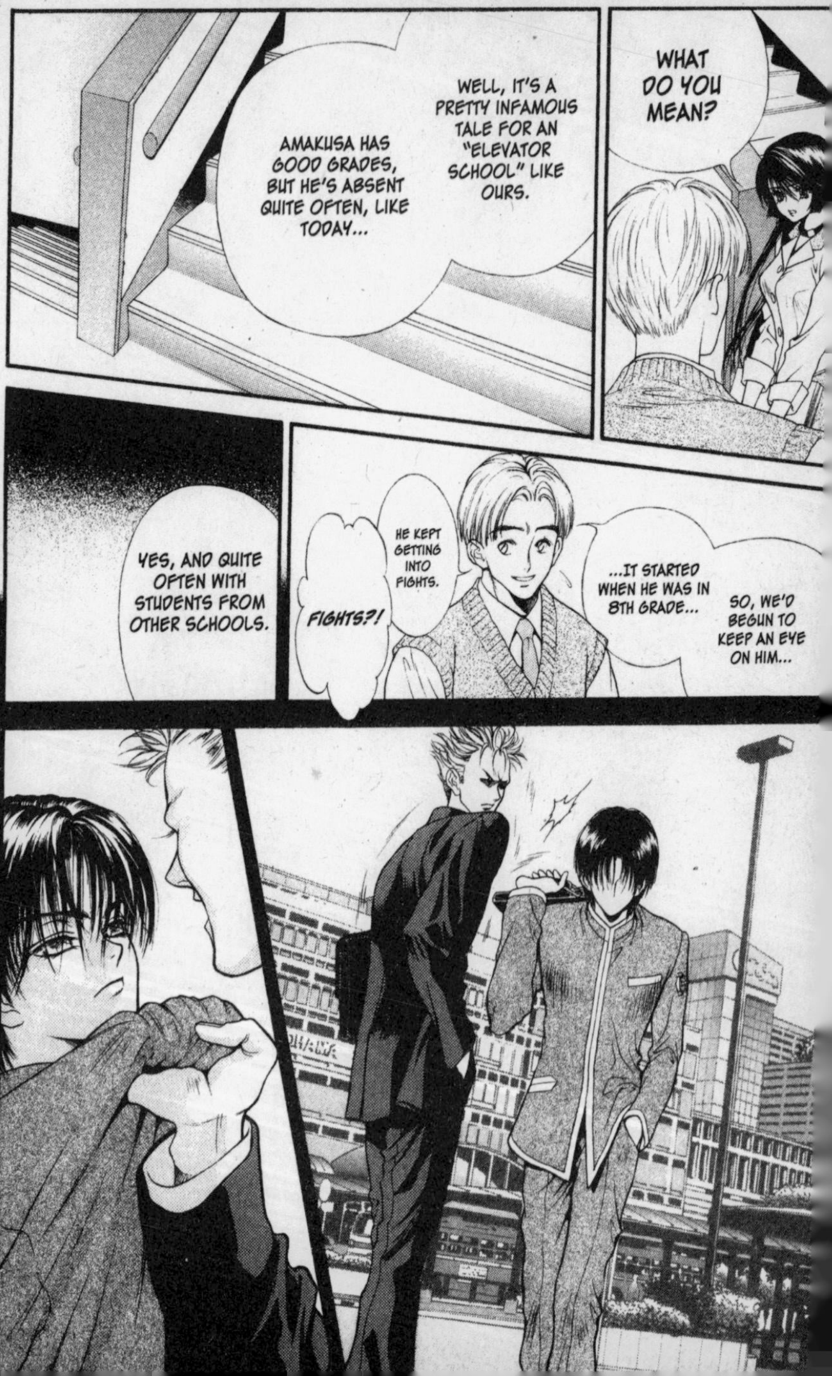
WHAT DO YOU MEAN?
WELL, IT'S A PRETTY INFAMOUS TALE FOR AN "ELEVATOR SCHOOL" LIKE OURS.
AMAKUSA HAS GOOD GRADES, BUT HE'S ABSENT QUITE OFTEN, LIKE TODAY...
SO, WE'D BEGUN TO KEEP AN EYE ON HIM...
...IT STARTED WHEN HE WAS IN 8TH GRADE...
HE KEPT GETTING INTO FIGHTS.
FIGHTS?!
YES, AND QUITE OFTEN WITH STUDENTS FROM OTHER SCHOOLS.

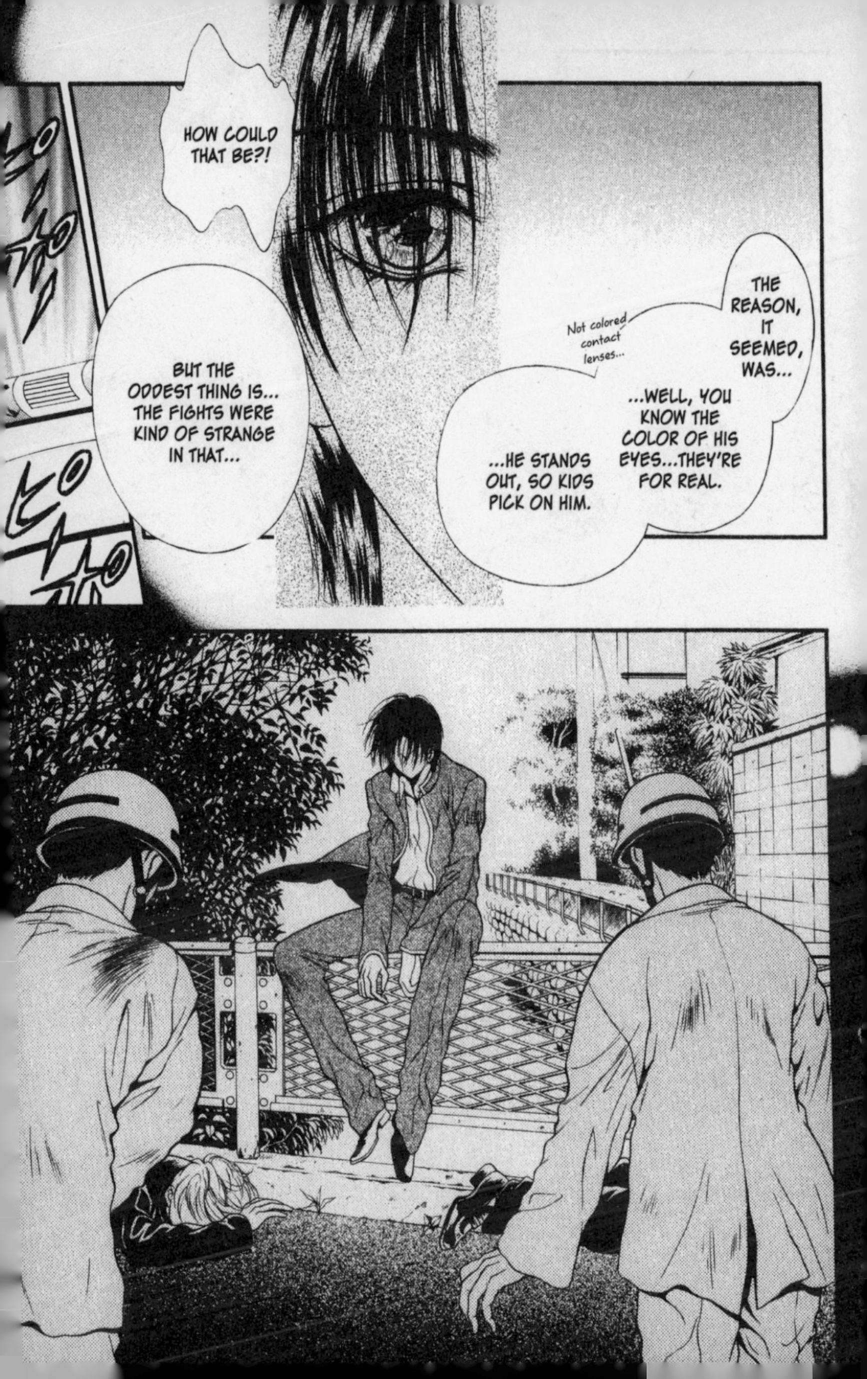
THE REASON, IT SEEMED, WAS...
...WELL, YOU KNOW THE COLOR OF HIS EYES...THEY'RE FOR REAL.
Not colored contact lenses...
...HE STANDS OUT, SO KIDS PICK ON HIM.
HOW COULD THAT BE?!
BUT THE ODDEST THING IS... THE FIGHTS WERE KIND OF STRANGE IN THAT...

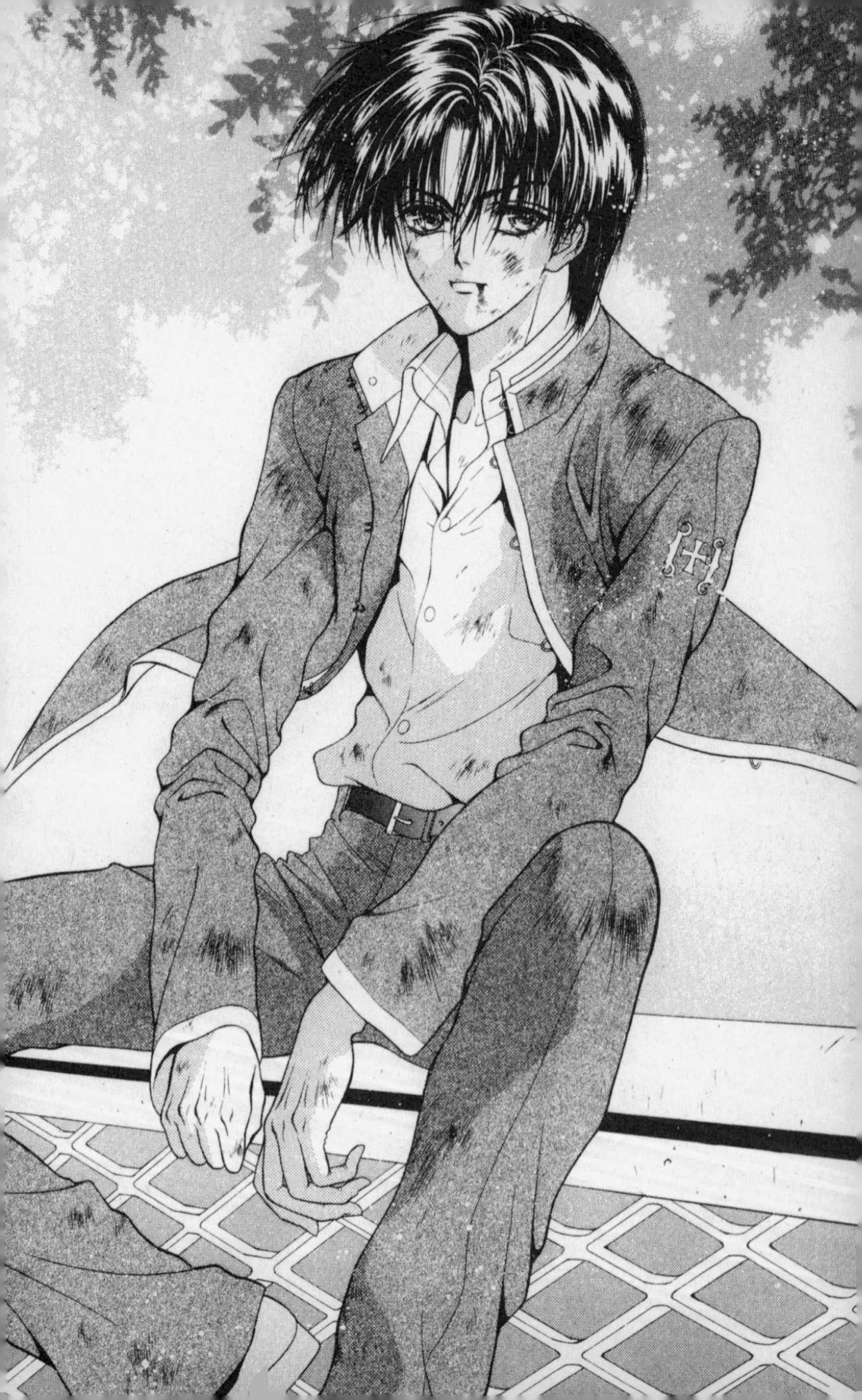

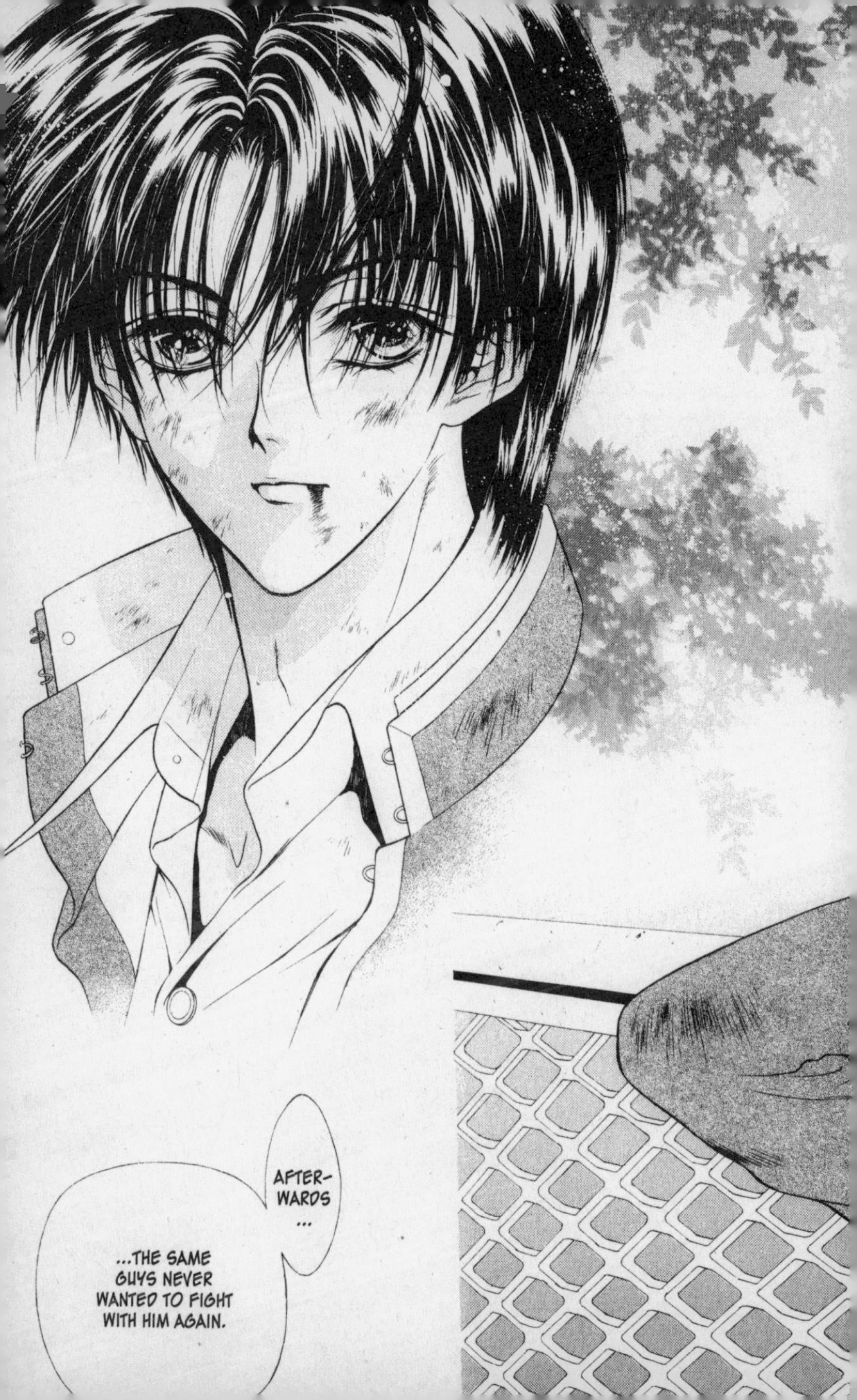
AFTER-WARDS ...
...THE SAME GUYS NEVER WANTED TO FIGHT WITH HIM AGAIN.

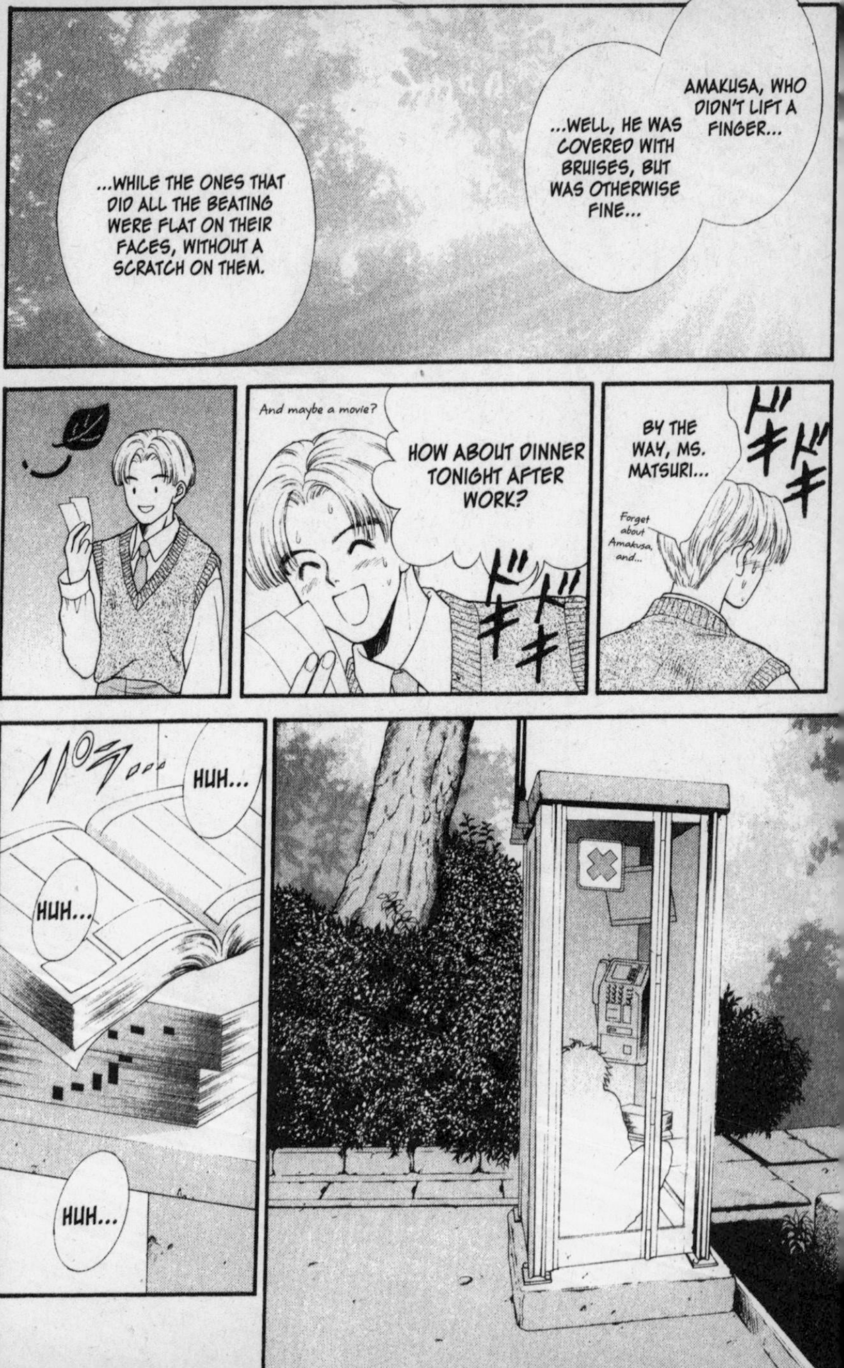
AMAKUSA, WHO DIDN'T LIFT A FINGER...
...WELL, HE WAS COVERED WITH BRUISES, BUT WAS OTHERWISE FINE...
...WHILE THE ONES THAT DID ALL THE BEATING WERE FLAT ON THEIR FACES, WITHOUT A SCRATCH ON THEM.
ドキドキ
BY THE WAY, MS. MATSURI...
Forget about Amakusa, and...
HOW ABOUT DINNER TONIGHT AFTER WORK?
And maybe a movie?
ドキドキ
HUH...
パラ
HUH...
HUH...

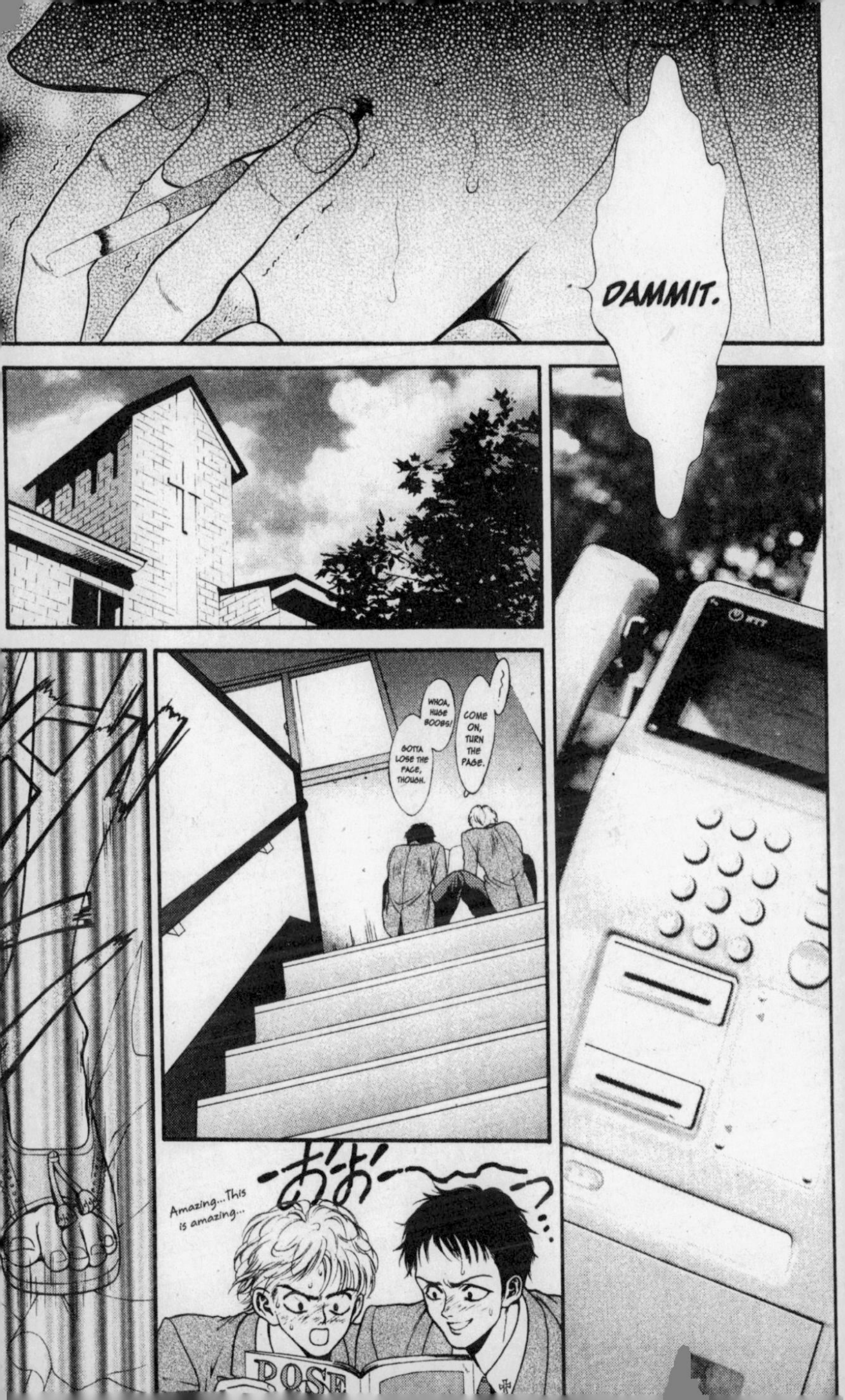
DAMMIT.
COME ON, TURN THE PAGE.
WHOA, HUGE BOOBS!
GOTTA LOSE THE PAGE, THOUGH.
おお～～～っ…
Amazing... This is amazing...

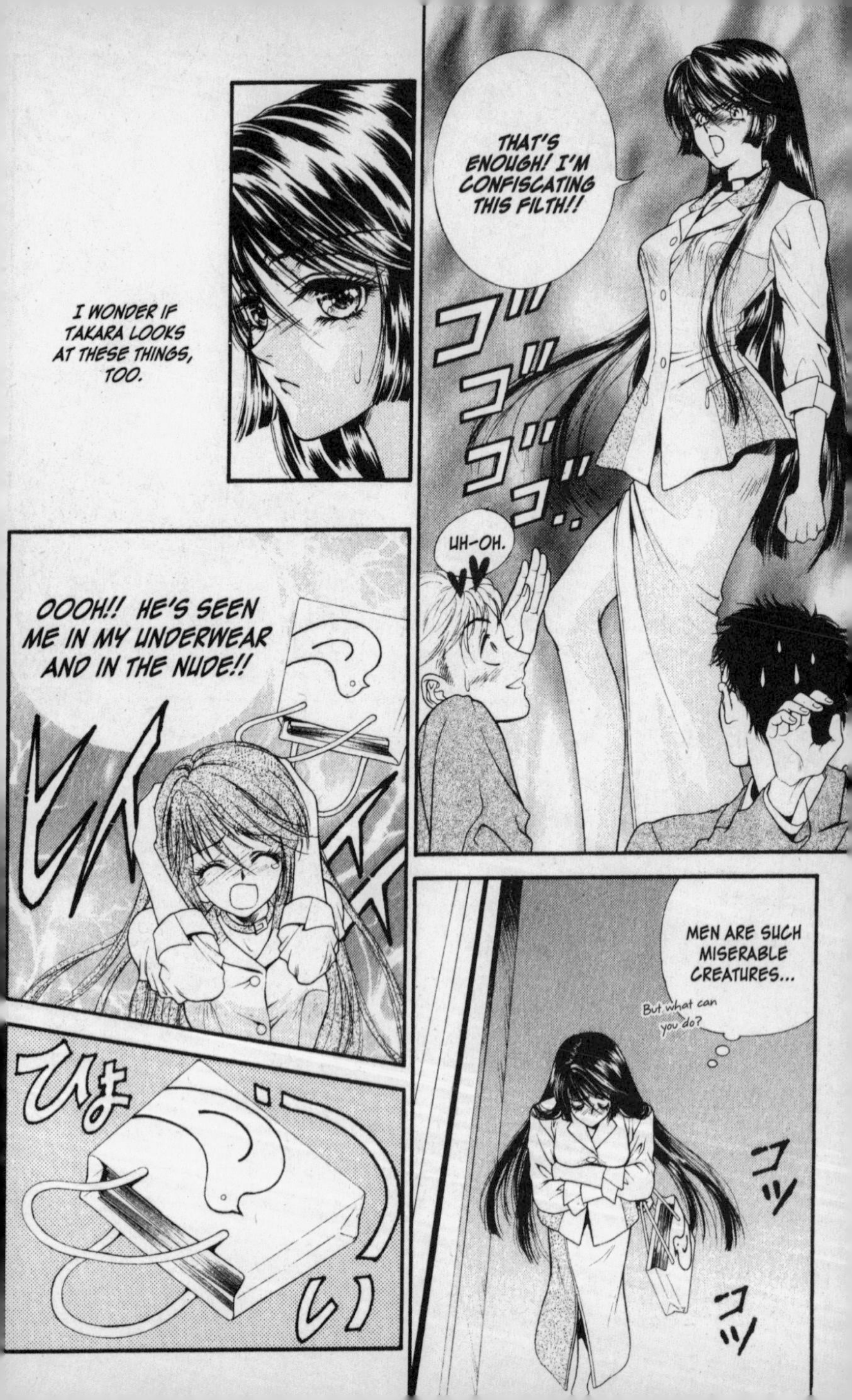
THAT'S ENOUGH! I'M CONFISCATING THIS FILTH!!
ゴゴゴゴ..
UH-OH.
I WONDER IF TAKARA LOOKS AT THESE THINGS, TOO.
OOOH!! HE'S SEEN ME IN MY UNDERWEAR AND IN THE NUDE!!
MEN ARE SUCH MISERABLE CREATURES...
But what can you do?
コツ
コツ
ひょい

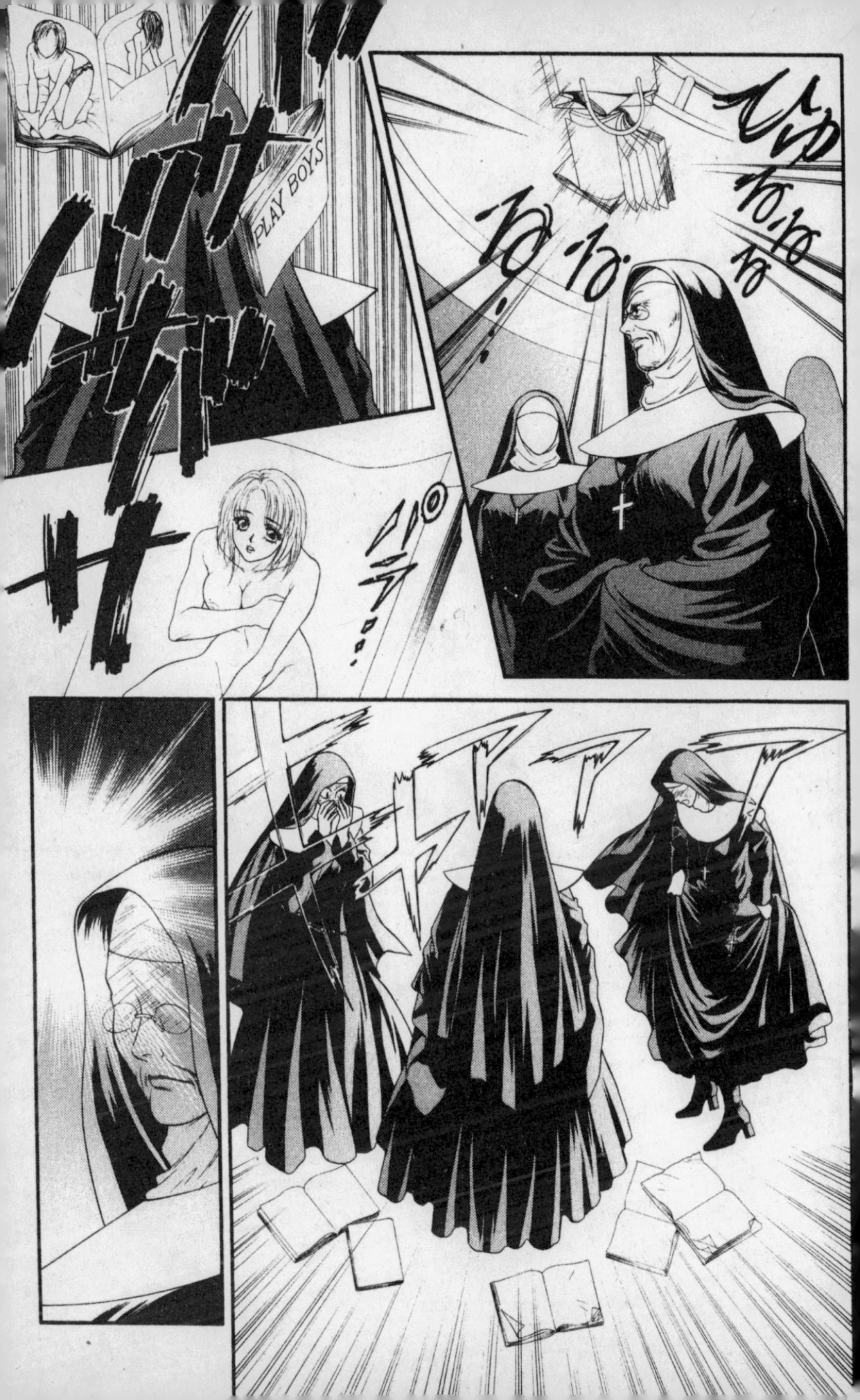
PLAY BOYS
パラ…

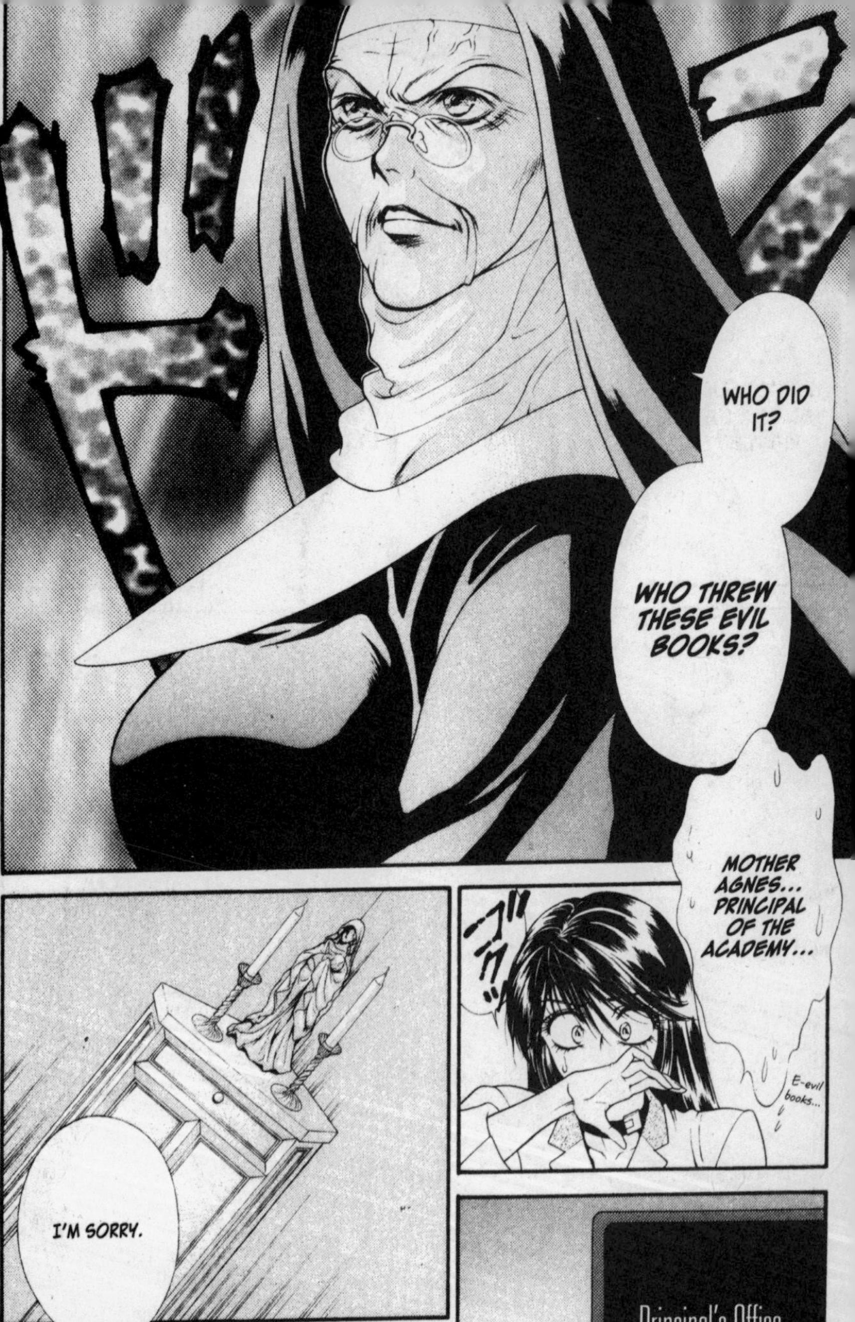
WHO DID IT?
WHO THREW THESE EVIL BOOKS?
MOTHER AGNES... PRINCIPAL OF THE ACADEMY...
E-evil books...
Principal's Office
I'M SORRY.

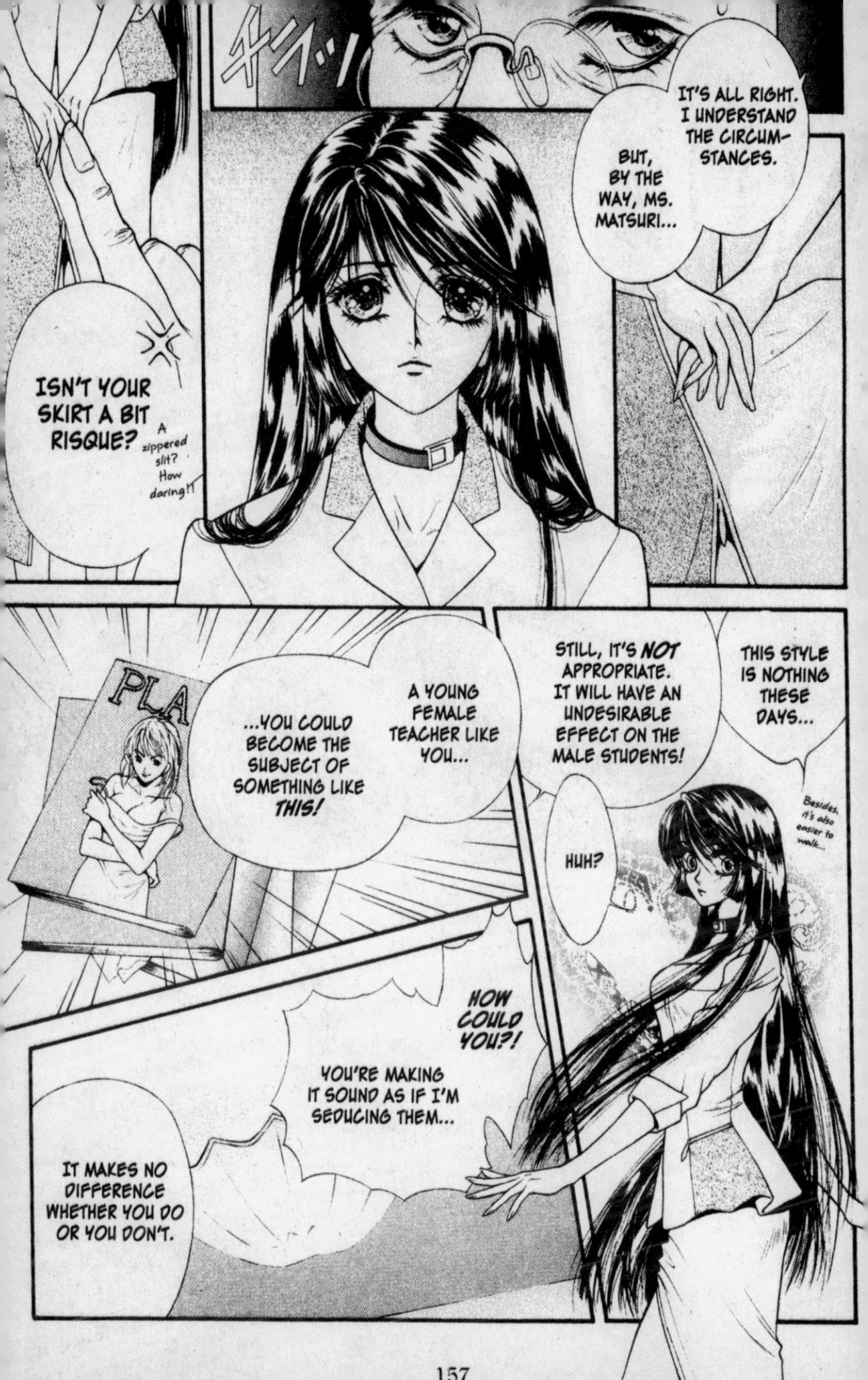
チラッ
IT'S ALL RIGHT. I UNDERSTAND THE CIRCUM-STANCES.
BUT, BY THE WAY, MS. MATSURI...
ISN'T YOUR SKIRT A BIT RISQUE?
A zippered slit? How daring!!
THIS STYLE IS NOTHING THESE DAYS...
Besides, it's also easier to walk...
STILL, IT'S **NOT** APPROPRIATE. IT WILL HAVE AN UNDESIRABLE EFFECT ON THE MALE STUDENTS!
HUH?
A YOUNG FEMALE TEACHER LIKE YOU...
...YOU COULD BECOME THE SUBJECT OF SOMETHING LIKE ***THIS!***
PLA
HOW COULD YOU?!
YOU'RE MAKING IT SOUND AS IF I'M SEDUCING THEM...
IT MAKES NO DIFFERENCE WHETHER YOU DO OR YOU DON'T.

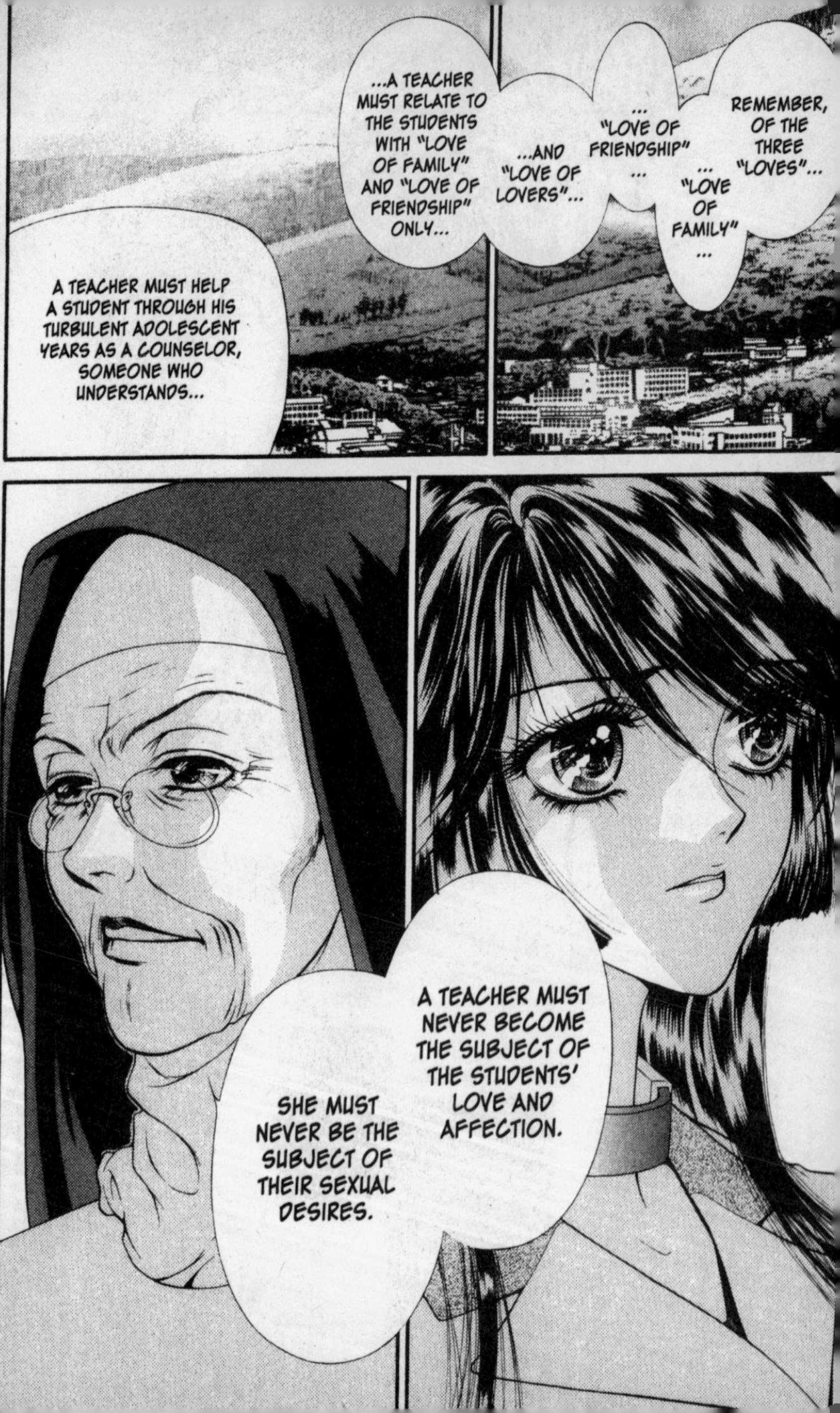
REMEMBER, OF THE THREE "LOVES"...
... "LOVE OF FAMILY" ...
... "LOVE OF FRIENDSHIP" ...
...AND "LOVE OF LOVERS"...
...A TEACHER MUST RELATE TO THE STUDENTS WITH "LOVE OF FAMILY" AND "LOVE OF FRIENDSHIP" ONLY...
A TEACHER MUST HELP A STUDENT THROUGH HIS TURBULENT ADOLESCENT YEARS AS A COUNSELOR, SOMEONE WHO UNDERSTANDS...
A TEACHER MUST NEVER BECOME THE SUBJECT OF THE STUDENTS' LOVE AND AFFECTION.
SHE MUST NEVER BE THE SUBJECT OF THEIR SEXUAL DESIRES.

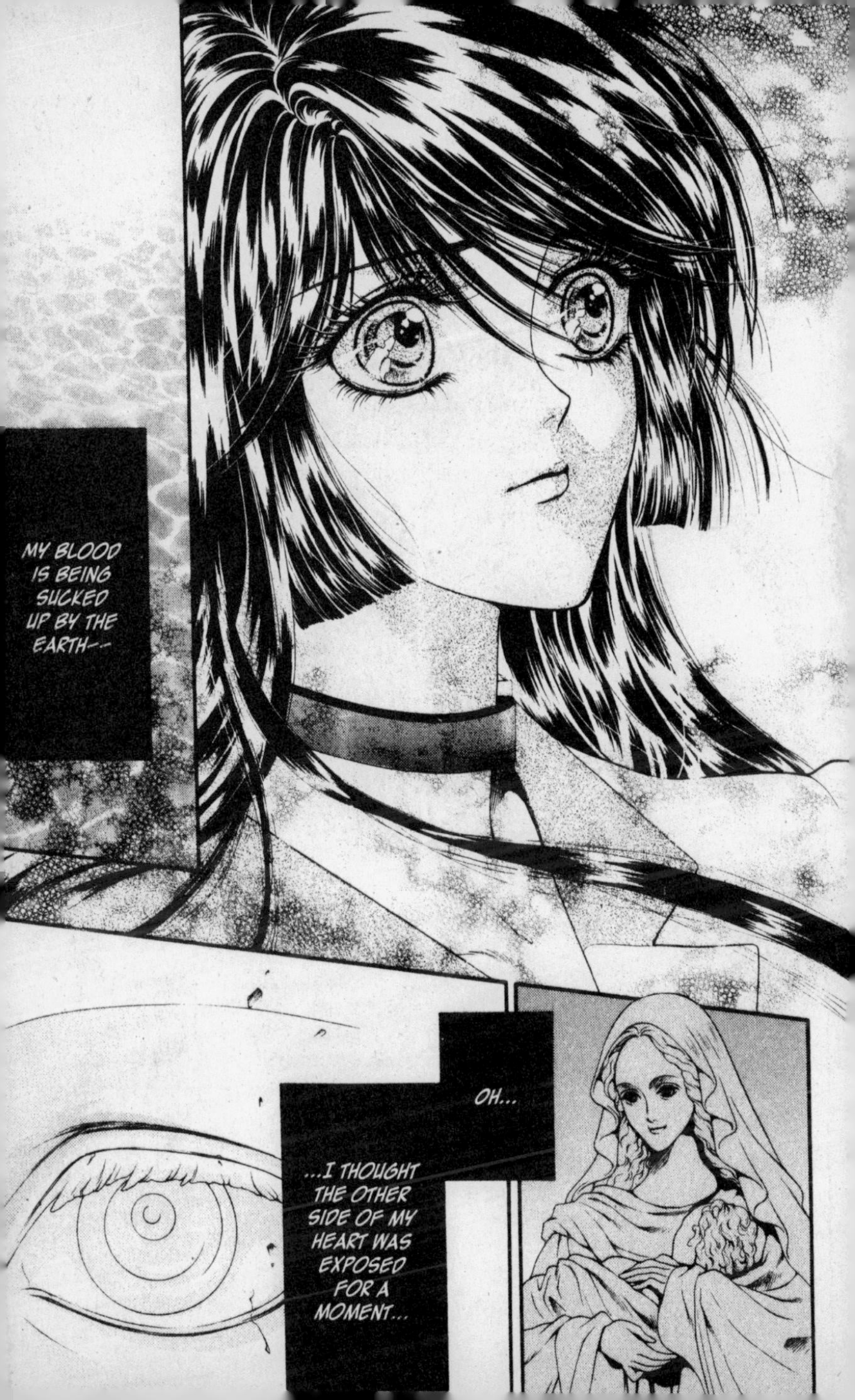
MY BLOOD IS BEING SUCKED UP BY THE EARTH---
OH...
...I THOUGHT THE OTHER SIDE OF MY HEART WAS EXPOSED FOR A MOMENT...

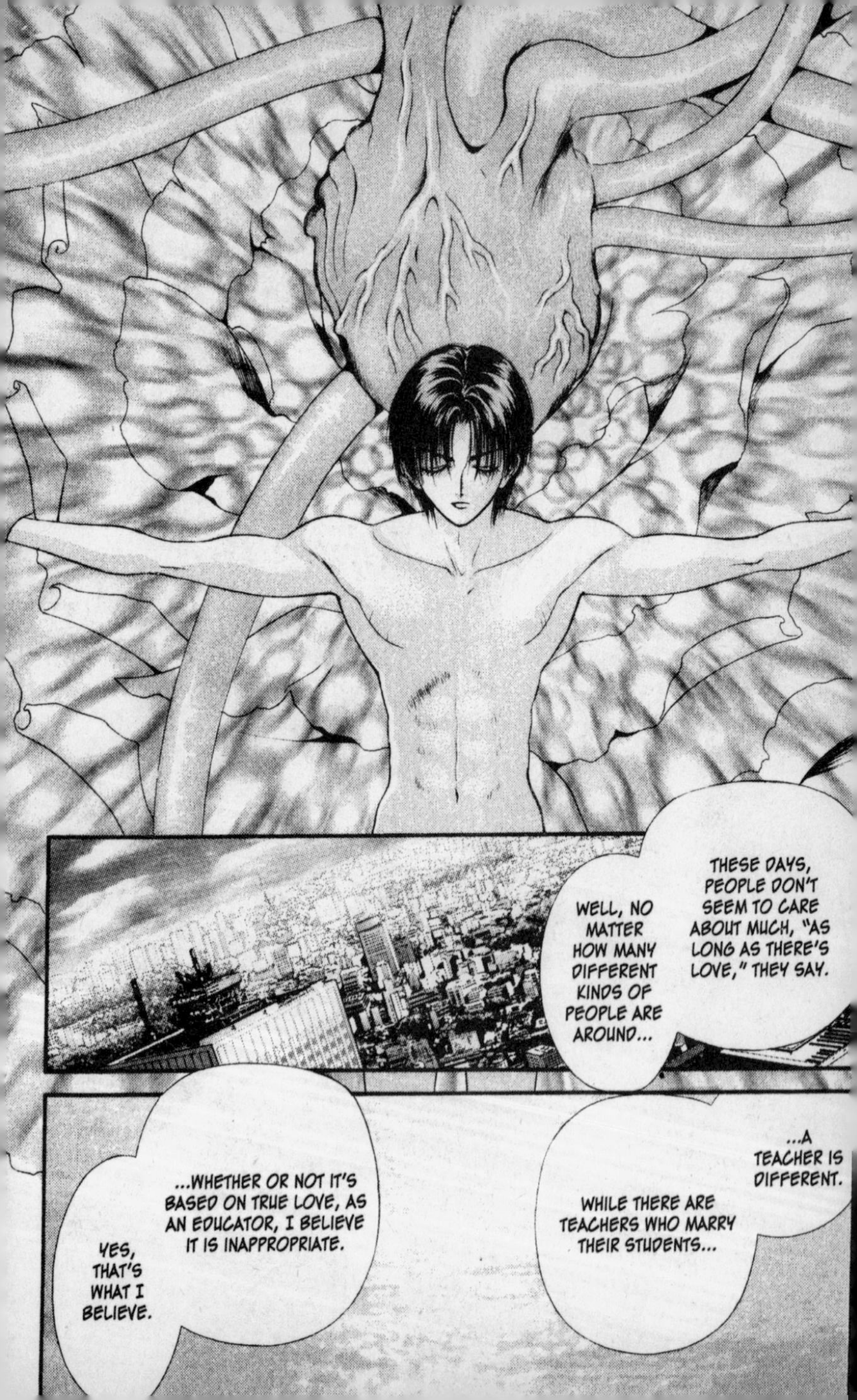
THESE DAYS, PEOPLE DON'T SEEM TO CARE ABOUT MUCH, "AS LONG AS THERE'S LOVE," THEY SAY.
WELL, NO MATTER HOW MANY DIFFERENT KINDS OF PEOPLE ARE AROUND...
...A TEACHER IS DIFFERENT.
WHILE THERE ARE TEACHERS WHO MARRY THEIR STUDENTS...
...WHETHER OR NOT IT'S BASED ON TRUE LOVE, AS AN EDUCATOR, I BELIEVE IT IS INAPPROPRIATE.
YES, THAT'S WHAT I BELIEVE.

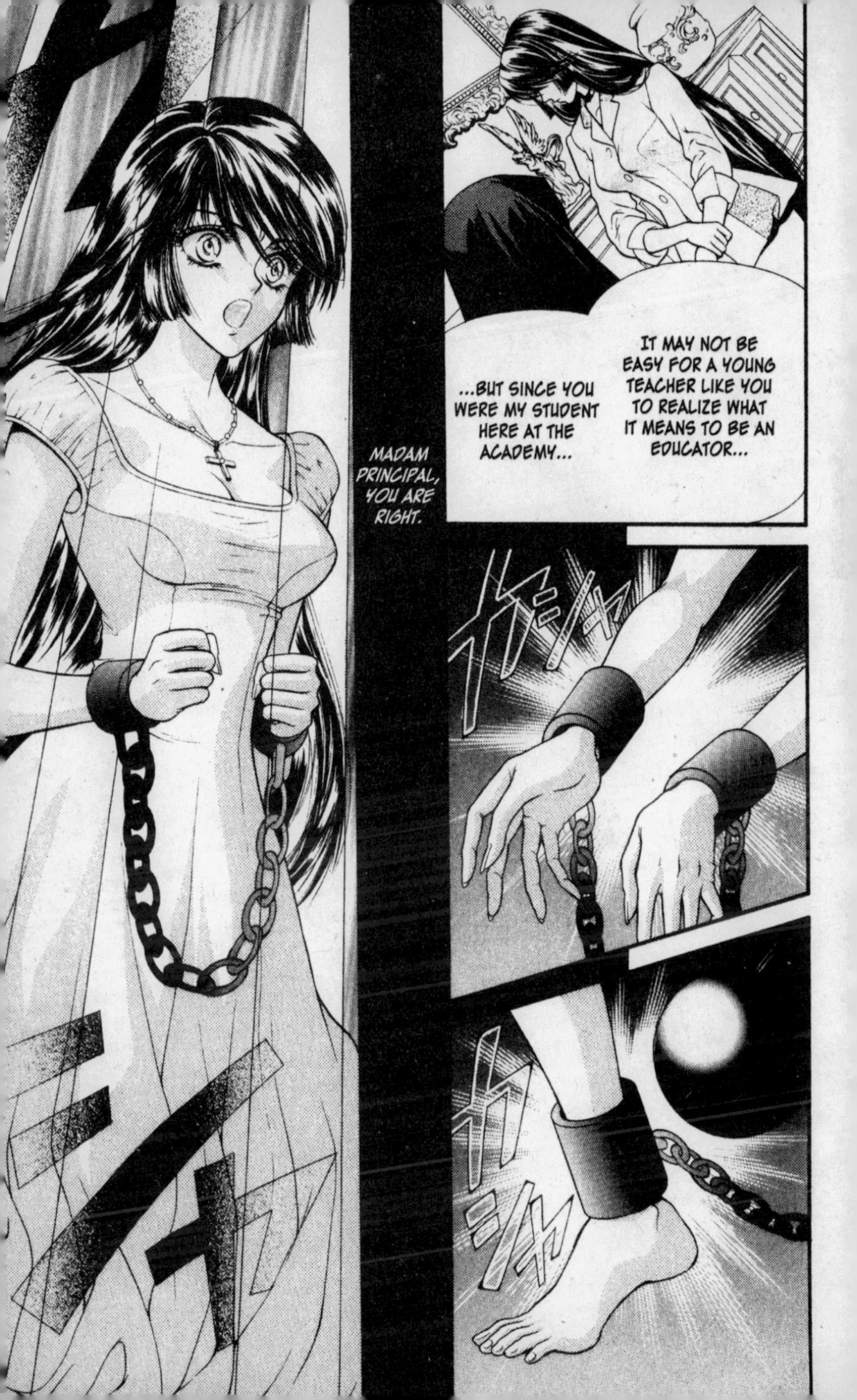
IT MAY NOT BE EASY FOR A YOUNG TEACHER LIKE YOU TO REALIZE WHAT IT MEANS TO BE AN EDUCATOR...
...BUT SINCE YOU WERE MY STUDENT HERE AT THE ACADEMY...
MADAM PRINCIPAL, YOU ARE RIGHT.

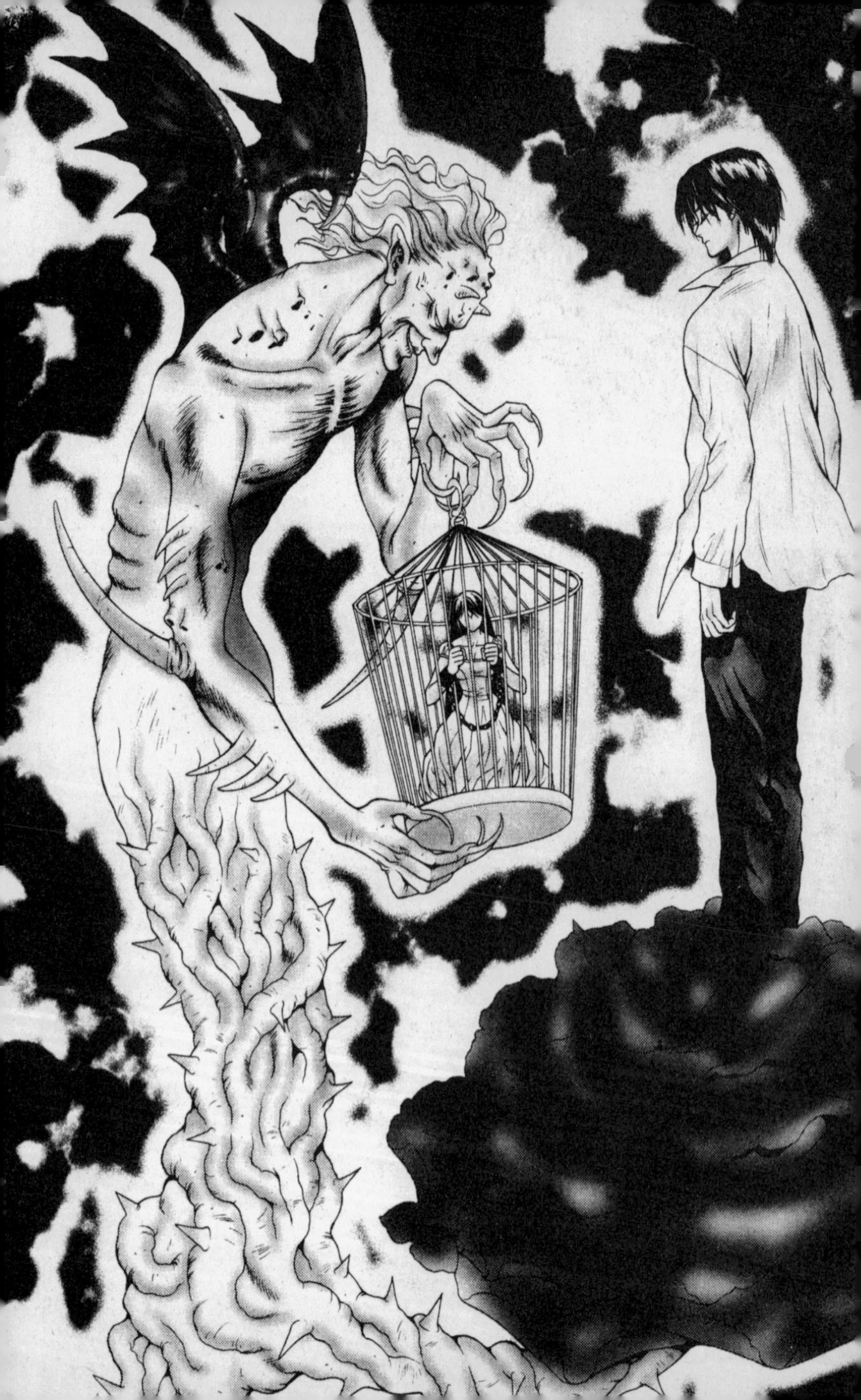

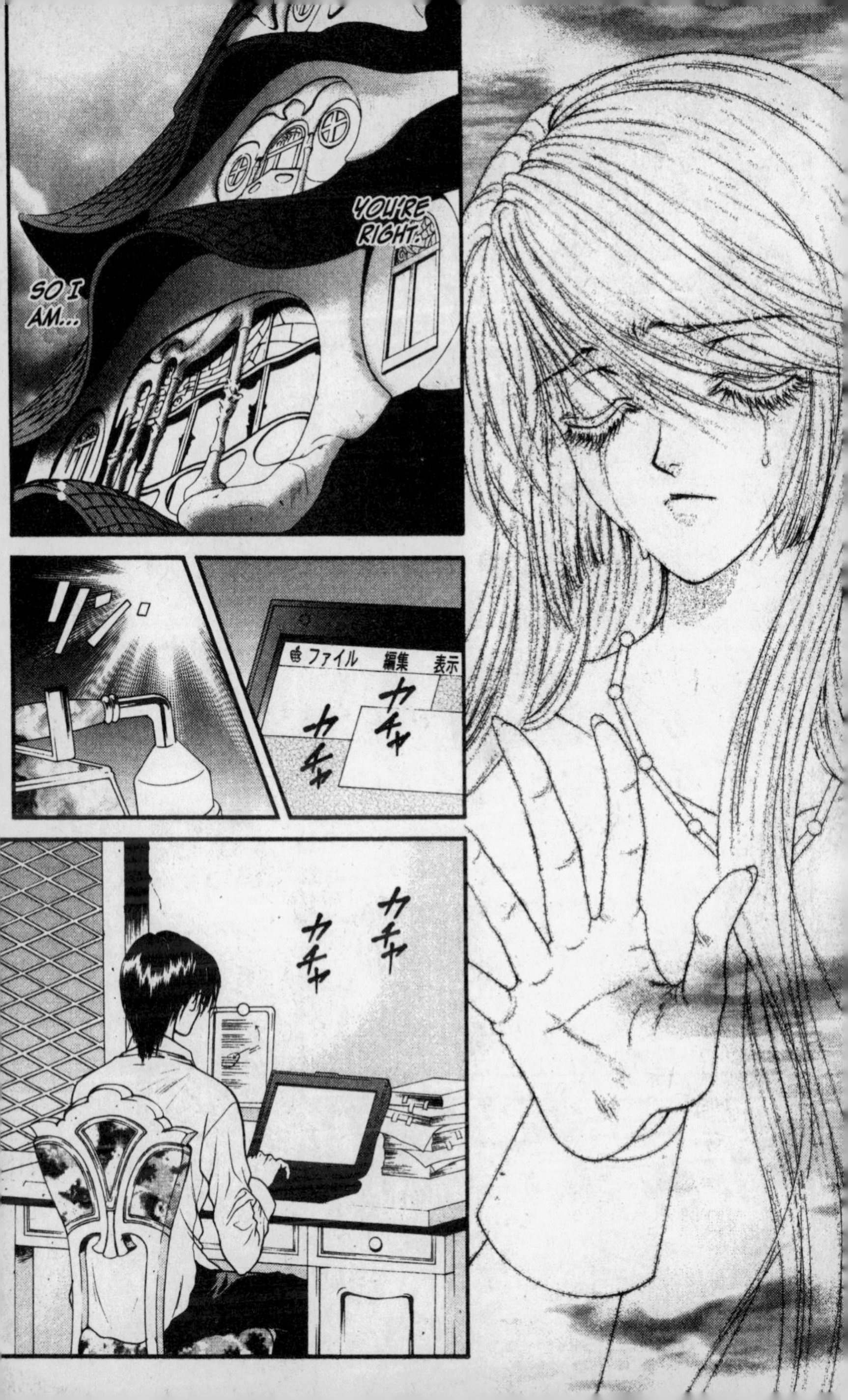
YOU'RE RIGHT.
SO I AM...
ファイル　編集　表示
カチャ
カチャ
リン゜
カチャ
カチャ

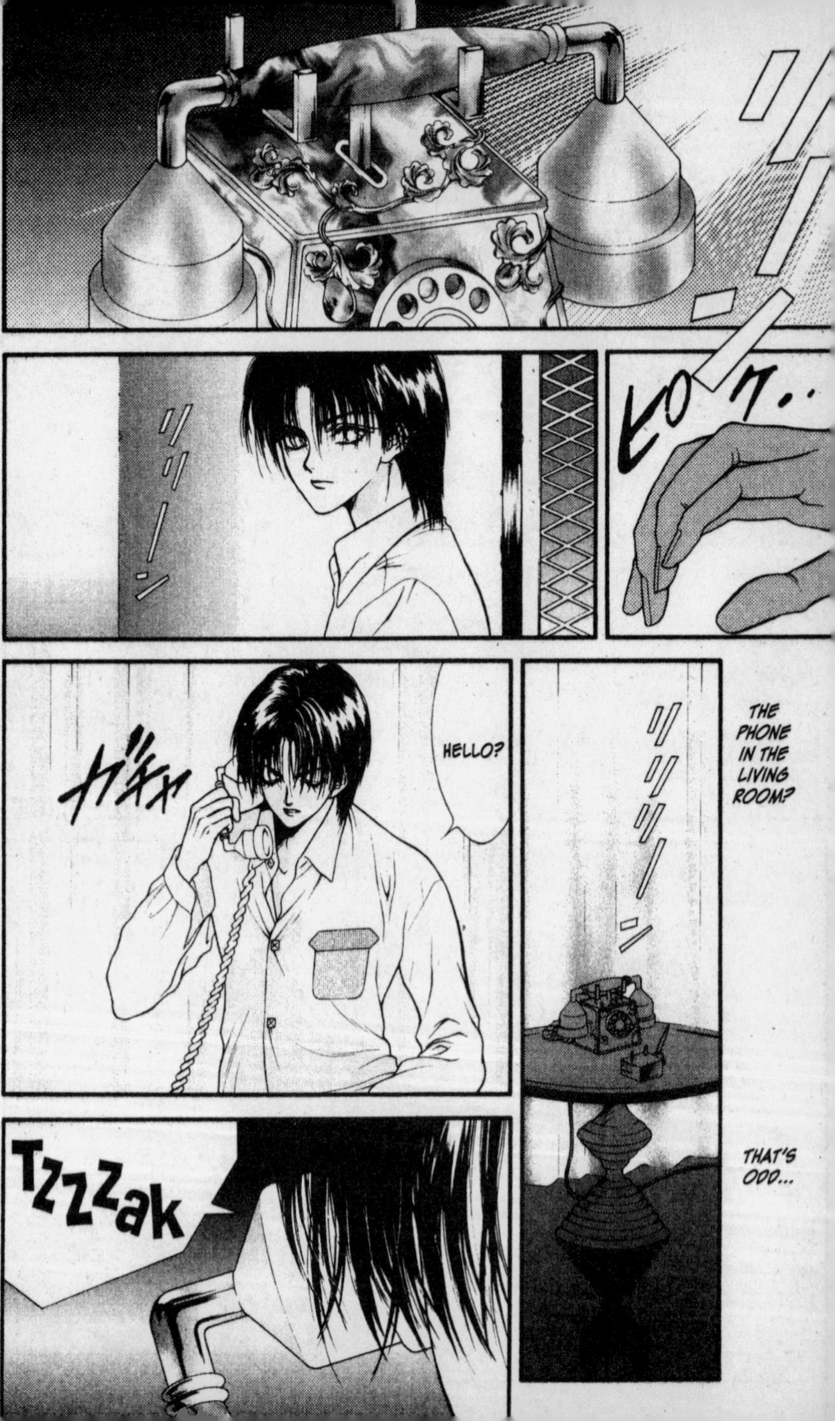
THE PHONE IN THE LIVING ROOM?
THAT'S ODD...
HELLO?
Tzzzak

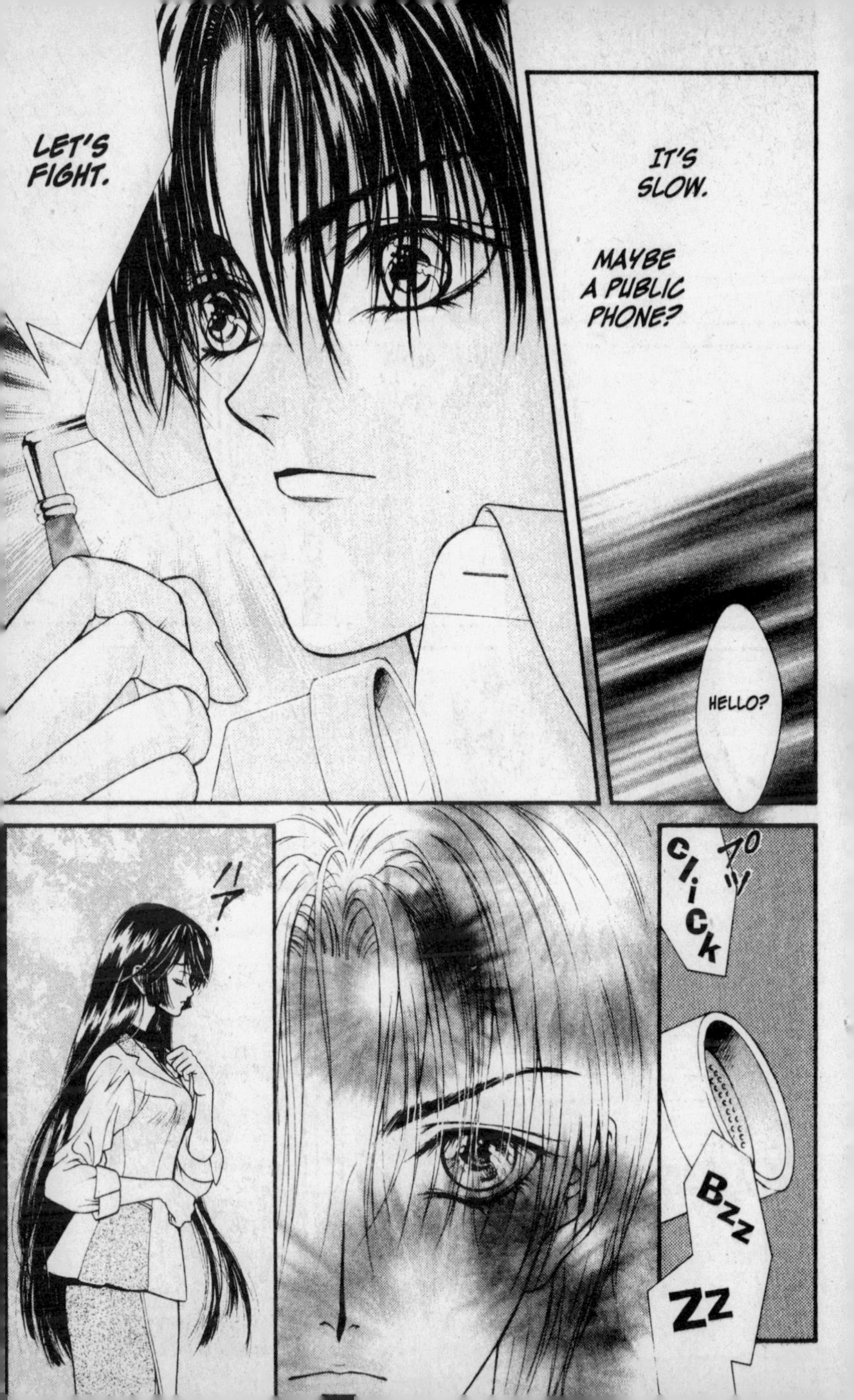
IT'S SLOW.
MAYBE A PUBLIC PHONE?
HELLO?
LET'S FIGHT.
CliCk
BZZ
ZZ

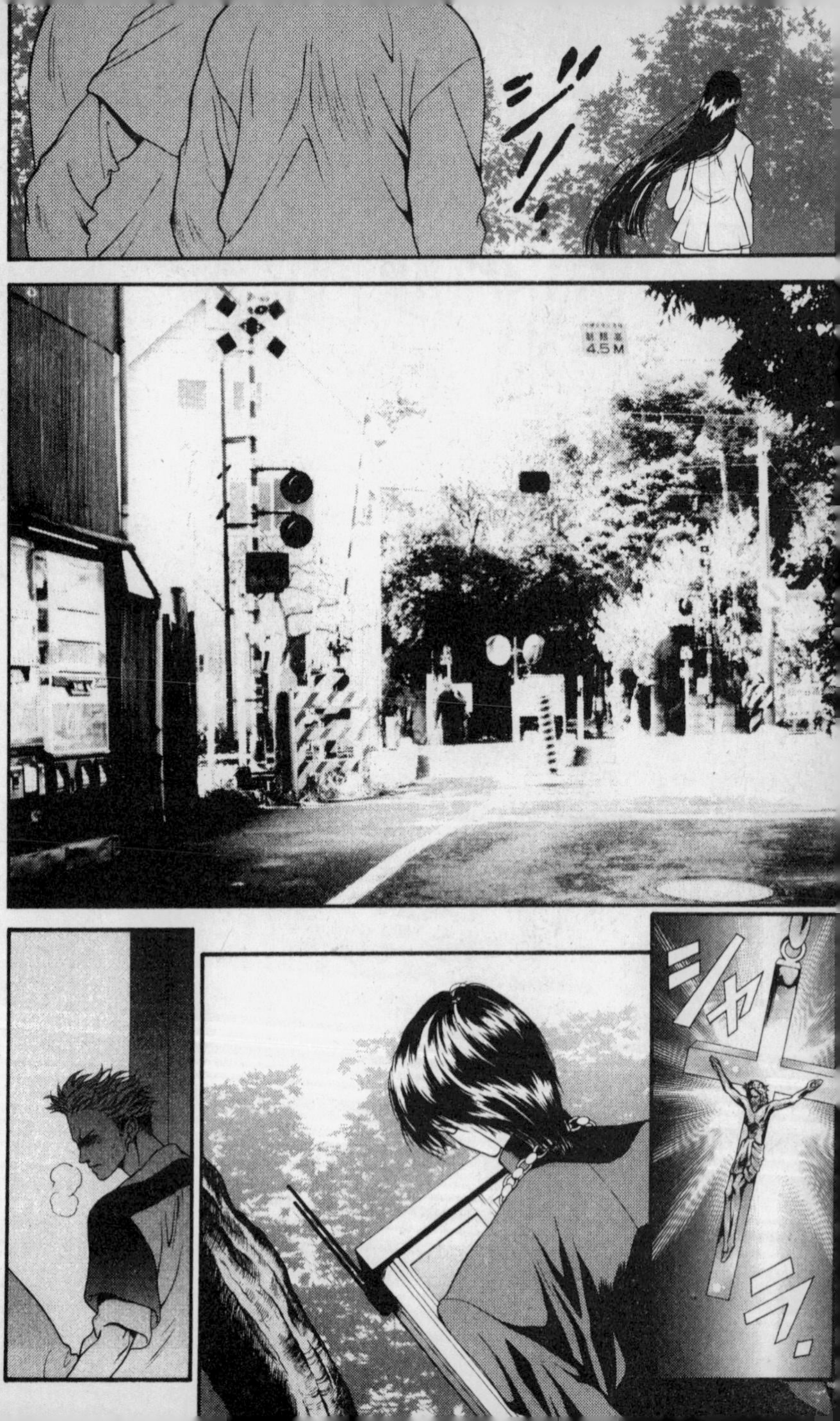
4.5M
シャ
ラ.

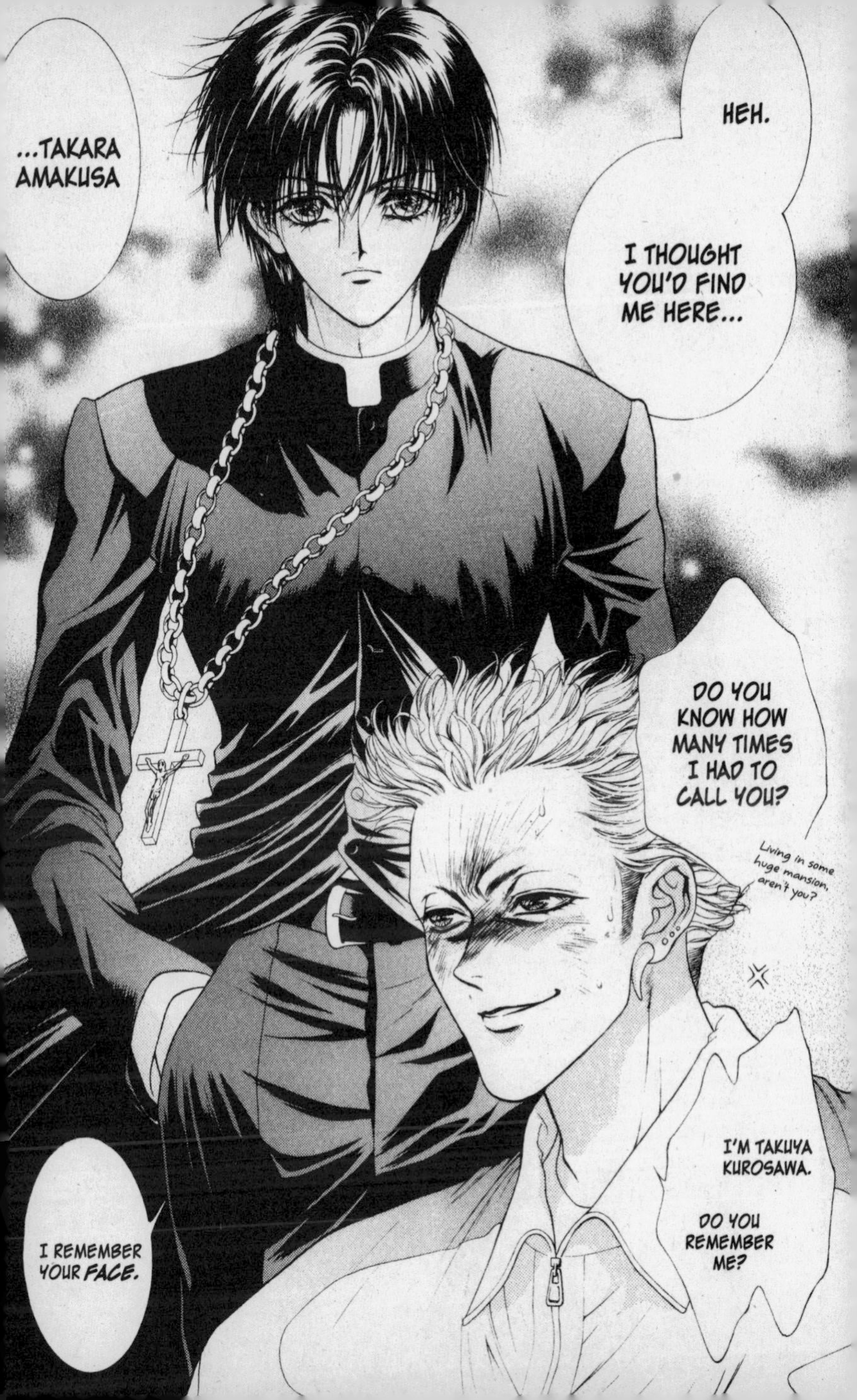
HEH.
I THOUGHT YOU'D FIND ME HERE...
...TAKARA AMAKUSA
DO YOU KNOW HOW MANY TIMES I HAD TO CALL YOU?
Living in some huge mansion, aren't you?
I'M TAKUYA KUROSAWA.
DO YOU REMEMBER ME?
I REMEMBER YOUR *FACE*.

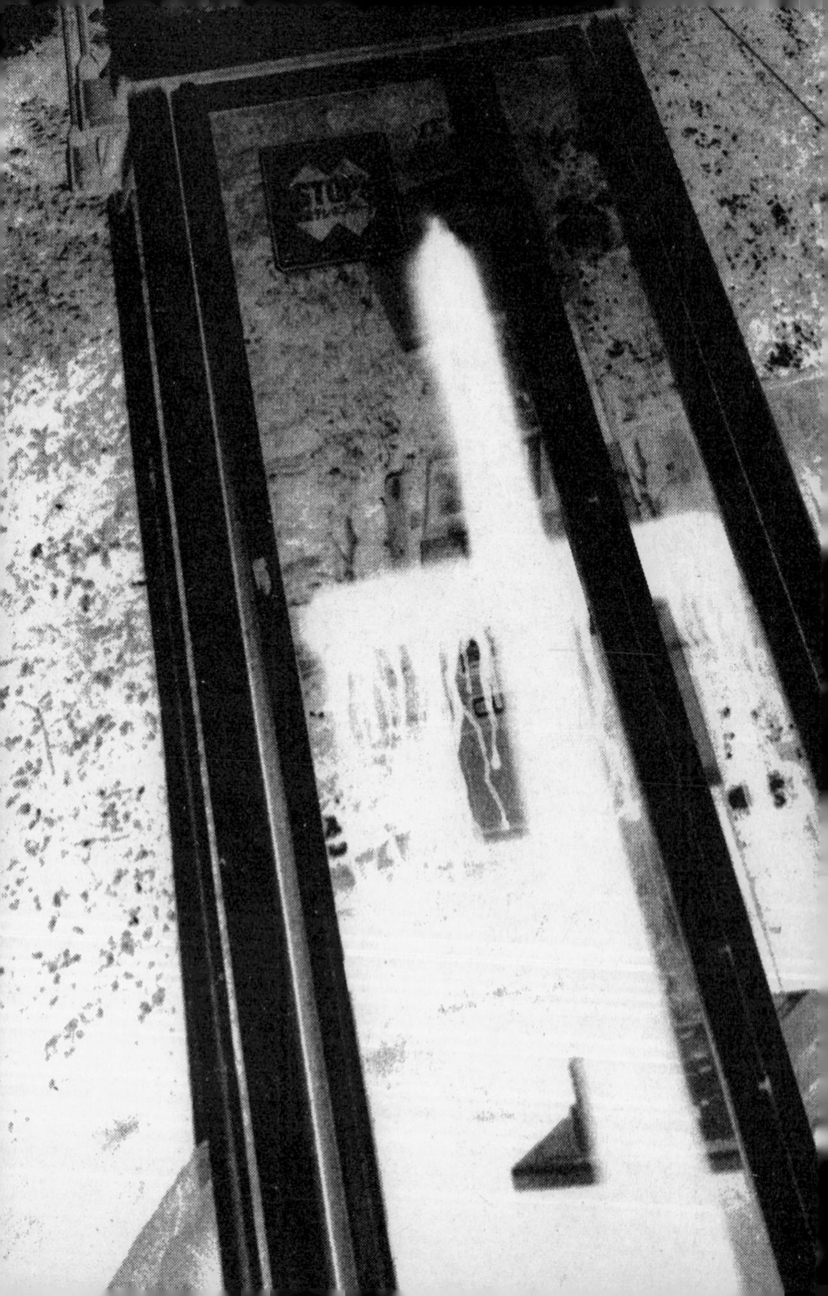

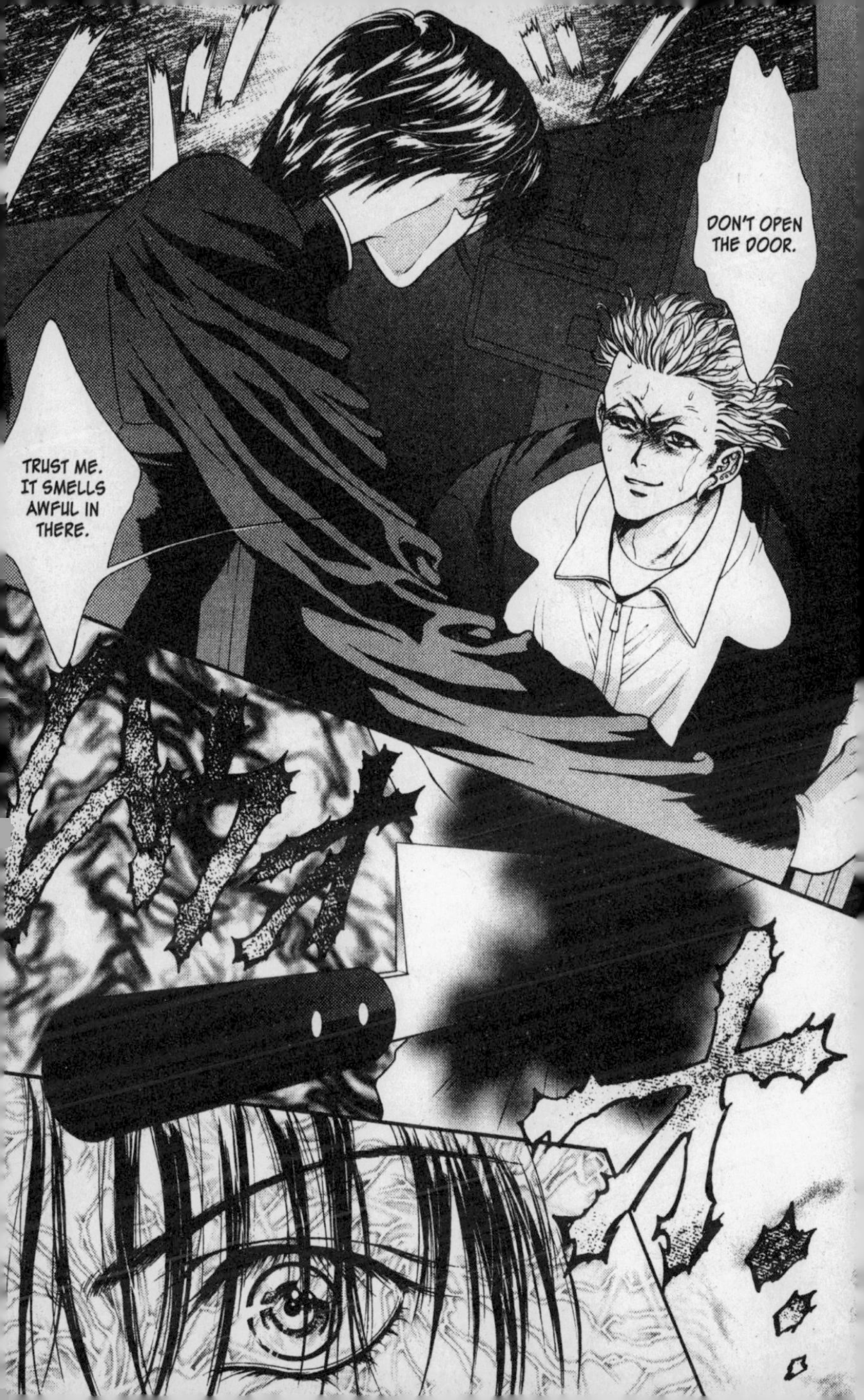
DON'T OPEN THE DOOR.
TRUST ME. IT SMELLS AWFUL IN THERE.

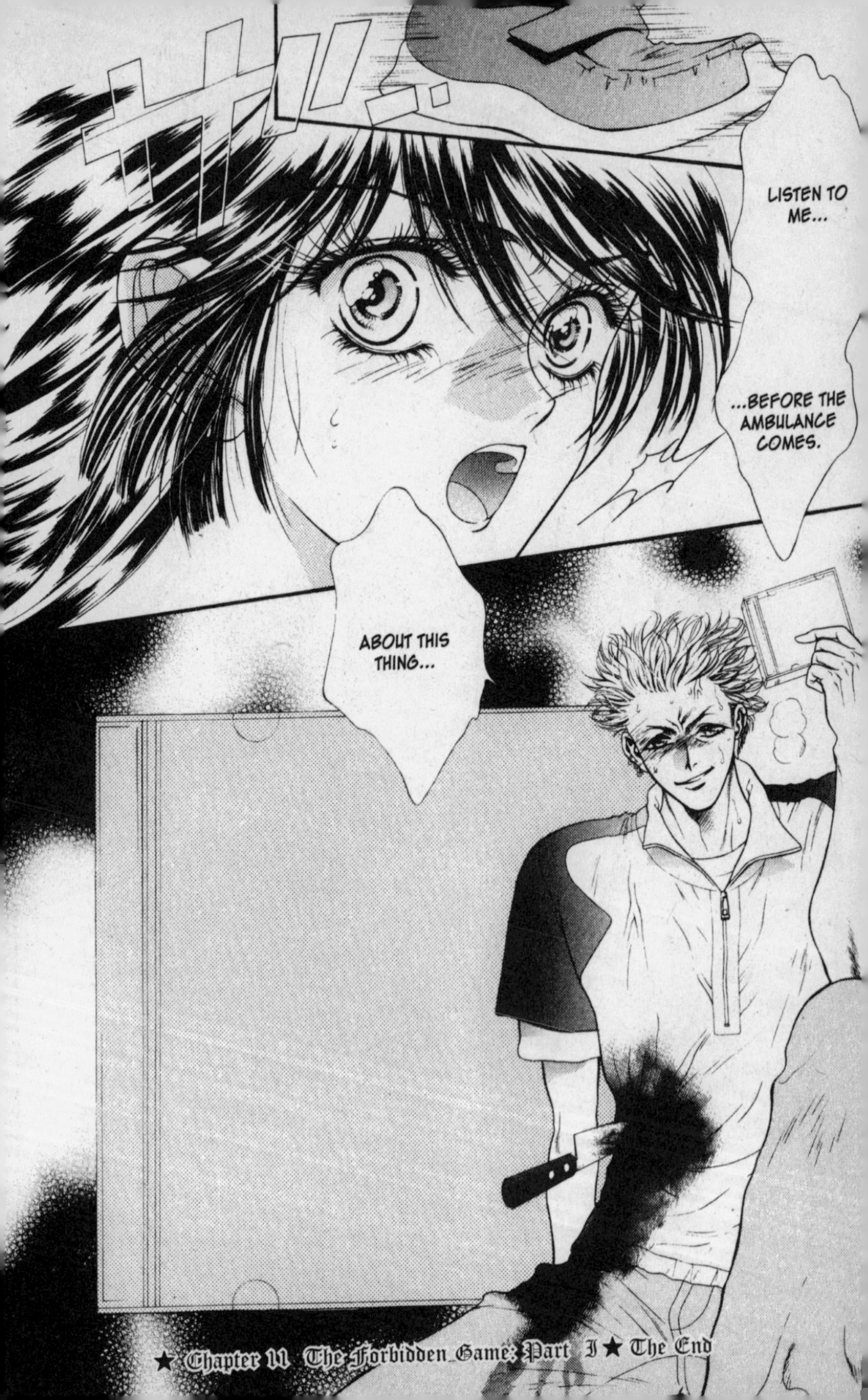
LISTEN TO ME...
...BEFORE THE AMBULANCE COMES.
ABOUT THIS THING...
★ Chapter 11 The Forbidden Game: Part I ★ The End

Oooh!

I worked up a sweat, breaking off a flower. I must change my silk shirt.

Let's take a bath. We'll fill the tub with red rose petals...

The difference in height is a lie.

I was finally able to create new characters, but sorry about all the mysteries. No lines, and no names. The color version first appeared in the magazine for telephone cards. Jumping to another subject, I couldn't help drawing Shizuha's maid costume. I wonder if you noticed that the fishnet tights are deformed. It took a long time, but I was very excited about creating real-looking legs. I love computer graphics! I was also able to draw Takara in his adolescent years. It was just a tiny bit, but maybe I wasn't able to give him enough of a boyish look. Maybe I need more practice. I'm looking forward to doing it again if I get a chance. But I must move the plot along. The new characters...they have a lot of lines. You just don't realize these things when you're designing the characters, you know. "The Most Difficult Hair to Draw" prize goes to Bartholomew and Fairyrose-chan. Whoa, wavy lines... Whoa, curvy lines... I pant as I draw these lines. But the most troublesome of all are Takara and Shizuha, after all. After inking it in, I still have to draw in the "shine." Since my drawing speed is slow, and it takes a long time, I'm hoping that digitalizing it will speed things up a little. My strength is waning, and I'm getting more prone to sickness. Even as I write, I'm coughing and wheezing from bronchitis. Human beings need sleep, I guess.

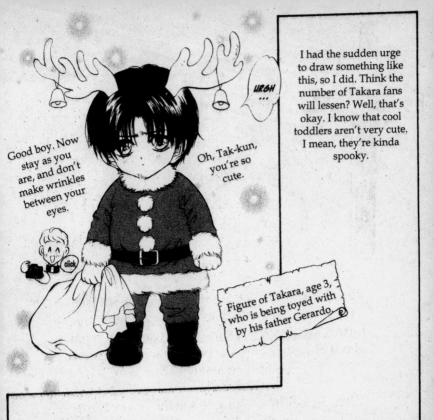

URGH ...
Oh, Tak-kun, you're so cute.
Good boy. Now stay as you are, and don't make wrinkles between your eyes.
click
Figure of Takara, age 3, who is being toyed with by his father Gerardo.

I had the sudden urge to draw something like this, so I did. Think the number of Takara fans will lessen? Well, that's okay. I know that cool toddlers aren't very cute. I mean, they're kinda spooky.

Because of my physical state and my family affairs, work has been really hard on me these past several years. I've been in a psychological black hole (I probably wasn't very nice to my friends either. I'm sorry!), but I think things are better lately. Maybe things are taking a turn for the better... Although it might just be me who thinks so, my power is back in my work. The story is even more full of mystery now, but it should get interesting (according to my plan). I'm so glad though that I didn't make a story out of the end of the century!! The evil 1999 went past so quickly, then 2000, and the 21st century.
Happy 21st century! See you in the next volume!!
P.S. I'm looking forward to hearing from you.

★ Afterword ★ The End

Next in the book of

Cross

What horrible secret could it be that the sinister Takuya Kurosawa wants to pass along to his former adversary, Takara Amakusa? And what about Shizuha? Has she been attacked by some unseen assailant?

Well, we're still waiting to see the next volume of *Cross* ourselves. But rest assured—when we know, you'll know!

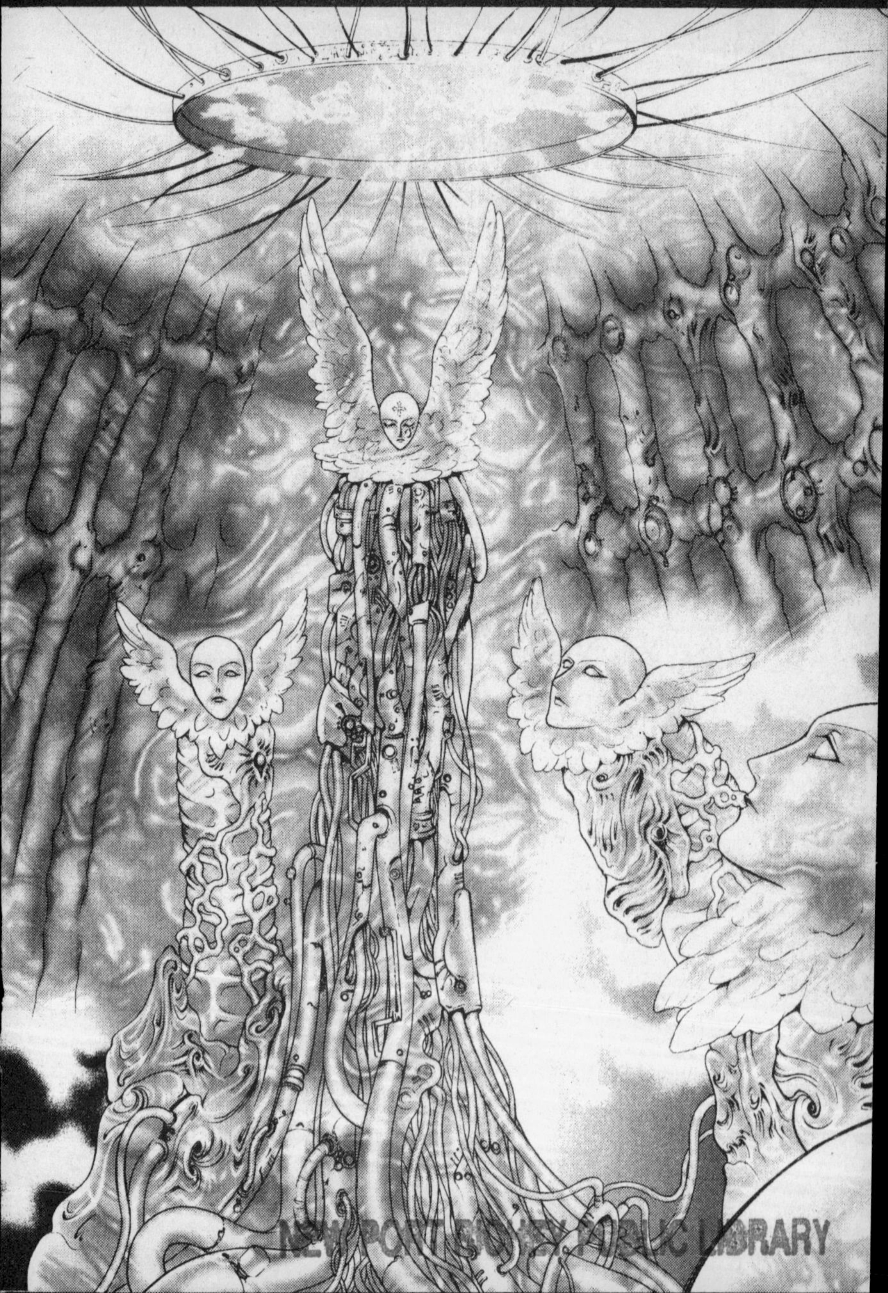

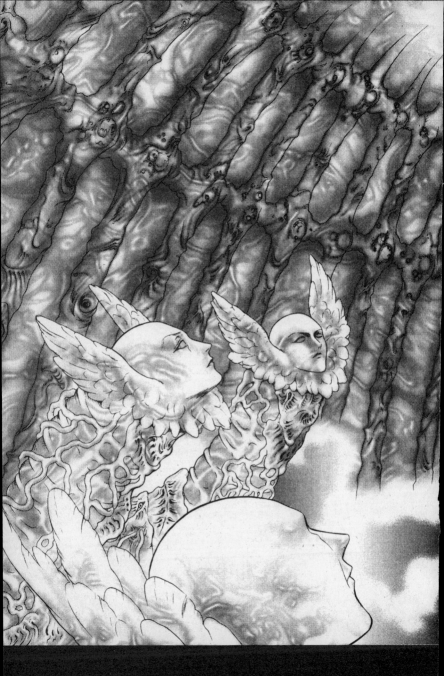

TOKYOPOP PRESENTS
MANGA 漫画
THE NEW SIZZLING HOT
FREE MAGAZINE
ZELDA AND FRIEND FROM
WAR ON FLESH
© Justin Boring, Greg Hildebrandt and TOKYOPOP Inc.
SIGN UP FOR FREE WWW.TOKYOPOP.COM

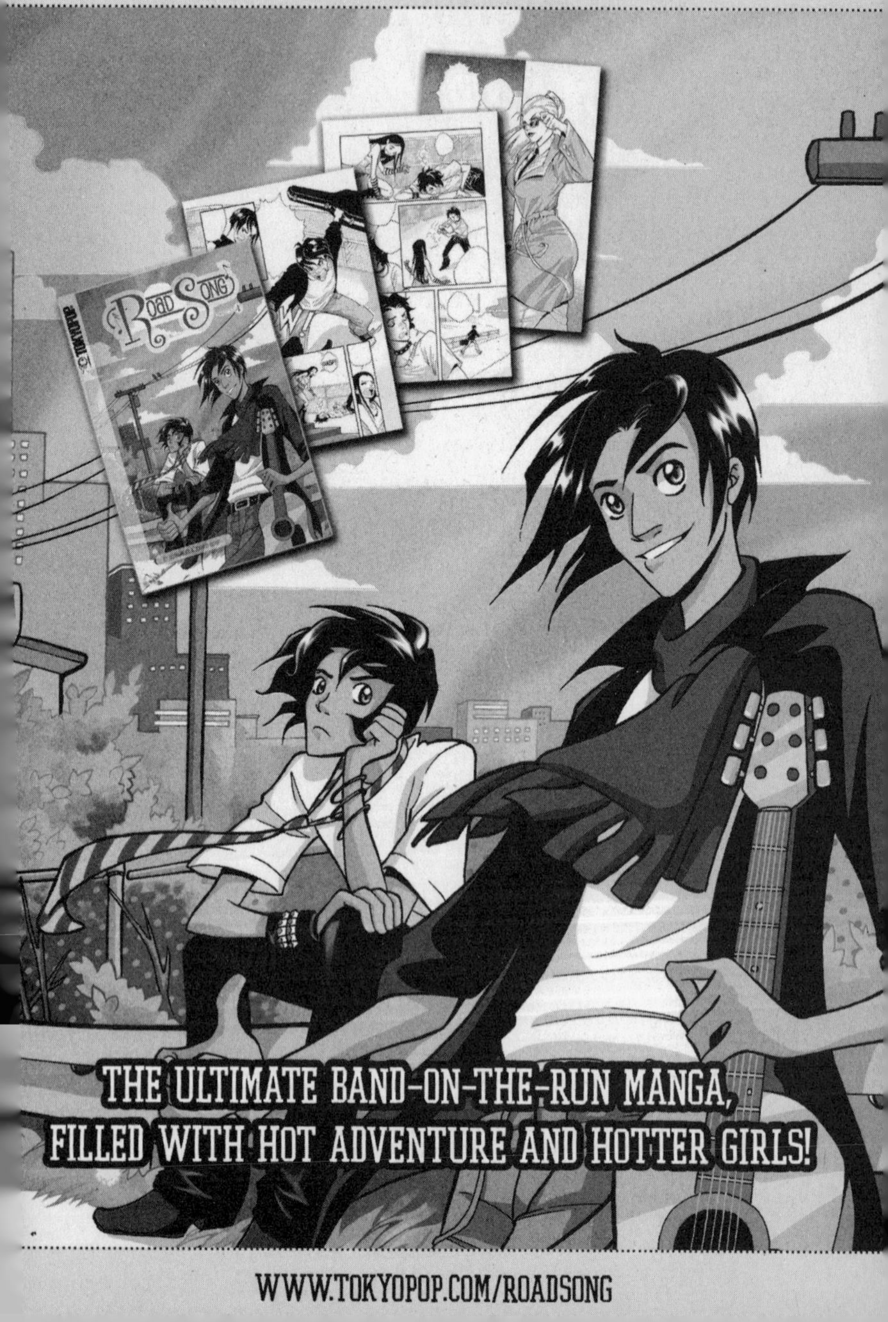
RoadSong
TOKYOPOP
THE ULTIMATE BAND-ON-THE-RUN MANGA,
FILLED WITH HOT ADVENTURE AND HOTTER GIRLS!

Music...mystery...and Murder!

RoadSong

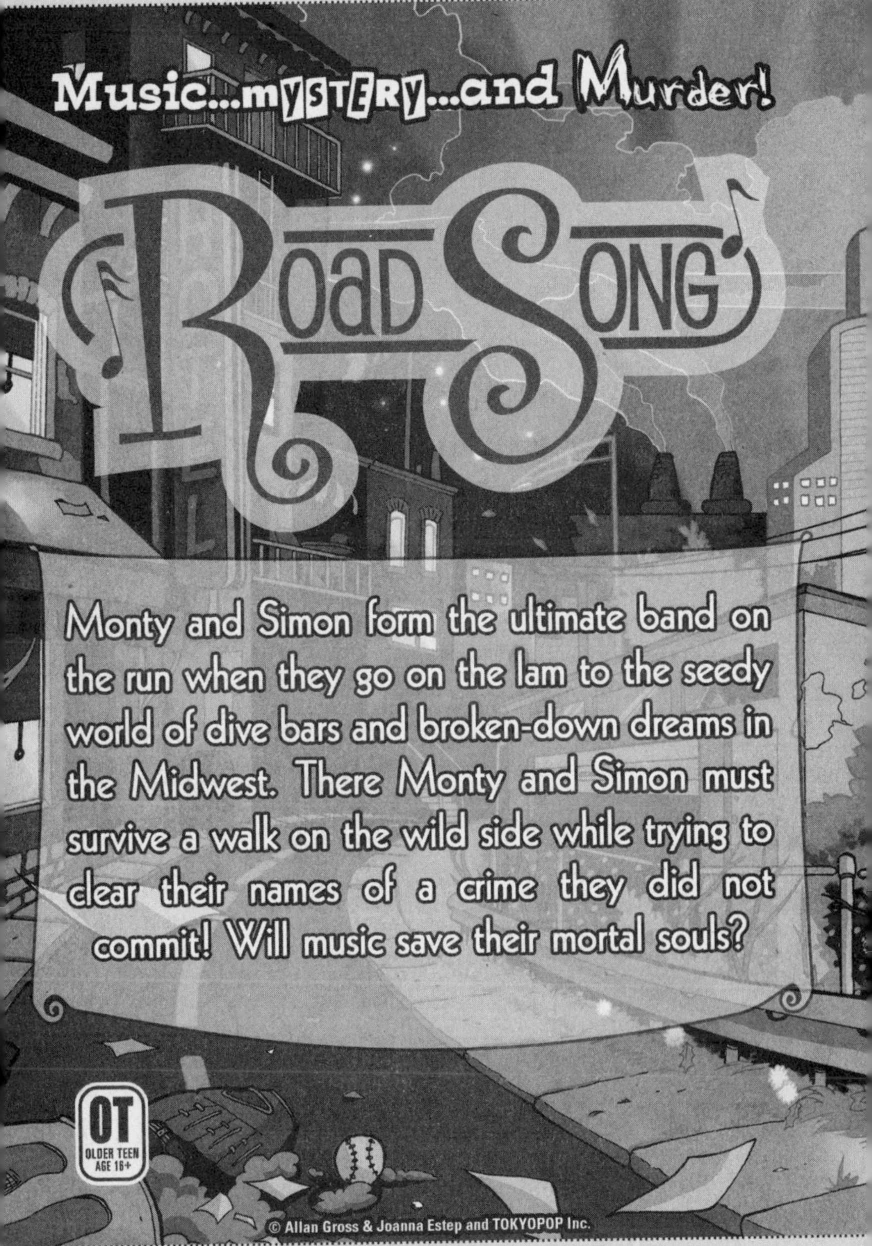

Monty and Simon form the ultimate band on the run when they go on the lam to the seedy world of dive bars and broken-down dreams in the Midwest. There Monty and Simon must survive a walk on the wild side while trying to clear their names of a crime they did not commit! Will music save their mortal souls?

OT
OLDER TEEN
AGE 16+

© Allan Gross & Joanna Estep and TOKYOPOP Inc.

READ A CHAPTER OF THE MANGA ONLINE FOR FREE:

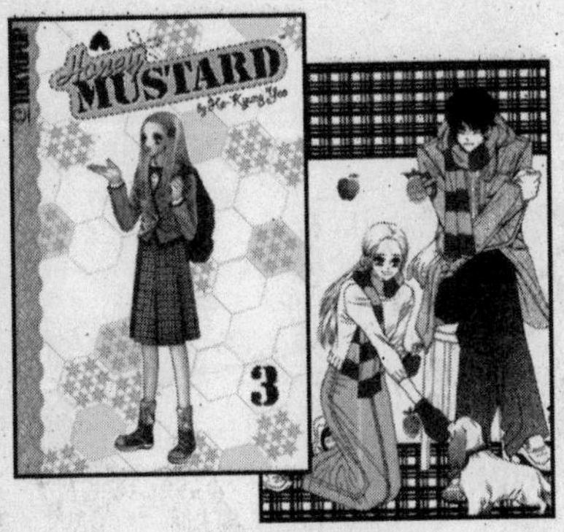
Honey MUSTARD
3

BY HO-KYUNG YEO

HONEY MUSTARD

I'm often asked about the title of *Honey Mustard.* What does a condiment have to do with romance and teen angst? One might ask the same thing about a basket of fruits, but I digress. Honey mustard is sweet with a good dose of bite, and I'd say that sums up this series pretty darn well, too. Ho-Kyung Yeo does a marvelous job of balancing the painful situations of adolescence with plenty of whacked-out humor to keep the mood from getting *too* heavy. It's a good, solid romantic comedy...and come to think of it, it'd go great with that sandwich.

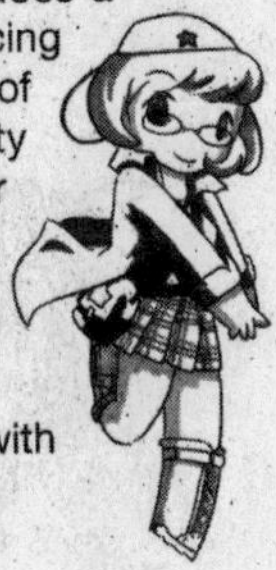

~Carol Fox, Editor

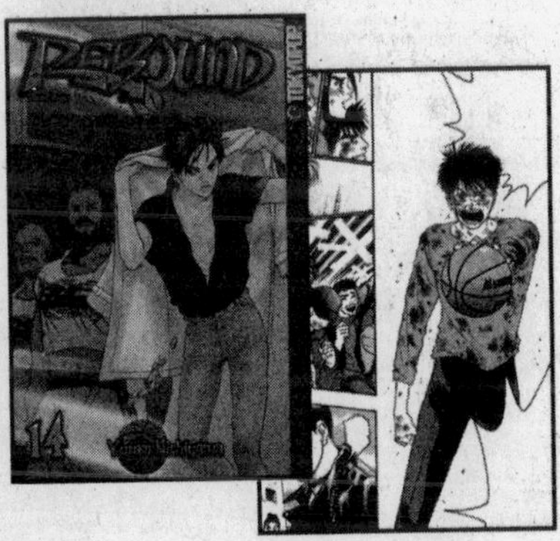
REBOUND
14

BY YURIKO NISHIYAMA

REBOUND

At first glance, *Rebound* may seem like a simple sports manga. But on closer inspection, you'll find that the real drama takes place off the court. While the kids of the Johnan basketball team play and grow as a team, they learn valuable life lessons as well. By fusing the raw energy of basketball with the apple pie earnestness of an afterschool special, Yuriko Nishiyama has created a unique and heartfelt manga that appeals to all readers, male and female.

~Troy Lewter, Editor

SHOWCASE TOKYOPOP MANGA SUPPLEMENT

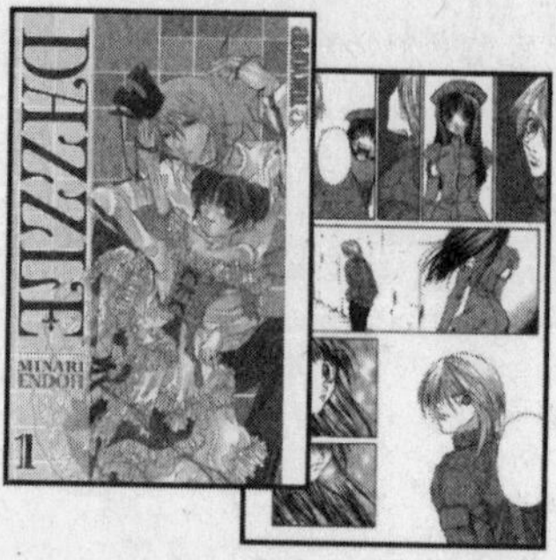
DAZZLE
MINARI ENDOH
1

© Minari Endoh/ICHIJINSHA

DAZZLE

BY MINARI ENDOH

When a young girl named Rahzel is sent off to see the world, she meets Alzeido, a mysterious loner on a mission to find his father's killer. The two don't exactly see eye-to-eye, until Alzeido opens his heart to Rahzel. On the long and winding road, the duo crosses paths with various characters...including one who wants to get a little too close to Rahzel!

An epic coming-of-age story from an accomplished manga artist!

T TEEN AGE 13+

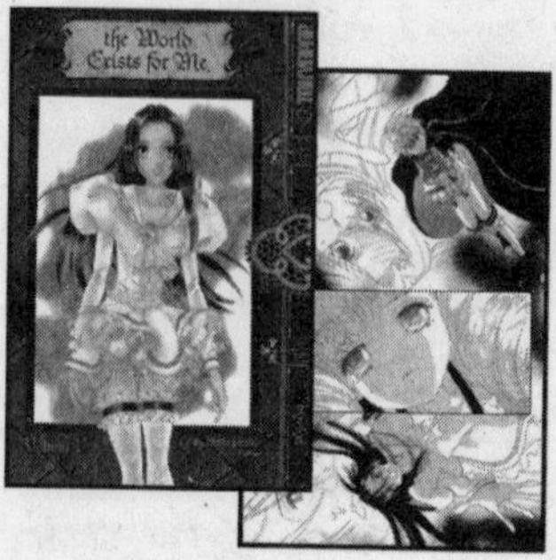
the World Exists for Me

© CHIHO SAITOU and IKUNI & Be-PaPas

THE WORLD EXISTS FOR ME

BY BE-PAPAS AND CHIHO SAITOU

Once upon a time, the source of the devil R's invincible powers was *The Book of S & M.* But one day, a young man stole the book without knowing what it was, cut it into strips and used it to create a girl doll named "S" and a boy doll named "M." With that act, the unimaginable power that the devil held from the book was unleashed upon the world!

From the creators of the manga classic *Revolutionary Girl Utena!*

T TEEN AGE 13+

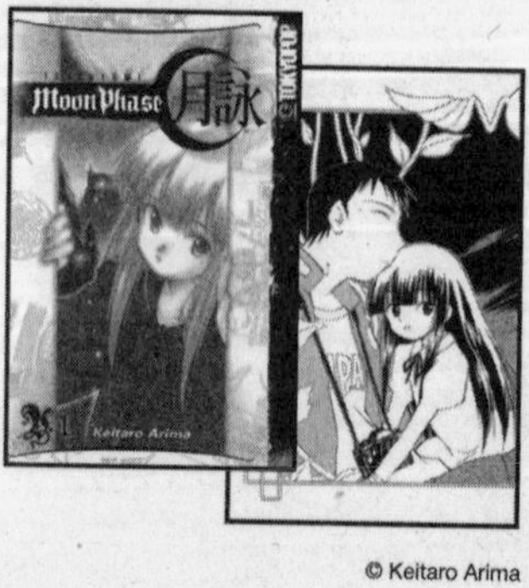
Moon Phase 月詠
TOKYOPOP
1
Keitaro Arima

© Keitaro Arima

TSUKUYOMI: MOON PHASE

BY KEITARO ARIMA

Cameraman Kouhei Midou is researching Schwarz Quelle Castle. When he steps inside the castle's great walls, he discovers a mysterious little girl, Hazuki, who's been trapped there for years. Utilizing her controlling charm, Hazuki tries to get Kouhei to set her free. But this sweet little girl isn't everything she appears to be...

The manga that launched the popular anime!

T TEEN AGE 13+

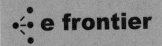

STOP!

This is the back of the book.
You wouldn't want to spoil a great ending!

This book is printed "manga-style," in the authentic Japanese right-to-left format. Since none of the artwork has been flipped or altered, readers get to experience the story just as the creator intended. You've been asking for it, so TOKYOPOP® delivered: authentic, hot-off-the-press, and far more fun!

DIRECTIONS

If this is your first time reading manga-style, here's a quick guide to help you understand how it works.

It's easy... just start in the top right panel and follow the numbers. Have fun, and look for more 100% authentic manga from TOKYOPOP®!